CORPORATE STRATEGIES OF THE
TOP 100
UK COMPANIES
OF THE FUTURE

Corporate Strategies of the Top 100 UK Companies of the Future

Corporate Research Foundation UK

The McGraw-Hill Companies

London · New York · St Louis · San Francisco · Auckland
Bogotá · Caracas · Lisbon · Madrid · Mexico · Milan
Montreal · New Delhi · Panama · Paris · San Juan
São Paulo · Singapore · Sydney · Tokyo · Toronto

Copyright © Corporate Research Foundation

Corporate Research Foundation UK
Standbrook House
2 - 5 Old Bond Street
London W1X 3TB
Tel: 0171 - 4934919
Fax: 0171 - 4932545

First Published in Great Britain in 1995 by
McGraw-Hill Publishing Company
McGraw-Hill House
Shoppenhangers Road
Maidenhead
Berkshire SL6 2QL
Tel: 01628 23432
Fax: 01628 770224

A catalogue record for this book is available from the British Library.

ISBN 0-07-709213-9

The right of the Corporate Research Foundation UK to be identified as the
editor of this work has been asserted in accordance with the Copyright,
Designs and Patents Act 1988.

McGraw-Hill

A Division of The McGraw-Hill Companies

Printed in Great Britain at the University Press, Cambridge

PREFACE

One of the foremost features of the modern capitalist economy is the need for commercial organisations to keep improving their products, services and processes. The competition is continually doing so; and marketplaces change with increasing speed. As Lou Platt, CEO of Hewlett Packard, says in this book: 'What makes us highly successful this year, could be our downfall next year. Kill complacency'.

It is vitally important, therefore, to keep track of the practices and strategies of other businesses, even those that operate in widely divergent fields from one's own. Much practical benefit can often be gained from studying how successful companies think and act.

The most determining factor of success in business is quality of management. The vision, determination, values and thinking of senior management are in the end what make companies thrive. The Corporate Research Foundation has set out to identify and portray the strategic thinking of executives in the most forward-looking companies in Britain.

These managers realise it is also in the interest of their corporations that the United Kingdom has a thriving economy with world-class companies, practising best-practice management and creating leading-edge technologies, products and services. Therefore, they have spoken openly of the success factors specific to their organisations, and of what it will take for them to be successful in the future. In doing so they have generously contributed to what may well prove to be a very important book.

Robert C.R. Wolfe
Corporate Research Foundation

Sources & industry advisers

Robert Sandry — Price Waterhouse
Robin Linnecar — KPMG / Peat Marwick
Innovation Unit — Department of Trade & Industry
Dun & Bradstreet — Greig Middleton
Salomon Brothers — Paribas
James Capel — NatWest Securities
BZW — Panmure Gordon
Smith New Court — UBS
Investors Chronicle — *Financial Times*

Writers / researchers

Sam Ahmad — *Investors Chronicle*
Nigel Bolitho — *Investors Chronicle*
Adrian Bowden — *Investors Chronicle*
Rod Cant — *Investors Chronicle*
Paul Donkersley — Analyst / Independent writer
Paul Durman — *Mail on Sunday*
Nigel Hawkins — Analyst / Independent writer
Patricia Jennings — *The Telegraph*
Conor Joyce — *Investors Chronicle*
Roger Leboff — James Capel / *Investors Chronicle*
Alistair Osborne — *Investors Chronicle*
Bob Reynolds — Financial Times Management Reports/CRF
Humphry Smith — Global Fund Management
Peter Smith — *Investors Chronicle*
Paul Steenberghe — Euromonitor / Independent writer
Mark Taylor — Independent writer
Patrick Tooher — *The Independent on Sunday*
Martin van der Weyer — *The Spectator / Management Today*
Tom Winnifrith — *Evening Standard*
Robert Wolfe — Corporate Research Foundation

CONTENTS

Dr John Taylor, managing director of Hewlett Packard
Laboratories Europe, on the pattern of change in technology
and the implications for industry

Jim Clark, chairman of E&OP, on the working and business
environment of the future

INTRODUCTION

Whatever you do, do it with foresight; look to the end.
Marcus Aurelius, Emperor of Rome AD 161 - 180

Today, business is everywhere. It is at the centre of human life to a degree never before experienced. And with the new millennium speeding towards us and market conditions and competitive strengths changing more rapidly than ever, it is vital to keep a constant eye on the future. Much can be learnt from what works well in the present; but it also remains an imperative to look ahead, and this book has tried to look at those businesses that do that exceptionally well.

The Corporate Research Foundation's principal aim is to locate those businesses with best-practice strategic management and future orientation that are likely to have the greatest impact on the UK economy in ten to fifteen years' time. Implicit in our approach is an understanding that certain factors - customer demand, structural issues, people management and technology drivers - will cause substantial changes in the list of leading companies. Well-known names will disappear or cease to be relevant. Our aim is to find businesses - of all shapes and sizes, from all sectors and regions of the UK - that are truly companies of the future. British ownership is not a criterion; what matters is that selected companies should contribute to the welfare of the UK economy.

The Project

We have drawn from sources in all sectors - financial journalists, analysts and consultants - to establish a list of businesses that are advancing in key areas. Our team of 20 journalists has looked in depth at these companies and produced profiles according to our key selection criteria. We are concerned with each candidate's approach to future management in the following areas:

Structural Flexibility	Human Resources
Innovative Power	Growth Markets
International Orientation	Quality of Management

Our choices will be controversial. Some well-known names have been assessed and eliminated. We have cross-referenced against the current FT-SE 500 and taken extensive advice on the various trends in different industrial sectors. We have also sought to identify a group of 'business gazelles' that are highly innovative and work with the standard-setters in industry.

Around 250 enterprises were thus chosen and asked to assist in our research. A few turned us down for reasons varying from ongoing reorganisations, sensitivity concerning strategic issues and even a fear of the kiss of death by being marked out as one of tomorrow's highflyers. Members of our team then set out to visit and interview the CEOs and strategy experts. At times this resulted in eight separate interview-sessions with board members, and at times a pressurised half-hour at Heathrow in between flights; but the insights into their strategic thinking were obtained and duly reflected in reports. This book contains (in somewhat shortened form) reports on what are, by our criteria and in our judgement, the 100 companies best equipped to flourish in the next ten to fifteen years.

During the research exercise, many CEOs of British companies commented that they thought the project was exciting but that they did not envy us our task. Forecasting is an onerous job and any selection is bound to meet with criticism. Deciding on the last few places was very difficult indeed; and the differences between the companies that would have been included in a Top 120 selection and some of our Top 100 has at times been quite marginal. A book can only be so big, and our team has picked 100 well-managed businesses which demonstrate sufficient expertise, market appreciation, customer dialogue, structural and management flexibility, technological vision and application, financial stewardship and innovative people policies to take whatever the world has to throw at them.

Outcome

Some cardinal lessons, both timeless and topical, have emerged from the process:-

simplicity and balance

Business is at heart a simple endeavour. Its techniques, skills and technologies may be highly complex and complicated but the management of companies is essentially a simple activity. Many industry leaders - including Gerry Robinson of Granada, John Golding of Hewlett Packard, George Cox of Unisys, Steve Remp of Ramco, Martin Sorrell of WPP and Nick Butcher of DHL - echo the basic premise that when management moves away from being a straightforward activity then difficulties occur.

Balance is essential - between the short term and the long term, between entrepreneurial tactics and analytic strategy, between a framework of control and manager empowerment.

the here and now

In financial terms, the shift from a turnover- or volumes-based culture, redolent of the 1980s, to a profit-driven approach is among the most welcome developments. In the next ten years we will also see a move to cashflow valuation of companies. Analysts already assess companies on several measures of future cashflow rather than earnings-related methodology. The demise of earnings per share as the key assessment criterion is wholly welcome. Future cashflow gives a much better measure of the quality and source of profitability and is free from the influence of national accounting conventions.

Another major development, and one where British companies can excel, is the increasing demand for product quality. Customers are increasingly discriminative and demanding. They are acutely aware of their needs and they know, in considerable detail, the components of a good deal. Industrialists are expected to deliver to increasingly high quality standards, to provide greater value in products and services, to supply faster and to a wider range of locations, and to anticipate likely future demand. UK companies, especially in certain sectors, have a remarkable record of innovation in customer service.

The Future

Customer relationships are fundamental to the future. Traditional British product-based technical skill is no longer a surefire winner. 'What does the customer want?' is the only relevant question. Ways of supplying customer need are secondary. The customer is the key success element.

Speaking about the financial services sector, Ernst & Young's head of banking Mike Nelson remarks: 'The only core activity banks have is their relationship with their customers. Everything else is non-core'. This observation could easily be applied to any other sector. Those companies which do not regard their customers as core to their business might as well shut up shop today. The rigours of corner-shop trading will be applied to world class businesses of every size.

Being world class is not a function of size, it is an attitude of mind. Determination to be the best, employing the most innovative staff empowerment policies, using technology to enhance customer relationships, setting demanding objectives for profitability, ensuring the correct atmosphere exists - these are the key factors. When entrepreneurship, which is vital to give any business its energy, is matched with excellent professionalism to ensure that targets are met, customers are delighted and employees excel in their work. Such a combination will be remarkably profitable - so shareholders should be satisfied too!

Industry will become more European and global in character. The economies of scale which can be found by operating on a continental structure are impressive. Recent developments in the longstanding Unilever/Procter & Gamble rivalry are instructive in this regard. The Anglo-Dutch combine has several washing-powder manufacturing plants in each European territory; whereas P&G has just three for the whole of Europe, each of which can handle huge packaging runs in any requisite language. As well as brand resuming its key status in commerce, common European brands are achieving greater degrees of consumer acceptability.

The observer of the UK business environment should anticipate more transnational European ventures and policy and strategy being determined on a pan-European basis. Whatever the complexion of the political environment in the early years of the next century, business has accepted that closer commercial integration is desirable and even vital.

Being world class is also a function of the creation of an environment where excellent services and products can flourish. 3M is the innovator supreme in this regard but cultures as diverse as Hewlett Packard, BOC, and Unisys are excellent examples of this approach. This will become a crucial aspect of managing for competitive advantage. In many cases the cost of innovation is onerous and the establishment of joint ventures between former international rivals will become commonplace. There is an argument which suggests that these joint ventures will be the basis of subsequent mega-mergers. Certainly, industry as a whole believes that in each sector there will be three or four global players and increasingly the focus of attention will be on these companies. The trend will be away from national operations and towards regionally-based world players. The significance of national markets will be reduced in favour of regional jigsaws (see the Price Waterhouse profile) as contributors to a global picture.

The structure of the business of the future will emphasise the setting of policy at board level and devolving substantially to small teams. Within global businesses, the key regions will be major power points. And the long term R&D which is absolutely crucial to the longevity of enterprises will be co-ordinated worldwide. Prime examples of this are: Smith & Nephew, Sony, Hewlett Packard, 3M, BOC and SmithKline Beecham.

Ultimately the greatest operational challenges for our 100 companies are to introduce productive and responsive human resources policy and to harness technology. Since business lives in a period of constant change and renewal, the skilful corporation is looking at ways to encourage people to adapt to take advantage of advances in technology. This is not as easy as it seems because understanding the practical implications of changes in technology takes insight and expertise. Then applying this analysis to people management is fraught with difficulty. Some corporations have already lost morale because they rushed ahead with radical technology improvements without seriously considering the impact on employees. In the end employees are the heart of the business, its greatest asset and sources of its most significant potential. Managers ignore this at their peril.

Our alpha list of 100 is supported by separate pieces which attempt to display key developments in management thinking and create the settings for new developments. We have been in contact with some of the best brains in industry - and tried to reproduce much of the innovatory and revelatory in contemporary business practice.

Bob Reynolds
Corporate Research Foundation UK
August 1995

ECONOMIC OVERVIEW

The challenge of a global economy

Over the last 15 years the global economy has become increasingly fast moving and competitive. Modern telecommunications and computing technology has drastically shortened the effective distances between continents and transformed the way many businesses operate. Liberalisation and deregulation have opened up new opportunities for trade and created a 24-hour global capital market. Economic reform has greatly increased the links between the developed Western economies and the emerging markets in Eastern Europe, the former Soviet Union and China. South East Asia has emerged as the fastest growing area of the world, while Latin America has pulled back from the brink of bankruptcy. Closer to home, Europe has moved closer to a single market and has begun to plan for a single currency.

Over the next 15 years all the indications are that trends towards globalisation and more intensive competition will continue and in some cases intensify. Rapid technological change seems assured in areas like computing power, software development, multimedia and the Internet, biotechnology and healthcare. The rise of China and the Asian dragons looks unstoppable: by 2010 they could produce almost 30 per cent of world output (compared to less than 20 per cent in 1993), with China overtaking the US as the largest economy.

At the same time the developed economies will have to cope with a rapidly ageing population, with Japan particularly adversely affected and possibly set to become the sick man of Asia after years of post-war prosperity. They will also face increasingly severe competition as the low wage Asian economies move up-market and possibly leapfrog the established market leaders in their use of new generations of information technology. Continental European economies like Germany with high labour costs, regulated markets and unfunded pension schemes may find that their relative competitiveness is particularly adversely affected by these trends.

There are, of course, many risks and uncertainties concerning the evolution of the world economy over the next 15 years. For example:

. a split into protectionist trading blocs remains a threat
. the pace of technological advance and customer take-up is highly uncertain (e.g. for multimedia applications)
. the future size and degree of integration of the EU remains unclear
. the political situation in Russia and China remains potentially unstable
. the world economy will continue to suffer from periodic recessions
. environmental constraints on growth may become more pressing if adverse effects from global warming emerge more quickly than expected.

Implications for the UK

The UK, as a major trading nation, will clearly be significantly affected by these global trends towards increased competition and a premium on technology and skills. Recently, the UK's export performance has been very good, helped by a competitive currency, but it will be a constant challenge to sustain this export-led growth, requiring greater penetration of the fast growing emerging markets in Asia and elsewhere, as well as maintaining a strong position in lower risk, but slower growing, Western European markets.

The weakest link in the UK economy, not only in the last few years but over the whole post-war period, has been lack of investment in new technology, plant and equipment, infrastructure and skills. Only if these relative weaknesses are addressed is the UK likely to be able to sustain long term real growth of much more than two per cent p.a. (the average of the last 25 years) and sustain a lower rate of unemployment than the current eight per cent. Companies are only likely to invest more if they have higher profits, however, so there is a need here to establish a virtuous circle whereby the most successful UK companies improve their international performance and reinvest the gains in future expansion.

In addition to increased investment, however, lower unemployment will also require the UK to maintain and build upon its relative advantage, compared to other major EU countries, in terms of labour market flexibility. This has been a major factor in attracting inward investment to the UK from US, Japanese and Korean companies in particular over the last 15 years. Government policy will be a critical factor here, particularly as regards taxes on jobs and the regulatory burden on companies. In this context, the decisions of a possible future Labour government on the minimum wage and the EU Social Chapter remain an uncertain factor, although the latest indications are that the Labour leadership is well aware of the dangers to UK competitiveness of adopting inappropriate policies in these areas.

The UK also faces significant domestic issues, relating in particular to the large build-up of household debt in the 1980s, which has stabilised but not been significantly reduced in the 1990s. In a low inflation environment, with house prices particularly depressed and job insecurity tending to increase, this is likely to put a considerable dampener on domestic demand growth and increase the sensitivity of the economy to interest rate increases.

A continuing large budget deficit, despite reasonably strong growth since 1993, is likely to restrict the room for fiscal stimulus by any future government and increase the pressure for more fundamental reform of the welfare state. These domestic conditions emphasise the importance of maintaining a strong export performance if the UK is to sustain real growth in living standards. They will also increase the need for private sector provision in areas like pensions, unemployment insurance and healthcare, creating significant opportunities for companies which can win the trust of the public in these areas.

Greater public concern about environmental issues also seems likely to be a feature of the next 15 years if recent trends are any guide. Companies which make a genuine commitment to protecting or improving the environment can expect to reap a significant dividend if this assessment is correct.

Sectoral winners and losers

While it is very difficult to make precise projections of future growth rates for particular industry sectors, it is possible to identify in broad terms which sectors are likely to be the fastest or slowest growing in the UK. Three broad groups might be distinguished here based on the growth potential of Western European markets:

1 **high growth sectors**, which will tend to be those where there is rapid technological development such as telecommunications, computer software and hardware, electronic media, biotechnology, aerospace and healthcare; certain areas of financial services (e.g. insurance) may also be strong growth areas for the UK given our comparative advantage in this sector;

2 **the 'middle ground'**, which will include sectors like banking, retailing, leisure services, mechanical and electrical engineering, motor vehicle production and road transport which are relatively mature sectors but should still enjoy reasonable demand growth; and

3 **the 'slow lane'**, which seems likely to include traditional sectors like construction, steel and other metals production, bulk chemicals, textiles, food, drink and tobacco, and government services which are either stagnant or declining in the developed countries.

This does not mean, of course, that operating in the high growth sector is a guarantee of success - the competition will be fierce and the risks high. Similarly, a dynamic company could still operate profitably in the slower-growing sectors, particularly by focusing on the fast-growing emerging markets like China and Russia. The middle ground sectors will also continue to offer very profitable opportunities for companies that can achieve a leading position or find a suitable niche.

Qualities required of successful companies

Irrespective of the particular sector in which they are operating, therefore, the most successful companies will be those which:

. **take a global view**, exploiting the opportunities in fast-growing emerging markets in South East Asia, Eastern Europe and Latin America to offset probable slower market growth in the UK, the US and Western Europe (although there could be exceptions to this for some high value added products which only the richer nations can afford);

. **use technology efficiently**, both to ensure that product and service quality is continuously improved and to maximise the opportunities for achieving productivity gains and cost minimisation in core business processes;

. **invest in their people**, with a view to providing flexible career paths with ample opportunities for skills upgrading either through on-the-job training or subsidised learning breaks;

- **have flexible structures**, organised around project teams rather than functional hierarchies, to enable rapid, innovative responses to evolving market trends and opportunities;
- **have strong leadership teams**, who can develop a clear strategic vision, communicate this effectively to employees and motivate them to achieve the vision; and
- **recognise their wider social and environmental responsibilities**, which seems likely, as discussed above, to become an increasingly significant factor in maintaining a positive public image in the next 15 years if recent trends are any guide to the future.

This represents a formidable challenge, but it is one that any UK company must rise to if it wishes to achieve and retain a market position as a world leader. The companies included in this book have been selected on the basis that they have the potential to meet this challenge over the next 15 years.

John Hawksworth
Economics Unit
Coopers & Lybrand

July 1995

CORPORATE STRATEGIES OF THE
TOP 100
UK COMPANIES
OF THE FUTURE

Abbey National plc, London

A major UK financial services company which derived its distinctively innovative and direct relationship with customers from its origins as a building society

Outlook:

The flexibility of approach which characterises Abbey National will serve the group well as it encounters the anticipated revolution in financial services. Both in the UK and internationally but also through its capital markets operations the group is exceptionally well placed for strong performance

Scorecard:

Structural flexibility	★★★★
Innovative power	★★★★★
International orientation	★★★
Human resources	★★★★
Growth markets	★★★★★
Quality of management	★★★★★

Key figures:

UK turnover	n/a
Pre-tax profits	£932 million
UK staff	14,759

Abbey National plc
Abbey House
Baker Street
London NW1 6XL
Tel: 0171 612 4000
Fax: 0171 612 4010

Abbey National

There is something rather intimate about Abbey National. It is the UK's fourth largest bank but its closeness to its customer base and its integrated management approach means that it enjoys an homogeneity of approach which cannot be found in other banking institutions. It is also a rather surprising business. Within a few years since conversion from building society status it has moved definitively from almost total dependence on UK housing stock for its assets to a broad based financial services business.

The distinctive Abbey National culture which encourages and engenders creativity in its management and marketing will be a key success factor when the organisation responds to intensified competition in the decade ahead. Financial services is the industry which will experience a big shake-up in the coming years. It is a sector - perhaps more than any other - where the old world is making way for a new, and thus one where innovative and good management will make the difference. Finance director Ian Harley says: 'Financial services is 20 years behind manufacturing industry in terms of its measurement of profitability. In manufacturing there is an extensive history of the success or failure - and the degree of success or failure - of certain processes, markets, customer groups and products. Banking has never had these mechanisms and to a certain extent many key business decisions have been taken by instinct.'

Operations and markets

Where Abbey National has been distinctive is in its recognition of the requirements of the markets. In 1989 it was the first of the building societies - or savings banks - to apply for conversion to bank status. In the years which have elapsed the company has significantly extended the scope of its operation - it is now the world's fourth largest issuer of Euronotes. It has launched major developments in:

. long term savings   . savings accounts
. life and pensions   . treasury products
. banking accounts   . employee benefits consulting
. general insurance   . registrar services
. unsecured personal loans   . foreign exchange

In 1994, the company reported a 32 per cent rise in profits to £932 million. Its chairman Christopher Tugendhat told Alison Smith of the Financial Times: 'We intend to source more than 40 per cent of our earnings stream from non-traditional business by 1997.' It is a formidable target.

Few analysts really know what the future of branch banking will be. In the long term - with telephone banking, on-line services and ATM dispensers - it may become unneccessary, but at the moment Abbey National regards its network as a primary asset. 'Previously 75 per cent of our branch floor area was devoted to administration - now customer interaction commands 75 per cent.' The company has installed new technology systems which put all customer accounts on-line at the touch of a button and expand the range of services available.

Most services are conducted directly on screen which means that much of the paperwork is reduced or eliminated.

The company sees telephone banking as an important element in the future and it has made significant inroads into the telephone mortgage market. The telephone mortgage market is worth only two to three per cent of the overall market but it is growing and will become increasingly important. The company commands 40 per cent of the telephone mortgage market. It runs offices in Bournemouth and Glasgow which handle this activity.

Strategy and management

Managing director Charles Villiers says that its current strategy derives from the date of incorporation and conversion. 'We decided to convert to allow us to do a number of different things which were not possible under the previous regime as a building society. We summarised them like this:
- to free up our operational scope
- to have access to capital and wholesale markets
- to recognise members' ownership rights
- to clarify accountability
- to improve staff motivation

Greater professionalism has been the creed of the new business. New systems - both technological and management information - have been introduced. The quality and depth of management information is the best it has ever been. The branch network has been reformed to improve the quality of service, location of outlets, add to automated provisioning and make the service more relevant to the customer. Abbey National was always one of the first of the building societies to introduce new products and it is a core competence which it has continued in its new structure. Branches are open longer and more often. Customer operated locations are available 24 hours a day and seven days a week.

The company's five year strategic objectives were identified clearly:
- develop the core business, improve market share and use wholesale funding to grow the business
- diversify - by 25 per cent - from the UK housing sector
- become more broadly based
- develop a framework for selected involvement in other EU countries

This would be achieved while at the same time:
- enhancing earnings per share and shareholder value
- concentrating on keeping costs low
- developing a strong corporate image and customer service focus
- improving distribution channels

The results of the strategy have been generally positive and during the banking crisis of the early 1990s - where the bad debt provisions of the clearers were enormous - the Abbey National emerged relatively unscathed. In 1994 market shares in core markets improved and new business as a percentage of the whole increased to 18 per cent from 12. The market share on savings has fallen but the proportionate value of the business has risen. Two new major profit streams - life insurance and pensions, and treasury - have been created and are both major success stories. This success has enabled these core activities to account for more than 25 per cent of 1994 profits, within the five year plan.

Abbey National takes a positive approach to those exercises which have been less fruitful for the company. It has jettisoned its poorer quality investments such as commercial lending, housebuilding and estate agency. Its mixed performance on mainland Europe has encouraged a cautious approach. Mr Villiers says: 'We believe that we have products which could be valuable to continental customers but past experience has shown that financial products buyers are fairly nationalistic. Therefore the most effective way forward for us, we believe, is to take part in joint ventures with leading operators in our markets in national territories such as France, Spain and Italy to begin with.'

The company also intends to develop its opportunities in the distribution markets by joint ventures and improved relationships with intermediaries such as independent financial advisers.

The future

Peter Birch, chief executive, recently told staff : 'In 1986 Abbey National developed a mission statement. The company has changed a great deal since then so we have set a new vision: To be the outstanding financial services company in the UK. We want to be outstanding in terms of our returns to shareholders, in the opportunities we give our staff and in the service we give customers.' Brand has become very important to Abbey National; and it has become a leader in its sector in the distinctive use of marketing - especially advertising - to establish and enhance public recognition. Excellence of service and a reputation of integrity are vitally important in the much maligned financial services sector. One of the greatest challenges for the company in the years to come is to capitalise fully on its high standing among its customers to build a superlative financial services business.

Mr Harley says that the Abbey National's strength as a low-cost operator will be a key weapon in the struggle for market share ahead. Also the company's financial management systems are among the finest in the industry which coupled with a committed employee base and excellent training are major differentiators. But the shake-out in the sector will come quickly and it will lead to a hard battle for share.

Abbey National is well managed and positioned, respected, it enjoys clean and simple management structures, it is highly creative in its customer and market channels, it leads the industry in innovative products, it makes coherent use of its branch network, it has diversified convincingly away from its rather limited home base and has an enviable reputation among customers. It seems well set to be the UK's banking leader in the next ten years.

Allied Colloids Limited

Allied Colloids, Bradford

Allied Colloids is a leading speciality chemicals company, concentrating on environmentally friendly products

Outlook:
AC has been active, for 25 years, in a sector which has recently become vitally important. As the damage to the environment caused by irresponsible industrial practices has become more evident in the 1990s, Allied Colloids' range of products has shifted to centre-stage. Its spread of activities in Europe and North America has strengthened this company and emphasised its global base

Scorecard:

Structural flexibility	★★★★
Innovative power	★★★★★
International orientation	★★★★
Human resources	★★★★
Growth markets	★★★★★
Quality of management	★★★★★

Key figures:

Turnover	£356 million
Pre-tax profits	£50 million
Staff	2,965

Allied Colloids
Low Moor
Bradford BD12 0JZ
Tel: 01274 417000
Fax: 01274 606499

Allied Colloids

Among quoted UK companies, Allied Colloids is perhaps the best example of a true speciality chemicals company. It produces a range of products all of which are designed to enhance the performance of a product or process.

The group is an innovator, holding over 250 patents in the UK alone with expertise which crosses industry and geographical frontiers, enabling a valuable cross fertilisation of ideas. The breadth of its experience enables it to transfer technology across market boundaries.

Its portfolio of chemicals helps its customers find new ways to achieve better results and hence AC often works in close partnership on the development of innovative new processes. Unsurprisingly management regards constant contact with its markets and customers as the driving force behind all its research and development efforts. However closer investigation reveals a further stimulus which distinguishes the company from much of its peer group. In its words this is described as 'Caring Chemistry'.

Caring Chemistry is AC's commitment to its customers, workforce and the future. It aims to develop products which actually improve the environment and quality of life, for example its pollution control and water treatment processes which are used worldwide. The company demands the highest standards of design and manufacture, with safety and controls which comply with the toughest international regulations.

It hopes its customers can take for granted the highest standards of performance from any product, whatever role it was designed to fulfil. It also seeks to provide an unmatched level of service. It has a participation in a spread of industries; agriculture, personal care and hygiene, healthcare, oil and minerals, textiles and papermaking. This provides it with the insight to set new standards for integrity in an industry more often regarded as a polluter.

Operations and markets

AC supplies chemicals and technical support to thousands of different locations in over 90 countries worldwide. It is experienced in all aspects of providing systems which enable clients to use its products easily, safely and efficiently. It can design, install and maintain any technology on behalf of clients and the Caring Chemistry ideal is carried across all its divisions.

The fine chemicals division produces organic intermediate building blocks, essential to a wide range of pharmaceuticals, agrochemicals and light and colour processes. Its primary market is human healthcare as AC's intermediates play a key part in the synthesis of existing and new medicines. The division works closely with customers as it develops new products, hence it has the flexibility and speed of response required to service individual requirements.

Coatings and specialities combine expertise and practical knowledge from four sectors; adhesives, paints and coatings, inks and lacquers and personal care and detergents. AC is one of the world's largest producers of adhesives for pre-pasted wallcoverings and the polymers and additives that improve emulsion paints, such as dispersing and thickening agents, and gloss improvers. Its polymers have replaced the solvent-based resins used in printing inks and lacquers which produced harmful vapours. It has also developed environmentally safe alternatives to the phosphates used in a variety of detergents.

Similar thought has been applied to the papermaking industry, for products such as tissues, newsprint and fine stationery. Its chemical agents aim to improve product quality, reduce production costs and assist in environmental protection. Its most recent development, Hydrocol, speeds up the production process without compromising quality and won the company its second Queen's Award for Technological Achievement. As production of recycled paper continues to grow, AC is also applying new technologies to the art of papermaking.

The oil division promotes the use of environmentally acceptable water soluble polymers for all areas of exploration and recovery. It contributes to each stage of the production cycle, drilling, production and enhanced recovery. Its Alcoflood range of enhanced oil recovery polymers offers a cost-effective way for a producer to maximise the recovery potential of each well.

Its mineral processing arm has developed reagents which enable the removal of hazardous heavy metal pollutants in effluents and wastes from mineral processing operations. This lends itself to saving energy, generating less effluent and waste, maximising recovery of natural resources and achieving higher standards of pollution control. AC offers a complete mineral processing service from start to finish.

Pollution control provides advice on sewage and effluent treatment. In anticipation of ever more rigorous pollution control standards, it offers a complete service from the consultancy and analysis of specific needs to supplying necessary chemical agents. It designs and installs dosing equipment and inspects and monitors results. For both industry and the municipal sector it can help with the treatment of effluents, sewage and resultant sludges, with technologically advanced products and chemical treatment systems which can materially improve the performance of existing mechanical plant. Other products, flocculates and coagulants, improve the efficiency of solids/liquid separation and improve the quality of drinking water.

Its water treatment division helps clients such as offices and hospitals maximise the efficiency of heating and cooling systems, preventing scaling, corrosion and biological fouling of pipes and plant. Chemical treatment and control, design and installation of systems and backup support encourage more efficient use of water, reduced energy consumption in heat transfer and confidence in the continuing operational efficiency of plant.

The group's agricultural division researches ways to maximise crop production. Processes improve plant nutrition and soil fertility, and offer subtler and more selective methods of pest control. The role of polymers is growing in importance within this sector by aiding water retention, preventing soil erosion and enhancing the safe use of pesticide sprays, for example by reducing their drift.

Strategy and management

As AC's effect chemicals are typically used in controlled conditions to achieve precisely defined results, consistency and quality are vital to the continuously successful outcome. Its commitment to producing the highest quality of product is reflected in its practical endorsement of Total Quality Management and computer-controlled techniques. These infuse every part of its operation, from the technical expertise and chemical know-how of its representatives, to those responsible for identifying a customer's needs and solutions. Other areas such as the packaging, labelling and delivery of the product get similarly rigorous treatment.

The group is proud that its growth has mainly been organic rather than via acquisition, a reflection of considerable and continuing investment in research and development. New products and the programme of product and process improvement have both benefited from the introduction during the last year of specialised teams involving personnel from research, production, sales and engineering.

The recent investment in its processes has been relatively high both for a company of its size and by its own standards. Its UK plants in Bradford and Cleethorpes have been upgraded and rebuilt and it has also directed resources into additional polymer production in its US facilities in Suffolk and Albermarle. Last year it spent £57m on fixed assets and invested £3.3m in its joint venture with Courtaulds to produce superabsorbent fibres. This compares to a previous record spend of £26m in 1993/4 and it is expected to spend another £50m in the current year.

About 87 per cent of AC's sales are derived outside the UK, but mostly exported from the UK manufacturing base. Its Sterling sales and profits are therefore very dependent on the value of the pound against its key export currencies, the US, Australian and Canadian dollars, and Deutschmark. The company therefore hedges its net foreign currency exposure and has also put in place long-term contracts for the purchase of its major raw materials to protect itself from any repeat of some very wild swings in spot market prices.

AC makes a considerable financial and intellectual investment in the needs, safety and health of its employees. It carries this to the fair treatment of its neighbours, and the impact of its operations on the environment now and in the future.

Its policies and practices have been thoroughly reviewed with respect to these issues both internally, and using the services of independent experts and regulators. These reviews have led directly to improvements in safety training, storage procedures and stricter process control, an ongoing process. An allocation from its annual capital expenditure programme is directed into safety improvement and risk reduction.

This approach, allied to strong technical and manufacturing skills, has enabled the company to secure outstanding organic growth at excellent margins over the past twenty years. The majority of group products are still manufactured at its site in Bradford, but it has developed a manufacturing presence in the US since the mid- 1980s and is now investing in new capacity at a second UK site near Grimsby.

The future

AC puts a heavy emphasis on the production of products which meet the demands of an environmentally conscious society. As such concerns increase, the use of its products in all aspects of effluent treatment, for enhancing clean water recycling and for the secondary recovery of oil, can only increase. Demand for these products, which has grown 40-fold since the late 1950s, is likely to grow as more and more countries introduce environmental legislation.

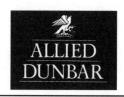

Allied Dunbar plc, Swindon

Allied Dunbar is a UK life insurer, owned by BAT Industries

Outlook:
Allied Dunbar has changed rapidly in the last few years. It has benefited from an identification with brand and brand management, it has significantly shifted its distribution approaches and has made powerful use of computer technology. The company has recognised that its industry is held in poor esteem by the public and rightly emphasised clear and straightforward service to its clients

Scorecard:

Structural flexibility	★★★★
Innovative power	★★★★★
International orientation	★★★
Human resources	★★★★★
Growth markets	★★★★
Quality of management	★★★★

Key figures:

Funds invested	£13 billion
Premium income	£1.5 billion
Staff	7,000

Allied Dunbar plc
Allied Dunbar Centre
Swindon SN1 1EL
Tel: 01793 514514

Allied Dunbar

Britain's insurance industry has received more than its fair share of criticism in recent years. Headlines have concentrated on the failures - largely of management - in the sector. So it is heartening to discover a company which is not only a focus of excellence in the field but also a standard bearer for British industry.

In a comparable survey to the Top 100 UK Companies of the Future in 1989, Allied Dunbar emerged as one of the very best British employers. Inspired by its demanding but caring creed, the company offered an outstanding environment for staff to achieve their full potential.

Six years later, Allied Dunbar has matured. It is still an excellent employer but the company has progressed as a business. In comparison to many of the other players in the life sector, Allied Dunbar is a young company. And its commitment to many of the values which motivated its founders has been retained. But its appreciation of the dynamics of a market-driven economy has sharpened.

This is a business which does not just talk about customers, it has a firmly-based realisation of customer-centred and customer-driven enterprise. For many years the insurance sector has lived on borrowed time. It has relied on market inertia and an incomplete knowledge of the needs of clientele for its prosperity. While the economy was advancing, a true appreciation of need was unnecessary. Even so, Allied Dunbar was holder of the title of the most innovative and creative life insurer in the UK. Its approach to winning and retaining business was leaps and bounds ahead of its rivals.

Operations and markets

Allied Dunbar is a markedly profitable component of BAT Industries, a FT-SE top ten company. It has more than one million clients, over £13 billion in investments and draws in £1.5 billion a year in premium income.

It provides financial advice to its customers, offering life insurance, pensions policies and a range of other related products.

It is regarded by many as one of the best employers in Britain, spending more than £7 million per annum on employee training. Its share of the market's new business grew by eight per cent in 1994 while that of its leading competitors declined. It is highly committed to brand, its customer-driven approach and its highly trained workforce.

The recession galvanised the sector and had extensive implications for the company. Brand re-emerged as a key criterion of success. And leading the field was Allied Dunbar. At precisely the right moment, the Swindon-based insurer engaged ex-Mars managing director George Greener as its chairman.

Mars is a company which understands brands and the top team at Allied Dunbar was quickly persuaded of the potential strength of branding for them. They perceived that in their case 'brand' could be equated with 'reputation'. Above all else customers were looking for integrity and reliability. The poor performance of the industry, generated by self-interest rather than concern for customers, meant that the market was wide open for companies which respected the wishes of their customers and supplied products which they could depend upon. Allied Dunbar had already proved itself as a creative and high performance insurer, offering a range of valuable insurance, savings and pensions products. The challenge ahead for the company was to build on its high quality name to allow customers to discriminate between its products and those provided by other businesses.

Strategy and management

Chief executive Sandy Leitch comments: 'Consumers are looking for peace of mind and value for money. They want to deal with people they can trust, and to feel confident that anything that they buy from them will be right.' He says that the company has made a commitment to its customers, which is published in many of the company's documents. It is composed of four main determinations:
. providing value for money
. delivering advice which can be trusted
. tailoring specific solutions for particular customers
. being a company which can be relied upon

'The financial marketplace is changing at an unprecedented pace, consumers are becoming more financially aware and press coverage of the industry is increasingly negative. There's never been a higher level of interest in our industry; and never a lower level of confidence. Reputation could be described as a consistent set of expectations in clients' minds about what we stand for. It gives clear and constant reference points to differentiate us from our competitors. A consistent reputation is based on two factors: what we promise and what we deliver,' Mr Leitch remarks.

The recognition - by customers and potential customers - that Allied Dunbar is a name which can be relied upon for superb quality insurance-related products and honest and open dealing is at the heart of the company's commercial objectives.

Allied Dunbar has launched an initiative to familiarise all staff with the main tenets of its brand-building strategy. It has capitalised on the experience of Scandinavian Airlines System which deployed its Moments of Truth philosophy with great success. This states that reputation is developed in the few seconds that convince consumers that a brand is distinctive.

The company recognises that reputation is not created overnight. Jerry Grayburn, marketing director, says: 'We are driving forward a series of measures related to our behavioural performance and a business model, which in time, will become very powerful. We are also monitoring the market much better than we have ever done before. Additionally, our market-led approach is working in key areas of the business such as product development and distribution. Deadlines on the development of new products are much tighter than at any time in the past. This is a remarkable achievement because the quality of products must also be much stronger. Finally, our identity is becoming much more consistent.'

Finance director Brian Thomas shares Mr Grayburn's view that the brand initiative is a potent force in the business. 'In the 1980s we ran a successful business but it was a more predictable business. It has to change because the environment of the 1990s is so different. Now, properly satisfying the market is a key business driver.

'If you think the Allied Dunbar brand is merely about products, then you would be wrong. In my own area of finance, our approach to product design and pricing is much more flexible. Among my recent concerns has been driving the disclosure strategy. Here a strong proposition based on our agreed brand character allows us to move forward. In financial services, I see few brands among the banks and building societies but not one in life insurance. So we have a formidable opportunity to differentiate ourselves from the rest.'

Armed with a powerful brand, Allied Dunbar has begun the next stage of its growth as a life company. At present the business is the fifth largest life insurer in the UK up from number eight only 18 months ago. But a whisker separates the company from its next two largest rivals - and AD has been experiencing above average growth while both of these businesses are declining.

The league table of life insurers, in fact, shows wholescale decline with a scant few advancing. Allied Dunbar, in contrast, has seen growth recently and aims to reach the number three slot. The top two are also leaking market share but the climb is steeper here and Dunbar managers are sufficiently cautious not to predict an early ascent to top spot.

Consumers can now expect the company to be more responsive to their needs. This can be seen in many ways; for example, the numbers of direct sales staff have been reduced but their quality, always high for the sector, has been substantially enhanced. Equally, the information available to policyholders over the telephone when ringing through to Swindon has been extended. The company has refined its database to integrate further easy access to portfolio information on particular clients.

Managers recognise that the demands of the marketplace are becoming more vigorous and so the fixed barriers between departments are being eroded. New classes of executives are being developed who can appreciate the benefits of cross-functional working and drawing on skills in different sections of the company. This process will accelerate. It has always been an open culture which encouraged employee participation and growth. But it has recognised that the future lies in highly flexible organisations populated by highly talented people.

Another main catalyst is the pace and source of competition. Traditionally, financial services has compared unfavourably with manufacturing in its capacity to understand and meet market demand. With a more discriminating customer base and international operators on the horizon, the entire sector will be put through the hoops to achieve efficiencies and quality of service. New competitors can be expected to emerge in coming years with the advantages of efficiencies created by technology and with none of the infrastructural handicaps of bank-led insurance activities. However, Dunbar is in a good position to withstand assaults from new operators. It is building a reputation for honesty and reliability, its investment performance is good and it has the most highly committed workforce in the sector.

The future

This is a healthy company with a sound investment strategy and a clear vision of the future. The clarity of its market perception, its reputation and its distinctive delivery will be powerful weapons in the competitive war ahead. Its policy of building both its direct sales approach, where it is market leader, and its relationship with independent financial advisers (IFAs) will also pay dividends. Allied Dunbar is a real player of the future.

ANDERSEN CONSULTING
ARTHUR ANDERSEN & CO. SC

Andersen Consulting, London

Andersen Consulting is the world's largest global management and technology consulting organisation. Its mission is to help its clients change to be more successful. It does this primarily through its business integration approach which helps clients to link strategy, processes, information technology and people

Outlook:
Andersen Consulting will continue to work throughout the world to deliver greater value and service to its clients. Its financial growth will continue in recognition of its ability to deliver value to its clients. Its market leadership and innovative approach means that that it is regarded by many companies as the leading thinker in these areas

Scorecard:

Structural flexibility	★★★★★
Innovative power	★★★★★
International orientation	★★★★★
Human resources	★★★★
Growth markets	★★★★
Quality of management	★★★★★

Key figures:

European turnover	$1.142 billion
Global turnover	$3.45 billion
UK staff	2,858

Andersen Consulting
2 Arundel Street
London WC2R 3LT
Tel: 0171 438 5000
Fax: 0171 831 1133

Andersen Consulting

Few of the candidates for inclusion in this book are self selecting. These are the tight minority of businesses which embody effective change in every aspect of their operation. They are the companies against which the rest of industry benchmarks. Andersen Consulting is one of these. It became the world's largest consulting firm by reading and anticipating client demand and developing services which help its clients change to become more successful. This is at the heart of why Andersen, rather than its rivals, continues to stand head and shoulders above the consultancy market. Other leading practices struggle to achieve comparably flexible operating structures, service delivery methodologies and the financial returns of the Andersen Consulting business. Andersen has consistently reconfigured itself to help its clients be more effective in their own enterprises.

Among the leading lights in Andersen there is constant - even daily - pressure to review the nature of its business, its markets and its products and services. This alert and responsive philosophy keeps the company finely attuned to movements - greater or lesser - in its principal markets. It allows Andersen to construct a highly functional appreciation of markets and clients. Then it is able to translate trends among individual clients and specific market sectors into analysis of the future of the corporate sector. Given Andersen's detailed expertise and understanding of the information technology environment, its total strengths contribute to a clear picture of future business.

This determination to interpret the processes of change in business and to harness them for the benefit of the practice and its clients is a major aspect of the rationale for success at Andersen. It has evolved beyond the more traditional consulting services which are offered by the accounting-led practices and the strategy players such as PA and McKinsey. Andersen's vision of the future suggests clients will buy less of the discrete assignments which are currently their preference. Instead they will sponsor joint ventures with suppliers, closer supply-chain partnerships and outsource non-core elements of their businesses. This is a substantial movement from the sector's approach as recently as a decade ago.

Operations and Markets

Consulting was one of the major growth industries of the 1970s and 1980s. Industry grasped the nettle and made extensive and increasing use of management advisers. The larger accounting- based consultancies were the real winners. Armed with financial muscle and global organisational power, the big six accountants displaced the traditional consulting firms. Arthur Andersen's consulting arm raced to the top of the pile. It was so successful that in 1988 it became a separate business around the world. Today Andersen Consulting is the UK, European, US and world number one.

According to figures published by Management Consultancy and Management Consultant International, Andersen Consulting is twice as large as its nearest UK competitor Coopers & Lybrand. Andersen booked £247 million in 1993 on fee growth of 15%. In MCI's survey of European consultancies -

including the EU, EFTA and Eastern Europe -Andersen Consulting was twice as large as runner-up McKinsey & Co. Andersen reported fees of $1,016 million.

In the Americas during 1993 Andersen reported a 14% rise in fees to $1,573.9 million. Worldwide income in 1993 topped $2,880 million, more than double than McKinsey which came second and almost three times larger than revenues at third-placed Ernst & Young. During the recession of 1991 to 1994, when most UK consultancies were fighting to achieve growth in single figures, Andersen regularly booked 30% a year. This staggering feat was achieved by relentless commitment to servicing target markets, and was mainly arrived at by organic growth.

Andersen Consulting is currently structured along industry lines. Its major market strengths are in financial services, manufacturing and distribution, telecommunications, healthcare and utilities. Within each industry sector, the firm offers business and operational strategy, business process design, change management, and information technology architecture services as its core competencies.

Strategy and Management

Vernon Ellis, European managing partner, has no doubts why the firm is so successful. 'There are four elements. Together they make up our heritage. Many years ago - even before IBM - someone at Andersen saw the impact computers were going to have on business. So we developed considerable information technology expertise before many of our competitors.

'Our common background in Arthur Andersen has allowed us to develop a set of shared methodologies which we practise throughout the world. Our training systems are built on these models. Our third strength is our common core of trained people who talk the same language. From this comes an integrated approach to serving clients.'

Andersen Consulting is beyond the leading edge of thinking in terms of future demand. The pursuit of assignments in unfamiliar territory has brought with it new rivals. Among them EDS (Electronic Data Systems) and Hoskyns.

Mr Ellis explains that Andersen examined the sources of traditional business and projected that since many corporations were planning to outsource non-core activities, the need for traditional consulting services would decline. So in the tradition of great strategic thinkers Andersen Consulting turned a negative into a positive. It has gone into facilities management.

He gives four examples of Andersen assignments, initiatives or joint ventures which show the headway which the company has made in these markets. The London Stock Exchange in the early 1990s decided it had to overhaul its whole approach to computing if it was to regain a leadership role for London in international capital markets. Its computer operations urgently needed rationalising and its development track record was not good (culminating in the much publicised failure of the TAURUS project). In consequence, IT development and operations have been outsourced to Andersen Consulting with 300 staff transferred over. Andersen is held to a service contract which calls for very tight operations service levels at lower cost while on the development side, Andersen Consulting is building the new trading systems under a new fixed price contract.

The second example features an arrangement between Andersen Consulting and BP Exploration. 'BP Exploration came to the conclusion that its core competence was oil exploration and not managing a complex accounting function. So we have established an initiative which now employs 250 ex-BP accounting staff. We handle all the internal accounting work for BP Exploration and Accounting Centre Aberdeen is now doing work for other oil companies.'

The third example involves the agricultural equipment supplier Fiat New Holland. Andersen was already working on new distribution systems. A logical extension of this was to create a joint venture company which has taken over the entire operations for spare parts distribution and storage.

Another area of development occurred in the US. 'One of the most difficult administrative tasks for airlines is revenue accounting. They cannot record revenue until they match the ticket coupon listed on check-in with the original sale. It is an administrative nightmare. On an assignment for North West Airlines we created our own processing centre for coupon reconciliation. Now this utility handles 60% of all airline coupon processing in the US.'

Andersen Consulting believes that the configuration of industry will change radically in the future. Information technology advances will accelerate this restructuring and in many industries we will see the emergence of new info-enterprises taking up their positions in restructured industry chains. The airline revenue and the oil accounting centres are two early examples. Andersen is in an excellent position to provide such services on a solo or joint venture basis.

The Future

Andersen Consulting is one of the most remarkable business successes of the last 20 years. At twice the size of its nearest competitor, it is the source of a steady stream of advanced concepts on the future of industry. Internally its daily examination of its business purpose breeds a culture of excellence, innovation and vibrant thought.

Many rivals get to grip with ideas as Andersen discards them and moves on to the next level. In the 1980s cultural philosophers talked about paradigm shifts - Andersen Consulting is a living example of a business which creates and exploits such phenomena. In the business environment where every company needs to assess the future, Andersen's continuity is assured.

Apple Computer

Apple, Middx.

Apple is one of the world's leading international computer hardware and software companies. Its most famous product is the Macintosh which is one of the most creative and easy to use computer systems

Outlook:
The introduction of the Power Mac is a major step forward for Apple. Its traditional heartland of committed Mac users in education, communications and creative disciplines is now being expanded in a bid for the wider commercial and business market. The big growth area in the next decade is domestic systems and Apple is exceptionally well placed to exploit this trend

Scorecard:
Structural flexibility	★★★★
Innovative power	★★★★★
International orientation	★★★★
Human resources	★★★
Growth markets	★★★★★
Quality of management	★★★

Key figures:
Turnover (global)	$9,189 million
Pre-tax profits	$1,920 million
Worldwide staff	14,592

Apple Computer (UK) Ltd
6 Roundwood Avenue
Stockley Park
Uxbridge
Middlesex UB11 1BB
Tel: 0181 569 1199

Apple

'Macintosh is far too good a computer to be left in the hands of Apple,' used to be a common, if exaggerated, quip in the computer industry. However, that feeling is now changing, with Apple's dynamic management installing new priorities and strategic aims, aimed at taking the group into the 21st century. Apple was 18 years old in 1994, and like most teenagers has enjoyed a bumpy ride during some of those years. Throughout the journey to becoming a multi-billion dollar corporation, and one of the best-recognised global brand names, Apple has retained that quirkiness which at times has infuriated, but which has made the company stand out in an increasingly bland corporate world.

Even the circumstances of Apple's founding provide a clue to the group's nature. Steve Wozniak and Steve Jobs, two young computer engineers working for Hewlett Packard and Atari respectively, founded the company on April Fool's Day in 1976, with the plan of making pre-assembled circuit boards. Mr Jobs sold his Volkswagen van and Mr Wozniak his programmable calculator to finance their first production run, which was assembled in the Jobs family garage. A sign of the two young men's confidence came in the original business plan, which predicted turnover of $500m after 10 years - in the event it only took five.

By 1980 Apple had grown to a company employing some 300 people, and when it joined the stock market in December of that year, demand was so strong it became the largest Initial Public Offering since Ford in 1956.

That innovative spirit which defined the company came to the fore in the development of Macintosh, the most outstanding computer of the age. Recognising that innovation is hard to maintain in a corporate atmosphere concerned with existing products and problems, Apple's management isolated the team working on the Mac some half a mile from the main company campus. The tactic worked brilliantly, and the startling new computer was backed up by a unique advertising campaign.

During the 1984 Super Bowl, Apple ran an ad entitled '1984'. The ad only aired the once, but went on to win nine awards, including *Advertising Age's* Commercial of the Decade. An intensive print campaign was commissioned, including buying every page of advertising in *Newsweek's* special post-election edition.

Operations and markets

Since the launch of the Apple, and its initial stunning success, the marketplace has changed however. Giants such as Microsoft and Intel have sprung up, and taken dominant roles in the design and marketing of personal computers. For much of the past decade Apple was content to do its own thing, aware of an enormous base of customers who liked and admired its product, and who weren't interested in moving to IBM compatible systems. Others moved on though, and Apple failed to realise that in such a market software is king. Some 90 per cent of the world's PCs now come equipped with Microsoft operating systems, even though many experts regard the system as inferior to the Mac. Perhaps it was only the excellence of the Mac computer which helped Apple to come this far. As one long-term industry observer quipped, 'Apple won the argument, but lost the war. IBM lost the argument and the war. Microsoft won the war because Bill Gates [the Microsoft supremo] wasn't interested in arguments'.

But Apple is still a significant player in the PC market, supplying around 10 per cent of all PCs. And that market is growing at a phenomenal rate - over a third of US households already possess a PC, and that figure is expected to reach half the nation by the end of the decade. Elsewhere in the world the proportion of PC owners is smaller, but the rate of growth is even faster.

Apple is entering a crucial period for its future success. The changing nature of the PC market has conspired to give the group an almost unparalleled opportunity to cement its strong position. Dataquest, the industry research agency, expects home PC sales to match business sales this year for the first time, and home computer sales are forecast to be double that of the business PC market between 1993 and 1998. The principle beneficiary of this surge should be Apple - already world number one home computer supplier (market share 23 per cent). Apple's product mix is perfectly matched to the years ahead. There is an installed base of 15-16m Mac units, and a growing number of new customers in markets such as Japan, which are no longer the sole domain of local producers. In the battle for the hearts and minds of the consumer Apple has a huge advantage from its pre-eminent position in the education market. A world market share of 28 per cent (50 per cent in the US) is a great introduction to home PC buyers. Parents generally look to see what hardware their children are using at school before purchasing a computer for the home. The fastest growing sector of the home PC market is multimedia, where Apple is number one with a near 25 per cent market share.

Strategy and management

Three huge steps have been identified as the key to Apple's strategy into the 21st century. The first, which has already been implemented has proved to be a roaring success, but the jury is still out on the next two:

1) A 1991 agreement laid the foundation for the latest of Apple's award-winning models, the Power Mac. This computer is based on a new type of microprocessor which should set the standard for years to come. The Power PC provides developers with a mainstream platform for advanced software solutions in two ways: new versions of current applications (such as publishing, word processing, spreadsheets, databases) will run faster, and the creation of a new generation of applications will bring new capabilities to the PC which were once the preserve of much more expensive workstations. Speech recognition, voice control, text-to-speech translation and video will be far more widely available. The launch of the Power Mac has been a tremendous success - 20 per cent more than budgeted targets have been sold, more than 1m in the first ten months. By the end of 1995 Power Macs should make up around half Apple's predicted 4.4m unit shipments. The software industry's reaction has been just as favourable as consumers', and there are more than 500 native versions of Power Mac software on the market now, up from only 67 when the product was launched.

2) The second leg of Apple's strategy is more of a quantum leap. The company's

jealously guarded proprietary technology, the subject of countless lawsuits through the 1980s and 1990s, is going to be licensed, allowing the production of the first Mac clones. This step flies in the face of accepted wisdom at Apple over the last decade, but is management's response to what one expert has called the computer industry's new creed: 'Software is king, and entertainment software is God.'

Three producers have already signed up to license Mac products, among them Pioneer, which will provide an additional boost in Japan. Creating a clone market for Macs is intended to make the format even more attractive for software developers, ensuring the future of the Mac. To really get the process going Apple needs to sign up one of the top ten PC manufacturers. This eventuality has become more likely with increasing resentment among producers such as Vobis and Compaq, who fear the power of the Microsoft/Intel partnership at the hub of the PC market.

3) The third and most revolutionary step for Apple is the development with IBM and Motorola of a common hardware platform. Known as HRP (Hardware Reference Platform) the new machine will be able to run virtually any operating system including Windows, UNIX, NetWare and IBM's Warp, as well as the Mac operating system. The Power PC-based machine will be easily configured to any of these systems, and in some cases will come with a choice of pre-loaded systems which the consumer can use or discard as required. Not surprisingly, the HRP, which should debut in 1996 is expected to bring about a massive shake-up in the PC market, perhaps similar to the shockwaves felt when the first Mac hit the market back in 1994.

CEO Michael Spindler has been running the show since 1993, after cutting his teeth as head of the European operations. The group has a history of incisive appointments, even if the dynamic nature of the industry has sometimes necessitated a quick turnover of staff - few other technology companies would have had the insight to appoint John Sculley as president back in 1983, a man who had made his name at soft drinks giant Pepsico. In fact, marketing-led expertise was just what a company staffed by technology-focused executives required. A tribute to the new stability at the group is the smooth transition to the Power Mac - no other computer company has successfully managed the radical restructuring of its crucial microprocessor architecture.

The future

After years of sometimes brilliant but often erratic progress Apple now looks to have secured a bright future, with a steady pair of hands on the tiller. 'We are committed to licensing the Macintosh operating system,' says Michael Spindler. 'We believe that our first licensing agreements together with the creation of a common hardware reference platform for Power PC based computers, lays, a foundation for broader acceptance of the Macintosh.' Revolutionary decisions have been taken, and although there is still a long road to travel, Apple looks well set to remain the dominant player in the PC industry into the 21st century. After several years of playing catch-up, the group looks to have a credible strategy and products to lead the next generation of computers.

ASDA, Leeds

ASDA is the fastest growing UK supermarket chain offering
good honest value always

Outlook:
The pace of change in retailing is remarkable. At the top end Tesco has edged
past Sainsbury and ASDA has moved into third place. The appointment of
Archie Norman as CEO has done wonders for this previously rather
lacklustre company. Now ASDA is roaring ahead. The business is
concentrating on higher margin areas and experiencing outstanding increases
in sales

Scorecard:

Structural flexibility	★★★★
Innovative power	★★★★★
International orientation	★★★
Human resources	★★★★
Growth markets	★★★★
Quality of management	★★★★

Key figures:

Sales	£5.7 billion
Profits	£246.2 million
Staff	36,000

ASDA Stores Ltd
ASDA House
Southbank
Great Wilson Street
Leeds LS11 5AD
Tel: 0113 2435435
Fax: 0113 2418660

ASDA

ASDA is Britain's fastest growing retailer. The company has outperformed the industry - best specified as food retailing - for each of the last three years. It is no coincidence that this three-year period has witnessed a programme of comprehensive transformation and renewal initiated by ASDA's young, dynamic management team.

The core business is the ASDA superstore operation. ASDA has 202 stores in total, spread throughout the UK but with historical concentrations in the North and Midlands. With 8,345 square feet of sales area, these stores generated sales of nearly £5.7 billion in the last financial year (1994/95), on which pre-tax profits of £246.2m were achieved.

While the food retailing sector is not without its problems - overcapacity and pricing pressure are just two examples - ASDA has a number of factors in its favour. Its superstores are on average 60 per cent larger than those of its competitors and it sells a wider range of clothing, entertainment and general merchandise. The superstore niche of the industry is a growth area at present, experiencing both inflation and substantial volume gains. And with only half of its stores renewed so far, ASDA has left itself ample scope to realise good returns in its immediate future.

Operations and markets

ASDA's principal activities are described as the retailing of food, clothing, home and leisure goods, and property development, and the ASDA superstore lies at the heart. The group has been transformed in recent years, as management set about creating a leaner, more responsive business focused on customer service and capable of sustained profit growth. The measures taken have been fairly substantial, and a sizeable exceptional charge was made on profits in 1994.

This recovery plan was necessary because ASDA had somehow lost touch with its traditional, working-class customer base. Furthermore, many ASDA stores were crying out for investment. 'ASDA Price' had always been synonymous with outstanding value - that means quality as well as price - but previously loyal customers had turned their backs. It was this falling customer count that formed the roots of ASDA's weak trading performance. Chief executive Archie Norman: 'The business paid a high price for the loss of customer focus and this is not a mistake that will recur under this management. Since launching the renewal programme, customer numbers are up three quarters of a million a week and continue to grow.'

That is a good performance, and a quite necessary one given the current background to the food retailing sector. ASDA management has labelled it 'Industry in the Treacle' with just cause. Low growth, superstore saturation, pricing pressure from the discounters, an industry continuing to add capacity faster than growth in demand, static to declining margins and the additional costs of marketing and service initiatives all feature.

ASDA can continue to make good inroads into the competition by winning back customers and adding new ones, and clearly has a better opportunity to boost sales and productivity because it is starting from a lower base. That is only part of the story. ASDA stores are on average 60 per cent larger than those of its competitors, and the company makes great virtue of its non-food sales. And why not? In a crowded food retailing market, many have not appreciated that the superstore sector is still a growth market. This is a niche area of retailing that is exhibiting both price inflation and substantial volume gain, in terms of proportions of total consumer expenditure.

So what of the trumpeted ASDA 'difference'? Archie Norman: 'The ASDA "difference" is the people we employ, our larger stores, our market-style fresh foods, our "George" brand clothing and a unique range of general merchandise. We intend to make this difference count in a market which continues to get tougher.'

The combination of store rejuvenation, sharper customer focus, and the non-food dimension, is behind ASDA's superior performance. Like-for-like sales are up by 8.4 per cent; market share increased to 9.7 per cent (making ASDA the third largest in UK food retailing); sales per full time employee have been improved by 10.5 per cent. Since 1992, comparable sales growth has outstripped the industry average by 16 per cent and customer numbers have increased by 31 per cent to 5.2 million per week.

Strategy and management

ASDA's strategic focus is on expanding its higher margin areas. Quality of fresh foods is one of the main determinants of customer choice and a main thrust of ASDA's recovery strategy has been an increased emphasis on fresh foods in a market hall environment. This is where the virtuous circle begins. By improving its quality, ASDA has strengthened its own brand value and increased sales accordingly. This allows for a more rapid stock turnover, more dedicated suppliers, and improved quality. The results are self-evident - in the last three years, sales of fresh meat have increased by 61 per cent, fruit and vegetables by 80 per cent, and bakery goods by 44 per cent.

Another high margin activity - own brand participation - is also on an upward trend. At 32 per cent, ASDA's brand penetration is at its highest ever level, and with rivals Tesco somewhere nearer 60 per cent, there is a lot more to play for.

In the so-called 'non-food' activities, ASDA is perhaps best known for its unique 'George' brand of clothing. The legend of George Davies, formerly of 'Next' fame, lives on. ASDA claims leadership in the out-of-town market for clothing and, driven by ladies fashions and childrenswear, annual sales growth and sales per square foot have raced ahead.

ASDA's management is also committed to a penetration strategy, reinvesting gross margins to boost sales. There is still a lot further to go, and as a high priority, the company is investing some £70 million over three years in systems infrastructure not only to catch up with, but probably to leapfrog the competition.

There has been an increasing emphasis on improving productivity and the gains have been impressive. Sales per employee have increased by 34 per cent in three years, while the central headcount has been reduced by 18 per cent. In reducing the headcount, which followed a salary freeze in the first year of the three-year programme, the company has taken difficult decisions with frank, honest communications.

ASDA is financially sound. Previous investor concerns about cash flow and depreciation policy have been allayed, with the group now in a net cash position and generating positive cash flow. Tight financial disciplines have been introduced and depreciation policy brought more into line with the industry norm; indeed, observers suggest that some of ASDA's write-backs of earlier provisions are probably conservative.

The management team, led by Archie Norman, is very young and relatively new. This would appear to be exactly what the company needs, and one that is well-suited to a fast-moving, ever changing industry. ASDA claims that its management structure is 'flat', based neither on hierarchy or status. More than 170 of ASDA's 202 stores have new managers, and nearly all of the top 200 managers at ASDA House have been recruited or promoted during the 'change' period.

Hardly unusual for a retailing business, ASDA recognises the importance of not only customers' opinions, but also its own staff commitment (whom they refer to as 'colleagues') in delivering outstanding customer service. Motivation is a key factor in helping deliver the best value and service, and ASDA employees at all levels are encouraged to participate in the success of the business. The company is proud of its self-styled ASDA personality.

An awful lot of time and effort has been devoted to engendering this culture, and the evidence is that it is working. Employees seem happiest when they are identifying closely with customers and their requirements and comments. Real responsibility leads to real commitment. The concept of listening groups held at each store is just one example of a range of initiatives taken to ensure that ASDA never again loses sight of its customers. Selling does not always come naturally to everyone, and it is possible to make a case that many people in large organisations shy away from it if at all possible. This is not the case at ASDA, where all staff seem to have a very clear idea about the selling process and the methods by which it is maximised.

Motivation and empowerment are not idle words at ASDA. The company has just introduced the Colleague Share Ownership Plan to extend share participation to the majority of ASDA's 36,000 employees - to be taxed as income, not capital gain, of course.

The future

The initiatives taken over the last three years have undoubtedly put ASDA in a strong position. ASDA has effectively re-invented itself and in so doing, has secured its future for the mid to late 1990s. New stores can now be opened at an acceptable rate of return, and over half of the existing stores have still to be renewed. And the non-foods business in its superstores is enjoying a phase of healthy resurgence.

If there have been concerns about future growth beyond the renewal stage, including planning restrictions for out-of-town sites, then this would appear to be of greater hindrance to ASDA's competitors. ASDA's vigorous management team is under no illusions as to the competitive pressures facing the industry and will not shy away from confronting these head on.

ASDA looks set for continued strong performance over the next few years, and much of this can be attributed to catching up its peer group. But if business decisions are taken with the same vigor as the programme of renewal has been, Britain's 'fastest-changing retailer' has every chance of being Britain's 'fastest-growing retailer' in the foreseeable future.

BAA plc, London

BAA owns and operates seven UK airports - Heathrow, Gatwick, Stansted, Glasgow, Edinburgh, Aberdeen and Southampton.It also manages shops and restaurants at Pittsburgh Airport

Outlook:
BAA emerged from the public sector with impeccable speed and efficiency. This is one of Britain's most innovative former public sector businesses and is warmly regarded by analysts. In the next decade through Terminal 5 at Heathrow and its international expansion BAA has a rewarding future

Scorecard:

Structural flexibility	★★★
Innovative power	★★★★
International orientation	★★★★★
Human resources	★★★
Growth markets	★★★★★
Quality of management	★★★★

Key figures:

World turnover	£1,097 million
World pre-tax profits	£366 million
UK staff	7,800
Total assets	£2,845 million

BAA plc
130 Wilton Road
London SW1V 1LQ
Tel: 0171 834 9449
Fax: 0171 932 6699

BAA

BAA chief executive Sir John Egan has set his company on an ambitious flight path. 'Our mission is to make BAA the most successful airport company in the world,' he says.

This is no idle ambition. BAA, which operates two of the world's busiest airports, Heathrow and Gatwick, is already planning well into the next century. It is investing more than £1m per day for the foreseeable future at its seven airports. And it plans to spend another £1.2bn on the proposed Terminal 5 project at Heathrow. This against a background of ongoing world aviation growth, with passenger traffic forecast to increase by five per cent annually for the next decade. Throw in the opportunities for BAA from a number of airport privatisations overseas and it is easy to see why market analysts call BAA 'an excellent long-term growth story'.

As Chris Avery, aviation analyst at stockbrokers Paribas, puts it: 'BAA offers all the growth potential of world aviation, without the risk of investing in individual airlines.' BAA's skill has been to capitalise on the growing numbers of passengers coming through its terminals, enticing them to spend increasing amounts of money in airport shops. Indeed the rapid development of BAA's retail arm has largely underpinned its profit growth, up from £122m in 1987 to £322m in 1994.

From this formula, shareholders have more than trebled their money since BAA came to market in July 1987, with the shares outperforming the All-Share Index by over 150 per cent. Today BAA has a market capitalisation of around £6m putting it comfortably in the top 40 FT-SE100 stocks. According to Mike Powell analyst at NatWest Securities, 'BAA's status as a core transport sector holding is unquestionable'.

Sir John's business philosophy starts with the premise that the customer is always right. So he is a true champion of the service ethic. BAA conducts 100,000 interviews a year with passengers to ensure they get what they want from using BAA airports. But Sir John is also a capitalist through and through. His belief is that people will spend more - as long as they get value for money.

Operations and markets

BAA is a hybrid company. Part utility, part transport company, it draws its single largest proportion of income from retailing. And, on top of this, it also has growing property and construction businesses. But basically it has four main sources of revenue: airport charges, retail income, property income and construction. Crucially, only one of these is regulated.

Airport charges: BAA earns revenue each time a plane lands or is parked at each of its seven airports - Heathrow, Gatwick, Stansted, Glasgow, Edinburgh, Aberdeen and Southampton. It also gets a handling fee for every departing passenger using the airports. This income source is partly regulated by the Civil Aviation Authority, with charge increases held below the retail price index. Every five years the regulatory regime is reviewed. In 1994, airport charges accounted for £367.10m of BAA's total £1.1bn revenue. But it is not a particularly lucrative source of income.

This is, however, deliberate. It is not BAA's strategy to make a killing on airport charges. Sir John wants to encourage airlines to use airports, not put them off. And the regulator would not permit BAA to make fat profits from charges. As Sir John points out, charges at London's airports have fallen 20 per cent in the last three years. 'In Heathrow we operate the largest and most profitable international airport in the world,' he says. 'Yet its landing charges are among the lowest, making it an ideal base for profitable airline operations.'

Retail income: But the more airlines that use the airport the more opportunities there are for BAA to profit from the passengers they bring. This has been steadily achieved by an aggressive expansion of retail activities, with revenues from passenger shopping rising from £150m in 1987 to £468m in 1994. BAA will double the retail space at its airports over the next five years. Stockbroker Charles Stanley estimates that by 1997, 12 per cent of BAA's airport terminal space will be devoted to retail activities.

Crucially this income stream is not regulated, and operating margins are wide. This is because airport shopping is a much higher quality business than high-street retailing. As Rowan Morgan of Nikko Europe puts it: 'Passengers are a captive and often bored audience, capable of being relieved of their cash given a suitable inducement.' Moreover they are some of the world's richest people.

BAA's inducement has been to improve the quality of the goods on offer. As Sir John says: 'Passengers wanted a wider choice of restaurants - so the range now extends from burger bars to caviar and oyster bars.'

BAA works in partnership with concessionaires to bring high standards of customer service. And both BAA and the concessionaires reap rewards. While spend per passenger in the high street has risen by only 10 per cent since 1988, spend at BAA's airports is up 50 per cent, showing compound growth of around 7 per cent annually. With these kinds of growth rates, it is no surprise that Heathrow's Bally shoe store, for example, sells more shoes per square metre than any other shop in Britain.

Property income: Third in importance behind these two sources of revenue is income from property rentals. This increased to £180m in 1994. 'Wherever we have applied our philosophy of choice, quality and value for money we have seen our income increase and property should be no exception,' says Sir John. His aim is to give airport tenants real value for money, so they base themselves at the airports rather than elsewhere. To achieve this goal, BAA has been steadily building up its property portfolio. In the last three years, BAA has added over 1m square feet of property, raising the value of the book to £6bn. It plans to make available another 1.5m square feet of prime airport rental space over the next three years. And it recently announced a land deal with British Airways at Heathrow which radically increases the amount of rental space available there.

BAA is targeting all big users of the airports - airlines, handling agents, customs and immigration, the police and cargo handling companies - with the view to locking them into attractive rental contracts on a long-term basis. So in January 1995 it announced that it was freezing rents at its terminals until March 1996, directly benefiting around 90 airport tenants.

Construction: Construction is BAA's youngest revenue activity. Its colossal spend on terminals makes it one of the UK's largest contractors. But it is also paying close attention to honing up its own building skills, employing the latest techniques. Its aim is not only to bring down the costs of its own projects, but to develop a skill base that it can market elsewhere.

Sir John believes the British construction industry is both backward and too expensive. He reckons more sophisticated techniques could shave at least 30 per cent off project costs. One of BAA's core skills is redeveloping airport buildings while keeping them in operation. But the company's developing skills do not stop at the perimeter fence. It is working in partnership with British Rail, for example, to build the £300m high-speed rail link between Heathrow and central London.

Strategy and management

Modern construction techniques will be a feature of the planned £1.2bn Terminal 5 project at Heathrow. But first BAA has to win planning permission - vital to its growth prospects in the UK.

BAA's case is that south-east airports will only be able to meet growth demand until 2002. Failure to build Terminal 5 will mean UK airports lose traffic to European rivals. And this will cost 16,500 jobs. Sir John calls Terminal 5 'essential for the continued economic well-being of London, the south-east and the UK'. There is bound to be some opposition on environmental grounds. But, with so much at stake economically, BAA is expected to get the green light.

But BAA's future is not only on Terminal 5. The company is already heavily involved in airport consultancy on most continents, advising on prestige projects such as the new Hong Kong airport. Moreover, it has already demonstrated that its airport retail skills can be transported elsewhere. Today it operates the shopping malls at Pittsburgh International Airport, US. Within six months of opening, sales reached $1m a week, more than doubling the amount passengers spent at the airport.

Similar retail opportunities are being explored. But BAA is also targeting something more ambitious: ownership and operation of airports abroad. More governments are following the UK example of privatising their airports. Most recently Australia announced that it would be selling off 22 airports, including Sydney, Melbourne and Perth. Shrewdly, BAA has already gained a listing on the Australian stock market and joined forces with two local fund managers to advance its claims.

Such expansion is essential if BAA is to maintain the earnings growth it has demonstrated since its flotation. And not all of it will be funded through cashflow. Terminal 5 and projects overseas will involve a call to shareholders. But BAA's strong track record suggests that financing shouldn't be a problem.

The future

'BAA is the quality player in both the European airport sub-sector and the European transport sector as a whole,' says Matthew Stainer, analyst at Morgan Stanley. 'It has high quality earnings and we estimate that underlying earnings growth should be 13.1 per cent a year over the next four years, substantially higher than our forecasts for the UK market.'

Baxter Healthcare Ltd

Baxter Healthcare, Newbury

Baxter Healthcare is a major international healthcare manufacturer

Outlook:
The globalisation of markets is nowhere more apparent than it is in the healthcare sector. The outstanding levels of investment which are required to ensure long-term viability mean that concentration will occur around a handful of key operators. The global players will need to be market leaders in key product areas and geographical regions. Baxter has the capacity to be a significant force

Scorecard:
Structural flexibility	★★★
Innovative power	★★★★★
International orientation	★★★★★
Human resources	★★★★
Growth markets	★★★★
Quality of management	★★★★

Key figures:
Sales	$9,324 million
Operating profits	$801 million
Staff	67,500

Baxter Healthcare Limited
Wallingford Road
Compton
Newbury RG20 7QW
Tel: 01635 206 000
Fax: 01635 206 115

Baxter Healthcare Ltd

Throughout the world the system of healthcare is under close inspection. Governments unable to cover the increasing costs of an ageing population and the advanced methods of treatment are looking for ways to reshape their systems of medical support. Hospitals are closed down or rationalised and the allowed prices for treatments and products are cut.

This poses strong challenges for healthcare companies: How to continue funding the long-term development of new products whilst transforming themselves into flexible, cost-efficient and service-oriented organisations. Only a few global players will be able to meet these challenges and the leading-edge medical equipment manufacturer Baxter Healthcare has shown it will be one of them.

Operations and markets

Baxter Healthcare originates in the United States. It is the world's leading manufacturer and marketeer of healthcare products and services for use in hospitals, other healthcare settings and with patients at home. Baxter is present in over 100 markets, employs some 60,000 staff and provides a spectrum of products covering over 70 per cent of the supplies needed in hospitals.

Operations are divided between United States (70 per cent), Europe (15 per cent) and the rest of the world (15 per cent). The growth prospects in developing countries should increase the significance of the rest of the world substantially over the next decade.

Baxter's activities are focused in two industry segments:
. medical specialties:
   highly specialised products for treating kidney and heart disease and blood disorders and for collecting and processing blood, which include dialysis equipment; prosthetic heart valves and cardiac catheters. This segment accounts for approximately one third of the company's sales.
. medical/laboratory products and distribution:
   supplies and equipment for laboratories and medical institutions including intravenous systems, diagnostic-testing equipment, surgical instruments and a range of disposable and reusable medical products. Customers include hospitals, blood banks, veterinarians, offices, dentists and home patients.

Strategy and management

The three main aims of Baxter Healthcare's strategy are:
. creating a customer-focused organisation providing superior service
. bringing to market innovative products through internal development and external partnerships
. increasing global market penetration

In early response to the changing market place, Baxter has committed to transform itself into a service-focused organisation which according to its corporate statement will 'provide the undisputed best service to customers in both distribution and manufacturing'. It has recognised that the ways of doing business in its market-place are going to change through changing customer needs and that they will be changed by those that understand these changing needs best. Special account teams have been set in place in order to create closer customer relations and so to enhance customer understanding.

Baxter has recognised that in a business where the customer is under strong pressure to reduce costs, long-term competitive advantages can be created by generating special services and programmes that help the customer rationalise costs.

The best example is perhaps Baxter's ValueLink (TM) stockless inventory-management service. Valuelink allows hospitals to eliminate the large cost of storing and maintaining supplies without sacrificing their level of service or increasing the risk of out-of-stock. Baxter manages a hospital's inventory, delivering supplies several times a day, on a just-in-time basis. ValueLink helps hopitals to save money through inventory reduction and reduced costs of handling, and enables the hospital to put to full use its often expensive spaces by transforming warehouses into revenue-generating areas.

'Baxter has helped us save more than $ 100 million over the last five years' says Mr Trout, chief executive of AmHs, which represents more than 1,000 non-profit healthcare facilities throughout the United States. 'Working with your customer for your customer. Baxter has put in enormous effort and investment over the past years to change into a modern customer-driven organisation, fully exploiting the need for more efficiency in the healthcare industry.'

Another example is the Quality Enhanced Distribution (QED) system aiming at hospitals not yet ready to implement the rigorous changes of the ValueLink services. In hospitals where Quality Enhanced Distribution has been implemented, it has reduced the amount of labour associated with the receipt and storage of supplies by an average of 90 per cent. Baxter itself benefits through increased business at QED accounts and a more predictable distribution schedule, resulting in fewer but larger deliveries among other efficiencies.

Underpinning these new services is the philosophy that the customer truly is a partner in the whole exercise, as is well demonstrated in the ground-breaking contract with Duke University Hospital in the US. Here Baxter set up the industry's first risk-sharing supply agreement, meaning that if supply costs fall below a certain cost per procedure then the Hospital and Baxter share the cost-savings, but if supply costs exceed the target, Baxter pays half the difference.

True partnerships also eventuate in the research and development of new products, where Baxter ensures it maintains its leading position by various alliances with leading-edge companies. This enables Baxter to master new and complex biomedical technologies and market new products timely and competitively. For its partners Baxter is a source of leading-edge medical and technical know how, while providing the expert knowledge and experience in the equally important fields of production, procedures and marketing.

The global penetration strategy of Baxter Healthcare entails that Baxter has presences in all countries with governments that are committed to attaining economic stability and improving healthcare. Corporate vice president Carlos del Salto: 'There is an exciting undercurrent of change and opportunity for Baxter to expand its leadership. The challenge for us is to get into these markets early on and establish a strong presence.'

The newly industrialising and developing countries contain the majority of the world's population and they will see their healthcare expenditures rise even more strongly than the western countries. With vast markets developing in China, India and Indonesia, Baxter has been right in globalising its operations further. The contribution from these markets to Baxter's sales and profits will substantially increase over the years.

The future

Baxter has shown itself to be able not just to provide the excellent products neccessary to be successful in the competitive healthcare market, but to read the signs of the times properly and to create win-win situations together with its customers. Its lead in state-of-the-art materials management services is now widely recognised, creating opportunities to offer these services through other healthcare companies. Baxter nowadays provides a range of products well beyond its own scope of research and development, thereby increasing the service offered to its customers and earning extra income from distribution.

The healthcare market is still expanding even in the troubled markets of the United States and Great Britain. This will continue as the population ages - in the U.S. there will be 70 million senior citizens in 2030, compared to 30 million in 1990 - and new methods of treatments and products are introduced at rising costs. Baxter is sure to profit from the growth in these markets having displayed the ability to move ahead of the competition and adapt to customer needs.

BICCGroup

BICC, London

BICC is a world market leader in the cable and construction sectors

Outlook:
BICC is a highly respected company worldwide which has experienced considerable development in the last few years. BICC is at the forefront of technological advance in an industry which is in increasing demand throughout the world. But the company recognises that continuous improvement in all of its activities is the key delineator of world class success

Scorecard:

Structural flexibility	★★★★
Innovative power	★★★★★
International orientation	★★★★★
Human resources	★★★★
Growth markets	★★★★★
Quality of management	★★★★

Key figures:

Turnover	£3.97 billion
Pre-tax profits	£131 million
Staff	35,708

BICC plc
Devonshire House
Mayfair Place
London W1X 5FH
Tel: 0171 629 6622
Fax:0171 409 0070

BICC

One company that needs only to go that extra mile to achieve promotion to the top flight of quoted UK stocks is BICC. With a market capitalisation of £1.2bn, the cables and construction group already stands on the threshold of inclusion within the FTSE-100.

Operations and markets

BICC was formed in 1945 through the merger of Britain's two leading electrical and cable companies. Over the next 25 years, it expanded abroad, mainly in Commonwealth countries, and in 1969 acquired the Balfour Beatty power construction and engineering group. Subsequent acquisitions took BICC's cable interests into North America, continental Europe, Asia and Australia, while Balfour Beatty moved into civil engineering and other contracting businesses and now has an annual turnover in excess of £1.7bn.

With annual sales approaching £2bn, the cable business is one of the largest in the world, and provides about three-quarters of group profits. Operating in a market worth more than £30bn, it is the biggest power cablemaker in North America and is the leading manufacturer of optical fibre outside the US.

However, Sir Robin Biggam, the chairman, recognises the challenges BICC faces in markets where steady growth cannot always be guaranteed. 'The long-term success of businesses like BICC, operating in largely mature markets for infrastructure development, comes not from massive step changes in technology or market dynamics, but from the relentless pursuit of total continuous improvement.'

According to the chairman, examples of this approach include responding to the market's need for contracting out non-core activities, upgrading manufacturing facilities in Germany and on Merseyside, and transferring UK-based technology into the US market.

Concentrating on areas of competitive advantage is another area for attention. 'We are leading the response to the growing market for privately funded infrastructure projects and building on established reputations for quality work in Hong Kong and specialist cables in the US,' he says.

Strategy and management

BICC has made mistakes along the way. Cable and construction were once regarded by investors as 'sunset industries' - primary industries offering little growth. This prompted BICC in the eighties to develop a third leg, known as BICC Technologies, a division which at its peak in 1987 had sales of around £200m.

However, dwindling profits by the turn of the nineties forced BICC to rethink its foray into the world of electronics. Last year, this chapter in diversification was effectively closed when its Vero Electronics group was sold to management for £33m.

Property development was another area which once held attractions for

BICC, being linked to Balfour Beatty's construction activity. Now the policy is to sell developments once they are completed and invest the proceeds in projects which offer far better returns as Sir Robin Biggam explains. 'It remains our priority to reduce our capital tied up in property and progress will be made in 1995. The group is looking at a number of management programmes aimed at maximising profit growth over the next period.'

Foremost among these are enormous opportunities for power and telecom cables in the Asia and the Far East. BICC ranks second only to Alcatel in the provision of cables worldwide and one of its most important assets is the breadth of its geographic reach and product range.

'We want to rapidly develop a major cable manufacturing and trading business in the Asia-Pacific region, where cable sales have more than doubled to £173m over the last five years,' says Sir Robin. This could treble to £500m by the end of the decade if the growing infrastructure market is successfully exploited. To that end, BICC recently formed an Asia-Pacific Cables division to handle business in the region. The UK company will have a 50 per cent stake with the rest held by Metal manufactures, the 61 per cent-owned Australian subsidiary.

Of course, riding the Asian tiger exposes BICC to greater political risk as the company found to its cost over the Pergau Dam affair. Balfour Beatty and Trafalgar House, its consortium partner, failed to win a £30m project management contract for the new Kuala Lumpur airport when the Malaysian government controversially placed a ban on public contracts to British companies.

The ban was later lifted, and BICC remains confident Balfour Beatty can recover any lost ground by trebling sales in the region to £300m over the next three to five years as many Asian countries like Malaysia continue their programmes of rapid industrialisation.

This expansion is part of a strategy to reduce Balfour Beatty's dependence on the depressed UK construction market, where prospects are bleak given the uncertain outlook for many infrastructure projects, especially road building. Balfour Beatty is increasing the proportion of its overseas business and last year 22 per cent of the division's £1.7bn turnover came from overseas, compared to a 9 per cent share in 1993.

The most obvious growth market by product rather than area is fibre optic cables, which are rapidly taking over from traditional copper wires. The growth is being driven by rising demand for mobile telephone networks, cable TV, video libraries and home shopping. But the main source of demand comes from telecomms companies, especially in the deregulated UK market. With BICC already boasting about a third of the European fibre optic market, it is particularly well placed to benefit as continental European telecomms markets open up. Group fibre optic sales of £123m in 1994 are projected to hit £300m by the year 2000.

In the short term, BICC has to grapple with higher raw material prices. In the case of copper and aluminium - two of BICC's biggest costs - they rose by over 70 per cent in 1994, an increase which meant some customers delayed orders. Passing on higher selling prices for cables is proving very difficult, so the emphasis is on pushing through volume increases.

The higher raw material prices put a strain on working capital requirements, which rose by £60m last year, leading to a net cash outflow of £112m. As a result borrowings increased - exactly by how much remains the subject of some debate, but under the strictest interpretation net debt was 100 per cent of shareholders' fund.

However, BICC did move towards producing a more transparent accounting policy, bringing most of the property-related, off-balance-sheet debt on to the balance sheet. And analysts believe the high level of borrowings will come down over the next few years as capital expenditure falls by a fifth with the completion of heavy investment in Germany and Spain and the peaking of raw material prices.

Cash flow will also be improved by the recent decision to cut the 1994 dividend by almost a quarter to 14.6p. Few would dispute that a policy of paying more to shareholders than the company actually earned - as BICC did for three years on the trot - was not a sustainable policy.

But there are many in the City who swear that the dividend cut was not entirely unrelated to the imminent arrival of new chief executive Alan Jones, formerly of Westland and Plessey. Although BICC is at pains to deny it, the feeling remains that Jones applied pressure to have the dividend cut to ensure his regime presided over a rising rather than a stagnating payout.

The arrival of Mr Jones, who joined BICC at the start of April 1995, may herald a revival in BICC's share price, which has consistently underperformed the stock market. Certainly, he appears to have the right credentials. While at Westland, he presided over a 60 per cent increase in the company's pre-tax profits and a tripling in the share price.

'He is a tough and experienced manager,' says Sir Robin, 'whose background in electrical engineering and major projects equips him admirably for handling our two core businesses of cables and construction.' Mr Jones will take charge of the day-to-day running of BICC, though Sir Robin remains chairman.

The future

Sentiment towards BICC is also likely to improve with further significant property disposals. With the introduction of new management, the belated dividend cut, the tidying up of the balance sheet, lucrative exposure to the high growth fibre optic sector and hopes that base metal prices may have peaked, BICC seems to be pressing all the right buttons.

Notwithstanding a difficult UK power cables market and intense price pressure on UK construction contracts, the group's stock market fortunes may be on the verge of a significant revival.

BLACK& DECKER®

The New Generation

Black & Decker, Berks

Black & Decker is a highly respected manufacturer of power tools for both domestic and industrial markets

Outlook:

B&D is the best known name in power tools in the UK. In the rest of Europe it encounters severe competition but is slowly winning the battle. Its manufacturing operation in Spennymoor is one of the most respected plants in Europe. B&D is building directly on its enviable reputation through internal quality enhancing initiatives

Scorecard:

Structural flexibility	★★★★
Innovative power	★★★★★
International orientation	★★★★
Human resources	★★★★★
Growth markets	★★★★★
Quality of management	★★★★

Key figures:

Worldwide turnover	$5.2 billion
Pre-tax profits	$190 million
Staff	36,000

Black & Decker Ltd
210 Bath Road, Slough
Berks SL1 3YD
Tel: 01753 511234
Fax: 01753 551155

Black & Decker

To the uninitiated, Black & Decker's approach to employee empowerment seems excessively complicated. Cloaked in the jargon of Total Quality Management, it is littered with phrases such as 'Excellence, Liftshafts, Vital Few Priorities and TQ Dashboards'.

However as the results of these efforts begin to emerge, its strategy deserves further consideration. Black & Decker is actually far from vague about its objectives and the contribution it expects from its workforce. Investors are seeing results and analysts now recognise the potential of a combination of leading products and innovative management thinking. Both must have been sceptical post B&D's patchy record over the last decade.

Between 1984 and 1993, although sales rose three-fold to peak at nearly $5bn, profits were unpredictable, lower at the end of the period than the beginning. There were two expensive restructurings in 1985 and 1992, the second following the expensive acquisition of Emhart Corp. in 1989. Dividends were cut in 1986 and 1987 and have been slow to recover.

However in recent years B&D has put a stronger emphasis on reducing debt via cost cutting and sweating its working capital. It has set itself some stiff targets; to annually increase its earnings per share and operating efficiency by 20 per cent and 5 per cent respectively.

Operations and markets

Black & Decker is a global manufacturer and marketer of products and services in more than 100 countries worldwide. It is the world's largest producer of power tools and accessories, security hardware and electric lawn and garden tools. It is also the world leader in golf club shafts and glass-container-making equipment and has leading shares in industrial fastenings, plumbing products and small appliances.

Operations fall into three main categories: consumer and home improvement, industrial and commercial, and information services and systems. The first of these is dominated by its consumer and professional power tools and accessories, but other areas contribute. These include garden and lawn care, security hardware, leisure (it is the world leading manufacturer of golf club shafts), plumbing and certain service activities. It owns a broad spectrum of major brand names and is the worldwide market leader in power tools and accessories.

That market presence is B&D's fundamental strength. To quote recent analysis, Black & Decker's 'manufacturing makeup, distribution channels, major push with new products, customer service levels and brand franchises with the global consumer are assets which cannot be reflected in the group balance sheet'.

Commercial and industrial products comprise industrial fastening systems and glass-making machinery. It has a superb range of brand names in the former sector but this division has been hurt in recent years by recession in the car industry.

Information systems is built around PRC, a consulting operation. PRC's business is directed largely towards government work, but recent years have seen efforts to diversify into commercial sectors. It designs, develops, integrates and supports computer-based systems that handle and process information. A volatile earner in the past, PRC is expected to produce good returns short term, as two new major contracts begin to build up earnings momentum. These are the US government's Super Minicomputer Procurement contract and a new weather system.

Strategy and management

As is often the case with the most compelling strategies, the basic objectives are very simple indeed. They fall into four categories. The first, customer satisfaction, aims to exceed its customers' expectations and to 'delight its customers'. Next, employee satisfaction is intended to enhance the motivation and personal growth of all its employees. The final two are equally sensible: increase market share by beating the competition and provide shareholders with a satisfactory return on their investment. B&D's approach to achieving its strategic visions involves constant change and enhancement of operations through a Total Quality process.

Its European operations are kept informed by internal documents such as 'Visions and Key Strategies 1995-97' and 'Business Improvement Through Total Quality - The Customer', the latter issued as part of 'Liftshaft 1995'. All of them are inextricably linked by B&D's fundamental desire to be recognised by every single customer as being the best in sustained total customer satisfaction.

The 'Liftshaft Process', despite the jargon, simply describes the process of ensuring that everyone works in the same direction, and in a practical way takes each employee through the process from business objectives to implementation. The Liftshaft is intended particularly to shift the focus of all employees to satisfying the needs of its customers. Each employee establishes their 'Vital Few' priorities, i.e. the high priority business improvement activities (up to a maximum of five) which will move the business forward from its current position to the business vision.

The Liftshaft is based on measurement and wherever possible every 'Vital Few' should be structured so that its progress can be objectively monitored. Measurement, as B&D stresses, is fundamental to improvement and group systems measure its current performance, assess desired performance or goals and measure its progress towards those goals. B&D's procedure for measuring the progress towards its business objectives is called the 'Total Quality Dashboard'.

The TQ Dashboard is a measure of eight key business indicators of customer satisfaction, market share and profit, defined in terms of the return on assets. A key measurement is 'Strike Rate to Order', a figure which reveals the percentage of customer order lines satisfied completely at the first attempt. The principle can be applied to any segment of the business.

The process of customer satisfaction is an interactive one. B&D market research interviews end users after it introduces new products to understand their needs. It hopes to be responsive to market conditions. Consequently being able to determine the optimal timing for the development and production of new products, and the method to select, develop, evaluate and implement them into production, are all critical to maintaining and improving quality, cost and productivity.

In its statement 'Business Improvement Through Total Quality' the company defines its strategy towards its employees. 'We know there is enormous people potential within our business - intelligence, commitment, loyalty, innovation, motivation, creativity and initiative. We will harness this fantastic power and apply it in a single, forward direction, towards our customers. As a result, our customers will be satisfied, we will increase market share and profits, employees will be fulfilled and shareholders satisfied because our performance will be superb '.

Employees are provided with a supportive culture which enables them all to feel free to contribute their best. They are well aware that any achievements will be recognised and rewarded. This befits its business vision to be regarded by all of its employees as a 'great place to work'. Its way of working and behaving is based on core values, basic principles of behaviour, a sense of urgency, a passion for product quality and an obsession to produce results.

Teamwork is not a new concept, but B&D intends to do more than just pay lip service to its establishment. Its structure includes an open-door management style and the promotion of a coaching and learning environment to help everyone to fulfil their aspirations. It acknowledges that learning from its mistakes is a key part of continuous improvement. One of its basic principles of behaviour is to focus on the work process, issue or behaviour, not the person. Thus it recognises contribution, not status, which in turn helps maintain the self-confidence and self-esteem of all workers.

The results are tangible. The QIT which handles the objective analysis of any failures helps B&D to take a lateral view of product breakdowns, and a creative approach to finding an ongoing solution. Over the past two years its team has put together a network of sources such as service centres and authorised repair agents, which has allowed to assemble data on some 22,000 products.

The future

The elusive turnaround in operating results appears to have arrived. Management has managed to gear up the performance of its world leading product lines without putting the balance sheet under the kind of strain seen in the past. By achieving this via manufacturing efficiencies the group has operational rather than financial gearing and there should be more to come short term as B&D approaches its target of $100m of cost cuts between 1994 and 1996.

Black & Decker's market driven philosophy has puts the emphasis in the right place, customer satisfaction. New products are constantly being introduced to optimise the combination of quality, cost and value for money. Innovative thinking is genuinely a feature of its working environment.

It describes itself as 'unconventional and unlimited in its thinking, applying a creative mind to issues in order to discover possibilities for new solutions'. This means it is ready to crystallise its entrepreneurial spirit and take calculated risks. It will do things differently if this helps it meet the needs of its customers. As its future relies less on macroeconomic recovery than management actions, its determination to take advantage of opportunities for improving productivity, cutting costs and introducing an empowering employee culture augur well.

BNFL, Cheshire

BNFL is one of the world's leading nuclear power services companies, with operations in the UK and throughout the world

Outlook:
BNFL is profoundly confident about its future both in the UK and around the world. It has a formidable level of contracts agreed and it is extending its service provision to new markets. The company is convinced that nuclear energy - at present still a controversial issue - will become recognised as environmentally friendly

Scorecard:

Structural flexibility	★★★★
Innovative power	★★★
International orientation	★★★★
Human resources	★★★
Growth markets	★★★★
Quality of management	★★★★

Key figures:

Turnover (global)	£1.2 billion
Pre-tax profits	£81 million
Worldwide staff	14,000

BNFL
Risley
Warrington
Cheshire WA3 6AS
Tel: 01925 832000
Fax: 01925 822711

BNFL

The future of energy provision in the next century will be led by environmental issues as much as the effective supply of power. Hydro-carbons which have long been the primary source of energy are increasingly being seen by world leaders as net contributors to a decline in environmental quality. The search for an efficient and environmentally clean alternative has been underway for many years. The nuclear industry argues that it provides the only realistic option. Nuclear power is already a significant contributor to the world's energy needs and it is used extensively in many countries.

If nuclear power is the replacement - and the sector's claims are convincing - well-managed and safety conscious companies in this field will have an outstanding advantage. Among the few world leaders in the sector, BNFL is in an enviable position. Its prosperity for the next decade is assured, it enjoys a formidable reputation in overseas markets and even the contentious nuclear power debate may turn in its favour. The company has signed contacts which guarantee that its key THORP (thermal oxide reprocessing plant) installation at Sellafield will be at full capacity for the next 14 years. After investing more than £2.75 billion in the facility, senior executives at the UK's safety-first nuclear energy services provider must be relieved. But they also know that they face challenges from an increasingly demanding international marketplace.

Corporate communications director Colin Duncan says: 'Our immediate investment strategy is largely complete. We know that we have extensive expertise to offer world markets. It is now up to us to win the business.' His remarks are typical of the directness of BNFL. This is a pragmatic company with more than 40 years' history in the nuclear industry. Despite being at the centre of controversy from time to time, BNFL is confident that its reputation for quality, effectiveness and, above all, safety will help to secure its targets, especially in the global arena.

Recently, BNFL has entered a new phase in its development. In common with other major industrial sectors, the nuclear industry has become increasingly global in orientation. Domestic strength is vital, but the distinguishing factor for sector companies will be their capacity to operate to excellent standards around the world. The UK company's management believes that it is one of the few nuclear industry businesses which can be a significant worldwide player. For example, there are only two operators with sufficient critical mass, investment and experience to enter the fray in the worldwide reprocessing sector. Excluding domestic markets, BNFL commands 50 per cent. Its only other competitor - a French company - takes the other half. The commissioning of THORP has been a major step forward in growing international business - one half of all orders are from overseas.

Operations and markets

The company originated immediately after the Second World War in the UK Atomic Energy Authority which was created to manage the UK's nascent nuclear energy industry. The present business was established from the former production group of the UKAEA in 1971. It operates with all the disciplines of a private company but is in fact 100 per cent government-owned.

With headquarters in Risley, near Warrington, BNFL employs around 14,000 people in the UK and runs offices in many locations around the world. Its most famous site is Sellafield in West Cumbria which handles nuclear reprocessing, waste management and the Calder Hall Magnox power station. It also operates centres at Chapelcross, southern Scotland (Magnox power station), Springfields, near Preston (fuel manufacture), and Capenhurst, close to Chester (uranium enrichment). Its main activities are nuclear fuel management and reprocessing, reactor operation, waste management, uranium enrichment and transportation.

The financial performance of the company is impressive. Sales have grown from £950 million in 1988 to nearly £1.2 billion in 1994. Return on sales is around 8.5 per cent. Profits took a back seat in 1994 when BNFL produced pre-tax figures of £81 million. This was partly due to the costs of regulatory delays in getting the THORP plant on stream. This hiatus was caused by the political consultation process which is a key operational factor. There is no denying that nuclear power is controversial but BNFL thinks that the argument may be swinging its way. The Rio environmental conference, BNFL argues, was a turning point. Should global warming be convincingly and empirically substantiated, the hydro-carbons industry - chemicals and petroleum - will be seen as the main enemy of the environmentalists and nuclear power as the only safe alternative.

'We are one of Britain's leading exporters,' says Mr Duncan. 'We have been active in the international market for many years.' At present between 60 and 70 per cent of profits are generated in the domestic environment but in the future overseas income will become increasingly important. 'BNFL has been present in Japan since the 1960s and we have taken time to develop strongly-based trading relationships with Japanese industry. When [President of the Board of Trade Michael Heseltine] visited Tokyo the chairmen of Tokyo Electric and Mitsubishi Heavy Industries both congratulated the government on commissioning the THORP facility.' The Japanese have a very high regard for BNFL, valuing the company's approach to its business and its style of relationship with countries around the world.

It is this long-term commitment to building dialogue with clients in different cultures which BNFL believes has paid dividends. 'We see the Pacific Rim, the United States and Eastern Europe as areas of strong growth potential,' says David Bonser, company development director. Relationships with Japanese industry and with developing countries such as China and Korea are expected to blossom as demand for BNFL's services continues to expand rapidly. In the United States as operators look for solutions for their nuclear industry, BNFL is ready to exploit market opportunities. It perceives particular opportunities in the waste clean-up and plant decommissioning markets.

The former Soviet bloc provides different challenges - not least an inherent unfamiliarity among customers there with western concepts of accountability, cost or income. 'Some installations need attention but we do not try to impose western solutions to eastern problems. We work with the local administration. In the west, you would expect the plant manager to be able to make decisions about how to run his installation. This is not always the case in the former Soviet Union. Our aim is to be pragmatic and help local people solve problems in their own way. We do not impose western approaches but listen carefully to local needs and work with the manager to find suitable answers. We believe in building up relationships of mutual trust.'

Strategy and management

The future in the international nuclear industry will be governed by a series of factors where BNFL can demonstrate decisive market advantage. Safety is central. The anti-nuclear constituency makes considerable efforts to demonstrate that the industry's safety standards are poor. BNFL adamantly refutes this assertion. The company maintains that it has an exemplary record on safety. Even minor safety considerations take precedence over revenue. 'Recently a production manager at one of our sites noticed that something was not right with the facility. He was not sure about the nature of the failure but he faced two choices: shut the plant down and lose hundreds of thousands of pounds in revenue or do nothing and hope that the problem would rectify itself. He shut the plant down. As it happened the problem was not serious and he could have carried on. He may have felt embarrassed but senior management applauded the decision,' says Mr Bonser.

More than 30 years of problem solving in the UK has made the company light on its feet when it comes to providing customer solutions elsewhere in the world. 'We believe that it is important to have a strong domestic base for many reasons - it shows our stability as a business, it confirms our government's commitment to the nuclear industry and it means that we have a proven track record which we can draw on for solving issues for our customer wherever they may be.'

BNFL is also a long-term investor. Many of the contracts running currently were secured as a result of investments made in the 1960s and 1970s. The company has recently devoted £10 billion to its capital investment programme, and about £50 million a year to basic research and £30 million to plant support. According to its 1994 annual report BNFL has spent 7.5 per cent of £1.13 billion turnover on research. 'Many companies do two or three year plans but we commission a ten year plan because we need to project that far in advance,' comments Mr Bonser.

The future

'We know that the nuclear industry can have an unfavourable impression with some people,' says Mr Duncan. 'At this stage perhaps the best we can hope for is "dealing with spent nuclear fuel is a filthy business but if anyone is doing it I suppose BNFL is the best choice." In the future, maybe, 15 years we can convert them to a more favourable perception of us and the industry. We are in for the long term. This industry is in its beginning phase and its role is growing.'

 **THE BOC GROUP**

The BOC Group plc, Surrey

BOC is one of the top three industrial gas companies in the world, respected for the extent of its management culture, technical expertise and quality of client relationships

Outlook:
BOC is distinguished by its clear application of global market principles. Its management believes in its role as technical adviser as well as supplier to clients. This is a decisive competitive advantage in its bid to secure complete worldwide coverage and high quality profitability. Customers want close supplier relationships and BOC is in a good position to exploit this trend

Scorecard:

Structural flexibility	★★★★
Innovative power	★★★★★
International orientation	★★★★★
Human resources	★★★★
Growth markets	★★★★★
Quality of management	★★★★★

Key figures:

Turnover (global)	£3.5 billion
Pre-tax profits	£435.4 million
Wordwide staff	37,557
UK staff	10,014

The BOC Group plc
Chertsey Road
Windlesham
Surrey GU20 6HJ
Tel: 01276 477222
Fax: 01276 471333

The BOC Group

The world of industrial gases is fiercely competitive. It is one sector of global business where all the key capacities of excellent production and technical skills, intimate relationships with customers and profound understanding of the art of salesmanship combine to differentiate the leading protagonists. There are three or perhaps four contenders for the claim to the title of the world's leading industrial gas company.

The dynamics of the industry have changed substantially in the last few years. No longer is the race simply to supply particular gases to specific clients. Customers now expect the global leaders to work with them to identify ways to enhance and extend their operations. The concept of value-added which echoed throughout industry for the last decade has found a true home in the industrial gases sector. It has become one of the real distinguishing factors in securing and developing client business. None of the majors can anticipate significant growth in business without a greater consultancy role with clients.

Nevertheless, despite the complexities of individual products, this is a straightforward industrial sector. Readily identifiable factors govern its operation. Customers want high quality products supplied in the quantity and at the delivery time stipulated. They want products which enrich their own processes. They want a good deal. The mechanics of the industry dictate that contracts tend to be large commitments - often multi-million dollar investments - which may involve establishing new plant in fresh territories. Winning contracts is grandmaster level chess, where the staying power for a long campaign and the experience to know when to press home are equally prized.

Advantage gained by technical superiority, skilfully managed client relationships and constant internal renewal put one of the top table companies - the BOC Group - in an enviable position to secure market leadership. It should be stated that BOC's objective is profitability and shareholder return rather than pole position; but its senior management recognises that critical mass which may generate world market leadership is desirable. Analysts suggest that BOC's current number two status would be exceeded if it were to acquire a second tier mainland European manufacturer or assemble a collection of third tier operators. The fusion would lift BOC above its immediate direct competitors.

Operations and markets

BOC is an international company with headquarters in the UK. It is emphatic that it is not a UK company with international operations. Income is drawn from all parts of the world. The group operates installations in every major territory across the globe and its management team is perhaps the most international of any major commercial player in the UK today.

In 1994 the group produced £3.5 billion in sales, £435 million in operating profits and new capital expenditure was £416 million. Some 71 per cent of turnover comes from gases, 16 per cent from healthcare products and 13 per cent vacuum technology. Geographically, BOC takes 35 per cent of its operating profit from Europe, 30 per cent from Asia/Pacific, 22 per cent from the Americas and 13 per cent from Africa. It has major operating companies in 50 countries worldwide. Gas does not travel; so installations need to be established locally, which requires substantial financial commitment by BOC but gives the company a base in each area to service additional customers.

The scope of the three main divisions of the business are:

. industrial gases - virtually all manufacturing processes use industrial gases. Quantities range from thousands of tonnes per day of oxygen and nitrogen to tiny amounts of very high value ultra-pure speciality gases and mixtures. Patenting technology for new gases production is a regular process for the companies. These new gases improve customer product quality, lower their production costs or solve their environmental problems. Innovation and high investment in R&D are key components of business developments.

. healthcare - through Ohmeda, BOC is a world leader in a wide variety of anaesthesia and critical care products and services. In the last year Ohmeda announced a joint venture with Hewlett Packard to grow its business in the medical equipment market.

. vacuum technology - this is a high growth area for BOC, profits rose more than 50 per cent between 1993 and 1994. The vacuum technology division embraces world leadership in vacuum systems, equipment and components. Around four-fifths of the world's output of energy-efficient coated glass is produced with BOC technology. The distribution aspect of this business has developed advanced systems for fast and safe handling of fresh foods.

Strategy and management

Two principal phrases summarise the BOC strategic approach: global orientation and world class quality. These two factors are interwoven in the group's philosophy. Group CEO Pat Dyer says: 'We are the most global of gas companies. We continue to be the strongest gas company in the Pacific Rim, having entered at a time when competitors were focused elsewhere, and we are the leading international gas company in China. During the past year, we have changed the name of our regional companies and the name of BOC Gases is being recognised around the world.

'To us being world class means not only holding our own against overseas entrants to the UK market but also being able to compete in any market we choose to enter around the world. Being globally competitive is not, regrettably, a permanent state. Nor is it some kind of corporate Oscar that we can display in a glass case at headquarters; it demands a continuous culture of reassessment, innovation, improvement and renewal. The plain fact is that in today's world, nothing less than continuing global excellence will underwrite our company's future existence.'

In 1994 BOC Group sponsored a Building Global Excellence research programme by London Business School. The conclusion of the research team was that companies can be world class - if they follow certain basic principles:

. long-term commitment to developing new capabilities and skills at every level in any organisation

. an ability to recognise and manage difficult dilemmas such as trade-offs between short-term cost reductions and longer-term investments for the future
. strong leadership based on a clear vision which stretches people and resources

The LBS team suggested that those companies which had travelled furthest along the road to global excellence share a range of common characteristics:
. high degrees of openness, informality and debate about common goals, creation of which encourages teamworking
. recognising the need to identify and share best practice, no matter where in the world it comes from

Mr Dyer says that the report is useful because it provides a benchmark against which the group can assess its performance in areas of key strategic performance:
. managing innovation successfully
. improving quality, safety and the environment
. building partnerships with customers
. regularly revisiting core values and first principles
. investing for the long term.

Its determination to realise and exceed quality goals is exemplified by its target to achieve registration under the international quality standard ISO 9000 at 100 of its sites worldwide by March 1994. The target was reached three months early and a further 80 locations were added by the end of that year. By mid year 1995 the total was in excess of 270 sites.

Communications within the group are superb - both at a management information level but also in employee contact terms. Its internal communications publications demonstrate in precise terms the scope of the success which BOC is achieving in its markets, the technological advances in various companies within the group but also the wider dimensions of management culture and changes in its mainstream markets. To work in BOC may be a tough and sometimes abrasive experience but it is also stimulating, rewarding and challenging.

The future

The dynamics of the world gases markets are evident: high quality production, better and closer client service and increasingly tougher targets. Companies which benefit from geographical strength, excellent client relationships, traditions of technical superiority and management quality are the ones which will survive. BOC is world technical leader; though second in size it probably has the most advanced management culture and sharply defined global strategy. The distinction for the group will be its high quality, technically innovative but low cost customer solutions throughout the world.

The Body Shop plc, West Sussex

The Body Shop is a retailer of environmentally-friendly, mainly small ticket, cosmetic items

Outlook:
This company is the unique dedicated network of environmentally-friendly cosmetics shops. It has majored on its green image from the outset and has expanded beyond the UK to achieve its remarkable sales growth in the US and mainland Europe. Popular with a wide target market, it has attracted critcism from certain commentators - especially in the City and on Wall Street - but has diffused these attacks and continues to thrive

Scorecard:
Structural flexibility	★★★★
Innovative power	★★★★
International orientation	★★★
Human resources	★★★
Growth markets	★★★★★
Quality of management	★★★★

Key figures:
Turnover	£255 million
Pre-tax profits	£37.3 million
Staff	3,327

The Body Shop International plc
Littlehampton
West Sussex BN17 6LS
Tel: 01903 731500
Fax: 01903 726250

The Body Shop

On one level, the inclusion of The Body Shop in a book about future top one hundred companies in Britain might appear to be a contradiction in terms. Although the company insists it is first and foremost a retailer manufacturing toiletries and cosmetics which combine ingredients with a history of use in many cultures with modern scientific research, one suspects inclusion in such a list might cause offence.

The Body Shop suggests that it has a higher goal than the pure profit motive - a total commitment to redefine the basic tenets of business. Time and again, The Body Shop restates its core values: concern for human and civil rights, care for the environment and opposition to animal exploitation. Its Mission Statement and Trading Charter include statements such as 'to dedicate our business to the pursuit of social and environmental change', and 'the way we trade creates profits with principles'.

While the debate rages about the spiritual values that underpin The Body Shop ethos, few would dispute that it has been a tremendous commercial success story. From its humble beginning in 1976, when Anita Roddick set up a small shop in Brighton selling 25 naturally-based skin and hair care products, The Body Shop now has well over 1,200 outlets worldwide, 80 per cent of which are outside the UK. Best-selling products include Cocoa Butter Hand & Body Lotion, Vitamin E Moisture Cream, Banana Conditioner, Peppermint Foot Lotion and the Colourings range of colour cosmetics.

Shares in The Body Shop have been among the best stock market performers of the last decade. Listed on the USM in April 1984 at 95p each, their value almost doubled on their first day of trading. A subsequent 32 share split means the original offer price was 5p against a current quote of 178p, which values the company at £338m.

Operations and markets

One of the key factors behind this rapid growth was franchising - in February 1995 only 43 of the 243 shops in the UK were company owned, while the comparable figure for the US was 91 out of 235 outlets. In the rest of the world, all stores are franchised apart from nine in Singapore. But a dip in profits in the year to February 1993, the first since the company was founded, added grist to the mill for critics who argued The Body Shop was just another retailing fad of the late eighties riding for a fall. From a peak of 360p early in 1992, the shares halved in value in less than a year. The fall from grace, brought on by the onset of recession on both sides of the Atlantic, coincided with a British television programme criticising the company's anti-animal testing stance. A libel action was brought by The Body Shop, which won £274,000 in damages.

Attacks on The Body Shop's squeaky-clean image continued, but they served merely to galvanise a company some investors - ethical or otherwise - feared was going ex-growth. Stung by criticism of its heavy-handed response to allegations made by a US journalist about its ethical credentials, The Body Shop accelerated the process of opening itself up to external scrutiny and providing outside validation of its claims. Its first response related to corporate governance, where the nine-member board of executives was beefed up with the appointment of two non-executive directors. More non-execs are being sought.

The issue illustrated one of the problems a growing, entrepreneurial company like The Body Shop faces when it is forced to adopt larger, more bureaucratic structures. 'It had reached the point where the lack of good structure was impeding creativity,' says Body Shop chairman Gordon Roddick. 'Ideas were taking a long time to come through.' The Body Shop also promised to publish its first full social audit. Expected in the autumn of 1995, the review will be independently verified. It will focus on general bench-marks specific to individual departments such as equal opportunities and pay, as well as looking at company values as they relate to various stakeholders - not just investors, but also suppliers, customers and the local community.

'We want to show that we're a company that is by no means perfect but that we have gone a long way on the road to social responsibility and that we have a high degree of integrity and principle,' says Mr Roddick. An audit of its anti-animal testing policy and procedures by a leading European agency has also been commissioned. There is now also a recognition that the company in the UK needs to establish a broader customer base as the pace of new store openings almost grinds to a halt. In particular, ways of pulling more customers through the door are being examined to ensure sales momentum is maintained.

One such initiative is The Body Shop Direct - a home-selling concept where customers (such as mothers with children), who would not normally go anywhere near a branch of The Body Shop are introduced to a selected range of The Body Shop's products in the home environment, with the aim that they will then visit their nearest branch of The Body Shop and become established customers. In the past, management has been reluctant to launch advertising blitzkriegs, but a more flexible approach to promoting products is on the cards. A hint of that came with the recent American Express campaign featuring founder and chief executive Anita Roddick, which helped lift like-for-like sales in the UK without costing The Body Shop a penny. The Body Shop's products may not be cheaper than rival ranges, but management is unlikely to enter into a price war to boost sales.

Strategy and management

One of the company's articles of faith is 'No one can beat The Body Shop at their prices.' But apart from stressing quality, The Body Shop continues to come up with lots of innovative products as well as re-launching existing ones. Moreover, overseas markets are nearing a size where it is economical to develop products for the local customer base, such as the Blue Corn range in the US. On the trading front, underlying sales growth remains strong and gross margins are being maintained despite rising costs. In the UK, store sales on a like-for-like basis rose by four per cent for the year to February 1995. Comparable Christmas store sales in the US fell by three per cent, for the year to February 1995, though this figure does not necessarily tell the whole story. The Body Shop has had a strategy in the US of opening a clutch of new stores in the same area. They eroded existing stores' sales but took time to show up in the like-for-like sales figures.

Nevertheless, critical mass in the US is being achieved, so margins should also increase over the next few years. But the strongest growth area of the future is likely to be Asia. Total sales to February 1995 leapt by 51 per cent with the biggest increase in Japan, where prices are set at a high premium to those charged in the UK. For all the furore over its image and ethics, perhaps the biggest challenge The Body Shop faces is the impact of competition in the US. Of course, The Body Shop is no stranger to competition. Copy-cat ranges sold at chains in the UK such as Boots, Sainsbury and Marks & Spencer have increased their market share and forced The Body Shop to sharpen up its retailing act. Perhaps its greatest test will come from Bath and Body Works, an effective rival in the US which recently opened its first batch of stores in the UK under a 50:50 joint venture agreement with Next. It is still early days, but in the five locations where Bath & Body Works has stores, The Body Shop says its own stores are, if anything, performing better than the average across its UK range.

The future

The Body Shop delivered compound earnings growth of 46 per cent in its first ten years. A repeat is unlikely in the next decade, but having stumbled several times, the company is now firmly back on the growth track. The aim is to double the number of shops around the world to over 2,000 by the end of the century. Assuming this period of expansion coincides with compound earnings growth of 20 per cent p.a. - less than half the rate previously achieved - and a stock market rating to match, The Body Shop may yet be knocking on the door of the elite club that comprises Britain's top one hundred companies.

Bookham Technology Ltd, Oxfordshire

This company has developed an innovative new technology for making integrated optical circuits which addresses the market demand for fibre optic communications components and sensors

Outlook:
The potential demand for Bookham's products is massive. The company's business rose by more than 200 per cent in the two-year period prior to June 1995. It is engaged in several research projects and intends to invest £5 million in manufacturing during 1995. Estimated sales for 1996 - £5.1 million

<u>Scorecard:</u>

Structural flexibility	★★★★
Innovative power	★★★★★
International orientation	★★★
Human resources	★★★
Growth markets	★★★★
Quality of management	★★★

<u>Key figures:</u>

UK turnover	£775,000
Pre-tax profits (loss)	(£1,792,000)
UK staff	30

Bookham Technology Ltd
Rutherford Appleton Laboratory
Chilton
Oxfordshire OX11 0QX
Tel: 01235 445377
Fax: 01235 446854

Bookham Technology

It should be no surprise to anyone that the field of multimedia technology will be one of the strongest growth markets of the future. In the vanguard of this revolution is Bookham Technology, an award-winning developer of optical chips from Oxfordshire. This is a company which commands a unique position in the sector - it is years ahead of potential rivals - and looks set to become a dominant player in the future developments in this field.

At the core of Bookham's breakthrough is the technology of manufacturing optical chips - integrated circuits which use photons (particles of light) rather than electrons to carry and manipulate signals. Using silicon as a base, Bookham has developed a way to make chips at a tenth of the cost of the existing methods that use lithium niobate and other compounds.

Operations and markets

This chip has multiple industrial applications in a diversity of commercial sectors. Among the most promising is its role as a key component to bring the information superhighway into everyone's living room. Bookham's silicon-based switches and transceivers will provide cable television companies with a cost-effective method of installing optical fibre instead of copper wire. Bookham's future, however, is not built around just one market or product but rather around a core technology. This patented technology revolutionises the cost structure of manufacturing optical processing units to such an extent that it will create numerous new markets and system manufacturers - and influence many others. Not only can Bookham now economically create customised processing units in very small batches, but this will also open up new high volume markets for applications with the qualities provided by optical technology, previously restricted to expensive bench-top equipment.

Strategy and management

Andrew Rickman, managing director and founder of Bookham Technology, is one of those unusual people who - in two years - manages to finish an MBA while doing his PhD in leading edge optical technology at Surrey University and spending an hour from six to seven every morning in applying for innovative-technology grants to develop the new knowledge in optics into manufacturing technology.

Coming from a family of entrepreneurs and businessmen, Mr Rickman knew at the outset how to plan a successful business. His concept envisioned a venture which would be aimed at a wide range of markets rather than a few, located in a field where strong growth was expected, and which would be capable of improving on existing technologies instead of creating a new technology from scratch.

Mr Rickman believed that the manufacturing future for optical technology lay in using the prodigious knowledge and experience in silicon-based chip manufacturing even though silicon was deemed academically to be a less attractive base than compounds such as lithium niobate.

Using various technology subsidies and grants Bookham Technology set to find a practical way of building integrated optical circuits at the government's Rutherford Appleton Laboratory. Beating such industry giants as AT&T to the race, Bookham came up with what is now called the ASOC - Active Silicon Integrated Optical Circuit. The ASOC is proving to be the next leap in the lower-cost/higher-performance trend in integrated circuits and will provide a wide range of system manufacturers with significant advantages in terms of cost, reliability, size and performance.

'We avoided the traditional approach of a British high-tech start-up, which is first to manufacture a product and then to seek a market. Instead we spoke to customers, discovered a need and then located a suitable manufacturing solution,' he comments.

By marketing early and bringing potential customers in to be part of the development phase, Bookham not only made sure that it is producing something it can sell, it is also getting potential customers to fund parts of the development of the ASOCs. At present Bookham is working on applications in the fields of environmental sensors, car collision avoidance, medical diagnostics, metrology, industrial measurement and control and of course data- and telecommunications.

While it intends to service all these markets, mostly in cooperation with the customers, one product has Bookham's major focus this year - the fibre optic switch market. By 1999, Bookham aims to draw around 50 per cent of its income from switches, another 30 per cent from sensors and 20 per cent from transceivers.

The fibre optic switch and the related fibre-to-home transceiver are now making it economically possible to connect homes to fibre optic cable networks. Fibre optic cables are replacing old-fashioned copper wires to bring hundreds of interactive channels into the living room for home-banking, home-education, video-on-demand and all the yet to be discovered pleasures of the information superhighway.

The cost of fibre transceivers has always prevented the optic cables to actually enter the homes themselves. Bookham's new technology created an optical tranceiver that will go to market in late 1995 and which at £200 will cost considerably less than existing products. This will make it possible to replace the copper used for the final link into the living rooms themselves. The total worldwide market for Bookham's products will grow from £1.5 billion in 1995 to an estimated £10 billion in 1999.

At present Bookham projects sales of £500,000 in 1995, which will grow to £5,000,000 by 1997. This growth forecast is based on the company's market research and its dialogue with existing customers, which have given detailed accounts of their future order book requirements from Bookham. This income expansion will fuel a rise in staff numbers from 20 in April 1995 to 40 by December 1995.

The small management team consists of internationally experienced people from the field hand-picked by Mr Rickman himself. He is a strong believer in empowering and stretching talented people. As marketing executive Mette Tholstrup says: 'He has a great ability of making you go out there and do things you didn't realise you could do yourself'.

Andrew Rickman emphasises the importance of the external relationships which appears to be one of the things Bookham is good at and derives value from. Not only does it have close co-development relationships with customers such as Ford Motors (US), British Aerospace, BNFL, Honeywell, MOD, Fuji, Dupont and CERN but Bookham has also created valuable links with other organisations through national and European governmental research programmes.

Bookham has a co-ordinating role in the European RACE project (Research in Advanced Communications in Europe) which besides providing funding for additional research has also led to working relationships with companies across Europe. In this context SOITEC of France is developing and supplying the SOI wafers on which the ASOC s are built, Optronics Ireland is creating low-cost laser diodes and the Danish national telephone company Tele Denmark is testing prototype components in systems. A proposal for a second pan-European project has been submitted, involving Bookham and French, Portuguese, Danish, German and Swedish players.

The future

Bookham is now working on a high volume manufacturing plant that will be opened in 1995 on the Rutherford Appleton laboratory site, together with new commercial premises for the growing company. The processing of ASOC wafers is to be conducted in the future by a subcontracted silicon foundry Semefab Scotland. Certain key process steps are still to be controlled by Bookham.

Mr Rickham describes Bookham as a typical high growth company. 'We show all the attributes of a successful start-up. We have a unique technology; we operate in markets, which although poorly served, are set for substantial growth. We have at least a three years' head start on our potential competitors. Our strategy is to grow by manufacturing our own products but also to license Pacific Rim and US companies in our technology. Our potential - if not limitless - is certainly vast.'

THE BOOTS COMPANY

The Boots Company PLC, Nottingham

Boots The Chemists is the UK's market leader in retail pharmacy

Outlook:
Boots is one of the best known brand names, respected for the quality of its goods, its persuasive marketing of its products and its diversification into related areas. Almost the entire portfolio of activities in the group is managed to high degrees of profitability and this situation looks set to continue

Scorecard:

Structural flexibility	★★★
Innovative power	★★★★★
International orientation	★★★
Human resources	★★★★★
Growth markets	★★★★
Quality of management	★★★★★

Key figures:

UK turnover	£4.3 billion
Pre-tax profits	£526 million
Staff	75,000

The Boots Company PLC
1 Thane Road
Nottingham NG2 3AA
Tel: 0115 9506111

The Boots Company

Boots ranks with Marks & Spencer and J Sainsbury as one of Britain's most respected and enduring stores groups, with sales of £4.3 billion for the year to March 1995, and pre-tax profits of £526 million. The engine of its business is Boots The Chemists, founded in Nottingham in 1877, the country's largest chain of retail chemists, a market leader in healthcare, cosmetics, toiletries, baby products and film processing, and an icon of the British high street.

Secondary interests include Halfords, the leading seller of car and cycle accessories, and ventures in DIY retailing - troublesome legacies of the boom-time late-1980s acquisition of the Ward White group. Boots home-grown peripheral activities include children's retailing opticians, manufacturing of consumer healthcare products, and investment in retail property.

The competitive threat to Boots comes primarily from leading supermarket chains, which now duplicate virtually all of the Boots product range alongside their food aisles. But - through cost control and attention to customer preferences - the group has performed steadily throughout the recession years. Most importantly, it has modernised and diversified without diminishing its name as a hallmark for reliability, particularly in beauty and healthcare products.

Measuring its own performance in terms of total shareholder return (comprising gross dividends paid and growth in share price), Boots was able to report 104 per cent growth for the five years to March 1995, ranking a close second to Marks & Spencer in its chosen league of ten competitors, but comfortably ahead of Sainsbury (78 per cent) and Tesco (47 per cent).

The group's investment decisions are driven by acute sensitivity to shareholder value. The business is cash generative - debt has been steadily eradicated since 1991, net bank balances in March 1995 standing at £517 million. If Boots' management faces one overwhelmingly tricky problem, however, it is the question of how, with a saturated retail market and a lingering public mood of post-recessionary thrift, to re-invest that cash for future growth.

One logical solution - and this is a company which places logic well ahead of market machismo - is simply to return the cash to the investors. In November 1994, Boots took the unusual step of buying back and cancelling £511 million worth of its own shares, the largest repurchase ever carried out in the London stockmarket and a more tax-efficient way of achieving the objective than paying a special dividend. As a demonstration of the admirable rigour which governs Boots thinking, that was a highly significant gesture.

Operations and markets

Boots The Chemists (BTC) operates 1,167 stores, many in long-established, town centre sites, and has a continuous programme of new store development and relocations. The division accounts for two-thirds of group turnover and a similar proportion of operating profit. Its core sales areas of healthcare (including dispensing pharmacy), beauty and personal care products are consistently strong, but additional lines such as computer games and music tapes have been less successful and space devoted to these areas is constantly being reduced.

Often located within BTC stores, Boots Opticians is the second largest operator in its field in Britain. A promising spin-off is Childrens World, a separate 48-store chain catering for parents shopping both for and with their offspring.

One of the keys to Boots' success, developed within BTC over many years, is retail engineering - that is, aggressive management of the product range to maximise margins, combined with monitoring of competitors in exhaustive depth. Direct product profitability is a refined management tool which allocates 90 per cent of group costs to individual products, taking precise account of labour, space, distribution and stock investment, so that managers have a measure of the profit contribution of every item on sale.

The application of this kind of technique is now bearing fruit in Halfords, which accounts for nine per cent of group turnover. This is another well-recognised high-street name, but a business which had been loosely managed and over-expanded under its pre-1989 Ward White management. Turning it around by the application of proven Boots methodology has been a lengthy project, but is now beginning to pay off. The effectiveness of the approach can be seen, for example, in a substantial market-share increase (to 25 per cent) for cycles, achieved despite reductions in product range and allocated store space. Halfords also operates a loss-making chain of service garages - but improvement may show through on the back of an innovative deal to service all Daewoo cars in Britain.

Also part of Ward White were the Fads home decorating chain, and the Payless DIY stores, subsequently merged into the Do-It-All joint venture with WH Smith. DIY was very much a 1980s story, linked to the property boom, and remains in desperate straits, with supply vastly exceeding demand at the superstore end of the market. Both these elements of the Boots group continue to make losses, dragging the contribution from the £900 million-plus Ward White purchase down to an operating profit of little more than £5 million for 1994/95.

Boots Healthcare International develops and markets over-the-counter drugs and medications, including well known brands like Nurofen and Optrex. This is the international growth area of the group's business, in pursuit of a trend in the developed world towards self-medication and self-management of personal health. A team of over 100 research scientists is dedicated to market-led product development.

The research, development and marketing of prescription drugs, on the other hand, was considered to lie outside Boots' core strategy: Boots Pharmaceuticals was sold in March 1995 to the German group BASF for £840 million, returning a profit of £273 million - a major contribution to the growing cash pile.

Boots also invests in retail property developments, and actively manages the retail divisions property portfolio. This has been skilfully handled through the property slump, and represents a significant element of group profit - £67 million at the operating level for 1994/95.

Strategy and management

The essence of Boots' strategy is adherence to the concept of value-based management. Divisional managers have a relatively free rein to expand their businesses within an agreed strategy, but there is no imperative to capture market share or conquer overseas markets. At every step, first and foremost, those managers must prove to their chief executive, Lord Blyth, that a return will be generated in excess of the cost of capital - creating added value for shareholders.

It is Blyth (formerly Sir James, a tennis-playing Scotsman with mid-Atlantic undertones) who is the dominant figure in the group. Unusually, he is not a lifelong Boots man: he has added his own special ingredients to the company's traditional formula. He joined Boots in 1987 from Plessey, the electronics group, having previously been head of defence sales for the Ministry of Defence - an unlikely background for a top retailer.

But Blyth's earlier career took in stints with Mars, General Foods and Lucas Batteries, among others, and (although shy of personal publicity) he is recognised as one of Britain's most disciplined and clear-sighted, hands-on managers - recognition reflected in his appointment by Prime Minister John Major to head up the Citizens' Charter initiative, which seeks to bring best customer-service practice to the interface between state bureaucracy and the public.

Colleagues attribute to Blyth the consistency of the market and product research applied to all Boots activities, and the value-based principles which guide strategic decisions. His approach is not, however, a radical departure from past practice: unlike many established retailers, Boots has long prided itself on analytical, market-led decision-making. Blyth's chief contribution has been to introduce focus and clear management accountabilities, and has set this firmly in the context of total returns to shareholders.

Above Blyth as group chairman is high-profile corporate heavyweight Sir Michael Angus, former CBI president and Unilever chairman. Underlining the social awareness which is part of Boots culture, and setting a lead for others to follow, Angus was one of the first chairmen to acknowledge adverse public sentiment on top people's pay. In June 1995 he announced that the company would issue no more share options to executives and would cut directors' service contracts to no more than two years.

Boots' provincial Nottingham roots, and the philanthropic tenets of its founder Jesse Boot (1850-1931), give the company a quite distinctive management ethos. Over £4 million per annum is dedicated to various forms of community support. Staff welfare and training are high priorities.

The homogeneity of Boots' management cadre, and the rigour with which investment decisions are addressed, are however by no means a disincentive to innovation. On the contrary, these factors provide collegiate trust, and a framework within which key managers enjoy considerable creative freedom. This can be seen in many examples, small and large: from the relaunch of BTC's 'No 7' own-brand cosmetics, to the success of the 'Shapers' range of calorie-reduced convenience foods, to the rapid development of the Children's World chain.

The future

As one of Britain's best-managed retailers, with a rock-solid, community-conscious brand image and a core business in the increasingly important field of healthcare products, Boots is certain to remain prominent over the next decade. Given its cash position, growth by acquisition must be a possibility. But the last major acquisition has not proved easy to digest, and disposals of peripheral elements - like the DIY interests - must be equally possible.

BRANN

Brann Ltd, Gloucestershire

Brann is a leading national direct market operation with a strong bias towards managed relationships with customers

Outlook:
Brann has enjoyed several metamorphoses but the company has never been stronger than it is today. This is an entrepreneurial business - emphasised by its management buy-out - with distinctive strengths as a client service provider in a range of marketing disciplines

Scorecard:
Structural flexibility	★★★★
Innovative power	★★★★★
International orientation	★★★
Human resources management	★★★★★
Growth markets	★★★★
Quality of management	★★★★

Key figures:
UK turnover	£29 million
Pre-tax profits	£2.3 million
Staff	600

Brann Ltd
Phoenix Way, Cirencester
Gloucestershire GL7 1RY
Tel: 01285 644744
Fax: 01285 654952

Brann

Creating loyal customers for clients. That is the stated purpose of Brann, one of the UK's largest and fastest-growing marketing communications companies. Marketing remains a fast-moving, innovative discipline, and one in which Britain enjoys a high reputation worldwide. Brann is oriented towards direct marketing and data-driven methods, rather than the heady 'above the line' world, and the former is an area of marketing that is advancing rapidly. Why? Because direct marketing consistently achieves measurable and profitable results.

The media spend in the UK exceeded £10 billion in 1994 and continues to grow. Within this, marketing communications is changing its focus dramatically. There is a swing away from high profile development of brands through the acquisition of customers, with companies instead seeking to build key brands in a fragmented market place. Brann is at this key interface between marketer and customer. Brann is also the fastest growing company of its type in this developing market.

While British marketing is revered in the world for creative, effective advertising, it is relatively underexploited in direct marketing methods such as telemarketing and direct mail, when compared to the US or Europe. Surprising? Perhaps, but it is encouraging for companies like Brann, because it flags tremendous growth potential. Many large companies, which typify Brann's client base, are switching increasing proportions of marketing budgets into this area of marketing communications. Marketing men are thinking more about customer management and less about product management, and Brann's expertise lies in managing this cultural shift.

Operations and markets

Direct marketing has become too narrow a term to describe what Brann does. The company has evolved into a business of three principal parts, with each focusing on a different aspect of creating customer loyalty; each also benefits from the experience, knowledge and ideas of the others. Indeed, the team approach is evident in all of Brann's work. Brann's main office is in Cirencester - it is a fallacy to contend that a big agency must be sited in London - with its new customer care centre newly located in Bristol. The company presents its three key skills under three Brann sub-headings:

Communications is effectively the direct marketing agency operation, the tangible product being targeted response advertising in all media. In addition to comprehensive implementation services, Brann's consultancy element does much more beforehand, in understanding, analysing and targeting markets and their behaviour, to devise an effective marketing strategy.

Systems deals with information. Brann is a great believer in data-driven marketing, and provides consultancy, solutions and packages in building, analysing and running databases for clients. The company's breakthrough marketing software, Viper, not only delivers an entire database onto the marketer's desktop PC, it reduces the analysis time to mere seconds.

Contact 24's business is customer contact management, sometimes known as response handling or fulfilment, where the interaction between client and customer is managed. Inbound and outbound telephone marketing is an inevitable consequence of response advertising and represents a major growth area of the future. Brann's capability in this area is comprehensive, and is succeeding in convincing clients to outsource this whole operation and concentrate on the more strategic aspects of the campaign.

Brann's turnover has risen steadily over recent years, but the greatest kick came in 1994 when the company went private. Turnover leaped by 40 per cent to £29m, and operating profits of £2.3m would have been higher but for Contact 24's relocation to new offices in Bristol. This performance did follow a couple of years of flat profits in the UK recession between 1992 and 93 - direct marketing budgets can survive a short recession of two years or so, but longer than that and discretionary marketing spends will be cut. While experts still argue whether the UK recession is over yet or not, Brann's accelerated turnover and profitability highlight the attractions of the direct marketing business.

It is this business that provides the best indicator to Brann's future success. The statistics point in the right direction: a rising UK advertising and marketing spend, with the top advertisers increasing their total spend in 1994 to £2.4 billion. Brann's impressive client list includes one in five of the top 100. An increasing proportion of this money is going on direct marketing. This market, in a survey by the Henley Centre for the Direct Marketing Association, was estimated to be worth £4.5 billion in 1994, with perhaps 10 per cent currently available to agencies. This proportion is rising. New users are entering this type of marketing arena and the major players are escalating their spend.

Brann works extremely hard for its clients to deliver intelligent solutions through consultancy, systems and marketing strategy. It focuses on the value of information and the application of technology - Brann people are extensive users and believers of data-driven marketing. And the company's breadth of comprehensive services, from consultancy and creative to database systems and telemarketing, sets it apart from much of the competition.

Strategy and management

Brann's management claims it can see no visible cap to market growth, and is convinced that Brann should increase its market share for the foreseeable future. Chris Gater, chief executive: 'Current trends indicate a shift from compiling customer databases to creatively applying this data. Telemarketing and customer-care lines offer prodigious growth, and in the systems market, demand currently outstrips supply. Technology therefore plays a key role, driving deep into the next generation of marketing communications and creating the opportunity for the nimblest operators to develop new products and services. This is precisely where Brann is focusing its development.'

Clients are actively involved in the planning process, a partnership approach based on mutual interest but which has the advantage of making it more difficult for them to switch to another company. Other barriers to competition include Brann's heavy investment in technology and databases, and its compelling track record in advising new entrants into this field of marketing communications. While many of Brann's clients are multinational, the company's activities are primarily focused on the UK, although it is considering its options for extending overseas. But the marketing tools and processes that the company owns are easily applied across frontiers, and with less emphasis on global brands, the potential is clearly there.

The strategic management process is well organised, employing the usual methods of annual budgets, three year plans, annual strategic reviews, and targets. Margins are more important than absolute numbers. Each individual operation is responsible for examining its own markets, opportunities and threats. Their reports are scrutinised by senior management at the next stage, where the best opportunities and also any common elements between the operations are identified. In implementing strategic plans, milestones are deemed important as well as financial returns.

Brann's policies in human resource management are expansive and committed. The MBO delivered the platform to instil a new culture and to encourage employees to participate and innovate. Everyone has a chance to have their say and is genuinely empowered in a climate of encouragement, open management and counselling. The 'virtual team' approach, which creates front line client teams of multi-disciplines and managerial positions, would seem to breed mutual respect.

Not surprisingly, training is crucial. A number of training programmes are used, aimed at developing both common and specialist skills. Feedback is a valuable part of this process and is used to shape future modules as part of a management learning contract. Brann would seem to enjoy leading-light or academy status in the marketing industry. Specialists in many disciplines are clearly attracted to join Brann, not least for the opportunity to gain hands-on experience across a range of leading edge marketing disciplines. But staff turnover is comparatively low.

A distribution of equity to many senior employees at the time of the MBO highlights not only a caring, conscientious, even generous employer, but also a positive commitment to real employee motivation. Additional equity was also retained for new senior people entering the business at a later stage so that this tool of motivation was still available. Alan Bigg, chairman: 'At the MBO we created a style of management with entrepreneurial spirit, but also with the humility to recognise that it would only work if our people are motivated. That was the reason they were given a chunk of the company - we believe it is highly appropriate for an unprescriptive business like Brann.'

The future

Brann is refreshingly realistic as to where the future will lead. Chris Gater, chief executive, views the key ingredients as 'the people we employ; expanding the level of competitive services we provide to customers; and technology. The present directors are custodians of this chapter in Brann's development. Our responsibility is to keep the company secure, keep innovating, and develop the next generation of Brann managers capable of taking the company to the next chapter.'

That underlines Brann's commitment to core values that have every chance of standing the test of time - a total commitment to creating loyal customers; an emphasis on developing new products and innovative solutions in data and direct marketing; an understanding of the applications of technology.

BRITISH AIRWAYS

British Airways, Middlesex

British Airways is the world's leading international airline

Outlook:
British Airways prides itself on being The World's Favourite Airline and indeed it is hugely successful. It invests heavily in customer care and staff training and has been extremely astute in marketing initiatives. This is an astutely managed company and it will need every ounce of its professionalism to compete in the deregulated environment which is certain to follow in the next decade

Scorecard:

Structural flexibility	★★★
Innovative power	★★★★
International orientation	★★★★★
Human resources	★★★★★
Growth markets	★★★★
Quality of management	★★★★

Key figures:

Turnover	£7 billion
Pre-tax profits	£327 million
Staff	53,000

British Airways
PO Box 10
Speedbird House
Heathrow
Hounslow
Middlesex TW6 2JA
Tel: 0181 759 5511

British Airways

British Airways is the world's most profitable airline, operating out of a well-defended hub at Heathrow, the world's busiest international airport. The next decade will see radical changes in the world airline industry. But BA is better placed than any other European airline to prosper in this changing market.

In financial year 1993/94, BA made pre-tax profits of £301m on a £6.3bn turnover. Today it has a market capitalisation of £3.8bn. To put its achievement into context, in 1993 the 230 airlines belonging to the International Air Transport Association (IATA) collectively lost $4bn. During the four years 1990 to 1993, they lost a total of $15.6bn.

This puts BA at the head of a very elite pack of profit-making airlines, which includes Singapore Airlines, Cathay Pacific of Hong Kong and Southwest Airlines of the US. 'BA is clearly the dominant international carrier in the world by a wide margin,' says Chris Avery, aviation analyst at stockbroker Paribas. 'It is a standard setter for the industry to follow, not least because it makes material profits in such a loss-making industry.'

That BA has shown consistent profits growth over recent years is all the more remarkable considering that the world airline industry has been through a swingeing recession. As BA chairman Sir Colin Marshall said: 'BA's results contrast well with the general picture. They reflect the airline's continued ability to counter economic and market forces while investing heavily for the future.'

IATA is now becoming more bullish about airlines' prospects. In 1994, its members showed a $1.8bn profit on $110bn of international ticket sales. Director general Pierre Jeanniot forecasts industry growth of 6.7 per cent to the end of the century, with IATA airlines making $5.5bn in 1995.

As Zafar Khan of stockbrokers Societe Generale Strauss Turnbull (SGST) says: 'To make a simple point, BA has continued to make money in very difficult circumstances and those circumstances are improving.'

But, while the outlook for aviation is improving, competition is increasing. Over the next decade, airlines are going to have to digest sweeping regulatory changes. Protected routes will be opened up to competition. And more state-owned airlines will be privatised. As the US experience of deregulation proves, such industry changes lead to a shake-out of poorly performing airlines, with only the fittest surviving.

In this increasingly competitive aviation market, only airlines with strong cost control will prosper. Deregulation in Europe means that the days of subsidy junkies like Air France and Iberia are numbered - unless they quickly bring their costs into line.

By contrast, BA's unit costs are less than half of its major European competitors. In 1993/94, it drove down these costs by an underlying 3.6 per cent, exceeding its cost-savings target of £150m. Even through the recession, BA achieved ongoing productivity improvements.

As Lewy Asrat, aviation analyst at Merrill Lynch says: 'BA is among the best positioned airlines in the world. It has a dominant position in the UK and a growing position in Europe, which will be a fast growing revenue region over the next few years. And it has much lower costs than its European competitors.'

BA has effectively stolen a march on its European rivals. While they spend the next decade struggling to adapt their cost structures to a changing industry, BA will be concentrating on its growth strategy.

'In terms of our network, product and service, and our focus on costs and asset utilisation,' says Sir Colin, 'we believe we are ahead of much of the competition and have the momentum to maintain that advantage.'

Operations and markets

BA has one of the best route structures in world aviation, with operations split into four regions: Africa, Middle East and the Indian sub-continent, where BA made most of its 1993/94 operating profits (£203m); the Americas (£129m); Far East and Australia (£95m); and Europe (£69m).

In the last financial year, all regions recorded improved profitability, with Europe's profits more than doubling and the Americas up by almost 50 per cent. BA carried 30.6m passengers and a record 607,000 tonnes of cargo. As Sir Colin points out, BA continues to improve its market share. 'Last year, our passenger numbers grew by 11 per cent, while the market grew by 5 per cent.'

Central to BA's success is its Heathrow hub. It holds many of the best slot positions at Heathrow, which SGST calls 'probably the best interlining hub in the world'. Heathrow is in the ideal geographical position between Europe and the North Atlantic routes. And plans to develop Terminal 5, which Sir Colin vociferously supports, could add capacity for a further 60m passengers a year.

But BA will not be able to sit for ever on its Heathrow hub. Aviation deregulation will gradually compel BA to relinquish some of its Heathrow slots. But it is not going to do this without ensuring it gets something in return. The trade-off could be increasing control of other airlines.

Strategy and management

In its structure, BA is developing as two types of airlines. It is building an aggressive presence in Europe, using low-cost subsidiaries to compete with lumbering national carriers. And it is constructing a worldwide strategy by taking equity stakes in other airlines, notably USAir and Qantas, with the goal of becoming the world's major global carrier.

Over the last couple of years, BA has been carefully constructing its European network. BA has acquired Dan Air and taken a big stake in TAT, a domestic French operator. It has transformed its Berlin operation into Deutsche BA, a fully-fledged German airline. It has acquired full ownership of the UK short-haul airline Brymon Airways and has a joint-venture with Maersk Air of Denmark. It has also entered into a new franchising agreement with the Gatwick-based independent commuter airline CityFlyer Express, which now flies under the BA brand.

'The overall effect,' says SGST, 'is to create a collection of low-cost operating units in Europe which are in a position to make good profits out of the current high yields and then to compete aggressively when deregulation really starts to bite. One has to question whether Lufthansa/City Line and Air France/Air Inter can hope to compete with these aggressive, low-cost operations.'

At the same time BA is building its global network. There are many advantages of strategic alliances with other airlines. Passengers deal with one brand worldwide, giving benefits of continuity, single check-in and ticketing and frequent flyer loyalty.

There is no duplication of costs at joint destinations. Short-haul passengers on one airline can switch to the partner airline for a long-haul flight, bringing benefits to both airlines. And there are economies of scale in joint-purchasing operations.

Of course BA is not alone in building alliances. But its approach differs to other airlines in one crucial respect. It has gone for ownership, with the aim of ultimately gaining control. Sir Colin believes that buying equity is the cement that holds relationships between airlines together.

So, BA has taken a 25 per cent stake in USAir and Qantas. This differs radically to the looser marketing relationships of Lufthansa and United or even the older Delta/Singapore/Swissair alliance. Here the members have cross-shareholdings, but not big enough stakes to stop them individually pursuing other competing alliances.

While the Qantas alliance is performing well, no-one can pretend BA's $400m investment in USAir has reaped immediate rewards. In an increasingly competitive US aviation market, USAir's high cost base has caused escalating losses. BA stresses that even during this rough patch, it still gained £70m worth of benefits from the code-sharing agreement with USAir on 57 routes. And BA has always said that the real benefits of the alliance would come through in the second half of the 1990s.

Geographically, the BA/USAir/Qantas alliance is the only one that really girdles the world. Moreover, when political pressure builds on BA to relinquish some of its key slots at Heathrow, it has a trump card to play. It can trade them for the right to raise its stake in its two global partners to over 50 per cent, making it the world's only round-the-world airline operator.

From Concorde to the latest Boeing 777s, BA is at the forefront of technical innovation. But its ability to consistently increase staff productivity speaks volumes about its innovative management approach.

In the summer of 1993, Operation Brainstorm invited all staff to make suggestions for generating additional revenue or trimming costs. More than 5,500 suggestions were received, many of which were acted upon. Profit-sharing schemes give staff an incentive to work as efficiently as possible. And 62 per cent of employees have shares in the company. As part of the Opportunity 2000 initiative, percentage targets have been set for the employment of women and ethnic minority managers by the year 2000 and a dedicated Equal Opportunities executive has been appointed to monitor progress.

The future

BA has consistently made profits in a predominantly loss-making industry, and analysts believe these will continue to increase by 10-15 per cent annually over the foreseeable future. It already has the low cost base competitors can only dream about. Its European strategy is sound. And it is further along the path of becoming a truly global carrier than any other airline. In five years time it could even have a Chinese partner. On top of this, BA has an innovative approach to both marketing the company and motivating its staff.

All this suggests it will be one of the dominant forces in world aviation over the next decade and beyond. As Sir Colin says: 'Our strategy is to keep in the forefront of the globalisation of the airline industry - resulting from increasing deregulation around the world, along with more privatisation, as governments recognise the high cost of retaining control and ownership.'

British Biotech plc, Oxford

British Biotech is a significant biotechnology company

Outlook:
The biotechnology sector is one of the most difficult for non-specialists to penetrate and to assess in strictly business terms. Much of its activity is far-future research developing the sources for new drugs. British Biotech is a respected company with the resources and the relationships to succeed

Scorecard:

Structural flexibility	★★★★
Innovative power	★★★★★
International orientation	★★★
Human resources	★★★★
Growth markets	★★★★★
	★★★★

Key figures:

Investment funds	£25 million
Staff	300

British Biotech plc
Watlington Road
Oxford OX4 5LY
Tel: 01865 748747
Fax: 01865 781047

British Biotech

In February 1995 British Biotech admitted that trials of its lead product, the cancer drug Batimastat, had been delayed by manufacturing problems. Its shares plunged by 24 per cent on the news - but British Biotech is still worth £235m even though it has yet to deliver one compound to market and it is bound to lose money at least until 1998. So even at this relatively early stage of its corporate history British Biotech is already Britain's largest biotech company and the 10th largest in the world. Despite the Batimastat hiccup it is still well regarded by investors, is exceptionally well run, is fully resourced and has a strong portfolio of drugs under development. Shares in US biotech superstar Amgen have risen by 7,427 per cent during the past decade and it is now worth £5.6bn. British Biotech is already well down that path but there's still an enormous amount of upside.

Operations and markets

Founded in 1986, British Biotech is based in Oxford and has gleaned some of its ideas, if only a minority, from the eponymous University. It also has a growing US operation in Maryland. The company was first quoted in the UK and on Nasdaq in July 1992. Several rounds of fund raising have since 1986 brought in £151.5m and British Biotech still has net cash of £49m even though it is currently spending more than £25m a year on research and development and has no revenues as yet. Warrants exercisable at 525p in December 1995 could bring in another £47m.

That's not British Biotech's only source of income. The company has signed a number of credibility-enhancing deals with industry majors, such as Glaxo, which have brought in revenues of £8.8m since 1990. These agreements give the big pharmaceutical companies some rights to specific British Biotech products, should they come to market, but the Oxford firm will retain the lion's share of any future revenues.

Products:

1. Batimastat. British Biotech's lead product is a drug which it is hoped can combat late stage cancers of the abdomen (such as Ovarian cancer) and of the chest. A small scale trial involving 23 patients last year was successful and showed Batimastat to be highly effective against ovarian cancer. But in February 1995 British Biotech's chairman John Raisman admitted that in a large scale trial needed to gain regulatory approval for Batimastat for abdominal cancer some patients had experienced painful side effects. That is due to a change in the manufacturing process rather than an inherent flaw in the drug. But trials have been delayed and large scale trials of Batimastat, for both types of cancer, will probably not now finish until the end of 1996 - a year behind schedule. That would imply a launch in 1997. Stewart Adkins of the stockbrokers Lehman Brothers calculates that if Batimastat proves efficacious for both types of cancer, sales could peak at around £275m by the year 2003.

2. BB-2516. An oral (rather than injectable) drug of the same type as British

Biotech's lead drug, it is less proven than Batimastat but potentially far more valuable. That's because the human body finds it far easier to accept orally administered drugs and requires lower doses. However, BB-2516 is currently only at the stage of being tested for safety, and efficacy tests won't be complete until 1998. But the potential is enormous. In the US and Europe alone, BB-2516 could be of use to five million new patients each year. Peak sales could easily reach £800m a year by 2003 - if it works.

3. Lexipafant. A product designed to improve tissue oxygenation and organ function. The drug could prove very useful in treating pancreatitis and heart disease and is British Biotech's second most advanced product. Pancreatitis alone effects 260,000 patients in the Western world each year, each of which cost more than £800 per day to treat using conventional therapies. A small scale (80 patient) trial last year indicated that Lexipafant in its injectable form was of considerable benefit to patients. So the drug is currently undergoing a full, pre-registration, 300 patient trial for pancreatitis. It is also being put through a small scale trial among heart patients. In either form Lexipafant is unlikely to be launched before 1998 but peak sales could quickly reach £50m.

4. Oral Lexipafant. An oral form of Lexipafant is being worked on as a possible treatment for the world's fastest growing disease - asthma - in conjunction with Glaxo. A large scale trial will take place this year. Small trials were encouraging. This market is highly competitive, oral Lexipafant is still largely unproven and won't be launched until 2002 at the earliest according to Lehman Brothers. But though Glaxo would take a significant share of any profits, sales could reach £500m a year as by the year 2000 asthma could affect 15m Westerners every year.

5. BB 10010. This is a genetically engineered protein which British Biotech hopes, if injected can speed recovery from and minimise the side effects of chemotherapy. No clinical data on efficacy of this compound will be available until the end of 1995 when the results of a trial are complete. And a product launch is inconceivable before the millennium. But if it is launched BB 10010 could easily generate revenues of more than £500m a year and this market is growing at 13 per cent a year.

6. p24-VLP. A highly speculative project designed to delay or even prevent the onset of full Aids in HIV-positive patients. The drug is currently involved in a 500 patient efficacy trial but this remains an extreme long shot, albeit potentially an extremely lucrative one.

7. Arthritis compound. Another project which at this stage is highly speculative.

8. Multiple Sclerosis Treatment. British Biotech's wholly owned subsidiary Neures is working on a product for the massive MS market. Like the arthritis drug, even if successful, British Biotech's MS compound won't be launched until the next millennium.

Strategy and management

The key to British Biotech's corporate strength has not been so much its great ability to raise cash but its skill at using, by definition, limited resources prudently. The senior management team headed by chief executive Keith McCullagh and finance director James Noble are well regarded. Mr Noble was headhunted from the City and Dr McCullagh, who is chairman of the UK BioIndustry Association, has spent his entire working life in pharmaceuticals research. There is a relatively light senior overhead but key personnel (about one tenth of British Biotech's 300 staff) are given a generous share option scheme to foster loyalty.

British Biotech attempts to minimise its cash outflow in three ways which mark it out as distinct from the other UK quoted biotech companies and from most US firms in this industry. Outsourcing has been taken as far as possible in order to reduce overheads. Not only is the manufacture of chemical substances contracted out but so is its computer aided molecular design work, toxicology studies and even clinical trials of its drugs. Should any drug gain regulatory approval, production will be contracted out. James Noble stresses that his budget for sub-contracting exceeds that for staff costs - in this industry that's highly unusual.

British Biotech has also shown a willingness to drop programmes, such as its search for a prophylactic Aids vaccine, which don't show sufficient promise even though that doesn't always go down well in the City. With eight mainstream compounds still under development it can afford to cut the odd project but few biotechs are mature enough to admit failure at an early stage.

Another key to British Biotech's resource husbandry is the way it trains its staff to work flexible patterns. Apart from the most senior management all its workers can be switched both between the different stages of one development schedule or between different projects altogether. Thus no hands stand idle at any time.

Should one of its drugs come to market, British Biotech has committed itself to sell it either through a small dedicated hospital-only salesforce or via the existing salesforce of a joint venture partner. Such a strategy is designed to minimise future marketing costs.

This novel and mature approach to management means British Biotech is able to exploit its technology far more efficiently and cheaply than its peers.

The future

British Biotech has the resources to succeed, is run in an innovative yet prudent way and its technology has the potential to transform the company into a significant player in international medicines. As James Noble says, pharmaceuticals is the one area of industry where you can go from being a small company to become a mega corporation in one go.

Of course it's not certain that British Biotech's strategy for growth will succeed but if even one of its major projects comes to fruition the gamble will have paid off. One analyst believes its shares could soon be worth £15 - that could easily prove a pessimistic forecast.

British Gas

British Gas, London

British Gas is the world's leading international gas supplier and consultant on gas supply, exploitation and delivery

Outlook:
Despite a series of public relations gaffes in the UK, British Gas' reputation globally is remarkably strong and many analysts believe that worldwide the company will be the strongest sector player

Scorecard:

Structural flexibility	★★★★
Innovative power	★★★★
International orientation	★★★★★
Human resources	★★
Growth markets	★★★
Quality of management	★★★★

Key figures:

UK turnover	£156 m
UK pre-tax profits	£5.53 mn
UK staff	2,200
Worldwide turnover	£5.6 billion
Worldwide pre-tax profits	£1.4 billion
Worldwide staff	34,000

British Gas
Rivermill House
152 Grosvenor Road
London SW1V 3JL
Tel: 0171 821 1444
Fax: 0171 821 8522

British Gas

Few of Britain's leading companies are the world's largest in their sector. The days of the UK's economic supremacy in global markets are long since gone, but a handful combine the critical mass, resilience, product innovation, financial clout and reputation to assume the top spot.

The transformation of British Gas from a largely domestic supplier to standard setter for the world's gas companies makes a notable case study. In December 1986 it was privatised - including a few minor overseas assets and a tiny exploration and production arm. It retained the domestic monopoly of gas supply, employing some 90,000 people.

In 1995, it is the world's premier gas company and the UK's seventh-largest corporation. British Gas has restructured radically into five autonomous business units. The triggers for the changes were primarily the disciplines of private sector operation and an especially aggressive regulator who has forced the company to adapt in order to survive.

Operations and markets

1. Gas supply

The core UK gas supply business felt the brunt of the regulatory attack, headed by the combative Sir James McKinnon, Director General of Ofgas, and his successor Ms Claire Spottiswoode.

Larger markets for gas supply were gradually opened up to competition with Gas new competitors given advantages to help reduce Gas market share. Typically these meant that Gas had to pre-publish its prices allowing rivals, such as the BP/Statoil venture Alliance Gas Manweb Calor and Amerada Hess, to undercut it.

In 1995 53 per cent of those using more than 2,500 therms of gas a year buy from companies other than Gas. In some parts of the market, the utility's market share has slipped to 10 per cent. However Business Gas, the part of the utility competing in this market, will from now onwards be able to compete on a level playing field.

Meanwhile in the market in which Gas kept its monopoly, the supply of gas to customers who use less than 2,500 therms a year, it has been forced to cut its prices by up to 4 per cent in real terms every year.

From 1996 this market which is largely made up of domestic users will also be opened up to competition. Since Gas rivals can't cherry pick the best customers, Liz Butler, gas analyst at Panmure Gordon, doubts what impact the new rivals will make: most domestic customers are pretty inert and for marginal savings won't move their accounts. However it is clear that profits from gas supply will fall.

2. The gas pipeline

All suppliers of gas will have to continue to use British Gas £17bn pipeline and storage network. To ensure level competition this part of Gas, known as TransCo, will be separated from the rest of the company by Chinese walls. All pipeline users will pay the same prices which will fall by 5 per cent, in real terms, each year. TransCo's initial return on capital will be limited to barely 4.5 per cent.

3. Gas services and retail

British Gas owns small businesses which provide a range of appliance installation and services and which sell gas appliances through a retail network. Both have reduced their number of outlets dramatically and are moving to incentivise staff by altering the balance between basic and commission pay. However neither feature large in the greater scheme of British Gas. The shops may be sold.

The cost of insulating TransCo from the rest of Gas have been around £200m and this formed part of a £1.3bn restructuring charge taken against 1993's profits. That programme was aimed to strip £600m costs from the regulated UK gas businesses by 1998. That has necessitated a drastic reduction in the headcount which at the end of 1993 stood at 65,000. Already 10,000 workers have taken voluntary redundancy and another 15,000 will do so by the end of 1998.

Chief executive Cedric Brown admits that the enormous shake-up at his company has hit morale: 'Whenever you create uncertainty employees will be very concerned regarding their own positions. Until they know where they are they will be worried.' The company has tried to ease the process by consulting fully with trades unions, which are fully recognised at Gas. But Mr Brown is adamant that 'if you don't cut your coat to face the new situation the company goes down the plughole.'

Thanks to the drastic surgery, the constituent parts of UK gas will stay the main generator of earnings and cash for the rest of the decade. Operating profits should top £1bn until the millennium. That in its own right would make Gas one of Britain's top thirty companies.

Strategy and management

As the regulatory environment in the UK became increasingly tough, Gas moved to diversify and - unlike most of the former utilities - has been remarkably successful. Its attack has had two prongs:

1. Global Gas

World demand for gas is projected to rise by 40 per cent between now and 2005. To take advantage of this Gas has invested in gas supply and distribution systems in less regulated markets where it can make a greater return on capital than in the UK.

Its main assets are a 33 per cent stake in Argentina's MetroGas and a number of gas distribution and power generation projects throughout South East Asia. Gas consultants SERIS say that in terms of the number of international projects undertaken British Gas is the world leader.

However the company has resisted the temptation to grow merely for the sake of it and will only invest in projects where it can make a significantly better return on capital than it can in the UK. Last year it sold its 85 per cent stake in Canada's Consumers Gas for £609m, netting a small profit. A tighter regulatory regime would have limited future returns.

British Gas is one of the biggest, yet still discriminating, players in the field. That's important, Francis Gutman chairman of Gaz de France notes: 'in a market where barriers will progressively be lifting to become global, only major gas companies will be significant protagonists.'

This is a very long term investment and even by the millennium profits from Global Gas will have grown from more or less nothing last year to only £50m. Thereafter growth will be much faster believes Liz Butler.

2. Exploration & Production (E&P). Gas has also grown its E&P arm. Its contribution to group operating profit has risen from 2 per cent in 1987 to 28 per cent (£296m) in 1994. Initially centred on the UK North Sea, where Gas is now the largest player behind BP in terms of value, it now operates in 17 countries and by 1998 its production and profits are expected to double. Already its reserves are larger than those of Britain's two largest explorers Lasmo and Enterprise combined.

Following the disposal of Consumers Gas, British Gas balance sheet is pretty healthy with gearing down to 26 per cent. And with its cost cutting ahead of schedule it should be generating £2bn of cash each year by 1996. That will not only facilitate a progressive dividend policy (the shares already yield more than six per cent) but will fund its ambitious investment in unregulated activities.

But that's not the whole story. British Gas already has, according to chief executive Cedric Brown, 'a very sound foundation on which to build.' Mr Brown and his chairman Dick Giordano formerly of BOC, insists Gas culture must also change.

Before privatisation Gas was a centralised company operating through 12 regional units which often overlapped and encouraged the development of unnecessary tiers of management. The regions have gone and 12 layers of management have been halved to six. More importantly Mr Brown has tried to foster a culture of employee empowerment where responsibility is pushed down the line as far as possible. People are encouraged to stick their heads above the parapet with ideas; there will be a no-blame culture where success is rewarded.

In a pioneering scheme Gas is now setting up representative groups of workers in each of its business units to investigate their own pay and conditions. Given full access to outside pay consultants and to data on terms and conditions of employment at similar companies the teams must discuss their findings with focus groups of their colleagues. Then, without the presence of on-line or divisional managers, the initial groups present to full board members their ideas for improving conditions.

Workers are also being allowed to trade off benefits against each other, i.e. to take more holiday for less private health cover or vice versa according to individual needs. Such initiatives Mr Brown feels will encourage initiative and boost corporate loyalty and morale.

The future

There are icebergs ahead which may be circumnavigated. After recent PR gaffes a future Labour government may try to curb British Gas in some way. But with the pipeline earning a very modest return on capital and gas supply completely open to competition the socialists' room for manoeuvre looks limited. Other utilities are far more vulnerable.

More importantly, diversification is coming into its own. By 1999 less than 60 per cent of group profits of around £1.9bn will come from regulated activities. That should confirm and enhance British Gas's position as the world's leading gas company.

BP, London

BP is one of Britain's biggest companies and periodically its largest. It is active in the petro-chemicals sector

Outlook:
BP has taken the strategic move of aiming to reduce its operational base while achieving higher profitability. So far this has paid off handsomely. BP is on the forefront of new developments and sees its future growth in terms not of size but of shareholder return

Scorecard:

Structural flexibility:	★★★★
Innovative power	★★★★★
International orientation	★★★★★
Human resources	★★★★
Growth markets	★★★★
Quality of management	★★★★★

Key figures:

Turnover	£33.1 billion
Pre-tax profits	£2.28 billion
Staff	60,000

BP
Britannic House
Finsbury Circus
London EC2M 7BA
Tel: 0171 496 4000
Fax: 0171 496 4630

British Petroleum

As recently as 1992, a reckless dash for expansion had left BP's boardroom in disarray and the company unprofitable, heavily overborrowed, haemorrhaging cash and grossly inefficient. That's all changed. BP is now the most admired oil company operating in the UK. It has grasped the realities of operating in the petro-chemicals sector and decided to concentrate on those areas which are core disciplines, outsourcing a range of functions to preferred suppliers. Liz Butler of stockbrokers Panmure Gordon says 'BP has mastered the knack of growing by getting smaller'.

Though its revenues continue to fall its return on capital has increased rapidly since mid 1992 and is now among the best of the world's oil majors. Gearing has fallen from 101 to 59 per cent and the group is generating cash. And while employee numbers have halved to 60,000 in only five years, BP has turned a 1992 post-tax loss of £352m into a profit of £2.28bn in 1995. By 1996 net income should reach £2.25bn. Capitalised at £22.2bn, BP is set to remain one of Britain's premier companies. These returns show how the business continues to be a force to be reckoned within a sector which is fated to decline over the next half-century.

Operations and markets

The extent of the BP success can be seen by a close examination of the operating units - exploration and production; refining and marketing; and chemicals - which enjoy considerable autonomy within the BP strategic plan.

Exploration and production

Known as BPX, this arm has been run since 1989 by John Browne who will step up in July to become group chief executive. BPX has the been the flagship for the new BP instigating its cost cutting programme back in 1990. It also accounts for almost three quarters of group operating profits.

But it is still large, with net reserves of 6.538bn barrels of oil and gas reserves of 10,245 billion cubic feet. With a 78/22 oil/gas breakdown of reserves BP is more oil oriented than some of its competitors which, in an ever more environmentally conscious world, is generally viewed as a disadvantage. BP's main producing assets continue to be its massive, but declining, Alaskan oil fields. The largest single source of spending on field exploration and development (37 per cent of £1.6bn in 1994) continues to be the UK.

However, David Simon insists that BP will only develop a field if 'it can make a decent return assuming the oil price is only $14 a barrel'. Such a rigorous test means that BP is increasingly seeking larger projects to develop rather than the small more marginal fields of the North Sea. This strategy of 'elephant hunting' has paid off with large finds in recent years in Cuisiana Colombia, in the Gulf of Mexico and West of the Shetland Isles.

And a rigid attack on costs means that BP's costs per barrel have also fallen sharply making it one of the world's more profitable producers. This has been achieved partly by disposing of most of its older higher-cost fields; but BP has also spearheaded the introduction of new concepts such as the contracting-out of support services to the industry. Duncan Ritchie, chief executive of UK oil independent Goal Petroleum notes 'what BP has done to North Sea costs has transformed the industry dramatically'.

Refining and Marketing

Refining is a somewhat cyclical operation but BP has underperformed its rivals for some time. However, the disposal of low return assets, such as its Swedish and Irish petrol retailing chains, has helped it catch up. Some of its restructuring has been forced. Strapped for cash, it couldn't afford costly environmental upgrades to its US refineries. So it has been forced to sell sites such as Ferndale.

At its remaining sites cost control remains tight. Even in the fourth quarter of 1994 BP announced a further £30m provision for its US arm. As a result of selling old plant and investing selectively in newer sites reliability has soared from around 90 per cent in 1991 to 97 per cent today. Such an improvement is unparalleled in this industry. Last year the downstream division accounted for almost a quarter of BP's profits but that percentage should rise as economic recovery translates into higher margins.

Chemicals

The smallest and most cyclical part of BP, chemicals has taken more than its share of the pain of restructuring. Since 1992 the division's cash fixed costs have been slashed by a third, from $1.6bn to slightly more than $1bn. BP has dominant positions in areas including acrylonitrile - where its technology is used in 95 per cent of the world's manufacturing capacity - and in acetic acid. It is a leading player in other areas such as petrochemicals and polymers but less profitable operations such as its ethylene cracker at Baglan bay in South Wales have been closed or, where possible, sold.

The division now employs 13,700 people, 3,600 fewer than in 1992. That, and a dramatic about-turn in chemicals margins, enabled it to make an operating profit of £252m (loss of £68m) in 1994. Crucially almost half of last year's profits came in the final quarter and analysts believe that at the peak of the current cycle BP Chemicals can make a return on capital easily in excess of 20 per cent. That would not only amount to BP's best ever performance but would rank it among the world leaders in this industry.

Strategy and management

Much of the credit for BP's turnaround since 1992 has been ascribed to its top management team headed by its chief executive David Simon. Certainly back in June 1992 the board set rigorous targets, known as the 1,2,5 goals - debts were to be repaid at $1bn, net income was to reach $2bn and capital expenditure to be cut to $5bn by 1995. Given that in 1992 BP's debts grew by $1.2bn as its capital programme sucked in $5.3bn those were tough targets. But, ahead of schedule, all have been surpassed.

However, Mr Simon says there has been 'a fundamental change in the organisation - the individuals run the assets'. At the simplest level that means that the heads of BP's three main operating divisions (exploration & production; refining

& marketing and BP Chemicals) are given great leeway to run their businesses.

Gone are the days of Bob Horton when BP gambled on a $25 oil price and overpaid for acquisitions such as Britoil, wasted precious cash buying back its own shares and invested in low-return schemes. BP's return on capital at 13 per cent already puts it 'top of the class' according to David Simon. Only investments which can push that return even higher are being authorised.

The combination of lower interest costs, cost cutting and improved working practices helped push BP's underlying replacement cost profits up by more than a third to $1.52bn in 1994 despite a worsening operating environment. Equally, this strategy helped the group to turn cash positive to the tune of £404m (cash outflow of £1bn). That improvement was somewhat masked by BP's disposal of non-core assets (such as its nutrition business) and lower operational costs, which between 1992 and 1994 brought in £3.8bn.

That, and a reduction in dividend payments, has helped BP to reduce its borrowings by $6bn to $10.5bn in scarcely two and a half years. When, in 1996, John Browne hopes to announce net income of $3bn, Fergus MacLeod of NatWest Securities estimates BP is likely to generate around £5bn of cash. That means it can now grow both its dividend and its capital programme while still reducing its debts further. Mr Browne hopes they will fall to $8bn by 1996.

Throughout the group the concept of empowerment - devolving decision making as much as possible - is encouraged. David Simon estimates that more than a third of BP's underlying profit improvements last year came from what he terms Product Performance Management. PPM involves tackling bottlenecks and technical problems to maximise capacity and to improve yields and, only when that has been done, also investing in new plants. To encourage its employees to further the process of PPM each division runs internal competitions among its staff. For instance BP Chemicals' Awards for Innovation scheme last year attracted 166 entries. The chief executive of Chemicals, Bryan Sanderson, estimates the winning scheme alone will 'boost profits by £1m'.

Widespread downsizing has hit morale. But BP's policy of setting operational targets not only keeps the City informed but also ensures that the staff are aware of the company's goals and difficulties. The strategic uncertainty of the Horton era is gone. David Simon's slogan on arrival was Profitability, Reputation and Teamwork - BP's workers have taken all three ideas fully on board.

The future

In the rapidly growing Pacific Rim, BP is installing new refinery capacity in Singapore and Australia and growing its retail network throughout the region as well as in Eastern Europe. Chemicals will grow with new polyethylene capacity and the construction of plants in the People's Republic of China. Meanwhile BPX is searching out new opportunities in gas and is at the forefront of exploration in the former Soviet Union.

But once bitten twice shy. This time, the key to BP's future won't be size but shareholder return. In 1992 when BP made a clean replacement cost operating profit of £1.884bn that required $29.5bn of capital. In 1994, $28bn of capital produced a clean replacement cost operating profit of £2.725bn. That trend is good news for shareholders and seems set to continue, if not to accelerate.

British Steel

British Steel, London

British Steel is the third largest and one of the world's most successful steelmakers. It is regarded by many industry analysts as the premier low-cost producer

Outlook:
The future for steel producers will be conditioned by their capacity to manufacture to high levels of quality while maintaining a significant cost differential over subsidised producers.As the decade progresses the industry will probably regionalise strengthening the senior companies in Europe, America and Far East. British Steel enjoys a formidable reputation for superb quality and low-cost provision

Scorecard:

Structural flexibility	★★★★
Innovative power	★★★★★
International orientation	★★★★★
Human resources	★★★
Growth markets	★★★★
Quality of management	★★★★★

Key figures:

Global turnover	£6.23 billion
Pre-tax profits	£578 million
Employees	46,300

British Steel PLC
9 Albert Embankment
London SE1 7SN
Tel: 0171 735 7654

British Steel

The world's steelmakers live in testing times. Ever a cyclical business, steel production faces a range of fresh challenges in the next decade, one which promises to be among its most exacting. The industry rides, historically, in the backwash of economic trends and in 1995 had only recently recovered from the sustained reduction in demand during the recession. The sector as a whole and particular manufacturers have resumed profit profiles but their collective future is unclear as a complex set of factors is at work in the industry.

At present steelmaking is still a national business but in the next ten years competitive pressures will force more alliances, joint ventures and ultimately marriages between leading names. Competition is not straightforward in this business. Many of the senior international players wear badges of national pride and as such benefit from significant subsidies from their respective governments. Others, notably the UK's British Steel, rely only on their technical excellence and commercial skill. Issues of quality of output, creative use of technology, the nature of subsidies to competitors and the transition from production-led to market-led strategies will each play their part in shaping the steel industry of the 21st century.

Perhaps the single biggest trial for individual businesses is the capacity to achieve and maintain low cost production in comparison with direct competitors. This factor favours British Steel which is regarded by eminent US analysts as the premier low cost producer across the world. On *Metal Bulletin*'s 1994 steelmakers league table British Steel is placed fourth by tonnage produced, only half the size of leader Nippon Steel but not far behind the third placed candidate - Usinor Sacilor of France. According to *Metal Bulletin*, there are two senior players - Nippon Steel (25.50 million tonnes) and Korea's Posco (22.12 million tonnes), followed by Usinor and British Steel. The following seven places on the table are occupied by an assembly of US, European and Asian manufacturers each generating above 10 million tonnes. Although many sell their products outside their home markets, none can be classified as a truly international company.

Operations and markets

British Steel exports 47 per cent of its production. Its turnover in 1995 was £6.23 billion with pre-tax profits of £578 million. This tremendous project increase, up from £80 million in the previous year, is due to a combination of long-term favourable factors: rising prices for steel, better performance by British Steel associates, efficiency gains, and above all the ending of the continental recession Broker SG Warburg estimates profits of £1.05 billion for 1995/6 and £1.25 billion for 1996/7. The company believes that in the coming decade it will remain in the top three of both European and global producers. At present it employs some 42,000 people in the UK - concentrated at two groups of integrated works, Llanwern and Port Talbot in South Wales and Teesside and Scunthorpe. In 1995 it bought United Engineering Steels which has its headquarters in Rotherham.

The business has come a long way since 1980 when it employed 166,500 people and labour costs represented 37 per cent of the total budget. This was substantially reduced during the 1980s and now accounts for only 22 per cent of total costs. Furthermore, the company is making more steel today on only a quarter of the staff complement. It is a positive indicator to the progress - in management terms - of the enterprise. In market conditions which can change dramatically, British Steel has a cost advantage over loss-making state-run companies like Italy's Ilva and Spain's CSI. The European Commission has allowed national governments to prop up plants with subsidies or inject cash in return for limited cuts in production volumes, to the disadvantage of British Steel.

Strategy and management

The relative inefficiencies of other European producers have a direct bearing on the long term strategy for British Steel. In the short term, it can take competitive comfort from its clear cost advantage over continental rivals but in the longer perspective British Steel's global ambitions will almost certainly require improved competitiveness from European producers as a group.

This strategy has four principal points:
- staying competitive internationally on costs
- sustaining the move from production-led to market-led
- tightly targeted capital expenditure (spending £22 million at developments at Llanwern to add a million tonnes of capacity, 'ridiculously cheap' according to the chairman)
- a strong balance sheet; no gearing, cash-generation operation, tight control on stocks, working capital and investment.

Chairman Brian Moffat told Robert Heller in the June 1995 edition of *Management Today* that in the year 2000 'we will be an internationally based steel company. There's no such thing in the world today. For us Europeans to put our house in order, cross border alliances, mergers and joint ventures must be part of the answer.'

Joint ventures and investment often go hand-in-hand, For example, the LTV(US)/British Steel/Sumitomo Trico Steel joint venture (of which BS has 25 per cent) involves a total commitment of £275 million for a flat rolled steel production unit. This will eliminate the cold mill stage, saving a sizeable chunk of costs. A further £100 million has been spent by British Steel on its one million tonnes a year mini-mill in Tuscaloosa, Alabama.

These US projects are cutting the company's teeth for investments in other parts of the world. Mr Moffat says that British Steel needs local production facilities in overseas markets since transport costs eat too much margin on exports. His priority is Asia. First step is joint venture rolling or processing followed by manufacturing proper. India is the first port of call with China as a later objective.

Technological superiority, coupled with low cost production, is one area where British Steel is placing great emphasis. Technology director Dr Jeff Edington told Mr. Heller that technological innovation underpins British Steel's status as a low cost producer. More than 1,000 products variations are made at Scunthorpe alone, and the properties within steel are allowing secondary manufacturers like car companies to revolutionise their product lines. Dr. Edington argues that the company has caught up with - and surpassed - its principal rivals. It has 900 people active in research and development, and 1,500 in technology. In technology, the company has a clear direction: to work with customers to develop products, to buy steel technology and to draw greatest advantage from such acquisitions. Its electric arc furnaces at Trico Steel will be the first of their type. In construction British Steel has doubled its UK market share, winning business from concrete and expanding exports. Its applications are also a major part of the strategy, eliminating internal bureaucracy.

The management style at British Steel has been completely revamped in recent years. The civil service approach to corporate management had long since been ditched but the company held on to some of the more traditional aspects of British hierarchical personnel philosophies - strong indentity, high quality technical base, improving marketing abilities and proficiency on staff motivation.

Certainly under the present chairman the company has created an open culture where ideas are discussed and customer service considerations lie at the core of business activity. People have responded positively, demonstrating their support for the more focused approach. The new style sponsors innovation. It encourages employees to be team players and embrace the vision for British Steel in the future.

The future

British Steel is in a strong position to capitalise on market trends. It sets its sights high - to be a top three global player, supported by low cost production and technological superiority. Achievement of these ambitions in the long run will be influenced by the extent to which it can galvanise current rivals on the mainland to improve quality and cost efficiencies. The scope of joint ventures and futher advances in process, logistics and customer dialogue are also factors which will shape the company.

In many ways the company is fitter than most competitors to realise its goals, and British Steel in 1995 is characterised by verve, energy and drive to meet its strategic vision. Given the cathartic rollercoaster of the world economy, little in steelmaking is absolute but the company appears to be steering the right course. Few steel-users in the UK are world class so British Steel must look outward for its new business prospects. The world market is increasingly demanding and it requires excellent standards in every area of operation. This company is up to the task.

British Telecom plc, London

BT is one of the world's largest telecommunications companies. From its domestic base in the UK it has emerged from privatisation to be active around the globe

Outlook:
The future for BT is exceptionally promising - most analysts expect that there will be a battle of goliaths between the largest telecomms providers worldwide and AT&T and BT will slug it out. As a public sector company BT was poorly thought-of - it was flabby, bureaucratic, technocentric and a lousy employer. As a commercial company, it has shed layers of management and thousands of employees to make the company a much fitter and more agile operator. It has become a source of quality management thinking and also innovative practice in industry

<u>Scorecard:</u>

Structural flexibility	★★★★
Innovative power	★★★★
International orientation	★★★★★
Human resources	★★★
Growth markets	★★★★
Quality of management	★★★★★

<u>Key figures: (31 march '95)</u>

Turnover	£ 13,893 million
Pre-tax profits	£ 2,662 million
Staff	137,500

British Telecom plc
BT Centre
81 Newgate Street
London EC1A 7AJ
Tel: 0171 356 5000

British Telecom

The telecommunications industry stands on the threshold between two worlds. There's the gradually disappearing world of state-run telephone companies operating as protected monopolies purely within their national boundaries. Then there's the emerging world of trans-national, private sector suppliers competing with one another in every significant market across the globe. BT has moved decisively into the modern world of competition, innovation and customer orientated thinking. It is, indeed, one of the leaders of the telecomms revolution.

In the liberalised future for telecomms, the pressure to compete will inevitably limit to a mere handful - probably no more than half a dozen - the number of suppliers which can claim a truly global role. Few doubt that BT will be a prominent member of that group.

Operations and markets

The company which began life as the telephonic arm of the UK Post Office embraces the idea that in the future, the role of a telephone company will go far beyond handling telephone calls.

The distinctive factor which will create winners of the future is the capacity to add new services to the industry's traditional strengths. This forces companies to think creatively, as BT chairman Sir Iain Vallance explains: 'Technological change is encouraging the convergence of once separate industries; not just telecommunications and computing but publishing, entertainment and consumer electronics.'

With trials already under way in areas as diverse as interactive television, electronic payment systems and tele-working, BT is leading from the front, and foresees further large scale changes to the role it can play. Sir Iain again: 'Successful telecomms companies of the future will be retailers of everything that can be converted into digital form, not only operators of the network.'

Strategy and management

To ensure that it takes its place as one of the world's dominant telecomms companies at the start of the 21st century, BT has espoused a strategy which can broadly be described under two headings. On the one hand it aims to do an ever better job of providing its traditional UK customer base with telephone and related services, in the face of rapidly mounting competition. On the other, it is taking determined steps to establish itself as a viable player in new technological and geographical markets. What is more, BT is pursuing both of these goals while keeping sight of the necessary objective of constantly improving its productivity and cost-effectiveness.

The signs are that BT is ideally positioned to realise its ambitious goals. The key factors in building the company's present strong position are: the UK government's early move to privatise BT and remove its protected status; the decisive measures taken by a cost-conscious and customer-orientated management; and the co-operation of a highly regarded workforce which, despite undergoing drastic cutbacks in numbers in recent years, has contributed immeasurably to its company's much enhanced reputation for delivering the goods.

BT's strength in the UK is the springboard from which all future expansion must start. Perhaps the most vivid illustration of this strength came in December 1994, twelve years after Cable & Wireless plc was awarded the first licence to offer public telecommunications services in competition with BT. It took those twelve years for C&W to decide that Mercury, its UK operating subsidiary, could never become a viable competitor across the full range of telecomms services in the UK. Mercury said it would discontinue marketing to residential customers, and axe its public telephone kiosks. More than a decade after competition was introduced to the UK telecomms market, BT still commanded a 95 per cent share of residential phone calls within the UK, and 83 per cent of business calls (as at March 1994).

These market shares will inevitably fall. Despite Mercury's retrenchment, competition to BT is mushrooming. Whereas in 1991 only five operators, including BT and Mercury, were licensed to offer public telecommunications services, now some 150 are. The bulk of these, numerically, are cable television providers, who frequently offer keenly priced telephone services as an inducement to customers to subscribe to cable TV packages.

In line with Oftel's policy, more competitors will chip away at what was BT's near monopoly. BT's task in the UK, therefore, is to ensure that its operations are sufficiently cost-effective that it can still make acceptable profits from a reduced customer base. 'The whole idea in the UK is that we have to be the most efficient operator,' says Sir Iain Vallance. 'If we have that, then we have security against almost anything the regulator or politicians can throw at us in the long term.'

BT sees two sides to this problem: the need to reduce costs in line with attrition of its UK market share; and the need to expand the market, by encouraging customers to make ever more use of BT's greatest tangible asset, the BT network.

As far as cost-effectiveness is concerned, BT has undergone a revolution since privatisation. While improving its responsiveness and widening the range of services offered, BT reduced its workforce from 240,000 to 140,000 between 1990 and 1995, with another reduction of around 10,000 expected by March 1996. Although not entirely ruling out compulsory redundancies, BT has so far succeeded in cutting its payroll by means of generous voluntary redundancy packages and natural wastage. The cost has been considerable: approximately 2 billion in redundancy payments were charged to profit in the three years to March 1995. As an investment for the future, however, BT sees this expenditure as indispensable.

The resulting improvement in productivity is appreciated by industry experts. Chris McFadden, telecoms analyst at stockbroker Smith New Court, says: 'We believe BT will have fewer than 50 employees per 10,000 lines by 1996, a 50 per cent improvement on the 1993 figure.' Based on the rate at which Mr McFadden expects rivals to take customers away from BT, the company is doing more than enough to compensate in terms of lower costs for the expected reduction in revenue. The other side of the coin is BT's campaign to increase customers' tendency to use the network. Here, the company has three related tools at its disposal: marketing, pricing and service innovation. Higher-profile marketing has been a feature of the past five years, but advertising campaigns are now increasingly associated with special offers, permanent price cuts and information about new services. These have succeeded in expanding residential call volumes, says BT.

The development of BT's pricing policy is an interesting illustration of how a company with, by now, an acute feel for marketing has turned a seemingly harsh regulatory environment to its advantage. It is obliged by Oftel's 1993 pricing edict to keep annual price rises below the prevailing rate of inflation: from 1993-97, the formula is for price changes of 7.5 per cent less than the change on the Retail Price Index (RPI). With UK inflation hovering between 2 and 3.5 per cent for the first half of that period, BT has been forced to make absolute price reductions.

By concentrating the price cuts where they have the maximum competitive effect, however, BT both makes it harder for rivals to steal custom, and bolsters its own efforts to stimulate call volume. Thus, 1994 saw the abolition of the peak charging rate for calls between 9am and 1pm on weekdays; in 1995, BT has already announced its intent to switch all business and residential customers for the first time to a system of charging by the second, which should further reduce bills in comparison to the traditional 'per unit' charging method. BT says that since privatisation in March 1984, the average residential customer's bill has come down by 29 per cent in real (i.e. inflation-adjusted) terms, while business bills have seen a real terms fall of more than 50 per cent. This isn't mere hype: the International Telecommunications Users Group concluded in February 1995 that the UK had the lowest charges for telephone calls of any of the world's main industrial nations.

As this accolade suggests, BT's operating performance is first class by the most rigorous international standards. That's just one of the reasons why observers of the global telecomms scene have little doubt that BT can more than hold its own outside the UK, as well as at home.

International partnerships will be a key feature of BT's efforts to gain access to new markets. In this regard, the company's most significant move so far in the 1990s has been its 1994 link-up with MCI Communications, the second-largest long-distance telecomms carrier in the US. BT paid $4.3bn (2.7bn) for a 20 per cent stake in MCI, the two companies forming a joint venture called Concert, which will invest £1 billion in the medium term in what is already the world's largest and most advanced data network

While many telecoms providers with global pretensions may emulate the move, Sir Iain Vallance has no doubt that BT and MCI are leading from the front. 'While our competitors are still talking about alliances, BT and MCI are out there talking to customers,' says Sir Iain. 'We've left the starting blocks well ahead of the field and we intend to remain there.' BT followed up its MCI alliance with the January 1995 announcement that it would begin offering telecoms services in the German market, Europe's largest, via a joint venture with energy-to-engineering conglomerate Viag, one of Germany's largest industrial companies.

The future

For a company acknowledged as a class act at home, and a force for any of its global rivals to contend with overseas, the future is as tantalising as it is challenging. BT seems certain to take a key role in the development of new services and new technologies which will dictate the future shape of the communications, media and entertainment industries. It is already looking to the potential of interactive technology, conducting trials of a video-on-demand service along with other offerings such as home banking and shopping. Indeed, by the end of the century, the distinctive BT piper should have plenty of cause to blow his own trumpet.

Burford Holdings plc

Burford Holdings plc, London

Burford has established a reputation as one of the UK's most dynamic and entrepreneurial property companies

Outlook:

What has endeared its management to investors is its uncanny timing and an ability to generate very attractive growth without compromising financial security. Its property portfolio is well diversified, with a long term income stream from a range of quality tenants. Borrowings are predominantly long term and at fixed rates

Scorecard:

Structural flexibility	★★★
Innovative power	★★★★
International orientation	n/a
Human resources	★★★
Growth markets	★★★★★
Quality of management	★★★★★

Key figures:

Rental income	£26 million
Operating profit	£13 million

Burford Holdings plc
20 Thayer Street
London W1M 6 DD
Tel: 0171 2242240

Burford

A steady record of sector outperformance distinguishes Burford from its peer group. Throughout the recession it sailed above the turmoil of the property crash and as the economy recovered, its management team's creative and entrepreneurial approach to the property business has become highly valued by investors. Burford has never forgotten the risks inherent in the property business. Almost every visionary UK property developer of the 1980s eventually lost everything by ignoring the need for cashflow. Some of London's most exciting buildings, for example Canary Wharf and Broadgate, are monuments to the failure of many in the property industry to recognise that crucial ingredient. In some respects Burford's management has more in common with the property entrepreneurs of the post-war era. The majority of these supported a considerable development programme over twenty years, relying on the income from an investment portfolio accumulated gradually.

The trader-developers of the 1980s failed en masse because they attempted to speed up this process. They hoped to fund hugely ambitious speculative developments by property trading or via methods of 'financial engineering', such as off-balance-sheet finance. When the property market ground to a halt reality struck. Trading is no substitute for regular investment income from rents. Burford restrained its exuberance while the sector boomed in the late eighties. As it is not its style to 'bet the farm' on a single speculative project, as the market over-heated in the late 1980s it acted contracyclically, and actively sold properties to financially insulate the group from the severe downturn to come. When rents and capital values went into sharp decline, £95m of sales meant that Burford had no gearing and could therefore comfortably fund all of its costs, administration, salaries, property management and dividends from the income stream generated by its portfolio.

Conversely as companies in financial straits became distressed sellers, the group was one of very few in a sufficiently strong position to buy properties at their cyclical lowpoint. In 1990 it bought around £48m of property which yielded a very attractive $11^{1}/_{4}$ per cent per annum. In 1993 the pace of acquisitions was stepped up, partly funded by a £42m rights issue. A second rights issue in March 1994 raised £100m to part fund the acquisition of a portfolio from Ladbrokes. Between early 1993 and June 1994 it bought around £315m of properties, including its largest single purchase ever, the Trocadero in Piccadilly Circus for £94m.

Operations and Markets

Burford is a property investment company with a portfolio of properties worth approximately £435m at its last year end, yielding annual rents of £34m. The portfolio, although weighted to the south east, is spread geographically and by sector. Around half is office space, a quarter retail with the rest split between leisure and industrial. Nearly 40 per cent is in London, a sixth in the Midlands and the remainder spread across the UK. The executive team of Nigel Wray and Nick Leslau have shown superb timing during the most testing period for the property industry since the second world war. They shrewdly degeared the group by 1990, and acquired over 80 per cent of the current portfolio in the last two years and acquired many buildings with unique opportunities for management to add value. Yet even as it has built up that proportion of its portfolio where it can make things happen, it has simultaneously added to its holdings of institutional quality buildings which balance and secure its strategy. The clearest example of this was its acquisition of the Ladbrokes portfolio in February 1994. This was typical of Burford's previous acquisitions, concentrated around four new buildings of institutional quality bought for their predictable, secure long-term income.

Strategy and Management

Considering its innate financial conservatism, Burford's growth over the last decade has been remarkable. Gross property assets have grown from £81m in 1990 to £435m in 1994, while gross rental income rose from £3m to £35m. The property acquisition strategy has been risk averse, yet has delivered results in both bull and bear markets. Burford's net asset value per share has increased by around 700 per cent since 1987, compared with a negligible increase in the property sector.

Specifically it looks for properties to be well located in an established business area. They must be capable of producing a double figure yield within the short term, yet where typically 60 to 70 per cent of the income stream is secure and long term. It looks for properties which it can purchase at low capital values per square foot, in order to provide space at very competitive rates. It never invests abroad, speculatively develops or invests in areas which it does not understand. Investors can take comfort from the fact that it has no intention of changing its strategy.

The next criterion is perhaps the most important, yet also the most idiosyncratic. Any acquisition must contain opportunities for Burford to add extra value by exploiting 'angles'. The track record of identifying under-utilised assets and adding value by active management is the key to understanding the group's unique potential.

The above is, in itself, an intelligent strategy, but it does not make Burford unique. What does, is its focus in its financial statement on what it describes as its 'Armageddon Scenario'. This analysis of its financial stability does not take a conservative, but a nightmare view of the future progress of its property holdings. It assumes that all its tenants depart when their leases either expire or breaks are available, and that the resulting space is never relet. A scenario which is highly improbable, yet under this extreme case the group will still produce sufficient rental income to service all its existing debt until the year 2013. Its views on borrowing are also extremely cautious and it wishes to protect the company from the cost of adverse interest rate movements. Its average cost of borrowing is 9.3 per cent, some 94 per cent of which is at fixed rates. It has established long-term repayment profiles; some 69 per cent is not repayable for another 20 years. Its accounting principles are extremely straightforward. It does not capitalise any interest; rental income alone is sufficient to cover, by 1.2 times, all operating costs, financing charges, taxation and dividends. Extracting value through active management can take place in a number of ways. Rent reviews, lease renegotiations, moving tenants around, new planning permissions, refurbishment and joint ventures are all used. For example, although Burford is not interested in speculative development, at least two of its income producing properties contain useful development angles which it could unlock by a sale to or a partnership with a pure development group.

The Future

Were it not for its purchase of the Trocadero, one would define Burford's future in terms of continuation of a strategy which has served it exceptionally well up to now. However this leisure scheme is more significant to the group than any other of its properties and the group's public profile has become very closely allied with the scheme. Burford acquired the Trocadero in September 1994, as a leisure scheme which had been something of a disappointment over the last few decades. Hence its acquisition by a group which had previously focused on more purely commercial properties, raised eyebrows. The Trocadero had suffered since the war by having owners who were relatively uninterested or cash strapped. In addition, although it attracted astounding numbers of visitors, approximately 16m per annum, and was one of London's leading tourist attractions, the method to translate that into commercial gain had always eluded the operators. Burford has managed to quickly silence its doubters. It has announced a bold and exciting joint venture with Sega of Japan to build the UK's first urban theme park. Some analysts have estimated that Burford could have secured some £3m per annum by letting the 100,000 sq ft of vacant space to conventional users. It has instead invested £15-25m of its own money into a 50:50 joint venture to offer, on four floors, six high-tech, interactive ride attractions plus many other entertainments and restaurants, all scheduled to open in 1996. The plans, which have received permission, include a much needed facelift for the building's facade, improvements to the common parts and extension of the atrium. The prospect of the Segaworld park opening has also attracted further leisure tenants to the centre which by the time the scheme is completed will be fully let. According to analysts all this could increase the value of the Trocadero, purchased for £94m from the receiver, to £250m or more.

Burford has taken this one step further, In August 1995 it acquired The London Pavilion, an adjacent leisure and retail centre, for £13.2m. It has tentatively mentioned plans to join the two schemes (which are already linked underground) by building a bridge above Windmill Street. The London Pavilion is another indifferent performer but the two centres have considerable potential in the right hands, and together the 'marriage value' means each should leverage the returns from the other. Nick Leslau has referred to The Pavilion as 'a front door to the Trocadero' making its flagship property probably London's leading draw. It is difficult to be precise about the potential of a centre which will be unique in Europe. However estimates of around 15 per cent of the Trocadero's usual visitors spending, say, £13 apiece (less than half the Tokyo fee) on the entrance to the theme park, suggest that the scheme could add £10m to Burford's annual income from November 1996.

BURMAH CASTROL

Burmah Castrol, Wiltshire

Burmah Castrol is one of the UK's leading oil companies

Outlook:
Burmah Castrol is strongly positioned for impressive growth. Leading analysts agree that the company's financial strength will be enhanced by its astute strategy of cautious acquisition. Profits are anticipated to double within four years. This is partly due to significant international spread

Scorecard:

Structural flexibility	★★★★★
Innovative power	★★★★
International orientation	★★★★★
Human resources	★★★★
Growth markets	★★★★★
Quality of management	★★★★

Key figures:

Turnover	£3 billion
Pre-tax profits	£219 million
Staff	22,000

Burmah Castrol plc
Swindon
Wiltshire SN3 1RA
Tel: 01793 511521
Fax: 01793 513506

Burmah Castrol

On the eve of Christmas 1974 Burmah Castrol was a diversified oil conglomerate with interests ranging from tanker transportation through exploration to caravans and Do It Yourself. It was also on the verge of a spectacular bankruptcy which necessitated a bail-out by the British government.

Almost 21 years later it is one of the most highly regarded and focused lubricants and speciality chemicals businesses in the world. Its brand names and margins are the envy of its competitors and its prospects and strategy for organic growth are bright and well mapped out. It also has the balance sheet strength to enhance its position through acquisition.

Capitalised at £1.935 billion, Burmah Castrol sits comfortably inside the FTSE-100, but seems certain to improve its position over the coming decade.

Operations and markets

In the calendar year 1995 more than two thirds of Burmah Castrol's pre-tax profits, which will reach £270 million according to Fergus MacLeod at NatWest Securities, will come from its lubricants business.

Of that, more than three quarters will come from sales of lubricants for automobiles. Brand names such as Castrol GTX give Burmah a leading position in the British and German market.

In the US it is gaining market share steadily and currently ranks second behind Pennzoil. Indeed it already leads the consumer rather than the corporate market. In 1994 its volumes grew by seven per cent in a market which grew by only one per cent. Its brand strength means that Burmah Castrol has always been able to charge a significant premium for its automotive lubricants because customers perceive that its products are of a higher quality than competing lubricants produced generally by the international oil majors such as Shell and Elf. Thus, Burmah Castrol's gross margins are, by a long chalk, the highest in this industry.

However the company is adamant that its brands will not lose their value as have other retail brands and supports its products with an unusually high promotional and marketing budget.

The remainder of the lubricants division provides products for a wide range of industries. Often these products enjoy relatively low volumes as they are designed for specific small markets. But that means that the oil majors are unlikely to bother to compete which is reflected in Burmah Castrol's very healthy margins.

The lubricants business is organised on a country by country basis with management usually drawn - as far as is possible - from the local workforce. Thus Burmah's different operating units often employ vastly different strategies.

In the US auto lubricants are targeted at the end-using customers whereas in the UK garages and other larger users also receive considerable marketing attention. In the developing world Burmah Castrol adopts wholly different strategies. Hence in Vietnam Burmah Castrol's managers have targeted the washshop market for motorcycles, which not only generates income but creates a valuable brand awareness when customers eventually get up to owning automobiles. In the more developed Indian market Burmah sells on a UK garage style model rather than to end users as in the US - but the decision to adopt this strategy was largely taken at a local level.

Burmah Castrol is a major player in five areas of speciality chemicals: metallurgical, construction, mining, screen printing inks and coatings. In each of these markets, bar construction chemicals, it is the world's leading producer by volume according to its own 1992 Report and Accounts. In construction it is ranked number four.

Chemicals is organised into five divisions along product lines and each operation is given a considerable degree of management autonomy.

The chemicals division has been expanded greatly since the mid 1980s, largely through the hostile £260 million bid for the mining and construction products company Foseco, which was completed in December 1990.

Though less cyclical than pure petrochemicals these niche products were all hit by the recession as major customers especially in the German steel industry and in construction cut back orders.

Hence Fergus MacLeod believes that divisional operating profits, which stood at barely £11.5 million in the depths of the downturn in 1991, will reach £80 million at the peak of this economic cycle in 1996. That means the division will have achieved its target 10 per cent return on sales.

Burmah Chemicals sets out to be a lead player so if a part of the organisation does not look set to command a lead role in the world market it is disposed of, as was the water treatment products business several years ago.

Alternatively the company has sought to build up its businesses through a series of small strategic infill acquisitions either complementing the product range or to strengthen its position in a particular market. Excluding Foseco, Burmah Castrol's chemicals business made 19 acquisitions of which 14 were deals costing less than £1 million.

Until early 1995 Burmah also owned a UK based chain of petrol stations but this was a low return legacy from its pre 1974 oil company days. And after years of minimal investment which left the operation without critical mass it was sold to Frost Group plc. Small operations in six other countries including Turkey, Belgium, Chile and Sweden make a minimal contribution to profits and are essentially run as cash cows. Any reasonable offer to buy them would undoubtedly be accepted.

However Burmah still retains a 50 per cent stake in a fleet of ships used to transport liquefied natural gas from Indonesia to Japan. The ships are contracted to transport cargoes until well into the next millennium by which time their book value will have depreciated to almost nothing. However they are likely to generate a steady contribution to pre-tax profits of around £7 million a year.

Strategy and management

Burmah Castrol's top management team lead by chief executive Jonathan Fry are all based at its tightly run, relatively low cost head office in Swindon, Wiltshire.

The Burmah Castrol culture is one of cautious promotion from within. Though succession will not be an issue for quite some time since Fry is only 57, it is likely that potential candidates to take over have already been earmarked and are being groomed. All bar two of Burmah Castrol's executive directors have been with the company since the late 1970s. The two newcomers have both served more than a decade in Swindon.

Lower down the corporate pecking order all staff are kept informed of the company's progress via the 'People Management Plan' which, according to Fry, is based on 'open, two-way communication.' This involves regular briefings and surveys of the opinions of all Burmah Castrol's 22,000 employees world-wide.

Its cautious approach to internal advancement is reflected in Burmah Castrol's strategy for growth. Other than the Foseco deal, new Burmah has never made a hostile bid and such a move is unlikely in the future. Instead its inorganic growth will continue to be based on using its enormous power to generate cash to fund a series of very small infill acquisitions on an agreed basis - which often keeps the local line management in place.

However Burmah Castrol also has three stratagems for expanding its core lubricants and chemicals businesses organically: brand enhancement; new product development; and exploitation of developing markets, notably in the Far East.

In 1994 Burmah Castrol's lubricants operations spent £48.3 million, almost one sixth of its operating profits, on marketing and research and development. The results are very high brand recognition and the launch of a stream of new products.

The most notable of these is Syntec, a synthetic automobile lubricant which though more expensive than conventional products has been the driving force behind its rapid gain of market share in the US.

The exploitation of developing markets is made easier for Burmah Castrol by its international nature. Its spread of operations in more than 150 countries makes it less vulnerable to pronounced economic downswings or currency fluctuations.

Burmah looks to hire local management in its infant Asian operations where it hopes to take advantage of a forecast 300 per cent increase in consumer buying power over the next five years. By applying western marketing techniques such as branding, adapted to local needs, it has already chalked up impressive gains.

In Vietnam it has a 20 per cent share of the lubricants market, in India it has a 10 per cent share of the automotive lubricants market and in Thailand its profits have increased by 600 per cent over the past five years. At present the Far East accounts for only a small percentage of group operating profits but this region will make a significant contribution by the year 2000.

The future

Burmah Castrol is financially strong - its gearing is now less than 30 per cent and falling. That leaves it well positioned to continue its cautious acquisition policy.

But it is its organic growth which is more impressive. Simon Trimble of Lehman Brothers expects its pre-tax profits to reach £438 million by the year 2000, compared to just £219 million in 1994. This year it is expected to generate almost £400 million of cash. That allows it to reward its shareholders immediately through impressive dividend growth and for the long term through heavy investment in research, marketing and in bolstering its presence in the growth regions of the future.

Cadbury Schweppes, London

Cadbury Schweppes is one of Britain's most respected companies, operating in the confectionery and soft drinks sectors

Outlook:
Cadbury Schweppes is the senior name in confectionery in the UK. It has also adapted its worldwide strategy to take in joint ventures and license agreement with for example Coca-Cola and Hershey. The company is in the forefront of the debate on ethical business practice

Scorecard:

Structural flexibility	★★★★
Innovative power	★★★★
International orientation	★★★★★
Human resources	★★★★★
Growth markets	★★★
Quality of management	★★★★

Key figures:

Turnover	£4 billion
Pre-tax profits	£478.5 million
Staff	40,500

Cadbury Schweppes plc
25 Berkeley Square
London W1X 6HT
Tel: 0171 409 1313
Fax: 0171 830 5200

Cadbury Schweppes

In Britain, the name Cadbury is virtually synonymous with chocolate. Internationally, too, Cadbury is growing strongly with confectionery sales in nearly 180 countries. The cover of the group's latest annual report pictures a Cadbury's advertising bill-board from Moscow's Red Square - highlighting the jump in Russian sales from five million bars of chocolate in 1992 to more than 280 million in 1994.

On the drinks side of its business, the group's international brands include Canada Dry, Sunkist and, of course, Schweppes. Through CCSB, it also holds the UK franchise to Coca-Cola.

Cadbury Schweppes took a further huge leap forward in early 1995 when it acquired Dr Pepper/Seven-Up, the number three American drinks business. Dr Pepper is the fourth biggest brand in the US soft drinks sector, while Seven-Up is at number eight.

Combined with its existing US business, the £1.6 billion Dr Pepper deal gives Cadbury Schweppes a 16 per cent stake of the carbonated soft drinks market. Dominic Cadbury, chairman of Cadbury Schweppes, regards the purchase as the most important development for the group since the merger of the Cadbury chocolates and Schweppes drinks business in 1969.

Operations and markets

The group was already one of the world's leading beverages and confectionery companies, employing more than 40,000 people. In 1994, it made pre-tax profits of £478.5 million on sales which for the first time exceeded £4 billion. The addition of Dr Pepper/Seven-Up is expected to help lift 1995 profits to around £525 million.

The business divides naturally into the two 'streams' of beverages and confectionery. Even before the Dr Pepper deal, the drinks side was slightly the larger. Last year it made profits of £269 million on turnover of £2.2 billion. The group makes and bottles drinks in 15 countries, and licenses its brands to another 84.

In the UK, Cadbury Schweppes' products are bottled and distributed by Coca-Cola and Schweppes Beverages, the joint venture company which also handles Coke. Despite the high-profile assaults mounted by Virgin and Sainsburys, Britain's premier supermarkets group, CCSB, had an 'outstanding year', with record profits and sales volumes.

Although the group has substantial businesses in Europe and the Pacific Rim, in recent years its expansion has been concentrated on North America. The £218 million acquisition of A & W Brands in 1993 gave Cadbury Schweppes control of the best-selling root beer. The addition of Dr Pepper/Seven-Up will make the Americas the group's most important territory. The profit contribution from the UK will, for the first time, fall below 40 per cent.

In 1994, Cadbury Schweppes made a £235 million profit from its confectionery business, whose sales rose by 10 per cent to £1.8 billion. The group makes chocolate and other confectionery in 23 countries and sells its products in a further 156.

The purchase of Bassett Foods and Trebor at the end of the 1980s greatly strengthened Cadbury Schweppes' position in sugar confectionery, which now represents more than a third of the stream's sales. More recent moves include the acquisitions of Bouquet d'Or, a leading French brand for chocolate assortments, and of Industrias Dulciora in Spain. Cadbury Schweppes has also announced a joint venture to produce chocolate in China, a £75 million contract to set up a factory in Russia and a £20 million investment in confectionery production in Poland.

In the US, Cadbury's products are made under licence by Hershey Foods - an arrangement that stems from the group's recognition in the mid-1980s that it was fighting a hard battle with the American confectionery giants, and this arrangement would give a better return.

Other well-known brands include Fry, Milk Tray and Roses. It is continually adding to an already-strong portfolio. The group claims its TimeOut chocolate bar is the most successful confectionery launch of the 1990s.

Confectionery is less susceptible to the own-label threat than soft drinks. Consumers like the chocolate they know and grew up with, which is why it is often difficult to transfer brands from one country to another. Different grass, different cows and different milk can produce important differences in taste. Never the less, confectionery companies are highly competitive and increasingly global in scope.

Strategy and management

Cadbury Schweppes aims to be the largest and most successful brand owner operating in the non-cola sector of the worldwide soft drinks business. The acquisition of Dr Pepper/Seven-Up takes the group much closer to securing this ambition, though Coca-Cola retains leadership of the non-cola market.

The US carbonated drinks market is the largest in the world, accounting for about a third of total world volume. The market is dominated by Coca-Cola and Pepsi-Cola, who between them control just over 70 per cent of the US market.

With its flagship brands, the distinctive fruit-based flavour of Dr Pepper and the Seven-Up lemon-lime drink, Cadbury Schweppes' new acquisition has the third biggest slice of the huge American market. Perhaps more importantly, the non-cola market is the fastest growing part of it. This has helped make the Dallas-based Dr Pepper/Seven-Up one of the fastest growing companies in the sector. Sales growth over the last five years has been more than double the industry average. Last year it made profits of $203.6 m (£129.7 m) on sales of $769 m (£490 m).

Cadbury Schweppes has already begun integrating Dr Pepper/Seven-Up with its own American beverages operation under the leadership of John Brock, formerly president of Cadbury Beverages North America. The enlarged business will have greater purchasing power, and will be able to command better access to shelf space in stores. The group believes there is scope for increasing volumes through a joint approach to distribution and by linking brands to create more effective promotions.

In confectionery, the company aims to be one of the top three producers. With an estimated 8.5 per cent share of the world market, it currently trails Philip Morris (11 per cent), Mars (12.5 per cent) and Nestle (14 per cent). Cadbury Schweppes sees huge potential markets in the former Communist countries and other liberalising economies - hence its investments in Poland, China and India.

Dominic Cadbury, who took over as chairman in 1993, is the great-grandson of John Cadbury, who founded the business more than 170 years ago. Yet he takes great pains to stress that Cadbury Schweppes has long ceased to be a family business. The family shareholding has dwindled to a very small level. Mr Cadbury expects to be the last Cadbury to head the group and he is confident that he rose to the top of Cadbury Schweppes thanks to his abilities, not his name.

While this prompts a few wry smiles among outsiders, no-one doubts Dominic Cadbury's ability. As chief executive for nearly ten years from the end of 1983, he was responsible for reshaping the group's activities and spear-heading the thrust into international markets.

An early step was to sell off peripheral interests such as Typhoo tea, Kenco coffee, Hartleys jams and Jeyes cleaning fluid. This allowed Cadbury Schweppes to focus on the two streams of soft drinks and confectionery.

Cadbury was then able to drive the business forward through a series of acquisitions and partnership deals. The 1986 deal with Coca-Cola which gave Cadbury Schweppes the UK franchise for 'The Real Thing' was a particular coup. Cadbury has also won praise for his patient wooing of an initially reluctant Dr Pepper. This year's takeover came nearly eight years after Cadbury Schweppes took its initial stake in Dr Pepper.

One striking feature of the group board is the length of service of its executive directors, most of whom have spent 20 years or more with the company. Cadbury Schweppes is alive to accusations of insularity. However, it believes the steady flow of acquisitions provides it with a ready source of new management talent.

The board can also draw upon the diverse experience of its non-executive directors, who include Thomas Hutchison a former ICI director and deputy governor of the Bank of Scotland, and Dr Franz Humer, who was chief operating officer of the pharmaceuticals giant Glaxo.

Cadbury Schweppes is widely regarded as a model employer - no doubt a key reason for the loyalty of its senior management. This reputation was founded on the Quaker beliefs and social conscience of the 19th century Cadburys, most famously demonstrated in the building of the village of Bournville for their factory workers.

The company remains committed to its open management style and invests a lot of time and effort to secure good employee communications. This includes company conferences and regular staff meetings to explain the group's aims and performance.

The future

Cadbury Schweppes has built powerful positions in two of the world's largest markets, with combined annual sales worth an estimated £125 billion. Both are still growing even in mature markets such as the UK, where confectionery sales are growing at two per cent a year.

CAPITAL RADIO plc

Capital Radio, London

Capital Radio in London is the world's largest metropolitan radio station. Its parent group is the acknowledged market leader in UK commercial radio, operating the leading stations in Birmingham, Southampton, Brighton, Maidstone and Canterbury

Outlook:

Having led the industry for more than 20 years, Capital is exceptionally well placed to benefit from effective deregulation and radically improved shares of UK advertising. It faces enhanced competition in its core markets but its emphasis on quality production and strong links with its communities will be important weapons in its armoury

Scorecard:

Structural flexibility	★★★★
Innovative power	★★★★★
International orientation	★★★
Human resources	★★★
Growth markets	★★★★★
Quality of management	★★★★

Key figures:

UK turnover	£52 million
Pre-tax profits	£22 million
UK staff	450

Capital Radio plc
Euston Tower
London NW1 3DR
Tel: 0171 608 6080
Fax: 0171 387 2345

Capital Radio

Britain's accelerating commercial radio industry is about to embark on another phase of growth which will ensure that its recent progress as a credible advertising medium is confirmed. Until the recent past, the sector drew barely two per cent of all UK advertising budgets; but its elevation to four per cent, projected increase in revenues and rapid expansion in terms of outlets will move the industry to new levels of profitability. According to industry statistics, the third quarter of 1994 was a watershed. All commercial radio exceeded all BBC radio and local commercial radio surpassed network BBC radio in share of listening for the first time.

This is a major milestone. In April 1995, the industry's trade journal Broadcast commented: 'A number of factors have contributed to the resurgence in radio's fortunes. The arrival of national commercial radio had a decisive impact on perceptions of the medium. However, improved marketing and research aided that development.' This greater professionalism was spearheaded by the industry's leaders, notably London's Capital Radio.

Operations and markets

Capital - the longest established franchise holder in the sector - is the touchstone of commercial radio. It is the greatest innovator in independent radio and is generally regarded as the standard setter for the sector. It has a formidable grip on the London market - with more than 26 per cent of the city's audience. Its two outlets, Capital FM and Capital Gold, are market number one and two respectively.

But the story does not end there. Its scope has extended to embrace licences in Birmingham, Southampton, Brighton and Kent. In every locality where the group holds commercial radio franchises it is market leader. In addition, it is a widely respected and profitably managed company, reporting an 89 per cent increase in profits in 1994 to £22 million. This represents 43 per cent return on sales which was exceptional but Capital regularly brings in 35 per cent.

By any business measures, the Capital Radio achievement is an instructive one. It is a company which has stayed close to what it knows best and it has excelled by being exceptionally good at its core activity. No serious consideration of Capital Radio and its future contribution to its industry can be made without analysing the rapid development of commercial radio and its prospects during the next decade.

Strategy and management

Commercial radio in Britain is a young industry - launched in October 1973. It is only since the late 1980s that the real growth in the network has taken place. In Spring 1995, there are three national commercial stations (plus Atlantic 252 which covers most of the UK from Dublin), a raft of as-yet-unproven regional commercial operators and an explosion of local independent stations. Every major conurbation now has five or six commercial signals - or at least they all will have before too long - and the industry's regulator the Radio Authority is committed to 'extending listener choice'.

However, the forces of enhanced professionalism and commercial economics have also been at work in the industry. A consolidation of local and regional franchises into four or five substantial groups has been taking place. Sector analysts say that Capital, GWR, EMAP and either Metro or Scottish Radio Holdings will be the key players in local and regional commercial radio in the next decade. CLT should not be forgotten either - this is the dominant radio and television force on mainland Europe - which has 80 per cent of Atlantic 252 and a significant share of London's Country 1035. More important is that this financial powerhouse is actively seeking licences in the UK.

Since 1992, commercial radio has transformed itself - certainly in the eyes of media buyers at advertising agencies. The two per cent medium spent £2.5 million marketing itself - especially through the Radio Advertising Bureau, which Capital had lobbied the industry to create. The result was that it suddenly became the four per cent medium and immediately arrived as big business. Since costs had not increased dramatically, clearly most of the difference went straight to the bottom line. Capital's MD Richard Eyre, who spent 16 years in advertising agencies before enlisting at Euston Tower, knew exactly what the media buyers wanted and set out to deliver it. This could be summarised as quality, consistency, delivery and validation.

In 1987 management radically changed the format of the station and then split the FM service from the AM - increasing the company's overall audience. On FM, Capital concentrated on newer material while the Gold service played the hits of the 1960s, 1970s and 1980s. This is standard practice today but at the time it was a bold move. Another key factor in the Capital programming philosophy is the employment of the most talented presentation and production people, and it has an outstanding record for retaining able broadcasters. The FM service roster of daytime presenters has remained unchanged for several years and Gold employs some people who have been with Capital since the 1970s. This is at once testimony to the quality of the broadcasting staff, their rapport with their listeners and Capital's industry reputation as a great place to work.

Mr Eyre says: 'We have two groups of customers - our listeners and our advertisers. If we do not serve our listeners, we cannot convince agencies or companies to advertise with us. To reach our listeners we invest in people and programmes. We have more than 150 people in Euston and another 300 around the country. This is high for commercial radio but our market position is due to the quality of our output.'

The company's management has spread its approach to its holdings in key markets in the West Midlands and on the south coast. Director of programmes Richard Park - regarded as the best in the business - was charged with turning around the company's acquisitions in Birmingham - BRMB FM and Xtra-AM. 'When we arrived, BRMB was number four. Within a few months we had resumed the area's number one spot. We did it by appointing enthusiastic local management who know their turf well and believe that they should have world class radio, and by putting experienced local broadcasters in key slots. I am particularly proud of what we achieved in Kent with Invicta. This is a station which has never enjoyed the rapport with its market and audience which Kent deserves. Shortly after acquisition we installed local management and broadcasting staff and it is now market leader.'

The future

Much of the group's future is - remarkably - not contingent on its performance as a business. Unlike many other industries, radio is still dependent on the whims of its regulator, which does not have an unblemished reputation for its understanding of the dynamics of the sector. Despite a recent change in the chairman and CEO of the Radio Authority, there is no sign that it intends to relax its control over the operation of individual stations. This is all the more remarkable when the number of commercial signals is anticipated to rise by a factor of three in the next decade. The RA has an inversely small secretariat so the problem of assessing suitable candidates for particular licences seems a Herculean task.

The influence of the regulator is crucial in other areas. Capital believes that its hugely successful Gold service deserves an FM licence. 'We say that all music services should be on FM and all speech on AM,' argues Mr Park. 'Gold is head of the queue when it comes to the granting of an FM frequency. But the legislation at the moment does not allow one company to operate two FM licences in the same location. We believe that the proven success of Capital Gold demonstrates the validity of our argument.' The regulator would be making a positive contribution to the development of the industry if he adopted a more flexible approach to this. There is a commercial aspect to the question because at present advertisers regard FM services with greater seriousness than AM outlets. So Capital clearly wants to improve the returns of one of the most successful radio stations in the country.

In the next two years Capital will move out of its London landmark Euston Tower headquarters to Leicester Square. Mr Eyre says the station has always occupied only two floors of the building and now needs to expand. 'We must still be at the heart of the city and a central location is a necessity,' he says.

The company will face greater competition as the years progress. Originally, Capital challenged the RA's decision to grant FM licences to Heart and Virgin in London. But pragmatically the management in Euston believe that they will be the net beneficiaries of the move. They have set the standard to beat and their listeners have remained enormously loyal against the attractions of Kiss, JFM, Spectrum, Country, Melody and the other London operators. Heart and Virgin are direct competitors for Capital FM but Mr Park's philosophy of quality and stability at a time of change will probably emerge triumphant. Excluding a rash of madness by the Radio Authority at the next licence review, Capital will continue to dominate the industry in the next decade.

Close Brothers, London

Close Brothers is a specialist UK merchant bank but one which has a balanced spread on activities

Outlook:
Close Brothers has avoided the devastation which has afflicted the rest of the UK merchant banking scene. It has done this by application of sound business principles and high quality management, two qualities which have been absent in the sector. Close Brothers continues to be highly profitable and there is no reason why it should not continue to be so

Scorecard:

Structural flexibility	★★★★
Innovative power	★★★★★
International orientation	★★★
Human resources	★★★★
Growth markets	★★★★★
Quality of management	★★★★★

Key figures:

Total operating income	£76.9 million
Pre-tax profits	£33.1 million
Staff	445

Close Brothers
12 Appold Street
London EC2A 2A
Tel: 0171 426 4000
Fax: 0171 426 4044

Close Brothers

An intelligently run UK bank makes a refreshing change. The population of independent UK merchant banks has dwindled over the last decade as the urge for global expansion has drawn many into the ever more capital intensive territory occupied by the US investment banks and securities houses. Some have ultimately concluded that they could not survive independently. By contrast Close Brothers has eschewed this strategy and may be the City's last example of a traditional merchant bank. That appears to have been the right course.

During the last two decades its peer group has experienced varying degrees of trauma, while Close Brothers has sailed through market crashes and economic downturns with its profit growth record intact.

Operations and markets

Close Brothers is an independent merchant bank, a group of around a dozen separate financial services businesses. These range from corporate finance advice and commercial lending, to personal financial products, credit management and, via Winterflood Securities, smaller company market-making. The apparently unrelated nature of these businesses is in part deliberate. Close does not set out to be an integrated provider of financial services and its individual divisions are not necessarily intended to have a common customer base.

Although the bank can trace its history back to 1878, the organisation in its current form dates from the mid-seventies, when most of the existing top executive management came on board. The bank became independent via a management buy-out from Consolidated Goldfields in 1979, giving the management a significant minority stake. It then went public in 1984 by reversing into a quoted investment trust. Close has recently become a constituent of the FT-SE 250 (MidCap) Index.

Strategy and management

Close Brothers' philosophy is to build a balanced portfolio of businesses, intended to produce a blend of steadily growing profits. It believes it can best achieve this over time by including businesses, at least a proportion of which can be expected to prosper in each different part of the business cycle.

For example, the early cycle beneficiary of an economic recovery would be its market maker, Winterflood, which thrives during the inevitable high volumes generated by a leading indicator such as the stock market. It also has a corporate finance division, which benefits from similar influences and advises medium sized public companies.

Towards the other end of the economic cycle is its credit management division, which offers debt factoring and agency debt collection services. Business Advisory Services, the commercial debt-collector, was acquired in 1992. Its business is inevitably quiet during and immediately post recession, when debt levels fall with lower turnover and companies become more efficient at collecting their own debt. In between are a range of businesses which have produced Close's target, although it is always looking for ways to optimise the balance.

The acquisition of Winterflood in 1993 appeared to take Close into a higher risk profile than any of its existing business. The experience to date is that this has not been the case although management would not argue that group profits are harder to predict. Winterflood is a smaller company market-maker and is a business which Close originally helped to structure when it was acquired by its previous parent, Union Discount.

Although Winterflood is a business which cannot predict business flows (unlike the quite predictable nature of the rest of the group), it is not the high risk venture that the large market makers often tend to be. It is more of an old-style City jobbing firm, much less capital intensive than even Close's banking divisions. It is a niche business, the only one in the UK to cover 1,250 or so stocks, some 50 per cent of those in the market.

The customer base is principally stockbrokers, hence there is minimal danger of bad debts. It does however make money according to the flow of deals and market volumes. However, as Winterflood, which cost Close £19m (a reasonable multiple on the previous year's £4.5m profits) made an estimated £13.6m contribution in its first full year within the group, it is difficult to argue with the logic of the acquisition.

Close Brothers, like any of its type, is a risk taker but it takes a carefully considered approach to new investments. It avoids homogeneous, commodity style banking services, and concentrates on areas where it has a competitive advantage.

When the investment banks attempted to move away from capital intensive activities such as lending, Close remained committed to this area of business.

Close lends secured on specific assets earning a margin plus fees. Yet it faces a dilemma when determining its lending strategy. In global terms it is a small bank, with limited capital, yet it aims to earn a high return on capital. It refuses to spread its capital dangerously thin, in order to play on that global stage. Effectively it needs to find a way to lend to secondary covenants, for above average margins, yet without taking secondary risks. The answer it has found is to lend only against a very specific and limited range of assets.

Unlike most banks, which lend on the strength of a covenant and are prepared to accept low margins, Close regards the asset as the key, not the covenant. It therefore chooses only assets which it believes will hold their value. Loans are secured, predominantly in Sterling and around 50 per cent of the loan book is repayable within 12 months. Interestingly only six per cent of the book is property related. The bank had a total loan book of £405 million at its last year end, the largest segment of which was secured on printing equipment, an area in which it has particular expertise, and which elegantly encapsulates Close's approach to lending.

The group has built a close relationship with German company Heidelberg, the world's largest manufacturer of printing machines. It does not finance newspaper presses, for which there may be relatively limited demand, but rather sheet fed machines. There are many of these high precision off-set machines in the UK and they are always in demand. They are renowned for reliability and engineering quality, capable of running for 24 hours a day, seven days a week for perhaps 20 years.

There are two special advantages with this asset. Firstly Heidelberg normally prices them at a constant DM price worldwide, making them a truly international asset. Secondly Heidelberg UK will generally not offer discounts to the end customer. These combined mean the machines hold their values superbly. In some instances, as the prices of new machines rise, a press can actually after five years of use still be worth what you paid for it. Heidelberg machines have unsurprisingly been nicknamed 'the printer's pension'.

Even during the recession used machines were in considerable demand internationally. When the departure from the ERM pushed up the Sterling price, Close simply increased the amount of second hand finance provided. Consequently it has been happy to lend, typically up to 90 per cent of the cost on straight HP terms over five years. After eight years in this business Close is the UK's number one provider of Heidelberg machines on finance. And when it provides the finance, it also bundles in other products, for example mechanical warranty insurance. This business is high margin, very secure lending.

Another example of its lateral thinking is its Prompt division which finances insurance premiums. Growth in this area, in which Close is UK market leader, has been impressive. The total value of premiums financed last year increased by 28 per cent to over £275m, around five times the level financed in 1990. Close pays the annual instalment on behalf of the borrower and collects repayments in regular instalments. It lends the full amount of the insured's premium, subject to the criteria that if a borrower defaults the policy can be cancelled. The surrender value, which should fully cover the outstanding borrowings, is then paid to Close.

It also has a significant consumer finance division which finances 25,000 mainly used cars with an average loan of £3,500. This business is experiencing historically low levels of bad debts.

An analysis of the lending activities shows how conservative Close is. It is also prudently financed, at competitive rates. The facilities mostly negotiated in the last two to three years, are either bilateral, or provided by bank syndicates led from the UK, or via a private placement among US insurance companies. All currency risk has been taken out by swaps.

In addition, as HP lending is at fixed rates but Close borrows mainly at floating rates, it usually swaps out any interest rate risk. It is not greedy, but simply protects what it sees as healthy margins. Other than on its free capital, Close does not take any proprietary risk on interest rate movements.

The future

In any risk taking business - and many of Close's divisions are capital intensive - it is hazardous to predict the future. Close Brothers has produced nineteen years of unbroken profit growth, but management is much more interested in growing the business than in turning away potentially remunerative opportunities in order to protect an impressive, but ultimately cosmetic record.

Consequently Close can be expected to invest in new ventures in the future, some of which may burn brightly for a limited time, leaving it to find a replacement for that contribution to earnings. That doesn't put off management, which appears to relish the challenge of inventing and developing new profit centres. However with its proven track record, that team should be relied upon to move the bank forward creatively and successfully over the next decade.

COATS

VIYELLA

Coats Viyella, London

Coats Viyella is the largest international textile company, specialising in thread, clothing, home furnishings, fashion and precision engineering

Outlook:
CV has gone through a remarkable transition in the last half-decade. Under Neville Bain, CV has ceased to be solely a holding company linking a group of otherwise unrelated businesses. It is now a coherent group exploiting market opportunities, technological advances and client service initiatives across all parts of the enterprise

Scorecard:

Structural flexibility	★★★★
Innovative power	★★★★★
International orientation	★★★★★
Human resources	★★★★
Growth markets	★★★★★
Quality of management	★★★★★

Key figures:

Turnover	£2.6 billion
Pre-tax profits	£105 million
Staff	76,000

Coats Viyella plc
28 Savile Row
London W1X 2DD
Tel: 0171 734 4030

Coats Viyella

The global textile industry is characterised by a multitude of small operators, several regional forces but only one major international business. Remarkably, the single worldwide player is not an American or East Asian combine but a British enterprise based in London. Coats Viyella is a commanding giant in a highly fragmented sector. The company is convincing market leader in threads, a dominant force in clothing, a leading player in fashion retailing and a key operator in homewares.

The group generates annual sales of £2.6 billion and pre-tax profits of £153 million. In this low-margin industry, Coats Viyella is achieving higher than average returns and chief executive Neville Bain sees the potential for considerable progress from economies of scale and investment in people and technologies. The average British business is strong on technical skills and delivery but Coats Viyella has also recognised the vital importance of effective human resources management and development of technologies which can improve competitive edge.

Mr Bain, with 27 years experience in Cadbury Schweppes, was appointed to restructure the group. He created five principal divisions which would enjoy considerable devolved authority. The centre would set a framework for the financial and commercial objectives of Coats Viyella and promote effective synergies and networking between the divisions.

Operations and markets

The group includes:

> thread - the original core business. It accounts for 40 per cent of total group sales. This business brings in £86.2 million on turnover of £1.05 billion. It is far and away the market leader. It is divided into two principal operating areas: industrial and consumer (crafts). Industrial provides thread for the clothing, footwear, luggage and automotive industries, and its products range from specialist performance thread to basic spun cotton or polyester. Consumer aims at the individual user at home and embraces: sewing thread (Sylko), embroidery thread (Anchor), tapestry and embroidery kits (Penelope) and zips (Talon, Opti).

> clothing - Coats Viyella is a major international player. This division generates £562 million in sales and £31 million in operating profit. Clothing gives a return on assets of 31 per cent and is a preferred supplier to Marks & Spencer and BHS. CV is the largest M&S clothing supplier and M&S contracts account for half of all Coats Viyella clothing sales. Significant volumes are also achieved in military and police uniforms, and careerwear. In 1993, Coats Viyella acquired Berghaus - a leading Dutch manufacturer which concentrates on coats and jackets with a large clothing activity in Russia where it has traded successfully for more than 20 years. This division has the most advanced computer-aided design facilities in Europe's - and probably the world's - clothing sector.

> home furnishings - this includes bed linen, curtains, table linen, towels and duvets. The division reported £11 million operating profit on sales of £169

million in 1994. It is the UK's largest supplier of bed linen (Dorma) and own-label products for M&S. Dorma France is supplied from the UK. According to Bill Drummond, corporate development director, 'our key success factors are design, response capability and managing variety, which are all critical.'

fashion retail - the Jaeger and Viyella retailing brands are two of the group's most important names. Fashion retail reported sales of £156 million and profits of £11 million in 1994. Jaeger is largely UK-based with 180 outlets but it does operate through 50 stores in the United States and a significant presence in Japan. Jaeger Man and Viyella are both UK businesses with an expanding group of outlets and good improvements in sales. Viyella Ladies is positioned at a lower price point than Jaeger and features an English country-living image.

precision engineering - it may seem surprising that CV runs an engineering business but this moulding enterprise exploits technology skills formerly used in the manufacture of zips. Dynacast is the world leader in die-cast zinc-magnesium-aluminium components which are small but effective units. This venture is highly profitable, delivering margins of 16 per cent and return on capital employed of 43 per cent. The company reports turnover of £171 million and profits of £28 million.

Averaged out, the sources of Coats Viyella's worldwide operating profits are:

UK	9 per cent
N America	30 per cent
Rest of Europe	13 per cent
S America	9 per cent
Asia, Africa, Australasia	19 per cent

Strategy and management

The Bain management team understood the strengths of the cultures of the individual business divisions. 'Managers and employees should feel their first loyalty to their company, next their division and finally to the group. But we do share a common set of values. We have eight statements of value which describe our mutual approach.'

The Coats Viyella statement of values embraces the following list:

. competitive ability - 'we must be competitive in the marketplace... maintaining our products' edge and identity against the competition. We compete on quality, service and value. This means innovating, analysing, taking risks and making decisions consistent with our values,

. quality, service and value - 'the key characteristics of the group's activities are quality, service and value. Our products sell on this premise and the best way to cement partnerships with customers is adding value in this way. We need to deliver value for money through manufacturing excellence coupled with appropriate commercially focused research,

. taking advantage of change - 'change is constant in markets, in ideas, in people, and in technology. We therefore need to have decisive leadership and fast management reaction to secure maximum advantage from such changes,

. committed people - 'committed people are key to our group's success. People must know what is required of them and should be given help to meet those expectations. Our standards should be demanding and this will require appropriate rewards,

. clear objectives - 'our group must have clarity of purpose to compete effectively. Its strategy must be clearly communicated and the objectives which flow from the strategy, both corporate and individual, must be understood. Objectives must be attainable and their achievement should stretch the abilities of those for whom they are set,

. simple organisation - 'we must concentrate on the key tasks of the business and all decisions as close as possible to the point of impact,

. openness - 'an openness of style and involvement of people in the decisions that affect them is of the greatest importance. It requires of management, trust and an ability to listen, ability to weigh up and decide,

. responsibilities - 'our group recognises its responsibilities to all shareholders, employees, customers, suppliers, governments and society. It will seek to keep its responsibilities to them in balance.'

The majority of Coats Viyella's 76,000 employees are based in the UK - 32,000. A further 5,000 are based on mainland Europe. Mr Bain says that he sources some of his products from the lower-cost-base economies of Asia. Coats Viyella has a large business in India and is active in Bangladesh, Indonesia, and China.

'If you take the UK as an employment base with salary and social costs as a base of 100, Germany is 225, France 145, Italy 140, Portugal 60, Turkey 40, and some far-eastern countries four. These costs represent between 15 and 25 per cent of production and so substantial savings can be made. Provided quality standards are the same as in the UK and the high level of response can be maintained there is room for improvement.' Mr Bain says that the company is investing heavily in appropriate technology. Computer aided design (CAD) is important. 'Recently, to see what we could achieve in terms of speed of customer service we ran an exercise based on the Italian fashion shows. We took a video of the latest designs. This was sent by satellite to our East Asian design centre. Our team completed CAD formats for a particular product. We were able to feed into our computer the details of the design and therefore we were able to prepare costs of production. Overnight we were able to create a specimen of the new line and generate a catalogue showing colour variations.

'The next day we were able to go to Marks & Spencer with our product. We were able to show its buyers how much the product would cost and how much the client could sell it for. This was all possible while the client's buyers were still in Italy.'

The future

Coats Viyella is an outstanding company. It is applying the latest management philosophy, concentrating on high quality service to customers, efficiencies from structural and technological advance and the development and empowerment of its people to achieve substantial business gains.

COLLEAGUES GROUP *plc*

Colleagues Group plc, Bath

Colleagues Group is a highly innovative and successful direct marketing company. Formed in the late 1980s, it offers a fresh approach to consumer direct marketing

Outlook:
This company has redefined the client-agency relationship. As it outstrips competitors in client-service performance with its innovative approach to service delivery, it is poised to build on its remarkable growth record. It has achieved its remarkable results by improving response times to mailings, cutting costs for all clients by buying media collectively and effective use of interactive technology

Scorecard:

Structural flexibility	★★★★
Innovative power	★★★★★
International orientation	★★★
Human resources	★★★★★
Growth markets	★★★★★
Quality of management	★★★★

Key figures:

Turnover	£36 million
Pre-tax profits	£3 million
Staff	80

Colleagues Group plc
Colleagues House
122 Wells Road
Bath BA2 3AH
Tel: 01225 447003
Fax: 01223 469988

Colleagues Group

Described by a leading journalist as the blueprint for agencies of the 1990s, Colleagues is one of the UK's leading providers of consumer direct marketing services. Effectively a super project manager, Colleagues adopts a controlled approach to handling the enormous logistical and production exercises inherent in direct marketing campaigns. Not only is this the part that clients are happy to outsource, Colleagues' emphasis on systems, technology and heavyweight buying power generates measurable cost savings for its clients in an industry that is already growing significantly.

Colleagues fits in somewhere between an agency and a provider of services. This is its strength. While Colleagues' habitat is in a marketing environment, the company's roots are in logistics, systems and production. It views direct marketing as an enormous control exercise and has a firm grasp of what it takes to make this activity more profitable. Colleagues treats its clients as outright marketing professionals, as business partners, and a virtually seamless join with its clients makes for a compelling package. Its successes to date, whether measured by profitability or client loyalty, more than hint at a successful philosophy.

Direct marketing, in its many forms, is certainly a growth business. All the indicators point to a continued acceleration in the marketing spend devoted to direct techniques, as advertisers migrate from high level, above the line brand support to more targeted, direct marketing of key brands in an increasingly fragmented, sophisticated market place. The direct marketing industry was estimated by the Henley Centre, in a study for the Direct Marketing Association, to be worth around £4.5bn in 1995, and growing rapidly. Although only around £300m of this total is currently spent through agencies, the trend to outsource is increasing. Colleagues is the UK's largest independent direct marketing agency and, more importantly, one of the fastest growing.

Operations and markets

Colleagues was formed in 1987 by James Robson, chairman and previously marketing director of the Damart Group, and was joined soon after by Andrew Bennett, managing director, who was also with Damart. The business has grown rapidly since its formation. It has added £10m to turnover in each of the last three years, to stand at £36m in 1994. Gross margins are of the order of 18 per cent. If higher margins can be found elsewhere, that is because Colleagues concentrates on logistics, not consultancy, and buys in an enormous amount of costs. But it generates these margins on very high turnover. Profit before tax of over £3m, which has also risen by around £1m per annum, equates to net profit margins of around eight per cent.

Remarkably, these levels of profitability are achieved with only 80 people, ranking Colleagues first in profitability per employee in direct marketing (*Marketing Magazine,* March 1994). This merits further consideration. James Robson: 'Our customers are principally high volume, experienced advertisers operating with large budgets and a strong commitment to the benefits that can be achieved through direct marketing. We provide a comprehensive range of services to these blue chip clients, but it is perhaps our emphasis on logistics and systems that distinguishes Colleagues from the competition, and the effective use of technology has become a core ingredient in our success. By approaching direct marketing as a rigorous control exercise, even the most complex programmes can be handled.'

This demands high levels of investment, and the company spends millions of pounds on information technology. Some 55 of its 80 staff are actively and exclusively involved in controlling direct-marketing programmes. Colleagues is effectively the orchestrator, buying-in and controlling an array of inputs and services to the production process. The use of online systems linking both customers and suppliers is a key feature of Colleagues-style of working.

Colleagues provides a comprehensive range of services and offers a 'complete solution' to clients. Its strengths are in the print, production and design of marketing material; media inserts and media programme management; and lists, databases and fulfilment.

Print, production and design is the most significant activity, accounting for around 57 per cent of gross profits. The company was responsible for the production and despatch of over 30 million direct mail items in 1994, and with print production representing the major campaign expense for many customers, the operation lies at the heart of Colleagues' business. All creative services are driven by the aim of making clients' marketing budgets work as hard as possible.

Colleagues is the UK market-leader in media inserts and media programme management, and is on target to place over one billion inserts in 1995. Working with five out of the top ten users brings exceptional buying power and priority access to key media. Such economies of scale will only increase with the number of inserts Colleagues places and the expansion of the range of potential carriers.

Lists and database management might not sound a glamorous aspect of marketing, but it is one of the fastest-growing. Colleagues derives just 15 per cent of its profits from these activities, but this figure reflects more the scale of its print production and media insert operations than a lower emphasis on lists and databases.

The 'competition' actually comes from the in-house marketing departments of potential clients as much as from other agencies. In persuading these departments to outsource, Colleagues has to demonstrate clearly that it does not form an on-cost, instead adding real value to a project by improving response rates and reducing costs. Some of its successes are spectacular, reflecting either the skill and expertise of its project managers, or simply by combining the requirements of several clients to drive costs downwards.

To describe Colleagues' customers as important is a massive understatement. To all intents and purposes, the two are the same - or at least the link between client and agency is quite transparent. Through online facilities, clients can monitor a project easily and precisely, and control Colleagues staff as if they were their own. This special relationship is at the heart of Colleagues' success and provides a clue to the origin of the agency's name.

Strategy and management

Colleagues remains a very ambitious company despite its low profile and has already demonstrated its ability to grow sales and profits consistently during a recessionary period. The company is now in the enviable position of being able to exploit its strong market position without any need to change a successful formula. Clearly the company is very comfortable in handling high volume direct marketing campaigns and should attract new business from companies switching budgets into this form of marketing communications as well as expanding services to existing clients.

Part of Colleagues' strategy is to build strong structural relationships with its suppliers, even to the extent of installing compatible systems. This cements confidence and tightens the vital degree of control that sharpens Colleagues' competitive edge.

Colleagues' strategy to maintain its leading position is to prescribe 'more of the same'. That means extending its strategic services, identifying and securing large, experienced or inexperienced clients with big marketing budgets. There is also scope to expand into adjacent areas of direct marketing, such as fulfilment, telemarketing and door-to-door distribution.

Colleagues floated 31 per cent of its shares (directors and employees still retain 54.7 per cent) on the London Stock Exchange in March 1995. In its flotation prospectus, the company suggested that future expansion could come through organic growth, acquisition or joint venture. Growth to date has been achieved exclusively by organic means, and the directors will almost certainly need to be convinced of a very compelling case in order to move down the acquisition trail. Colleagues is certainly not a marketing agency driven by large egos and is unlikely to make the same mistakes of some agencies in the late 1980s who believed big was beautiful.

At first, Colleagues appears to be very non-agency like in terms of culture and this is perhaps one reason why it has enjoyed considerable success and popularity with its clients. Systems and technology are more prominent than creative juices. The senior management is a tightly-knit team, comprising and supported by two non-executive directors. This lean structure permeates throughout the company. When 80 people are handling an annual turnover of £36 million, there is neither time nor room for baggage.

To motivate their high calibre staff, the founders of the business generously gave away equity to them. Employee shareholders are good allies of ambition and success - and creating them was a prominent reason behind the company's decision to list its shares. Despite heavy investment in technology, Colleagues did not really need the money - the company is cash positive and also cash generative. No acquisitions were planned. Instead, it provided a real market for Colleagues' shares and enhanced the company's important share ownership culture.

The future

A disciplined, controlled approach, and serious investment in technology, enables Colleagues to handle very large projects with small numbers of specialist staff. It can easily leverage this dynamic and expand business without copying agencies who pursued growth in size and scope that was unsustainable and uncontrollable. Colleagues is unlikely to make similar mistakes or hasty decisions.

Colleagues knows where it is going and its track record to date is superb. There appear to be few reasons why it should be restricted in its growth - the company can easily handle many more clients, direct marketing is a good business to be in for the identifiable future and the economies of scale should only improve.

COMMERCIAL UNION

Commercial Union, London

Commercial Union is a leading international UK insurer

Outlook:
The insurance industry has finally woken up to customer service and the more pro-active businesses in the sector have realised that they need to be more accountable and open with their clients and to offer a better range of products. This new realism has not been brought about by altruism but rather the demands of the market. Commercial Union is among those forward-looking companies which have seized the moment

Scorecard:
Structural flexibility	★★★★
Innovative power	★★★★
International orientation	★★★★★
Human resources	★★★★
Growth markets	★★★★
Quality of management	★★★★

Key figures:
Premium income	£7,671 million gross
Pre-tax profits	£413 million
UK staff	10,000
Total staff	25,000

Commercial Union plc
St Helen's
1 Undershaft
London EC3P 3DQ
Tel: 0171 283 7500

Commercial Union

Insurance is a funny old business. It purports to be about the sophisticated management of risk but like any other commodity product it is highly susceptible to swings in prices. It is very easy to write an insurance policy but making it pay is a different matter altogether. That's why management quality and the ability to stay ahead of the competition is so important. Commercial Union scores highly on both counts and is now firmly establishing itself as an industry leader.

CU is a composite insurance company. That means that it writes both general and life insurance. The general business, which underwrites policies ranging from private motor to employers' liability, accounted for 64 per cent of world-wide premium income last year. It is highly cyclical and its main markets are the UK, France and the US. Life insurance accounts for the rest. It provides more stable profits and, importantly, much greater growth potential.

The company's strategy is clear. If it is to improve returns to shareholders it must both expand the life insurance operation overseas and improve the earnings quality of its general business.

These are not mere platitudes either. In the last year, CU has proved its worth on both counts. It has successfully acquired the French insurance company Groupe Victoire and has responded to heated competition in the general insurance business far more swiftly than its peers. As the underwriting profit cycle turns against the industry, the quality of CU's earnings will shine through.

Operations and markets

Composite insurance companies recently announced a bumper crop of results for 1994. Driven by higher insurance premiums and lower claims costs' UK underwriting profits reached record highs. These fat profits will not last, however. The insurance cycle in the UK has peaked and new competition from direct writers, such as Direct Line, and foreign insurance companies is already driving insurance premiums lower.

That's important because the UK market generally accounts for 40 per cent of the general insurance business of the five composites. The cyclical downswing in the UK has led stock market analysts to predict a decline in insurers' earnings from this year. That is, with the exception of Commercial Union. Analysts expect its aggressive expansion into life insurance and its tight management of the general business to prolong earnings growth.

Most insurance companies have tried to assuage investors' fears of the coming downturn by arguing that this cycle is different. They have learnt their lessons, they say, from the grizzly year of 1991 when at their worst the five leading insurers suffered a collective underwriting loss of £2bn. Now they argue that they are no longer prepared to be sacrificed on the altar of cheap pricing and their commitment to underwrite for profit not market share has now become a well worn cliché.

Commercial Union is far better placed to live up to these promises than its peers. For a start it is the least exposed to the highly competitive personal insurance markets. Competitors Sun Alliance and Guardian Royal Exchange look most vulnerable here. More importantly, though, CU has planned for the downturn.

This is shown most aptly in its handling of the personal motor market in the United Kingdom. In the early 1990s, CU aggressively built up market share when premiums were on the mend. Now, as they deteriorate, it can afford to shed marginal accounts and to keep the profitable business for itself. In 1994 for example, CU gave up 16 per cent of its private motor book and wrote the lowest amount of business among the five composites.

As long as competition continues to bite, CU will pursue this strategy. It will not throw good money after bad and has wisely resisted the temptation to open a direct insurance operation to sell motor insurance policies. Such businesses have yielded low returns for its competitors.

In household insurance too, Commercial Union has acted swiftly to combat competition. Direct Line has also set its sights on this lucrative market which has up to now been the domain of the mortgage lenders. Late last year, however, CU edged out competitors Royal Insurance and struck a deal with Britain's second largest mortgage lender, Abbey National to provide household insurance products to its customers. This will mean that instead of Abbey's £250m annual premium income being shared by a panel of insurers, CU will pocket all the business itself. This deal alone will add £100m to CU's premium income and will substantially raise its share of the household market. Just as significantly, it will insulate the company from rate competition. CU has negotiated a fee structure with Abbey which guarantees a fixed rate of return on this business for the next five years.

Strategy and management

Commercial Union stands out from its peers due to its heavy involvement in the marine underwriting market. It is one of the largest corporate marine underwriters in the world and in 1994 wrote £354m of business, equivalent to 60 per cent of all that written by the other composites. Up to now this has been a handicap. CU has had to make sizeable provisions in recent years to boost its reserves. In the next few years, however, its persistence with this business will pay off.

Just as with Lloyd's of London, marine profits are booked three years in arrears. Recent results have therefore reflected the high losses incurred in the early 1990s. From 1992/3, however, marine insurance premiums recovered substantially. Moreover, an accounting change this year will allow CU to move from three- to two-year reporting of its marine account. That means that the improving profitability seen in earlier underwriting years will be booked in 1995.

Although premium rates for marine policies are softening in some areas, shrinking capacity at Lloyd's and the need to attract further corporate capital into that market will check the deterioration. Analysts believe that the medium term outlook in the marine underwriting market is encouraging.

The life insurance business is CU's ticket to future growth. Its £1.43bn acquisition last October of the French company Groupe Victoire provides an excellent opportunity for it to get its teeth into the underdeveloped French life market. Moreover, the acquisition reduces CU's exposure to the cyclical general business. Once Groupe Victoire is fully consolidated this year, analysts estimate that life insurance will make up 42 per cent of its total premium income. That compares with 23 per cent ten years ago and an average of 23 per cent now amongst its peers.

CU has picked its markets well too. With Groupe Victoire's life company, Abeille Vie, nearly half of CU's premium income will come from the French market which has far more potential for growth than in the UK. Here, for example, we spend on average $1,142 per capita on life insurance. In France the corresponding figure is only $831 and that is after the market has grown by 20 per cent a year over the last decade. Victoire has already made a substantial impact on group profits and is seen by many analysts as an extremely shrewd buy.

Although that rate of growth is unlikely to be sustained over the next ten years, analysts are expecting annual increases of at least 10 per cent. Moreover, with pensions deregulation likely after the French elections, a new market in personal pensions is set to develop.

Abeille Vie is the sixth largest life assurance company in France. In the first half alone it contributed £33 million in profits, boosting CU's total life profits to £105 million.

Abeille Vie sells two main products: unit linked, and an AFER savings contract which grew by more than 40 per cent last year. The future growth prospects for AFER are particularly encouraging. The product has TESSA-type tax advantages and will deliver improving margins from a management fee linked to the growing funds.

CU is also blessed with a low exposure to the saturated UK market. After the bad publicity this industry has received in the last year, notably over pension mis-selling, sales of life products have declined. That trend is unlikely to change in the near future as life companies now have to disclose to their clients exactly how much they make in commissions on each contract.

Analysts are not expecting great things from this market. At best UK life profits are set to stagnate and could indeed decline over the next few years. Thankfully for CU, its UK life premiums account for only 8 per cent of its world-wide book of business. Others are less well placed, notably Royal Insurance (22 per cent) and Sun Alliance (15 per cent). John Carter, CEO, speaking at the time of the group's half time figures, said 'worldwide life premium income for the last six months doubled and new business premiums increased from £463 million to £1,255 million. New single premiums rose substantially in the UK, certain European territories and the United States. In July (1995) we increase our shareholding in Commercial Union of South Africa from 36 per cent to a controlling interest of 51 per cent.'

The future

Commercial Union is the leading composite insurance company in the UK. It has diversified successfully away from the volatile general insurance market and has established a firm foothold in the expanding French life sector. It has also positioned itself well to cope with the vagaries of the underwriting cycle and new competition in personal insurance markets. These two factors will ensure above average earnings growth over the next five years. Its growth in key overseas markets places the group in an excellent position to compete in an increasingly globally minded sector.

Compaq, Renfrewshire

Compaq is one of the world's largest computer hardware and software companies

Outlook:
Compaq was the company which led the assault against IBM in the late 1980s. It is a remarkable business which launched in 1982 and now commands a sizeable slice of key sector markets. Technological edge and long-term planning lie at the heart of the Compaq success and it is this convincing management aptitude which encourages observers to have confidence about the future of the company

Scorecard:

Structural flexibility	★★★★
Innovative power	★★★★★
International orientation	★★★★★
Human resources	★★★★
Growth markets	★★★★
Quality of management	★★★★★

Key figures:

Global turnover		£10.9 billion
UK staff	manufacturing	- 1500 permanent
		- 700 temporary
	sales & marketing	- 190 permanent

Compaq Computer Manufacturing Limited
Erskine Ferry Road
Bishopton
Renfrewshire PA7 5PP
Tel: 0141 814 8000
Fax: 0141 812 7745

Compaq

The computer industry is a fast-moving world where to stand still means corporate oblivion. But among the multinational stars which sparkle in this dynamic universe, Compaq shines brightest of them all. It seems almost inconceivable that this enormous company, whose sales in 1994 totalled £10.9bn - a rise of 52 per cent on the previous year - only came into existence in 1982, when three former Texas Instruments employees met in a Houston cafe, and drew the blueprint for the company's first portable computer on a paper napkin.

But to remain at the top in an industry which is developing so rapidly requires special skills, and not just in terms of technology. Management must retain a capacity to adapt to the demands of the market. Such flexibility can involve painful decisions, it certainly did for Compaq, but these decisions were supported by a coherent and long term strategy aimed at keeping the company at the leading edge of one of the world's most exciting industries.

Back in 1982 Compaq was a mere irritation to the colossus that was IBM. Who would then have said that Compaq would become the computer world's David, slaying IBM's Goliath? Perhaps only those three original engineers, and Ben Rosen, the venture capitalist who backed their vision with his money.

Operations and markets

By 1983 Compaq had already notched up sales of £111m, and this growth rate was to continue, as an innovative and energetic management team, fired by a common vision and goal, continually beat IBM and others to the punch. From such humble beginnings Compaq has now outstripped IBM and its contemporaries to become the world's number one personal computer manufacturer. Compaq's global market share is now over ten per cent (compared with IBM and Apple both at around eight per cent) - thus it achieved the goal set by current chief executive Eckhard Pfeiffer a year ahead of schedule.

That global success is based on the ability to take a broad view of the industry. Even as the company was coming to dominate its domestic US market, the biggest in the world, opportunities were being sought overseas.

Rod Canion, one of the founders, gave Eckhard Pfeiffer, a former colleague at Texas Instruments, $20,000 to set up Compaq's operations in Europe. That was in 1984. The UK business which was set up then had sales of around £10m. In 1994 Compaq UK had a turnover of nearly £2bn - £1.3bn of which comes from exports - and is the most successful overseas business of a world-wide group encompassing factories in Latin America, Asia and Europe. Compaq is one of the ten largest exporters from the UK.

Production comes from a factory in Erskine, on the river Clyde in Scotland. This site supplies 80 per cent of Compaq's sales to Europe, and is working proof that manufacturing is still a skill to be found in Britain. Erskine was set the target of matching Compaq's Singapore plant in terms of efficiency, despite the latter's advantage in terms of cheaper labour, and more locally situated components suppliers. Today that target has been achieved, and Erskine generates turnover of some $3.5m per manufacturing employee, well above the company's average.

Strategy and management

But Compaq's success has been far from plain sailing. In 1991 the company hit a crisis, and profits fell by three quarters. The group had become complacent, and chief executive Mr Canion's theory that Compaq's superior technology would always command a premium had hit a rock. In what he later termed 'the hardest decision of my life,' Ben Rosen fired Mr Canion, and replaced him with Pfeiffer, then chief operating officer. At a computer trade fair Rosen had sent two unknown engineers around the stalls, with instructions to buy the parts to make a Compaq PC. He was shocked to find he could build a PC for 30 per cent less than Compaq, the leading player, was paying. Mr Canion's sacking was 'a shock, and a major, major culture change', according to Joe McNally, head of Compaq UK since its inception, and a friend of both men. He targeted volume growth as the way forward, and even though Compaq's gross margins fell from 40 per cent to 23 per cent, bottom line growth kept rolling on. Costs were cut aggressively, so much so that labour and development costs fell by three quarters in two years, and labour now accounts for only two per cent of costs for some products. Prices also fell, and the number of outlets for Compaq products went from 3,000 to over 30,000. In an extremely short period of time he refocused the goals and culture of the company; 'the key decision was to shift from being a product-centric company to becoming a customer-centric company,' says a senior Compaq executive.

Compaq's new strategy rocked the computer industry to the core. IBM was probably the hardest hit, and despite Big Blue's subsequent recovery in other areas of its operations, senior executives acknowledge that its PC activities are still struggling. 'There is an excruciatingly high sense of urgency there, this is one sixth of our business, and it's underperforming materially,' admits IBM's chief financial officer Jerome York.

IBM should be worried. Under Mr Pfeiffer's stewardship, Compaq burst into the number one position among PC makers in 1994, with a market share of over ten per cent. But that's not enough for Compaq: he is now preaching the kind of market dominance which IBM itself once enjoyed in the 1960s. He wants Compaq to have a market share twice the size of its nearest competitor, and that means around 16 per cent of the world's PCs.

As Joe McNally points out, the Compaq strategy is not just about having the cheapest product. 'Eckhard took the risk of extending the time for Compaq to become competitive again. He could have sacrificed the Compaq brand by buying a cheap PC from the Far East, and rebadging it, but instead we took more time and built our own.'

Nevertheless, Compaq's efficiency and production routines are the envy of the industry. Erskine was Compaq's first plant outside Houston, although it has since been joined by one in Singapore, and, last year, by factories in China and Brazil.

The Scottish plant employs some 1,400 full-time staff, plus up to 900 part-timers, and is busying itself turning out PCs and client-server systems 24 hours a day, seven days a week. The Erskine plant is a 'mirror-image' of the Houston facility, according to Joe McNally, and is therefore at the leading edge in terms of manufacturing efficiency. Production lines now take up one third less space, and the most advanced forms of 'cell' production have been introduced. This means small groups of workers are responsible for the whole manufacturing process, from bolting the parts together to bolting up the PC. Such practices give a greater sense of participation to the employees, and lead to considerable gains in the quality and quantity of work produced.

Erskine has also imported Houston's no-nonsense approach to components suppliers. The actual number of components per machine has been drastically reduced, and suppliers are obliged to have warehouses in the near vicinity to comply with just-in-time delivery procedures. In Houston some components manufacturers are actually setting up production on site. Compaq is not afraid of confrontations with its suppliers, and has rowed publicly with Intel, which produces most of its microprocessor chips. The new Presario line of multimedia PCs is being made with chips made by Intel's deadly rival AMD.

Compaq leads the computer industry in its working practices. The company was the first to employ the 'ABC' - activity-based costing - accounting system to apportion overheads accurately to individual products. The system has been adopted as a benchmark by the rest of the industry. But it is in price-cutting where Compaq has really come to the fore: after the mould-breaking reductions which shocked the market in 1991, the management team led by Eckhard Pfeiffer realised that this would be a fact of life in the commoditised world of personal computers. Compaq products are now designed and built on the expectation that prices will fall 25 per cent during their nine-month lives.

Even the timing of price cuts is carefully and thoughtfully planned. IBM and others are braced for more shocks, and are aping Compaq's strategy by sometimes leading with price cuts of their own.

Nevertheless, they were still caught napping last autumn, when Compaq dropped some product prices by 30 per cent, and then flooded the market with some £2bn of stock, during the peak buying period from September to December.

The phenomenal success of the company sometimes brings its own problems. 'We're growing so quickly, we've got to keep distribution and other systems right,' says Joe McNally, 'at some stage, something's going to crack.' Helping to overcome any problems is the open, unbureaucratic and non-hierarchical structure of the company.

The future

Compaq executives will surely be heartened by recent comments from Enrico Pesatori, the executive responsible for restructuring troubled competitor Dell Computer: 'I know of only one company to compare ourselves with, and that is Compaq,' he said. 'We can no longer characterise Compaq as just a PC company, it is a company that has perfectly interpreted the new style of computing that is emerging.'

Coopers &Lybrand

Coopers & Lybrand, London

Coopers & Lybrand is the largest accountancy-based professional advisory services organisation in the UK. It offers management consultancy, audit, tax advice, insolvency, corporate finance and human resources services

Outlook:
General consensus among knowledgeable commentators suggests that the largest three or four firms worldwide will race ahead of the other two or three among the big six. Demand for consistent quality of service across the world and the inherent globalisation of business will favour those firms offering innovative solutions which anticipate business need. Coopers & Lybrand is the largest practice in many key markets and is certain to be one of the senior players

Scorecard:
Structural flexibility	★★★★
Innovative power	★★★★
International orientation	★★★★★
Human resources	★★★★
Growth markets	★★★★★
Quality of management	★★★★★

Key figures:
UK fee income	£575 million
UK staff	9,400

Coopers & Lybrand
1 Embankment Place
London WC2N 6NN
Tel: 0171 583 5000
Fax: 0171 822 4652

Coopers & Lybrand

Coopers & Lybrand is an organisation for superlatives. It is - by far - the largest business advisory enterprise in the UK. This means that it is Britain's biggest professional services partnership. It also recruits more graduates than any other British enterprise. It has the widest spread of business services of any UK advisory concern embracing audit, tax, corporate finance, management consultancy, insolvency, growth businesses and human resources management.

Coopers & Lybrand audits more UK FT 100 companies than any of its competitors, it has the UK's largest general management consultancy, it has the greatest number of European FT 500 audit clients, Britain's biggest corporate finance, tax and insolvency advisory practices, and one of the most active corporate finance functions in the UK.

In recent years the organisation has achieved its *primus inter pares* role by a combination of rapid growth, merger and early identification of new market opportunities. In common with several firms in the so-called big six (accountancy firms) it reached its present size after merger - its 1990 tryst with Deloitte Haskins & Sells. The pre-merger Coopers & Lybrand boasted UK market leadership in management consultancy and insolvency. What Deloitte brought to the party was a prestigious audit client list, particularly in several areas where Coopers & Lybrand was not historically strong. These included construction, banking and some financial services sectors. Further expertise was also contributed in tax, corporate finance and certain areas of consultancy.

Operations and markets

In business terms the composite made remarkable sense. It created a professional services organisation with a high profile in all of its key markets, some of the most creative people in their sectors and professional expertise unmatched - in some business areas - by leading competitors. Being partnerships, the big six do not publish their profits but fee income in 1994 was reported as £575 million, way ahead of its nearest rival Arthur Andersen. In terms of the UK FT Top 100 companies Coopers & Lybrand holds 25 audit appointments - one ahead of Price Waterhouse. As tax adviser, it is also leader - in terms of fee income - by a slightly increased margin over KPMG, Ernst & Young and Price Waterhouse which are neck and neck for second place.

At the time of the merger UK staff numbers reached a peak of around 12,000 but now they are down to 9,400. The organisation has profited from an active programme of cost reduction, efficiency improvement and profit enhancement exercises with similar programmes being undertaken by Coopers & Lybrand International member firms in other parts of Europe and the US.

Strategy and management

Whereas audit was traditionally the core of the business, it has now emerged as one of several key services. Accountants have become business advisers. Instead of a simple compliance role, leading auditors aim to give added value to a process which clients have regarded as time-consuming, expensive and of little intrinsic strategic and operational value. Clients have been pressurising auditors to give more value for money in audits. Coopers & Lybrand has been among the leaders in devising audit-based packages, such as CLASS (Coopers & Lybrand Audit Support Software) which offer a broad range of business advice.

Clients now want greater involvement from their adviser, and greater understanding of their business and operational performance. In a climate where audit fees are reducing, Coopers & Lybrand has managed to retain its market share and gained two prestigious audit assignments in 1994 - Sainsbury's and Wellcome. Sainsbury's had been audited by medium-sized firm Clark Whitehill for many years and several big six firms nurtured hopes of securing Britain's largest grocer. But it opted for Coopers & Lybrand's international capability and retail expertise and experience. The leading pharmaceutical company Wellcome was apparently impressed by an extensive track record of consultancy in the pharmaceutical industry and the fact that it audits Glaxo. Since then these two giants have agreed to merger.

Although four of the UK big six have impressive audit client lists, Coopers & Lybrand's includes: BT, the Bank of England, Pearson, the Royal Bank of Scotland, Marks & Spencer, Pilkington, Kingfisher, Ford, Carlton, Digital, PowerGen and Unilever.

Three of the big six have substantial management consultancies - Coopers & Lybrand, Andersen and Price Waterhouse. Andersen Consulting is tightly focused on markets where the others generally do not compete. Coopers & Lybrand has cast its net widely and throughout the 1980s experienced exponential growth in its consulting practice. It was the earliest of the leading accountancy-based players to detect a need for its services and to develop a plan for growing the business. Partners would argue that a major part of their success has been due to its strategic flexibility and its approach to matching industry expertise to the work of traditional business divisions.

The UK organisation, like all other members of Coopers & Lybrand International, is a national partnership. It is linked through Coopers & Lybrand International - a Swiss *verein* - to firms which subscribe to the same international strategy and values around the world. In practice, like any of the big six, this means that for multinational clients a communality of service excellence can be achieved in all service areas at key locations. A major multinational would expect the same standard of service delivery anywhere in the world. If Coopers & Lybrand does not have an office in a particular territory and a major client needs coverage there, then the international organisation sets up an office.

The highly competitive nature of big six partnerships has revolutionised the concept of assignment targeting. As recently as a decade ago, the beauty parade emerged as the favoured method for selecting auditors and advisers. Today, competitive tendering is backed up by a complex mechanism of research functions, incisive strategy and senior partners responsible for winning specified targets. Professional institutes have relaxed the rules governing the process of winning business and the big six have responded with relish.

Two key facets of its organisational structure have helped Coopers & Lybrand to win business: its multidisciplinary focus and its industry-orientation. The two are really one and the same because part of the function of its focus is to capitalise on its industry strengths. It does not claim to be the first among the big six which saw industry expertise to be a key business asset but it suggests that its own is now one of the best developed.

As Coopers & Lybrand gathers pace towards the 21st century, expert knowledge and understanding of key industries will assume greater importance. Although still organised by service divisions (audit, tax, consultancy and so on), teams are structured with an industry focus. For example, all members of the insurance industry group sit together. So, in one geographical space all the auditors, tax specialists, actuaries and consultants which service the insurance industry constitute a whole. Their common interest and daily interaction builds a body of expertise which the organisation can draw on for all initiatives and assignments which involve that sector.

Its organisational matrix is a complicated structure but it allows the business to respond quickly and effectively to client demand. Within each industry group, competing clients will be represented by different lead partners and confidentiality is protected but expertise is shared by the group.

The firm acts as a strong advocate in contemporary business issues. In particular, it has played an important role in arguing for positive changes to benefit the business community. Six out of the eight key recommendations of the Cadbury report were advanced by Coopers & Lybrand. A spin-off has been a whole new business area advising companies on how to apply Cadbury recommendations to their own operations.

It has also concentrated on a market hitherto forgotten by some professional practices - the middle sized business. It has organised meetings with influential business leaders from these companies to discover which are the main issues for this sector. Coopers & Lybrand has created a marketing function for the medium-sized business and surveyed companies. Many are household names - some are high growth companies.

Coopers & Lybrand is also active in pension reform. Ten out of twelve recommendations which were adopted by the House of Commons investigation into company pensions emerged from the business' own inquiry into what went wrong with the Maxwell pension fund. Maxwell was a Coopers & Lybrand client. A new piece of software, created by the organisation, will enable businesses to ensure that they comply with pensions legislation. Nothing which the actuarial world has produced is nearly as powerful.

The future

The Coopers & Lybrand International network is the second largest advisory organisation in Europe - after KPMG - reporting revenues of US$ 2.6 billion. Its member organisations employ 29,700 people across Europe and together operate the second largest number of offices. European members of the network audit 29 of the FT European top 100 companies - and it is the largest audit practitioner in Europe.

Coopers & Lybrand is also the number one adviser on privatisation, and is particularly active in Eastern Europe and the former Soviet Union. In 1994, according to Privatisation International, the organisation undertook 379 assignments in 68 countries.

DAVIES ARNOLD COOPER

Davies Arnold Cooper, London

Davies Arnold Cooper is a leading firm of solicitors based in the City

Outlook:

Law firms are in general badly managed but there are some notable exceptions and DAC is one of them. This firm is run as a business rather than a professional practice. It has concentrated on its core strengths since the early 1960s and is remarkably profitable. The firm is based on high levels of service, strong HR policies and considerable professional expertise

Scorecard:

Structural flexibility	★★★★★
Innovative power	★★★★
International orientation	★★★
Human resources management	★★★★★
Growth markets	★★★
Quality of management	★★★★

Key figures:

Staff	405

Davies Arnold Cooper
8 Bouverie Street
London EC4Y 8DD
Tel: 0171 936 2222

Davies Arnold Cooper

A partnership structure and lack of publically available acounts makes it very difficult to accurately assess the financial health of any particular law firm. Yet a recent Coopers & Lybrand report suggests that times have rarely been tougher for the UK's legal profession. Its conclusion is that many firms are already in terminal decline.

Coopers' findings at least make it possible to take an objective look at the strategy of a legal practice as it has set out a formula which makes a successful firm. Unsurprisingly its conclusions are not that different from any other business. In that lies the fundamental weakness of many practices.

Many law firms have failed to take a commercial approach. Only rarely have they been well organised in a management sense and most of them only recognised that there was need to install management disciplines later than most other professions. An inability to be profit driven is at the heart of the problem.

The conclusion of Coopers' 1994 'survey of Final Management in Law Firms' report was stark. 'A quarter of all firms are seriously deficient in major parts of their strategic financial management, although a similar amount are performing extremely well. The gap between them is growing as the best performers use their superior management and profitability to invest in new services, technology, international links, training and development. Those whose inability to run a tight ship has robbed them of the same investment capacity face a clear message - time is running out.'

Davies Arnold Cooper is a medium sized firm, which stands out from its peer group because it is driven by a profit motive. It has always been the case at this firm. One of its recent reports quotes Lee Iacocca - 'volume at zero profit isn't too healthy'. That reassuring philosophy is part of the reason why the firm is solvent. Its management appear to regard themself as businessmen first and lawyers second and the strategy is direct and focused. The firm sticks to what it does best which means those areas where it has established a profitable competitive edge. Turnover is irrelevant unless it makes money.

It has put in place very efficient administration and management. A great deal of responsibility is devolved to the partners and from them to other employees. Everyone is involved, regardless of status, and that is an unusually egalitarian approach for any law firm. As all this is applied to its relationships with and advice to its clients, DAC has a compelling formula for success.

Operations and markets

Davies Arnold Cooper is a leading UK commercial law firm with an international reputation in litigation, insurance and reinsurance. It is a broadly based commercial practice with legal expertise in a wide range of fields. Its client base includes all sizes of British and international public and private companies in the manufacturing and service sectors - particularly insurance, pharmaceutical, construction and property. The firm also acts for professional partnerships of all disciplines and several of the UK's major public authorities.

Established in the City in 1927, DAC has 52 partners and over 400 staff. It has two City offices, one of which is in the Lloyd's building. Another office is based in Manchester, with two overseas in Brussels and Madrid and an associate in Hong Kong. It also has contacts with law firms throughout the world.

The firm has built a reputation on a practical and commercial approach. It has a campaigning and pioneering style which, coupled with its involvement in many of the UK's high-profile litigation cases in the past ten years, has generated considerable publicity for the firm.

It is perhaps best known for its involvement (usually on behalf of insurers) in defending most of the highly publicised personal injury actons tried by British courts in recent years. These include Abbeystead, Piper Alpha, the Bradford City and Hillsborough football stadium disasters, HIV/AIDS haemophilia and Opren. The firm's continuous organic growth, increasing by something like 75 per cent in the last three years, has largely been driven by the work it has carried out on behalf of the insurance industry.

Strategy and management

Coopers' report lists the most profitable areas for a law firm. For corporate firms most profitable is company/commercial work, litigation and commercial property. The lowest returns are generated from banking/insolvency and insurance work. Obviously even the most profitable area, litigation, requires a solicitor to win his cases and perhaps more crucially, the client to pay his bill promptly.

Since the 1960s, DAC's turnover has been generated predominantly (around 70 per cent) from litigation work. The remainder is divided two-thirds commercial law and, mainly for historic reasons, one-third commercial property. It has always stuck to its core activity, but that core has over time been refined and evolved. In common with good business practice, it emphasises the maintenance of excellent communication with its customers. It has looked at best practice in industry generally and applied those lessons to its own business.

DAC seeks to set the pace for its profession, spearheading campaigns to eliminate what it sees as unfairnesses in the existing legal system. Recent successes include persuading the government to change the law on commercial property leases, drawing attention to the disparity between European personal injury awards and exposing the negative attitudes of UK employers' organisations towards safety issues.

One unfairness it has gone some way to reform is the law of privity of contract in leases. This law effectively ties in a tenant for the length of a lease, usually up to 25 years, regardless of whether they have subsequently assigned that lease. In some cases, traders who relet their shop premises, possibly on retirement, have a decade later been presented with bills running into tens of thousands of pounds because a subsequent tenant collapsed. DAC's efforts, which received considerable attention in the press during the recession, generated the desired reforms, although they have yet to become law.

DAC recognises that like any business, it must offer 'unpretentious but quality services at value for money prices'. The biggest dilemma for any law firm is that legal services have seldom seemed to the public to be a fair buy. As it states, 'UK customers are more sophisticated and more aware of where a service adds value. Any professional practice which cannot match this need will go the way of the dinosaurs.'

The result is that some legal practices which have been slow to adapt to changes have already contracted. A few well-known legal names are likely to disappear over the next year or two, and not just by way of defensive merger.

Overcapacity is bad news for any profession. As businesses found they had to rationalise their own operations, they looked harder at the services they were buying from the legal profession. Law firms could no longer take the loyalty of their clients for granted, and had to drop a patronising attitude towards many of their clients.

The result is that buyers of legal services have become much more selective. Symptoms of this change include the beauty parades demanded by clients, fixed prices and tender panels. Lawyers themselves have had to relinquish their expectations of a partnership for life and face up to a more pressured environment.

DAC views this as a potentially healthy change for the industry unless bidding wars evolve which see lawyers undercut each other at uncompetitive rates. 'The discerning buyer should beware of any professional attempting to buy business. Loss leaders are often losers for everyone.'

DAC has refused to be defensive when its practices and prices have been questioned. It responded to its clients' needs for transparency and accountability by being the first City law firm to publish a protocol of costs and clients services, described by The Guardian as 'a tariff of fees and customer charter.'

Its introduction 'Legal fees, Getting more for your money' reassures clients of the firm's integrity. 'Providing an effective service depends upon avoiding costly repetition and unnecessary work. It requires careful staffing, using the right level and number of people for the job.'

However, most of its competitors remain reluctant to publish a similar tariff, other than quotes for specific jobs and clients. DAC's response is simple. 'One can only assume this is because they are embarrassed by their highest rates, reserved for the undiscriminating or unwary client. Too many firms of solicitors are living in the past. It is time for them to wake up to the new consumerist reality'.

The future

DAC is well placed to counsel and assist its clients on how to take advantage of prospects in Europe. It has an international perspective through its various offices and other well established legal business and client contacts throughout the world. It attempts to provide a solidly commercial analysis of the challenges and opportunities facing its clients. These will include traditional areas such as commercial property and construction issues, and legal and economic developments in Europe, but also extends to detailed studies on the opportunities for corporate capital at Lloyd's, the Cadbury report on non-executive directors, through to football litigation, Sunday trading and RSI claims.

Its ability to maintain a steady ship during the recession enabled it to stand by its longer term clients, to whom it believed it owed loyalty and support through a period when they suffered cash flow and other difficulties. As that accommodating attitude was not always matched, even by DAC's larger competitors, it was able to pick up some potentially important clients. This is the kind of consistent approach which will generate further growth in the next decade.

D·F·S
Furniture Company plc

DFS, South Yorkshire

DFS is the UK's largest independent furniture retailer in the UK

Outlook:
DFS has majored in customer service - a quality which was distinctly lacking in the sector. As a result this company has grown via a combination of entrepreneurial zeal and management capacity into a business which has grown rapidly. It is the market leader not only in financial terms but also in the quality of its relationships with customers and suppliers

Scorecard:
Structural flexibility	★★★★
Innovative power	★★★★★
International orientation	★★★
Human resources	★★★★★
Growth markets	★★★★★
Quality of management	★★★★

Key figures:
Turnover	£134 million
Pre-tax profits	£21.4 million
Staff	686

DFS Ltd
Doncaster
South Yorkshire DN6 7BD
Tel: 01302 337783

DFS

With a record of twenty-five years of unbroken profit growth through recessions and housing slumps, furniture group DFS undeniably has a winning formula. Yet the search for the 'x-factor', that special something which sets it apart from the field, is a frustrating experience. There is no one thing which defines why it is unique.

Executive chairman Graham Kirkham thinks you miss the key if you look too hard. 'Our success comes from having an edge in lots of different areas. Certainly a 16 per cent margin is attractive, but that's really a quarter-per-cent edge from each of the 64 things we do better. That's not a great deal of difference, but it's all the difference.'

Cynical analysts may be reluctant to accept it can be this easy. However management believes an outsider's main mistake is to assume DFS does something particularly clever when its recipe for success is actually remarkably simple, and lies in its attitude towards its customers, employees and suppliers.

Operations and markets

Based in Doncaster, DFS is the UK's leading specialist retailer of upholstered furniture (although it has only a seven per cent market share) with 26 out-of-town stores located mainly in central and northern England. Current executive chairman Graham Kirkham opened the first store in 1969, and since its inception the group has been vertically integrated, manufacturing around 15 per cent of its range in two factories in the UK. There is also a small dining room furniture arm with three outlets. The group was floated in November 1993.

Management's cautious approach is reflected in the fact that despite opening three stores last year, the group has no borrowings and holds around £27m in cash. Expansion is always funded from its own resources and very carefully planned.

Strategy and management

According to Mr Kirkham the company 'captures the best attributes of a private business, especially its customer service culture, and combines these with the strengths of a multiple'. He acknowledges that the barriers to entry in the furniture business are not insurmountable. Yet many leading retailers have tried and failed to make an impression on this market.

Mr Kirkham believes DFS has a competitive edge. 'Our competitors', he says, 'are actually facing barriers to success'. What he means is that 25 years of building relationships with customers, suppliers and employees have given DFS a head start which will prove tough for any new entrant to claw back in the short term.

Its relationship with its customers has the highest priority. As Mr Kirkham puts it, 'competitors are keen to emulate our example, but personal recommendation is tough to copy when it has taken us 25 years to establish. Our customers include three generations of the same families - parents, children and grandchildren'.

A customer can rely on DFS to nurse an order through to completion. DFS doesn't rely on its suppliers, most of whom are 'cottage industries', to do the job. It takes responsibility for careful inspection, quality control and delivery on an agreed date by its own people. It refuses to go self-service because this conflicts with its firm commitment to customer service.

For example 'the vogue in the industry is for manufacturers to deliver directly to the customer and in an academic sense, this results in cash savings'. DFS decided not to take that route because in its opinion the retailer, not the manufacturer, must care for the customer. Delivery is considered important, as John Massey chief operating officer, says: 'the presentation of our van crews counts as they are ambassadors for the company. We always use our own people and make sure we send sufficient people to do the job'. Service to the customer begins rather than ends with the order.

'We listen to our customers, because they provide our core market research. Our guarantee is twice as long as the rest of the trade and we back it up with a practical, quick response. Every branch has a service upholsterer in-house, because people have accidents and products can go wrong. We aim to sort out any problems with minimal aggravation for the customer'.

The second strand to its strategy is the considerable value it places on motivating its employees, generating enthusiasm with enjoyable work, something which is appreciated by the customer. 'Our showroom, prices and products are actually comparable to the competition, but we take the attitude that people buy from people, they don't buy a from a three-piece suite', says Mr Kirkham.

Job satisfaction means a loyal workforce. 'It's always going to be difficult to measure caring, loyalty and working in a fun environment, but we know that our staff are people, not machines and numbers. We expect them to be fallible, make mistakes, but when we recruit we take care to find the person that fits the bill'.

According to John Massey 'we see and get constant feedback from our staff, all of whom, from factory to salesroom can easily have a one-to-one conversation with all other levels. Employees are human beings, not numbers on a payroll. I'm appalled by the appearance of human resources departments which treat people as if they were numbers'.

Success is however the major spur to motivation for its employees. There is no ambiguity as far as employee targets are concerned. 'We are not in business to provide the best furniture or the best service, but to earn money. That's the measurement that counts'. It enjoys the challenge of going into new towns and generates healthy competition by pairing new stores with a similar size branch.

The third part of the DFS strategy is the way it manages its relationship with its suppliers. When he started the business, Mr Kirkham found it incomprehensible that during the summer retailers took advantage of suppliers' overcapacity to force down prices, only for the roles to be reversed during the winter as retailers became desperate for Xmas delivery. DFS acknowledges the need for order continuity in both camps. Being a manufacturer has helped it appreciate the need to keep a factory busy; it therefore offers its suppliers business 52 weeks a year and pays on time. This attitude is rewarded with keen prices. DFS recognises that its suppliers also need to make money. It prefers to take only a third of a supplier's output; that means that neither party becomes too powerful and upsets the balance of a relationship.

For DFS, innovation does not lie primarily in the application of high technology although it has readily adopted such techniques as Electronic Data Interchange computer links with its suppliers and Computer Aided Design in its factories. 'We can't stand still. The norms are challenged all the time and we look for ways constantly to improve.' Yet in the main its insistence on maintaining apparently old fashioned values is what has given it a competitive advantage without sacrificing margins.

The training of sales staff is an example of a 'small difference'. When a salesman joins, he begins a nine month training programme which takes him away from the sales floor for about 20 days. Each works at head office and the factory, where he will be expected to chase materials and production. He visits the hide suppliers, tannery, fabric suppliers and makes deliveries. This helps him to get to know products inside out and assess the process continually all the way through.

DFS expects their salesmen's criticism and feedback from its courses. Sometimes it has been 'very educational' and led to improvements such as the introduction of phones in cabs. Even the internal audit function is run with a commercial focus. It looks at processes, and questions why, for example, orders are delayed, or identifies where the company is losing money.

The future

The business thrived as a private company, but management believes the flotation has been good for DFS. 'PLC status has been positive for staff. They were loyal before but now feel part of a big league company. It has raised our profile as the "most successful upholstery manufacturer in the UK" which will help to attract the good people vital for our success as we expand.'

DFS plans to expand the business at a sustainable rate using only its own capital. 'The extra accountability to external shareholders, reporting to the City twice a year, is good discipline, but our strategy has not changed. We won't push store openings forward or delay them to smooth profit growth in an effort to please the City. We expect to maintain around 15 per cent a year growth, with new stores imminent in Norwich and Swindon, and plans for Bristol and Birmingham. A downside of being a listed company is that people emulate you faster. But we aren't perfect, and some have slavishly copied our mistakes as well.

'We won't worry if ratios may move up and down; this is a dynamic business.' Sales ratios can be manipulated, but such measures are really unimportant. The ratio could be improved artificially by shrinking stores and sacrificing profit.

Its out-of-town stores require strong advertising support and the group uses a full range of media such as TV, radio, local newspapers, posters, direct mail and doorstep drops. Store openings are planned in such a way as to maximise the impact of each campaign. Specifically this means grouping its stores within television regions, emphasising tight geographic areas and managing costs. As new stores are planned, locations are sought on the edge of its existing TV regions. 'We want some overlap to give us a flying start.'

Mr Kirkham is confident the DFS approach will remain a winner. 'Retail dynamics are constantly changing and we have to search for new edges. Our competitors have gone astray on service in the past, our area of greatest focus. But we are ahead in lots of other areas. In manufacturing we believe we hold an edge in fabric sourcing and the costing and design of products.' If it can maintain that attention to detail, by the end of the decade it will have a brand name in the south of England to match its reputation in the north.

DHL International UK Ltd, Middlesex

DHL is the world's leading international express distribution company delivering documents, parcels and freight across 200 countries worldwide. In 1994, DHL International (UK) Ltd carried 11 million shipments from the UK

Outlook:
The demand for its services is anticipated to grow rapidly in the next decade. The rapid expansion of the Pacific Rim and other global markets will boost its volumes by several multiples. Business in existing markets is also expected to increase as DHL continues to perform strongly against its rivals

Scorecard:
Structural flexibility	★★★
Innovative power	★★★
International orientation	★★★★
Human resources	★★★★
Growth markets	★★★★
Quality of management	★★★

Key figures:
UK turnover	£156 million
Pre-tax profits	£5.53 million
UK staff	2,200
Turnover (global)	US $ 3.1 billion
Worldwide staff	34,000

DHL International UK Ltd
Orbital Park
178/188 Great South West Road
Hounslow
Middlesex TW4 6JS
Tel: 0181 818 8000
Fax: 0181 818 8141

DHL International (UK) Limited

The international air express market is becoming more competitive. As in many other service sectors, customers have become more alert to the factors which distinguish between the leading operators. As a result buyers are now more demanding. This trend will characterise the development of the market in the next decade. And players are already shaping up for the challenges ahead. Whichever of the other leading companies has hopes of securing market advantage will need to take on DHL, which is the sector's best operator.

Operations and markets

DHL is the UK and world market leader in international air express traffic. The UK business is the second largest operation in DHL worldwide - the first being the United States. It is a highly profitable business which has grown between 15 and 20 per cent over the last five years, producing a turnover of £180 million a year. It has operations in 222 countries worldwide and is three times larger than its nearest rival in this market place. While DHL accounts for 67 per cent of the marketplace, UPS, Federal Express and TNT each have market shares of 10 to 15 per cent.

The company has reached this enviable position with a mixture of entrepreneurship, creativity and a high commitment to customer service. This is all the more remarkable considering that the business started only 20 years ago on the kitchen table of one of its largest UK investors. Today DHL UK has 44 depots, and employs 2,200 people. Its principal business lies in international documents where it has a 67 per cent market share and parcels under 50 kgs where it controls 46 per cent of the market. There are four so-called integrators in the worldwide market but the most profitable is DHL by a long way.

DHL was the first world class courier company around the world. It is distinctive from its leading rivals in that most of its offices around the world are wholly owned. DHL has more outlets around the globe than any of its rivals (or, for that matter AMEX or Coca Cola). It was also the first in the UK, started in the Putney in the early 1970s.

The original employees were a broad mixture of small business start up type personnel who were according to Mr Butcher, entrepreneurial types - 'jacks of all trades who will handle every aspect of the business. There were an awful lot of expatriate Australians and New Zealanders who used their camper vans to deliver the first DHL parcels,' he recalls. There was a work hard and play hard culture. There were quite a few sporting types in the organisation. But it was also characterised by a high degree of entrepreneurship. As the organisation has become more systematised and professional in its operation, management has striven to ensure that none of the original energy, dynamism and creativity of the business has been lost.

Strategy and management

Nick Butcher, managing director of DHL UK, says the reasons for its profound success can be identified as:

. reliability
. speed of delivery
. value for money
. simplicity of operation

'Our customers want to know that we will deliver their parcel, we will get there faster than our rivals, that they are getting value for money and that the access to our operation is as simple as possible. Our efficiency can be judged by the fact that we are suppliers to 96 of the FTSE Top 100 companies. For example nearly all of the UK high street banks - Natwest, Barclays, Lloyds, Abbey National and Midland - all use our services.'

And in customer survey after customer survey, DHL regularly scores higher than all of its major competitors. And there are cheaper operators, because DHL charges a premium price for its service.

'One of the guiding principles of DHL is our passion for customer service,' he says. 'This is a very personal business. We see one of the defining factors in the quality of our service as the high level of personal and direct contact between individuals at our customers and our personnel. Our customer contacts like to know that they can reach a named individual, with whom they are familiar at our offices. In previous years the chances of achieving this would be perhaps 1 in 150; today we are working towards ensuring that this will be 1 in 3.'

Around 50 per cent of DHL staff are based in its 44 stations around the country. Another 300 are organised in customer service teams. Two of these are at its headquarters near Heathrow Airport and the third is located in the East Midlands. When customers have a query about how long or how much it costs to send a package to another location around the world customer service staff are there to handle these queries. They are also engaged in tracking and monitoring of packages. For example, if a company is sending a parcel from Vancouver to a company based in the UK, the British company can telephone DHL to find out where the package is and when it will be delivered.

The market research which DHL conducts asks customers to grade the company on particular criteria. 'If we let a customer down and that does happen very occasionally - then we could quite easily lose the entire contract. So we cannot afford to make a single error. In order to improve levels of efficiency within our organisation we have established a quality department. This conducts quality audits on each of our stations around the country. We also send parcels through our system, unannounced, and also through those of our competitors to see who is faster and where the service needs improvement. Clearly we make mistakes from time to time but we would not retain our dominant market share without being very good at what we do,' says Mr Butcher.

On average the market for courier services has been growing at around 10 per cent a year. In contrast DHL has been growing at around 20 per cent a year. Mr Butcher believes that this pays testimony to the quality of his service and to the efficiency of his staff. 'We believe the market has substantial room for further growth. Companies are developing relationships with emerging markets in China, in the CIS, in Africa and other developing economies around the world. This means the number of packages going from and to these locations will increase. It means a substantial rise in business for our sector and also for our company.'

He also sees further opportunities for development in the UK. The current complement of 44 stations will grow to 50 in the next two to three years. DHL recently opened a new depot at Exeter. 'Formerly we ran the West Country out of Bristol. But the growth in the market suggested that we could open a further installation at Exeter. With local representation we have been able to discover more and more opportunities for new business. We believe that there will be at least five other such locations where we can open up and expand our business. So our penetration of the UK market will become deeper and deeper,' he comments. These are pockets of business rather than whole new areas but they remain extremely valuable for DHL. The company will be able to broaden its coverage and brand reputation.

It already has the strongest name in the sector for being the courier of emergency. If a company urgently needs to get a package to another part of the world - out of the run of normal assignments - then DHL is usually the first point of call. Mr Butcher believes that this is due to the company's excellence as a service provider.

The future

The capital investment required to launch an integrator the size of DHL or its key rivals suggests that no new operators are likely to emerge in the market. The management team at DHL UK expects that there will be new competition at the fringes of the market which will ensure that the heartland of the business continues to grow and prosper. Both the worldwide and European level organisations are based in Brussels. These operations are relatively small operations; high emphasis is placed on control - certainly at an operational level - invested in the managers of the national companies. Mr Butcher reports to an executive director for the northern European region. His patch includes Scandinavia, the UK, Ireland, the Netherlands and, perhaps unusually, Anglophone Africa. There are four such regional directors at the European level reporting in to the European CEO. Mr Butcher believes that responsibility for product and customer led initiatives of each national company will increasingly be found at the operating level. New relationships with other companies supplying niche market products will be an area of development for the company.

'We see that companies will become smaller and smaller as they stick to their core competencies and outsource many of their non-core activities. This means a wider number of relationships with an increasing number of smaller businesses. Also the growth in the international markets suggest that there will be increased dialogue with emerging economies.'

DHL has a bright and vibrant future. It continues to enjoy the confidence of its principal customers and it is building on the quality of its service delivery to its customers. DHL has a clear dominance in the market and this is set to continue.

ENGLISH & OVERSEAS PROPERTIES PLC

English & Overseas Properties

English & Overseas Properties is the leader among Britain's small property companies. It was one of the few property companies to survive the recession and is distinguished by its distinctive approach to its markets

Outlook:
The recession savaged property companies. The few which survived have anticipated that passive management would be adequate to achieving a return. E&OP will prosper in the next decade because it actively manages its portfolio, believes in customer service - an unknown concept in property - and has a formidable reputation for research and networking

Scorecard:
Structural flexibility	★★★★★
Innovative power	★★★★★
International orientation	★★★
Human resources	★★★★
Growth markets	★★★★★
Quality of management	★★★★

Key figures:
Turnover	£3,919,00
Pre-tax profits	£987,00
Staff	14

English & Overseas Properties
29, Buckingham Gate
London SW1E 6NF
Tel: 0171 828 9929
Fax: 0171 828 5767

English & Overseas Properties

The dynamics of Britain's property market will change fundamentally in the next decade. The high inflation environment which allowed property companies to indulge in passive management is already giving way to more rigorous economic criteria. Low inflation - and therefore low returns for owners and managers - is forecast to continue into the new century, forcing the property sector to re-examine its business objectives.

Anticipating lower income from core holdings, analysts argue that the focus of attention in the field will no longer be the property companies themselves but rather their customers. This represents an extensive change in direction and business approach for the sector which has traditionally considered client requirement and upkeep of holdings as low priorities. Many of the existing operators are ill-equipped to face the challenges of the new environment. They exhibit trading and operational characteristics which are the reverse of what will be needed in the next decade.

So property companies will need to be more flexible, customer- orientated and short term in their horizons. Only those players who are sufficiently nimble will stand a chance of survival - and ultimately prosperity. Few operators currently possess the distinctly different skills to thrive in the new market conditions. Given individual company cultural inflexibility, poor service orientation in the industry and sector overcapacity, observers anticipate that the numbers of players will radically scale down thus favouring a group of truly flexible, market aware and active operators. In particular, some smaller enterprises - with market capitalisations between £2 million and £50 million - which have neither the critical mass nor operational flexibility will face extinction.

Operations and markets

English & Overseas Properties is one of the smaller players but it will also be among the real winners. It is distinctive because it recognised at an early stage that the market would favour a thoroughly professional operator which would base its investment decisions by appreciating and meeting customer need and achieving short term rather than long term results. The company's unique blend of managerial innovation and conservative investment strategy allowed the business to execute a passage of safety through the darkest days of the recession. It also set E&OP in good stead to deal with the challenges of the future. Its preliminary financial results for 1994, issued in February 1995, show a company which has tripled its profits to a record £987,000 on a reduced turnover and which has £100 million of properties under management.

Jim Clark, E&OP's chairman, says: 'We have a small team in our headquarters in London but they are all professionals and we could easily double our property under management with no need to increase our team. We draw extensively on expertise within the industry and we believe strongly in putting together teams as and when we need them.' This is a key factor in the company's approach. It employs a highly skilled but small team at base and accesses people of ability as and when it needs. The source of income for the company since the recession has changed substantially. Mr Clark says that during the three years of the recession E&OP drew all of its new income from consultancy to client companies.

E&OP's business activities include investment in property, commercial and industrial sites, and consultancy to clients on property management. E&OP acts for a spread of clients - especially the banks and retailers. Among its investments 95 per cent are let; some 70 per cent of the holdings taken by listed companies. Its investments and developments largely involve smaller industrial and commercial sites but the company is shrewd enough to listen carefully to what clients need and to improve locations to meet customer requirements.

To examine the mettle and capacity for survival of any property company, it is instructive to look at its performance during the recession. This demonstrates its vision and management skill. It also shows what creative initiatives a business employed to stay afloat during the time when clients were shedding employees and dispensing wholesale with property commitments. Any property company which survived the recession deserves a round of applause. The sector was devastated by the economic collapse.

Famous name after famous name hit the dirt, some perished altogether. Even the survivors faced the rigours of sustained financial pressure. To emerge broadly intact and to have the strength to apply the new skills learned during the downturn, have become the defining factors for the industry.

Poor forecasting, multiple developments left unfinished or unoccupied, massive debt exposure and financial commitments which were unable to be met left the industry scarred. This trend was accelerated by the failure of client companies or businesses switching out of non-core activities to survive, thus scaling down their property requirements. In such an environment, it is remarkable that any property companies emerged on the other side but some were more astutely managed than others. E&OP was the only property company which was listed in 1988 to survive.

Strategy and management

Mr Clark says that E&OP's strategy is to grow as suitable properties and developments become available. Its sector knowledge is among the finest in the business which means that the company is alert to where these opportunities may arise. Unlike some of the larger players, E&OP believes that it should exploit opportunities to the full - and then sell on. This is not always appreciated by City analysts who look for long term holdings as a sign of stability. Mr Clark comments that the dynamics of the market will favour companies which have the capacity to be light on their feet and to exploit a potential gain. He suggests that the strategic priorities for the company are:

- . further investment in suitable holdings
- . further commitment to appropriate developments
- . reduction in core holdings
- . some 'opportunistic' ventures.

Resilience and flexibility are at the heart of the company and contribute - with its professional skill base - to the creation of the company's culture. The main operating areas of the enterprise are divided in terms of turnover:

- . investment (50 per cent)
- . development (30 per cent)
- . consultancy (20 per cent).

In investment, E&OP has £42.5 million in direct investment with a current rental income of more than £3 million. Prospects for the investment aspect of the business are rising rapidly. At the beginning of 1993 only 70 per cent of the portfolio was let, but by the end of that year, this had increased to 97 per cent.

The company has acquired more than £40 million worth of investment property for overseas equity investors - especially from the Middle East. E&OP has also been particularly active in an innovative deal which involved the conversion of Princes Court opposite Harrods in Knightsbridge. It is also active in two major joint venture companies - English and Overseas Assets (a 50:50 partnership with British Linen Bank) an office block in Finchley, and Institutional Property Holdings (IPH), 50:50 ownership with BZW. IPH is involved in small high-yield holdings where it has the capacity to add value.

Development is a principal on-going business for the company and although the properties which E&OP is involved in at any one time will inevitably vary from month to month it will always hold a portfolio of developments. The business is very active in using the latest and most innovative marketing techniques to attract interest in its developments.

Consultancy forms 20 per cent of E&OP's income but its impact on the enterprise as a whole is extensive. The relationships which the company develops with its clients broaden its access to decision-makers and extend its knowledge base. During the recession E&OP relied on consultancy as a primary source of income, but Mr Clark knows that long term this arm of the business will need to find new sources of business. The core of this aspect of the company is project management. Clients for this service include development companies, bankers and new investors in properties, and its expertise covers all market sectors.

The future

The challenges remain within the company as well as outside it. Mr Clark sees substantial opportunities to build on the skills within the organisation, drawing on cross-functional teams and thereby boosting fee-generation. 'We have already discovered that some potential strengths could be converted into profitability by exploiting the talents in different parts of the business.' Team building is an undiscovered science in property investment and E&OP is clearly going to experience advances if it capitalises on basic management theory. Property is still poorly managed as a sector, so it is a real delight to locate a property company which demonstrates all the characteristics of a well run business. E&OP has much to give its sector.

East Midlands Electricity

East Midlands Electricity, Nottinghamshire

East Midlands Electricity is a recently privatised company supplying and
distributing electricity in the Midland regions

Outlook:
In the challenging environment of a post-privatisation playing-field East
Midlands has set itself strong but realistic targets. With the determination
provided by a professional management-team and the ability to lead the field
in cost reductions East Midlands seems set to be among the key players of the
future

Scorecard:
Structural flexibility	★★★★
Innovative power	★★★★
International orientation	★★★
Human resources	★★★★
Growth markets	★★★★★
Quality of management	★★★★

Key figures:
Turnover	£1,369.0 million
Operating profit	£207.9 million
Staff	4,648

East Midlands Electricity plc
Corporate Office
PO Box 444 Wollaton
Nottingham NG8 1EZ
Tel: 0115 901 0101
Fax: 0115 901 8200

East Midlands Electricity

Since the privatisation of the electricity supply industry in the early 1990s, the sector is expected to be at the centre of considerable corporate activity in future years. Whilst market growth in the demand for electricity will be sluggish, the sector's remarkably strong balance sheet and its impressive dividend growth potential, notwithstanding the scope for mergers, should give investors good returns - political and regulatory risk permitting.

East Midlands Electricity is one of the 12 Regional Electricity Companies in England which were all privatised in 1990. Its major business is the distribution of electricity to over 2.2 million customers located mainly in Derbyshire, Leicestershire, Lincolnshire, Northamptonshire, Nottinghamshire and Warwickshire. Crucially this wires business - a natural monopoly - is subject to economic regulation by Offer.

East Midlands' other main activities are generation - notably the 40 per cent shareholding in the 350 MW station at Corby- and the supply of electricity - a high turnover and low margin business. It also owns an 8.4 per cent shareholding in the National Grid, which is due to be demerged shortly with the net proceeds being passed on to shareholders.

Whilst in structural terms all 12 RECs are broadly similar, East Midlands is seen as being the leader, along with Eastern, in achieving cost reductions in its core business. Overall employee numbers are now below 6,000, compared with 8,500 in September 1992: the core business reduction accounts for over 1,000. Moreover, after various unsuccessful diversification initiatives, there have been major Board changes, most notably the appointment of Nigel Rudd as non-executive chairman. The main emphasis now lies in generating further efficiencies from the core distribution business. In addition, the new management has demonstrated its declared priority in achieving shareholder value with its £187 million superdividend payment in 1994.

Operations and markets

In common with all RECs, East Midlands' monopoly distribution business will remain the key to future profitability. In 1994, this business contributed over 90 per cent of operating profits - equivalent to £169 million. Future profitability trends are very dependent upon the revised distribution formula which has been announced by Offer - it will apply as from April 1996. The original five year settlement announced in August 1994 has now been abandoned, except in respect of the present year. The revised formula of RPI-3, with a further one-off reduction in 1996-7, is undoubtedly tougher and places greater emphasis on cost cutting. Indeed, Norman Askew, chief executive, strongly backs incentive regulation, confident that East Midlands can outperform its peer group in cutting costs.

East Midlands stands to benefit from the above average load growth in its region with its comparative high level of new housebuilding. Furthermore, inward investment is important with over 200 foreign companies now located in the East Midlands.

Outside the distribution business, returns will be far less marked. The supply business is highly competitive, but East Midlands' performance has been amongst the best in the sector - in 1993/4, supply operating profits were £26 million. With the Corby generating plant being bid into the pool as a baseload station, there should be a useful contribution from this activity.

East Midlands' generating ambitions have now been cut back. The proposed investments in new stations at Rugby and Sutton Bridge have been dropped; there are no plans either to buy surplus plant from National Power or PowerGen, who are under regulatory pressure to divest of some of their plant.

After failing to earn adequate returns from both contracting and retailing, East Midlands has now exited these businesses. It is also taking a cautious approach to the gas market, which is being progressively deregulated. In particular, Mr Askew reassures investors by ruling out any upstream gas acquisitions.

More generally, the market has responded favourably to East Midlands' unequivocal priority to the development of its core businesses. The previous management team had undertaken several unwise diversifications. Its replacement, accompanied by a £130 million exceptional charge in 1993/4, has caused East Midlands to be partially rerated.

Strategy and management

Of all the RECs, East Midlands' strategy is probably the most clearcut. Last May, Nigel Rudd reaffirmed the group's aims - 'The continuing focus on the electricity businesses and the other actions taken over the past year will enable the group to release value to shareholders. Customers will benefit through good service and competitive prices in the years ahead.' The announcement last November of a £187 million superdividend - a sector first - was a vigorous demonstration of this strategy. Moreover, with underlying dividend cover of close to 3x and a gearing level of below 30 per cent, considerable scope exists for further enhanced returns for shareholders. Unlike several RECs, East Midlands has not specified a precise dividend growth target although Mr Askew has reaffirmed the aim 'to deliver real dividend growth'.

To generate adequate earnings, the group's strategy lies in developing the core electricity distribution business. Such a process has to be undertaken within the parameters of the pricing formula set by Offer. This strategy has been implemented over the last 18 months, most significantly through the delayering of the group's management process. Between 1993 and 1994, 13 cost centres were reorganized into seven profit centres. This process has reduced costs whilst maintaining close contact with customers.

Mr Askew also identifies scope for savings both from procurement - a director has been appointed charged with this reponsibility - and from a more focused capital expenditure programme. East Midlands will invest around £100 million a year.

In the longer term, East Midlands' efficient distribution business and success in the competitive supply business will place it in a good position to benefit both from further deregulation and from opportunities that may arise through mergers with neighbouring RECs, who have been less aggressive in seeking efficiencies. Although it is probably fanciful to suggest that REC consolidation will take place along the lines of that experienced recently within the TV franchise sector, there clearly will continue to be corporate activity.

Inevitably, the potential for cost reductions is finite. Given its unfortunate past of unsuccessful diversification, East Midlands is naturally cautious about overseas initiatives. Nevertheless, it has made a modest contribution, as part of a joint venture with Eskom and EDF, in using its core skills in electrifying a township in South Africa. In time, this could lead to greater involvement in a region with high load growth.

Compared with other RECs, East Midlands' board has wider experience in the private sector than virtually any other REC. Mr Rudd is well known - both in the City and in industry - as the chairman of Williams Holdings, while Mr Askew held senior positions within TI. By contrast, other RECs are more dominated by the public sector ethos and consequently have less experience either in achieving efficiencies in a competitive market or in participating in corporate activity.

Despite an expected capital expenditure bill of around £100 million per year, the scope for innovation in electricity distribution is limited apart from delivering improvements in IT and related areas. The costs of bill collection and metering can be substantially reduced in the long term although some initial capital expenditure will be necessary.

East Midlands' location near the heart of British industry has given it specific expertise in devising technology solutions for its industrial customers. With the region exporting 50 per cent of its output and with manufacturing accounting for 27 per cent of output - against a national average of 21 per cent - these skills are particularly valuable, especially with an increasingly competitive electricity market.

The future

Of course, like all RECs, Offer's revised distribution review will play a crucial role in determining the future finances of East Midlands. Since Offer declined to remove at a stroke some of the balance sheet strength built up by East Midlands since 1990, the main impact will be on the earnings line. Nevertheless, investors should stand to benefit from solid real dividend growth until 2000 and from the receipt of the proceeds from the demerger of the National Grid, unless the election of a Labour government results in a backlash against utilities.

From 2000 onwards, the prospects for the RECs are less clearcut, especially since regulatory and political risks will remain pronounced for the sector generally. But for East Midlands, its risk is below average. As a low cost operator, the group is less exposed. It benefits,too, from above average load growth in an area where the new housebuild in the 1980s was considerable. At the strategic level, its experienced management is well placed to position the group shrewdly for the inevitable consolidation within the industry.

Arguably, several of the smaller RECs simply do not have the critical mass to be major independent long-term players. Of the larger RECs, East Midlands stands out as having delivered shareholder value directly despite the difficult problems faced by the incoming management. If the REC sector consolidates in time to embrace perhaps three or four major players, along the lines of the TV franchise companies, it is almost inconceivable that East Midlands will not be one of the survivors. Its simple philosophy of generating cash to finance investment and returns to shareholders lies at the heart of its long-term strategy.

Esso, London

Esso UK is a leading oil company and part of the Exxon Corporation
- one of the world's largest companies

Outlook:
The oil sector does not have a long term future. However its short term
future is brighter than ever. New fields in the former Soviet Union, Africa
and in the Americas mean that companies in the sector remain profitable and
substantial multinational businesses. Esso UK is regarded as a standard bearer
for the sector

Scorecard:
Structural flexibility	★★★★
Innovative power	★★★★★
International orientation	★★★★★
Human resources	★★★★★
Growth markets	★★★★★
Quality of management	★★★★

Key figures:
Turnover	£7906 million
Pre-tax profits	£605 million
Staff	3,254
Global turnover (Exxon)	$113,904 million
Net income	$5,100 million
Staff	88,000

Esso UK
Victoria Street
London SW1E 5JW
Tel: 0171 834 6677
Fax: 0171 245 2201

Esso UK

At the top table of international oil companies, there are only a couple of players. These are Exxon and Shell. Exxon is the real winner between the two. A key measure in the business is return on capital employed and here Exxon is streets ahead of Shell. This is the oldest oil company in the world - having started as Standard Oil and being led by that consolidator of US oil interests - John D Rockefeller.

Exxon is the standard setter for the oil business - active around the world in both exploration and development. The UK business took its name from the original Standard Oil (SO) and has been retained as the company is the best known of the petrol venders. It has the reputation for the highest quality management in the sector and is the most astute operator in global oil. In the UK Esso UK plc runs two operating companies - Esso Exploration and Production (exploration and production of crude oil and natural gas) and Esso Petroleum Company (refining, distribution and marketing). Esso UK and Exxon Chemical operate together as the Esso Group of Companies.

Operations and markets

This is a top ten company in every market in which it operates. Throughout the world and indeed also in the US - it is seen as a classic multinational. Alongside other oil industry and computer sector companies it established the culture of the western multinational. Both Esso UK and Exxon are highly respected operators and a focus for ambitious graduates.

The operations of the UK company can be broadly divided into upstream and downstream. Downstream Esso runs the largest oil refinery in the UK at Fawley. It processes 300,000 barrels of crude daily and can run 20 different varieties of crude a year. In distribution, 90 per cent of the petrol, gas oil, jet fuel and diesel fuel sold in Britain reaches distribution centres through a 1,150 kilometres pipeline. The Esso distribution network delivers from 19 terminals and plants and uses 12 branded distributors. Esso owns and operates a fleet of around 100 road tankers to supply services stations.

Esso is an active participant in the exploration of the UK continental shelf since the first awards in 1964 and has interests in 73 licences involving 147 blocks and part blocks with an average equity level of 45 per cent. Since 1981 offshore oil and gas has exceeded domestic consumption so Esso and other oil and gas companies are net exporters to substantial net benefit to the UK economy. Some 95 per cent of UK need is met by North Sea and Morecambe Bay production. In 1994 Esso production of crude oil and natural gas was 347,000 barrels a day. Sales of gas were 500 million cubic a year.

The company has interests in 30 producing oil and gas fields. It holds 50 per cent interests in Auk, Barque, Brent, Clipper, North and South Cormorant, Gannet, Kittiwake, Tern and Eider, and lesser interests in Osprey, Dunlin, Fulmar, and Sean, all operated by Shell. In the Lehman and Indefatigable fields, Esso has a 50 per cent interest in blocks operated by Shell. In October 1994 gas started to flow from the Galleon field in the southern North Sea, where Esso has a 40 per cent holding.

Strategy and management

The quality of Esso's management is a major factor in the company's continued success and prosperity. Keith Taylor, chairman and chief executive of Esso UK, says: 'Competition in all sectors of our marketing and refining activities continues to put pressure on our earnings. Significant progress is being made in further reducing refining costs and our focus remains on operational integrity and further efficiency improvements to keep ahead of the competition.'

Operational integrity is managed through its innovative programme called Operations Integrity Management System, which is designed to ensure that all activities meet excellent standards. At the core of the company's environmental programmes, OIMS aims to prevent incidents through the effective management of risk. This is a structured and systematic approach to all aspects of safety, health and the environment. Mr Taylor says that Esso has had an environmental policy for 25 years which is dedicated to the long term protection and systematic reduction of pollutants in its products. Safety is a primary concern and a joint initiative with Shell offshore to ensure injury-free operation has achieved record results.

Oil sector companies are in a mature industry which is principally concerned with new exploration opportunities, competitive edge, operational - especially cost - improvements and efficiencies, safety and environmental issues.

Mr Taylor says that oil production has increased progressively for the last four years. A major part of Esso's production comes from the North Sea fields, especially the Brent, which were developed in the 1970s. Crude oil and gas production are at the highest level since 1988 although in 1995 prices are down ten per cent since 1993. The increase in production has been due partly to the coming on stream of new fields. The target in the UK is to improve production from the existing fields, add new fields and enhance cost and operational efficiencies.

'Work is well underway on the £1.3 billion redevelopment of the Brent field. It is one of the largest and longest-serving fields in the North Sea and its redevelopment will extend its life into the 21st century. This is due to be completed in 1998 and will increase production by 37,500 barrels of oil and natural gas liquids per day and 200 million cubic feet of gas per day. We are upgrading all four Brent platforms.'

He says that Esso is committed to spending more than £800bn on three new projects in the North Sea. The Schooner field in the southern North Sea will deliver gas via a third party pipeline system to an electricity power station and other customers. This is a medium-sized field due to come on stream in October 1996, producing 150 million cubic feet of gas a day. Pelican south of the established Shell/Esso Cormorant field will generate 25,000 barrels of oil a day from early in 1996. Esso's third project will produce oil from the Teal, Teal South and Gillemot A fields. Combined reserves are estimated at 90 million barrels of oil and 45 billion cubic feet of gas.

Mr Taylor says that one of the most advanced proposals to reduce costs is the £2 billion Eastern Trough Area Project. This is an integrated development of nine discoveries in the central North Sea which is currently being evaluated by Esso and six other companies.

In its retail activities Esso has met the 1.7 per cent reduction in demand for oil, by extending the range of the goods available in its service stations. Unleaded petrol now accounts for 60 per cent of demand of petroleum based products. The company has boosted interest in its products with its gifts catalogue The Esso Collection.

In 1995 Esso has 950 outlets - of which 600 now serve hot food. The sites are no more like mini-supermarkets rather than petrol stations which reflects the supermarkets' incursion into cheap petrol sales. The transformation of Esso stores was taken a step further when 400 became National Lottery sale points. Esso completed a deal with Rolls Royce to fill all new cars with Esso petrol on their departure from the factory.

Esso needs to invest heavily in long term research and development to prepare for the future. Its research centre in Abingdon is playing a key role in a joint programme backed by the European Commission and the European oil and motor industries. This provides technical input to establish a rational basis for the cost-effective vehicle emission limits in 2000. The company is working actively to extend further its quality management approaches and recently retained is Q1 status with Ford for preferred supplier of lubricants.

The future

Esso has the best return on capital employed in the oil industry. It sets quality standards for the sector and is determined to reduce costs and improve efficiencies. The industry faces short term growth but long term decline. Of all of the world's oil companies Esso stands the best chance of successful diversification.

First Choice

First Choice Holidays, W Sussex

First Choice Holidays is a leading tour operator, providing holidays in 400 resorts

Outlook:
First Choice has made a strategic decision not to buy a retail chain so that it can deal with all retailers. The company is aware of the concerns of buyers of holiday packages and has shaped a business which is accessible and responds to customer need. It is active in the development of technology to define and boost customer choice

Scorecard:
Structural flexibility	★★★★
Innovative power	★★★★
International orientation	★★★★
Human resources	★★★
Growth markets	★★★★★
Quality of management	★★★★

Key figures:
Turnover	£820 million
Pre-tax profits	£16 million
Staff	3,400

First Choice Holidays plc
Crawley
W Sussex RH10 2GX
Tel: 01293 588101
Fax: 01293 588109

First Choice Holidays

First Choice's previous history reads suspiciously like a pulp business soap opera, and has a plot reminiscent of the exploits of JR Ewing. In 1993, when still Owners Abroad, it delivered in short order, first a spirited defence to a hostile take-over bid from Airtours, partly achieved through an unusual 'strategic alliance' with a 'white knight' company who took a supportive stake; then a shock profits warning and the spectacle of erstwhile supportive shareholders doing a _volte face_ and booting out most of the Board.

Behind all this drama was a business which had strayed badly. Yet few people, apparently not even the management, seemed up until the crisis to have noticed the company's lack of focus and inability to respond to fast-changing travel markets. Now, less than two years after the bid and subsequent crisis, the re-organised and re-structured company, re-launched as 'First Choice', is once again a dynamic force in the industry, with a consistently increasing market share.

Operations and markets

First Choice is the UK's third biggest tour operator and provides holidays in 400 different resorts, via 80 airports in over 50 countries. Last year it looked after over 2.5m holidaymakers. Its subsidiaries include Air 2000, a charter airline which carries some four million passengers per annum and which in turnover is the world's 76th biggest airline, number 11 by profitability. Other group companies include ITH, Canada's largest tour operator with sales of over £200m, and Eclipse, the UK's largest direct holiday brand.

Unlike its two largest competitors, Thomson and Airtours, First Choice has not acquired its own retail chain, because it believes that the only way to maximise its retail distribution is in fact to remain non-aligned, which allows it to form good relationships with all retailers, rather than try to compete against its own customers!

Strategy and management

Ironically, the 1993 profit warning and departure of the chief executive and chairman brought in replacements without travel experience who were capable, precisely because of their broad experience of industries other than the holiday industry, of greater objectivity.

When Michael Julien joined in 1993 First Choice had no executive board. He asked Francis Baron to take over as chief executive at the end of 1993, but Baron was initially reluctant to accept as the systems were not in place to assess the commercial health of the business. He slowly changed his view. If the business was a complete mess, it was also inherently stable and appeared to have been ticking over for some months despite the lack of management or leadership. Francis Baron concluded that good management could turn it around.

There were other saving graces. There was net cash of over £100m and a substantial, though rapidly declining, share of the UK tour operating market. The group also owned a well regarded airline and in its alliance with Thomas Cook, had a useful defensive relationship with a travel agency distribution business. (Thomas Cook had taken its 21 per cent stake in Owners Abroad to help ensure adequate access to product, in response to Thomson's and Airtour's own major forays into travel agency ownership.') Existing operations provided scope for considerable economies of scale in a market in which demographic factors pointed to good growth over the next few years.

The first task was to recruit a new executive board. However as the company already employed many good travel industry people Baron was not out to recruit travel entrepreneurs. He wanted people who could run a company. With this in mind he reconstituted the board and senior management with people with the skills to find ways to differentiate in what was historically a quasi-commodity volume-driven sector. Mr Baron wanted innovative skills and ingenuity.

Over the following two years new management rationalised its brands and improved margins by altering its sales mix and price positioning, cutting the cost base and introducing efficiencies. It has deliberately not gone for vertical integration, i.e. acquiring a travel agent, a standard route for other leaders. First Choice's view is that many of the problems for which vertical integration is normally regarded as a partial solution can instead be addressed more fundamentally by effective brand building. Moreover, it believes that maximising trade distribution is vital, and its current strategy of remaining non-aligned has enabled it to form productive working relationships even with the agency chains owned by its major tour operator competitors.

First Choice aims to offer clearly-focused product ranges and to market them under brands which can generate strong consumer loyalty. The start was the name change from Owners Abroad into First Choice. This was an enormous and expensive undertaking. Owners' fundamental weaknesses demanded a complete reconstruction of its brands and their product ranges. Its organisation and delivery systems had to be streamlined. 'We needed to be much lighter on our feet, if we were going to be able to adapt fast enough to counter problems and to innovate to seize opportunities in an increasingly dynamic holiday market', explains Francis Baron.

In the process, the company halved its brochure range and invested in improved design, layout and production. It rationalised its brand and product portfolio into just three focused retail brands, targeted at each of the main clearly-defined market sectors identified by its research. The First Choice brand itself is aimed at the mass-volume family-orientated sector. Sovereign, a long established brand, was retained for the more sophisticated traveller looking for holidays with an emphasis on quality and service. A new brand, Freespirit, was also established to exploit the large and growing market for holidaymakers wishing to travel without children.

The company also changed its name to that of its lead brand to generate increased advertising and publicity leverage from the promotional budget. The name was also adopted as an umbrella brand to endorse its airline, Air 2000, and its direct brand, Eclipse. These changes were radical and some industry pundits felt the company might have been throwing the baby out with the bath water. But, after one year with the new brand line-up, fewer experts are now questioning this bold strategy, after some impressive market share increases for First Choice.

Although traditionally there has been little customer loyalty in the tour operations market, First Choice aims to make it the norm for its own brands. It has used advertising and creative marketing to drive its efforts to build a real consumer franchise. In First Choice's view, one of the keys to brand-building is innovation - to bring real customer benefits and a high 'quality of experience' even to mid-priced holidays. First Choice is the first tour operator to develop the concept of 'all inclusive' holidays for mainstream European resorts, for families, singles or couples. All meals, drinks, ice creams, sweets and watersports are included in the price. The price of these 'incidentals' can otherwise be very high, and the 'all-inclusive' concept enables people to budget for their holiday.

A culture of innovation and fresh thinking is encouraged by an enlightened employee policy. As part of its re-birth, First Choice has moved into newly designed premises providing its head office employees with a high quality working environment, congenial surroundings and good facilities.

The future

As over 90 cent per of distribution in the holiday industry is still via retail agents, only slowly being eroded as other channels near critical mass, it is critical that travel agents are given priority. First Choice has developed its information technology and other delivery systems and launched an upgraded view data system for travel agents which now sets the industry standard. Agents now have the ability to customise the system for their particular requirements and can access the database via precise parameters relating to types of family or location.

First Choice's anecdotal evidence is that agents find its viewdata system, First View, at least as efficient as the market leader, Thomson's, and more useful and user-friendly. However, the company spends considerable amounts each year on a continuing battle with its competitors to improve and upgrade screen-based selling systems for which travel agents have to pay nothing. It has similarly invested in brochure design for the benefit of agents and consumers and has improved clarity of the brochures via better internal page layout and organisation. The company's view is that over time, distribution channels will inevitably change - as they have already done in other industries - with greater opportunities for direct sell methods. Among the most exciting of these, although it is yet a few years off, is the use of inter-active technology by consumers in the home both to research and then book holidays direct, and First Choice's IT investment programme is already gearing up to enable the company to move swiftly in this area when the time is right.

Mr Baron is convinced the package holiday market still contains significant opportunities for growth. Demographic trends support this view, for example the greatest growth in package holidays in the last decade has been among AB socio-economic groups and the 35-54 year age group, which has increased the need to offer variety, new destinations and higher quality as well as the essential value for money.

In business terms, the key feature of the new management team's approach is to question whether the travel industry is really so different to any other industry. In Mr. Baron's view, for example, some structural weaknesses in the tour operations market can only be addressed effectively long-term, through the building of real brands and innovative marketing. "Without this the market is likely to remain as heavily price driven as before, plagued by the need both for heavy late-season discounting by operators and early-season by agents - at a grievous cost to each of them". First Choice are playing for high stakes, but if the company gets it right it will benefit not only First Choice itself but the whole tour operations industry.

GB Mailing Systems, Chester

GB Mailing Systems is a skilled niche market operator supplying software involving the compression of mailing lists and other related systems

Outlook:
GB started with the distinctive objective of achieving professional management as well as high quality products. This approach has paid dividends. GB is now staffed by skilled individuals recruited from world class companies. It is still relatively small in establishment but it commands preferred supplier relationships with hundreds of blue chip names. This is the key to its long term future

Scorecard:
Structural flexibility	★★★★★
Innovative power	★★★★★
International orientation	★★★
Human resources	★★★★★
Growth markets	★★★★★
Quality of management	★★★★

Key figures:
Turnover	£3 million
Profits	n/a
Staff	20

GB Mailing Systems Ltd
Herons Way
Chester Business Park
Chester CH4 9QR
Tel: 01244 683333
Fax: 01244 680808

GB Mailing Systems

The Americans use a term for growth businesses which show all the signs of being future world class companies. These are 'business gazelles'. Quality of management, originality of thought in product development, innovative management initiatives, flexible operating structures and customer-led orientation are all characteristics of the business gazelle.

Even though the term is unfamiliar here, there are numerous examples of companies which develop convincing commercial ideas and prosecute them with energy and commitment. Among the very best of these is GB Mailing Systems. Based in an elegant business park outside Chester overlooking the Welsh hills, GB has created a completely new market sector and fashioned products to service growing demand.

It develops niche market database software products for companies which conduct regular and intensive mailings. Database accuracy - especially lists bought in bulk - is notoriously unreliable. GB's initial product package was built around a software development in postcodes.

The idea for GB Mailing Systems was born in the autumn of 1989. Two men who had never met before - had separately arrived at the same idea for a business - combined to fashion a unique information management enterprise. One was a database manager; the other a technical director. Together they boasted more than 40 years' experience. Today they own one of the fastest growing businesses in the UK, creating markets of unlimited potential and attracting highly experienced employees from blue chip companies such as Digital, Lotus and Shell.

Operations and markets

GB was the concept of Bob Carter, an experienced software engineer, and Paul Chapman, a high level commercial systems manager. But in a move which characterises their pragmatic approach towards business they recognised immediately that their potential business venture needed a professional managing director to add to their own strengths.

Iain Johnston became one of the youngest managing directors of a substantial UK company - and his achievement will shortly be recognised by the Institute of Directors which will make him its youngest fellow. Only 24 at his appointment, he has already developed extensive experience in mergers and acquisitions and in change management consultancy. He saw a business with a unique capacity to devise innovative projects with unlimited market potential.

'We started with no money. But we committed to our products and principles. There is a form of evangelism here. Our people are energetic, enthusiastic and determined. Many of them have high class degrees and years of experience with leading companies, but their most important quality is their belief in GB and their conviction that we will succeed,' says Mr Johnston. Now the company boasts sales of £3 million and a roster of FT-SE 100 clients.

What is so convincing about the business is not so much its products - which are remarkably impressive - but the approach it has adopted to the management of the company. It is textbook good practice: high-quality people, strong belief in their core product and technology, devolved authority, planned growth and serious investment in research and development. In fact, GB balances the quality of thought of the best in industry with all the flexibility of a small business.

Strategy and management

Management is at the heart of the enterprise. The company's directors established guidelines for its people who are then free to achieve in their own way. This is a positive and supportive culture. 'The strategy is do what we are good at and outsource the rest. The production of CD-ROMs which carry our postcoder products, for example, is outsourced,' says Mr Johnston.

'We have established three core principles:
. understanding the real needs of customers
. ensuring that customers make the most of opportunities for significant productivity and customer service gains through the use of information management software
. striving to meet and go beyond customer expectation.'

What is distinctive about GB's approach to database management? Many companies - from banks to mail order businesses to publishers - have large databases of customers. In most cases these databases are substantially out of date - some even up to 90 per cent inaccurate. Using the Royal Mail Post Code Address System, GB's packages allow customers to review their databases for inaccuracies and to correct them.

This offers a tremendous cost advantage for companies, because - apart from having customers who are pleased to have received whatever communication is being sent - companies with accurate address lists can take advantage of the Royal Mail's Mailsort services. These can allow up to 32 per cent savings on mailing charges - provided the mail is properly addressed and presorted. This includes banks sending out statements, utility companies issuing bills, public companies dispatching shareholder information, holiday companies delivering brochures, and pharmaceutical companies sending out medical products to GPs and hospitals. The benefits are clear - a higher degree of accuracy in reaching customers and cost savings from bulk delivery schemes.

These systems were developed in conjunction with the Royal Mail and new products are advanced with joint venture partners such as the largest hardware and software manufacturers. The business has yet to report any substantial profit but this is by design rather than accident. Instead of paying large sums to the Treasury in corporation tax, GB has chosen to reinvest in the business.

So far turnover has grown from £500,000 in 1991-92, through £1 million in 1992-93, £2 million in 1993-94 and £3 million in 1994-95. To date it has tapped only one per cent of its postcode market where gross margins come in at between 75 and 90 per cent of sales. A good business to be in, in spite of the R&D requirement.

There is genuine freedom of opportunity at GB - regardless of age, creed, colour and sex. It also pays well for a small business. As a young culture, GB is highly flexible; most employees are capable of a range of jobs - with the exception of technical requirements. Salespeople, including the founders, take telephone calls or help out with the administration. Everyone is valued.

Since many GB employees have arrived from multinationals they are familiar with which best practice principles can be adapted for the small but fast-growing company environment. Its people policies must be working because the company keeps winning awards - like Granada TV's Flying Start silver award.

The future

GB may be on the threshold of great things with its postcode software but that is only the start. The directors know that they can apply their data compression skills to a wide variety of management information disciplines. GB is widely regarded by some of the leading names in industry and as such is forging joint venture arrangements to develop new product areas.

So far the company has attracted more than 1,000 customers - some as large as TNT, Marks & Spencer, Abbey National, Forte and Glaxo. 'The pleasing aspect about relationships with our customers is that they are so delighted with the products that they recommend them to colleagues,' says Mr Chapman.

Glaxo Wellcome plc

Glaxo Wellcome, London

Glaxo Wellcome is Britain's largest and most respected pharmaceuticals company

Outlook:
The takeover of Wellcome has put Glaxo in an outstanding position to capitalise on the increasing demand for improved and innovative pharmaceuticals. Glaxo has always been a highly esteemed business but in recent years has been looking for a successor to its phenomenal Zantac anti-ulcerant. The test for the future will be whether Glaxo has sufficiently strong management and resources to be a dominant player in world markets

Scorecard:

Structural flexibility	★★★★
Innovative power	★★★★
International orientation	★★★★
Human resources	★★★★★
Growth markets	★★★★★
Quality of management	★★★★★

Key figures:

Turnover	£2.4 billion
Pre-tax profits	£2.7 million
Staff	60,000

Glaxo Wellcome plc
Lansdowne House
Berkeley Square
London W1X 6BQ
Tel: 0171 493 4060
Fax: 0171 408 0228

Glaxo Wellcome

Glaxo's successful £9.4bn bid for Wellcome makes the combined entity, known as Glaxo Wellcome, by far the world's largest pharmaceuticals company. Combined sales of £8.25bn put it at 40 per cent ahead of its nearest rival, Merck. In 1994 the two separate companies made a total pre-tax profit of £2.7bn but a massive cost cutting programme as well as a strong new product pipeline means that this could reach £3.3bn by 1997, according to Peter Laing of Salomon Brothers. This is truly a company of the future.

Operations and markets

The key to the strength of Glaxo Wellcome is an extraordinarily diverse and powerful battery of world beating drugs. Both companies invest heavily in research and development (they spent £1.2bn between them in 1994 according to Stewart Adkins at stockbrokers Lehman Brothers). The current product portfolio is a testament to past investment and commitment to R&D:

1. Glaxo's Zantac. The world's leading ulcer drug last year generated revenues of £2.4bn making it the world's best selling product. The market for ulcer treatments is growing at around 10 per cent a year but Zantac faces stiff competition from Astra's Losec, from treatments which tackle the Helicobacter Pylori bacteria and from very cheap versions of SB's Tagamet, which has now lost patent protection. There is a fear that Zantac itself will start to lose patent protection from 1997 onwards but in probability it will be safe until the year 2002. Given these threats sales of Zantac are unlikely to grow by very much but it will remain the mainstay of G W's portfolio for some time.

2. Wellcome's Zovirax. The world's leading herpes, shingles and chickenpox treatment. In 1994 it generated revenues of £805m. Again there are problems with patents. The loss of protection in most markets over the next few years, culminating in the US in 1997, means rival firms can also produce Zovirax and sell it much more cheaply. The loss of patent normally cuts revenues by between 50 and 80 per cent. But Zovirax will be a useful drug for G W for several years. A successor product, Valtrex, should achieve sales of £320m by the end of the decade but is threatened by a rival SB product, Famvir.

3. Respiratory drugs. Glaxo has long been world leader in this field. In 1994 Glaxo's range of drugs achieved sales of £1.229bn with the asthma treatment Ventolin accounting for two fifths of that. Ventolin and the other anti-asthma compounds treatments Beconase and Becotide are mature drugs, sales of which have now peaked. But Glaxo has recently launched newer respiratory products, such as Serevent, Flixotide and Flixonase, sales of which are already strong and growing rapidly. Peter Laing expects that Glaxo's respiratory revenues will reach £1.79bn by the year 2000.

4. Aids treatments. Wellcome's dominance of the anti-viral market has helped it to establish Retrovir as the world's most effective treatment for Aids. In 1994 its sales were £206m, down slightly on 1993 after the Anglo-French Concorde study cast doubts on its efficacy among those who are HIV positive but were yet to develop full blown Aids. That is yet to be proven one way or the other but for

those with Aids, Retrovir (sometimes in combination with other drugs) remains the best available treatment and its sales are now picking up again. Glaxo's own Aids treatment, 3TC, also looks promising when used in combination - or cocktail - therapy, particularly with Retrovir and is due to be launched in 1996. Within 4 years of its launch sales should reach £450m.

5. Central Nervous System dysfunctions. Both companies showed some expertise in the CNS area. Glaxo's anti-nausea treatment Zofran generated revenues of £404m last year even though it was only launched in late 1990. The record of its migraine treatment Imigran is as impressive. Launched at the end of 1991 its sales reached £243m last year. Together these two products may generate revenues of £950m by 1998. Wellcome also brings something to this particular feast. Its epilepsy treatment Lamictal is viewed as 'genuinely superior' by Peter Laing and though only launched in 1993 it should generate annual revenues of £300m by the end of the decade.

6. Other pharmaceuticals. G W sold more than 30 other significant products last year which generated revenues of £1.849bn in 1994. However, many of those products are mature and income from them isn't expected to increase by much. G W is particularly strong in antibiotics, with products such as Fortum and Zinnat, and in cardiovascular treatment.

7. Over The Counter (OTC) drugs. A joint venture between Wellcome and the the non-prescription (OTC) drug specialists Warner Lambert is expected to generate annual sales of more than US$1.6bn. This global partnership will sell both parties' OTC products and develop and market other consumer health products, including OTC versions of Zovirax.

Strategy and management

Both Glaxo and Wellcome have traditionally fostered a culture based on research - new products are not often bought in. Indeed those products which look like making a low return or which it would be hard for the companies existing specialist sales forces to promote are often sold on to other companies before final trials are complete. As G W fights hard to increase its margins that practice is likely to increase.

The appointment of Sir Richard Sykes as Glaxo's chief executive has heralded a slight change of emphasis. Glaxo has increasingly also been investing directly in small biotech companies. Until recently this has been by funding collaborative ventures. Among its current projects G W is working on diabetes with the US biotech company Amylin and on influenza with Australia's Biota. It is also working with British Biotech on BB-882, an asthma treatment .

But for G W such investments totalling less than £100m since 1990 have been small beer. In January 1995 Sir Richard struck out bravely paying £350m to buy the entire share capital of the US/Dutch biotech Affymax. Glaxo is strong enough to engineer more such deals and with biotech out of fashion it is well placed to pick up novel technology on the cheap.

With its two strategies for drug discovery Glaxo is well placed to continue delivering new products to the market.

The pharmaceutical industry is undergoing a fairly tough time. The rise of bulk buyers and Governmental worries about healthcare costs mean that pricing levels have been under pressure for some time.

As a result many in the industry have already started to slash costs in an attempt to preserve trading margins which typically run at around 30 per cent. Bristol Myers Squibb has already cut its overhead by 14 per cent, Pfizer by 10 per cent and Warner-Lambert by 16 per cent. G W group has scope to reduce its £5.5bn cost base by far more.

The most obvious saving is to reduce staff. At the time of merger G W employed around 60,000 people but there are obvious overlaps in both research and, more especially, in marketing. Extensive consultation is taking place with the workforce but, in what is bound to be a painful process, the headcount could fall by as much as 15,000. Such dramatic cutting has led a former chief executive of Glaxo, Bernard Taylor, to call acquisitions such as this as 'a slash and burn operation'.

However the savings of the rationalisation process will be enormous. Stewart Adkins believes total cost savings could total as much as £1bn.

The future

The effect on G W of cost cutting and new product launches will more than offset the problems caused by patent expiries and general pressures on pricing.

By the turn of the decade brokers expect group profits to reach £3.5bn - a 90 per cent increase on last year's numbers. The issue of paper for Wellcome means that earnings growth will be more modest, a 57 per cent jump from 43p to 68p. Importantly, earnings growth will be accelerating thanks to new product launches as G W enters the 21st century.

The company will remain highly cash generative. Recent acquisitions have left it with significant net debts. But G W should generate £884m of cash in 1995 and £1.26bn in 1996. Even though its dividend growth and increase in R&D spend will surpass the market average, the company should find itself with net cash by the end of the century.

Both companies generated extensive pipelines of products which are due to be launched before the millennium. Most promising are the anti-cancer compounds Panorex and Navelbine and the Aids treatment 3TC. Didier Cowling of stockbrokers James Capel expects seven major product launches before the year 2000.

Glaxo Wellcome is a phenomenally cash generative company with an unmatched portfolio of drugs on the market and drugs under development. It has the financial muscle to maintain and improve that position and a management team imaginative enough to exploit new technologies. Sir Richard says he has 'the clear objective of building the world's leading pharmaceutical company of the future.' He starts from a strong base and few would bet against him.

GRANADA

GRANADA GROUP PLC

Granada Group, London

Granada Group is the largest television franchise and studio operator in the UK. It is active as a programme producer, it is the largest TV/video rental supplier and has major catering businesses

Outlook:
Granada is one of the best managed groups in the UK. It is widely respected as a programme maker, has significant interests in satellite/cable through Sky and is by common consent the leading ITV operator. It invests heavily in distinctive products but it is also adept at financial management

Scorecard:
Structural flexibility	★★★★
Innovative power	★★★★★
International orientation	★★★★
Human resources	★★★★
Growth markets	★★★★★
Quality of management	★★★★★

Key figures:
Turnover	£2097.7 million
Pre-tax profits	£265.4 million
Staff	33,841 - full time
	9,037 part time

Granada Group plc
Stornoway
Cleveland Row
London SC1A 1GG
Tel: 0171 451 3000

Granada Group

The future development of British industry will be dependent - far more than at any stage in the past - on the quality of its management. The pressure from global competitors, whose commercial strength is enhanced by advanced technology and telecommunications, will be relentless. This means that businesses will rely increasingly on the expertise, flexibility and adaptability of their managers. Companies will need to recruit the finest operators who are cautious risk takers, multi-skilled, courageous and alert, and who have the capacity to empower but also to lead.

In short, business in the commercial environment of the next ten years will be increasingly challenging. Few companies have yet reached a level of strategic and operational rigour which will equip them for the demands of the coming decade. Those that have will have found places in this publication. For a case study in how enterprises should be organised to anticipate the direction of future commercial trends, the reader should look no further than the Granada Group. This is one of Britain's best-managed businesses. Under CEO Gerry Robinson, the group has established a distinctive business philosophy which will be a model for UK companies eager to be world class.

A commitment to excellence in every area of the business is the hallmark of the Granada approach. Managers in the group are encouraged to seek innovative and rewarding strategies to extend customer service within a framework of tight control on costs and deep appreciation of the importance of cash - and cashflows - in the business. Targets are ambitious but based on sound knowledge of markets and the potential for particular products and services. Mr Robinson argues for extensive empowerment of talented and able managers but the scope of individuals will naturally depend on their capacities, experience and proven results.

He has assembled in the group a team of motivated, flexible but accountable executives who will be expected to perform. He gives considerable managerial freedom but he also expects officers to deliver.

Operations and markets

Granada has come a long way from its origins in the cinema business and in television as the ITV franchise holder for the north in the 1950s. It made itself a name for entrepreneurship, commanding television journalism and as a hothouse for the television talent of the future. Today, it has lost none of its zeal but has broadened out into a group which includes television interests, catering and other leisure activities.

Mr Robinson has created a group which includes:
. television broadcasting
. television production/programme making
. television programme sales
. television, video and multimedia rental
. motorway restaurants
. contract catering and other services businesses
. leisure operations.

In each of its markets, the group's interests are significant operators - if not leaders - and in every case the return on investment and capital employed is the best in the sector. Mr Robinson believes in excellent service to customers. He has a single watchword which embraces his approach to business - passion. This encapsulates Granada's determination to be the best in whatever it does.

It means that Granada managers are set demanding targets by the group, that they enjoy remarkable freedom to run their own businesses within the group strategic framework, that they should create innovative techniques for improved customer service and that they should believe - passionately - in their business. Customers and cashflow are king in the business methodology. Mr Robinson argues that the demands and potential demands of the customer are the driving force for group activities. 'We strive to be excellent in every area in which we operate. In television this means providing services with strong links to our communities and creating highly professional programmes which will appeal to the majority of our viewers. In our rental division, delivering unparalleled service and the finest selection of hardware. In motorway service, locating ways to enhance the quality of our outlets, which are already the best in the sector.'

In 1994 sales reached £2.1 billion - a 30 per cent increase on 1993. Pre-tax profit was up 51 per cent to £265.4 million. Earnings per share rose around 30 per cent and gearing was down to 58 per cent. Although all areas in the company increased their performance, television is now the largest single division. Its key components are:

- . Granada Television (north west ITV franchisee)
- . London Weekend Television (London Weekend ITV)
- . The London Studios
- . Granada's Manchester studios
- . Laser which sells TV airtime for LWT and the northern region (GTV, Yorkshire, Tyne Tees and Border)
- . Sky Television (where Granada has a 10.8 per cent holding)
- . GMTV - 20 per cent
- . Yorkshire Television - 14 per cent
- . London News Network - 50 per cent
- . ITN - 36 per cent

Its activities in this sector include the top-rated television programme in Britain - Coronation Street, the most widely used television production studios in the UK - The London Studios (70 per cent booked by external producers, 30 per cent by LWT and Granada), major contributions to the ITV network through programme production (especially drama, current affairs, documentary and light entertainment) and airtime sales for almost 50 per cent of ITV homes, adult viewers and ABC1 adults.

Strategy and management

Television's chief executive Charles Allen is clear that the future for ITV will be in making high quality programmes. In Granada and LWT, the group owns the two most creative programme-makers in the network. 'I explained to executives at LWT when we took over that cost control was not penny-pinching but ensuring that they achieved best value for their budgets. I believe fully in making excellent programmes. We have a considerable history at Granada of making superb programming and we have been prepared to invest in highly innovative series. But

I want producers to spend money on programme production rather than waste resources. Getting value for money is a stimulus to creative activity not a barrier.'

When he took over at Television he selected those executives he wanted to run the station and then completely changed their responsibilities. 'If someone is in charge of production and someone else runs television programming they tend to get entrenched. Talented executives should be able to handle any managerial role so I determined to switch individuals around to allow them to see the tasks ahead from different perspectives.'

Steve Morrison is managing director of LWT. He is firmly convinced that the commitment to programme-making is absolutely necessary. 'ITV is Britain's most popular television station. In years to come there may be hundreds of channels available through satellite and cable. To retain our distinctive identity - to remain attractive to our viewers - we must generate and initiate quality programmes. This is not only editorially desirable, it is the only sensible course of action financially. As a producer, this company determines the objectives of any particular programme project, it can share the production costs with co-funders and it benefits from the subsequent sales of the programme to other world markets. The number of television stations around the world is growing rapidly so the appetite for high quality programmes will increase.'

Before the takeover of LWT, rental was Granada's biggest division. But this business has not been slow to exploit the changing technological environment to give it market advantage. It remains the UK's most profitable television and video rental business. Granada, which absorbed Visionhire by 1990, is currently achieving more than 50 per cent of the new rental market. 'We have fewer shops than Radio Rentals but ours are considerably more profitable,' says divisional chief executive Graham Wallace. Former group finance director Mr Wallace is a firm advocate of effective cash management in the business and this business is a major cash generator for the group.

Human resources director Stephanie Monk assesses the effectiveness of structures and appointments, identifies critical success factors and ensures that the HR dimensions of business plans are sound and well constructed.

She says that the Granada culture can be summarised as:
. aiming for high levels of quality and service
. stressing teamwork and the ability of each individual to add value
. open - with little emphasis on status or bureaucracy
. tolerant of unconventional people and solutions
. encouraging creative approaches
. growth and results orientated but with a high element of fun
. welcoming change as an opportunity providing challenges and environment for people to take initiative and responsibility at all levels

The future

Granada stands on the threshold of an exciting future. This is an outstanding business which will lead the UK television, rental and catering businesses in the next decade. It helps that its competition commands few of the intrinsic strengths of Granada; but the management drive, commitment to customer service, integrity, clear and straightforward financial management, people empowerment policies, innovative approach and passion of the group lie at the core of its success.

The Greenalls Group

The Greenalls Group plc, Warrington

This leisure group operates managed and tenanted pubs, branded pub restaurants and lodges, quality hotels, off-licences and wholesaling businesses

Outlook:
In a changing brewing industry Greenalls has had the foresight and courage to make an early move to the areas where the profitability will lie - pub retailing and hospitality. Catering for all market segments with its different outlets and with a fresh professional management style, the Greenalls group is well positioned for a decade of growth ahead

Scorecard:

Structural flexibility	★★★
Innovative power	★★★
International orientation	★★★★
Human resources	★★★★
Growth markets	★★★★
Quality of management	★★★

Key figures:

UK turnover	£720 million
Pre-tax profits	£88 million
UK staff	21,418

The Greenalls Group plc
Wilderspool House
Greenalls Avenue
Warrington WA4 6RH
Tel: 01925 651234
Fax: 01925 413137

Greenalls

It appears that the future of the brewing industry lies in moving away from its roots. Michelle Proud and Graeme Eadie, of NatWest Securities in Edinburgh, say that the Office of Fair Trading's investigation into wholesale beer prices will encourage the changing trends in brewing. 'Even if it takes no action, the trends are now inexorable. Value has been transferred from the brewing side to the retailing side. Pub retailing has good growth prospects as consumers spend more eating out while modern retailers which have invested a lot in their outlets will also progressively gain share.'

Analysts maintain that those operators which are out of brewing, and into retailing, and which have set clear strategic objectives and invest heavily in their outlets are the ones that will be forces in the next decade. At present there are four majors: Bass (market capitalisation £8 billion), Allied Domecq (£7 billion), Scottish & Newcastle (£2.7 billion) and Whitbread (also £2.7 billion). Greenalls, which with greater critical mass could be among the leaders (£1 billion), and five regionals (Boddingtons, £0.5 billion, Wolverhampton & Dudley, £0.3 billion, Vaux, £0.3 billion, Marstons, £0.3 billion and Greene King £0.3 billion) complete the catalogue of main operators. Whitbread is warmly regarded in the City because of its accomplishments in retail but questions remain over its brewing activity. S&N may come forward as market leader, since it appears to have executed the best deals in the last decade. Bass is viewed with considerable disfavour since it boosted its brewing over its retailing and has previously set a higher margin on brewing - which it is likely to lose in the short term.

The future is not much rosier for the regionals. Increasing customer service demands and the expense of running vertically-integrated operations in current and future markets could force mergers between the principal regionals or absorption by one of the majors. The shining star of the sector is Greenalls. The Warrington-based operator set its strategic review in place in 1986 and has since moved out of brewing, concentrating on pub retailing, hotels and office licences.

Operations and markets

The management team showed considerable integrity and commercial courage by departing from what was the core business - having identified that retailing would be the future. This was especially tough in a sector where the heart often rules the head. Greenalls recognised that investment would be a major success factor and now invests more, proportionately, than any of its competitors in capital expenditure. As a percentage of retail assets, the Greenalls spend is more than nine per cent which is significantly higher than its nearest rival and almost twice that of the leading forces in the industry.

The composition of the group is concentrated in five areas:
. Pubs (1,923 outlets of which 42 per cent managed by the retail department and two-thirds tenanted through Inn Partnership)
. Restaurants and lodges (131 outlets managed by Premier House, including Millers Kitchen, Hudsons, Quincey's, Henry's Café Bar and Premier Lodge)

- Hotels (Greenalls concentrates on four and five star hotels including 21 De Vere Hotels and six US hotels)
- Off-licences (Greenalls Cellars operates 473 outlets including Wine Cellar, Berkeley Wines and Cellar 5. In addition Greenalls Food Store which stocks drinks as well as groceries and Night Vision, a video shop)
- Wholesaling. (In 1995 this division runs 24 depots, serving the free trade in England and Wales)

Strategy and management

NatWest Securities argues that Greenalls, more than any other company in the brewing sector, has found the key criteria for success. 'Investment and concepts (theme pubs) are the two most important keys to profitability in managed pub retailing, along with brand freedom in the pubs, which may have been a factor in the striking performance in average profit per pub which Greenalls achieved in 1990-92.' In this period, Greenalls achieved an average return on sales per pub of 27 per cent. 'There is no question that Greenalls has benefited enormously - in profit terms - from pulling out of brewing and concentrating on retailing.' The overall profit figures for 1994 are also nothing to be ashamed about. A 30 per cent growth in pre-tax profits to £88.2 million which represents 12.3 per cent return on sales of £720 million, itself up by 23 per cent on 1993. Capital investment in the business represented around 15 per cent of turnover.

Former Sunday Express City editor Christ Blackhurst is impressed by the Greenalls achievement. Writing in the April 1995 edition of Management Today, he remarked: 'A head of steam is growing for a major restructuring, for the industry to finally rid itself of the dross, to end the problems of oversupply of pubs and overproduction of beer. That, though, would require tough decision-making - which, traditionally, has not been the industry's strong point.

'One company which took such a step - and never looked back - is Greenalls. In 1990 Andrew Thomas and Peter Greenall, now managing director, ditched 230 years of history and stopped brewing to concentrate on running pubs. Five years later the courage of Mr Thomas and Mr Greenall is fully vindicated. From a large, regional brewer with a strong brand and 1,500 mediocre pubs in the north west, caught in a no-man's land between local and major player, Greenalls has become a focused, national group. While the brewers it left behind saw their profits remain flat, Greenalls rose by 30 per cent. The group is on course to break the £100 million barrier and, with one or two further acquisitions, to become Britain's first national beer retailer.'

Mr Thomas told the journalist that by quitting brewing, the flexibility of price and range is increased. More importantly, a psychological barrier was crossed - Greenalls' own Rubicon. By concentrating purely on customer demand, the company was able to offer an outstandingly improved and diversified service. As sales of beer have declined, food has become increasingly important and management is focused on providing excellent service to customers, rather than principally selling beer. The emotional bond with product is much stronger in brewing than in many other sectors and some of the other key operators may not be able to abandon their ancestry for modern commercial realities.

Greenalls, perhaps, had more reason than most to hang on to its heritage. Manufacturing has taken place at its Warrington site since Roman times and Greenalls established a brewery in Wildespool at the end of the 18th century which was still largely in family control into this century. In 1986 Greenalls faced up to the future. The management team took a series of steps which radically transmuted the business: it abandoned brewing; the family shareholding was rationalised and simplified to give equal representation to external shareholders; greater professionalism was introduced into the management of the business - recruits from other leading companies were drawn into the company; non-core aspects of the business were sold - Greenalls pulled out of areas such as Vladivar Vodka, brand ownership, bingo, international activities and soft drinks manufacturing.

The future

The pattern of development for Greenalls is by no means assured. However, it is a business which has been sufficiently pragmatic to jettison its emotional baggage and focus on the realities of a profitable future. Further acquisitions need to be made if Greenalls is to reach the top table. Mr Thomas says that there are gaps in its national coverage which need to be filled.

There is a greater business logic about the group as it is presently constructed. The pubs, restaurants and hotels, even the off-licences are retail operations. There is a natural symmetry about the arrangement. Management understands the necessity of sticking to core better than any other brewing business - and it has had the fortune to be initiator of a new phase in the development of the sector. As long as Greenalls retains its strategic vision, its flexibility of operation, its remarkable degree of innovation in a conservative sector, its powerful concentration on profitability and excellent return on capital employed, and its instinctive appreciation of the importance of brand leadership and market segmentation then the future for Greenalls will be better than its shareholders dare hope.

GUINNESS PLC

Guinness, London

Guinness is one of the world's most famous distilling and brewing companies, partly for its renowned Irish stout but also for its range of spirits

Outlook:
The worldwide drinks industry is one of the most competitive sectors. Brand leadership is a key factor and Guinness is a global force in both the spirits and stout divisions. The company's quality of management is also high in an industry where professionalism is not outstanding. Therefore this business is well positioned to be a keynote player

Scorecard:

Structural flexibility	★★★★
Innovative power	★★★★
International orientation	★★★★★
Human resources	★★★★
Growth markets	★★★★
Quality of management	★★★★

Key figures 1994:

Turnover	£4.7 billion
Pre-tax profits	£915 million
Staff	23,000

Guinness plc
39 Portman Square
London W1H 0EE.
Tel: 0171 486 0288
Fax: 0171 486 4968

Guinness

Guinness is quite simply the most outstanding collection of beer and spirits brands in the world. From Johnnie Walker whisky and Gordons Gin through to the group's eponymous Irish stout, most adults in the Western world and increasingly in emerging markets have drunk something brewed up by Guinness.

Spirits generally is one of the few industries apart from pharmaceuticals, where Britain has a number of world leading players, a fact that is largely due to the strength of the Scotch whisky industry. Guinness, with United Distillers, Grand Metropolitan, through its International Vintners & Distillers subsidiary, and Allied Domecq, formerly known as Allied-Lyons, make up three of the four top international spirits companies, along with Canada's Seagram.

Of the three British groups, Guinness is the largest and most profitable. The company is now one of the 15 biggest quoted on the British stockmarket, with a market capitalisation of around £9 billion and reported pre-tax profits of £915m for 1994.

Operations and markets

Guinness dominates the Scotch whisky industry. Last year the House of Walker shipped over 10m cases worldwide, making Johnnie Walker Red Label (more than 7m cases) along with the premium priced Johnnie Walker Black Label, the number one whisky brand in the world. Dewar's is the top seller in the United States and Bell's is number one in Britain, with White Horse the market leader in Japan.

In the single malt category, Guinness has a range of rapidly growing Classic Malts which have established themselves as brand leaders in three terminals at Heathrow airport. Duty free sales are also an important component of the group's leading gin brands: Gordon's and Tanqueray, which between them shipped 7m cases in 1994.

Overall, United Distillers accounted for 73 per cent of group operating profits last year and within that, analysts estimate that the leading whisky brands make up 70 per cent and gin much of the remaining 30 per cent.

The Classic Malts are one example of how Guinness has added a range of super premium priced whiskies on top of its more standard range of blends, with the result that their volumes rose 38 per cent last year when total Scotch volumes were flat. The repositioning of Bell's is another. Due to recession and fierce competition, Guinness took the unprecedented step in the run up to Christmas 1993 of cutting the price of a bottle of Bell's from around £11.50 to below £10, sparking a price war on the British high street and drawing criticism from the City at the time. The decision helped to improve volumes, but eventually Guinness relaunched Bell's as an eight year old blend at the previous price. Meanwhile, White Horse has been positioned as the cheaper brand.

Strategy and management

One of Guinness' strengths is the clarity of its strategic focus. There are only two divisions: United Distillers for spirits and Guinness Brewing Worldwide, both run by their own management teams, and organised on a matrix of geographical regions and worldwide brand management. There is a small head office based in London which oversees strategy, imposes financial targets and deals with corporate finance issues such as acquisitions and disposals.

Since early 1994, Guinness also has a 34 per cent stake in Moet Hennessy, the French champagne and cognac producer, which it received in return for selling its holding in LVMH, the huge luxury goods group that is Moet Hennessy's parent.

The prime focus for Guinness is to concentrate on organic growth in premium international alcoholic drinks, a market which is still showing overall growth every year. Add-on acquisitions, like the 1991 purchase of Spanish brewer Cruzcampo, are possible from time to time.

Management attempts to balance the rejuvenation of brands in the mature Western markets of America, Britain and Europe, with the building of brands and volumes in emerging markets in Latin America and Asia Pacific. To help enter new markets, the group is conscious that its efforts must embrace a broad range of price points and not just the premium end, though it will obviously attempt to move consumers upmarket as rapidly as possible.

Coupled with that, Guinness pays close attention to its cost base in spirits and, in particular, brewing, though it has recognised the need for ever greater marketing and promotional spend, especially in the developed world.

Talking at the announcement of the 1994 results, chairman Tony Greener summed up the group's strategy going forward: 'Price competition and promotional activity at the expense of long-term franchise building have been characteristics of our industry during the recession. As consumer confidence returns, we are determined to concentrate on the development of our brands to enable us to achieve pricing levels which reflect the strength of their franchise with the consumer.

'In the last two years we have made very substantial progress in equipping the company to meet the challenge of the increasingly competitive market place we expect during the balance of this decade. In the short term we have substantially reduced our cost base, flattened our organisation structures and we now have high calibre management teams in United Distillers and Guinness Brewing Worldwide and at the centre.'

Brand management is equally important on the brewing side, where Guinness stout is now sold in over 140 countries and brewed in 46, including Russia and Vietnam. Its popularity has been reinforced by extensive marketing, with modern-looking advertising which replaced the outdated Toucan with a bizarre range of surreal, stylistic, award winning advertisements, that highlight the intrinsic product qualities appealing to younger drinkers.

The fact that a 20 per cent rise in marketing spend was required to boost stout volumes by one per cent is indicative of the pricing pressure currently being experienced by management and explains the emphasis on productivity improvements and cost cutting. It was only through the latter that margins were slightly improved to 13 per cent, though that is still far better than the margins of 6 per cent to 8 per cent achieved by most of the domestic British brewers like Bass or Whitbread. Margins at United Distillers are far superior at

26 per cent, though again it has been cost reductions and higher volumes rather than price increases which have maintained them at such a level.

For a company that grew from the success of an obscure Irish stout, Guinness today has a remarkably diverse geographical profile. While the bulk of its production facilities are still in Britain and especially Scotland, it is a very different picture as far as sales are concerned. Last year a fifth of total turnover of £4.7 billion came from the United Kingdom, 16 per cent originated in the rest of Europe, 17 per cent in North America, 16 per cent came from Asia Pacific and the remaining 12 per cent from the rest of the world, principally South America.

It is the last segment where Guinness scores over the competition. While sales declined by one per cent in Britain during 1994 and by 5 per cent in the United States, they rose by 43 per cent overall in emerging markets like Mexico, Brazil, Columbia and Uruguay. In Asia, excluding the Japanese market which is still depressed, Guinness made rapid advances in Thailand, Taiwan and even China. It has just set up a Korean joint venture with Moet Hennessy and relaunched Johnnie Walker Red Label in that country.

Despite the investment needed in marketing and distribution, the relative lack of competition in emerging markets gives a fairly free hand with pricing and makes them highly profitable in a short space of time. Margins in the rest of the world at over 30 per cent are three times the level achieved back home, although that is partly due to the greater proportion of lower margin beer sales in Britain.

Trading in the developing world also brings risks with it: last year Guinness lost £30m worth of profits in Venezuela due to rampant inflation and political crisis and along with Allied Domecq it will suffer from the devaluation of the Mexican peso during 1995. Even so, however, these are undoubtedly the growth markets of the future, while the more mature areas like Britain and America will be used to develop new products and to hone production efficiencies.

The future

Guinness could not compete if it did not have the enormous size and strength needed to trade across 140 countries, fund huge investment and marketing and take the occasional hit on the chin. But as one of Britain's largest companies, with net assets of £4 billion, it can outgun most rivals. Following the £400m received from the sale of its shareholding in LVMH, net borrowings are currently down to £1.4 billion, giving gearing of 35 per cent. Stockbroking analysts point to the group's strong cash flow, which amounted to £460m before dividend payments last year, a new record. Dividends to shareholders were raised by 8 per cent for 1994 and analysts at NatWest Securities forecast ongoing growth of 10 per cent a year for the forseeable future. Pre-tax profits are expected to increase to £989m in 1995, £1,095m in 1996 and to reach £1,216m by 1997. With a robust balance sheet and a lower ongoing cost base, Guinness looks well positioned for the future.

G W R group plc

GWR, Wiltshire

GWR Group is the fastest growing group of commercial radio stations in the UK

Outlook:
Commercial radio is the fastest growing area of the media. Its share of national advertising revenues has doubled in the 1990s and is expected to grow even further. Key to capitalising on this trend has been the consolidation into major groups to share costs and resources, and the greater operational freedom allowed by the regulator

Scorecard:

Structural flexibility	★★★★
Innovative power	★★★★
International orientation	★★★
Human resources	★★★
Growth markets	★★★★
Quality of management	★★★★

Key figures:

Turnover	£32 million
Pre-tax profits	£5.3 million
Staff	675

GWR Group
Westlea, Swindon
Wiltshire SN5 7HF
Tel: 01793 422700
Fax: 01793 422772

GWR Group

At the end of May 1995, the Secretary of State for National Heritage Stephen Dorrell announced a series of proposals which will revolutionise the face of the UK media industy. Few observers anticipate that they will be adopted wholesale by Parliament but as opening shots they give a pretty fair indication of the direction of government thinking. For Britain's recently fashionable commercial radio industry, they canonise a set of trends which are transforming the sector from a fragmented collection of local operators into a cohesive and professional industry.

At the heart of the industry's recent growth is the generic promotion of the idea of radio as an advertising medium. Through the establishment of substantial radio industry groups, the sector was able to achieve such co-ordination as to convince advertisers that it is a viable and effective commercial medium. The dramatic rise of radio's claim on the UK advertising budget has enabled the industry to escape the derisive epithet of 'the two per cent medium' and secure, for the first time ever, around four per cent. Analysts anticipate commercial radio reaching six per cent by the year 2000 - and some even talk about seven or eight per cent in ten years.

Not surprisingly, the most professional and cohesive companies are the ones in the best position to capitalise on the opportunities presented by these changes. Chief among these are GWR, Capital, EMAP and Scottish Radio, and GWR is certainly ready for the challenges that lie ahead. One of the key suggestions put forward by Mr Dorrell was to lift the ownership restrictions on operating radio stations for one company, from 20 to 35. Within hours of the announcement GWR bid for Chiltern Radio Network and industry watchers say that it has its sights on East Anglian Radio. This combination would give the Wiltshire-based company a swathe of stations from Bristol across the Thames Valley and up through East Anglia to Nottingham.

Operations and markets

GWR is at the forefront of many of the decisive factors in the changing role of radio. It is the UK's second largest commercial radio group operating 20 franchises in the South West, Thames Valley, East Midlands, West Midlands and East Anglia. The company is based in Swindon where its original franchise for Wiltshire Radio - now GWR FM Wiltshire and Brunel Classic Gold 1161 - was awarded.

The group also owns 17 per cent of Classic FM, the national popular classical music station, and has significant minority holdings in radio companies as far apart as Salisbury and Harrogate. As the company waited for more franchises to become available in the UK, it broadened its operations overseas. GWR has 48 per cent of Radio FM Plus in Sofia, Bulgaria and in Poland it has formed a consortium with BBC World Service and four Polish media companies to establish Inforadio (GWR holds 33 per cent).

Group turnover in 1994 reached £21.7 million - a rise of 122 per cent on 1993. Pre-tax profits rose rapidly over the same period - £3.1 million which was an increase of 241 per cent. Virtually all of the profits are generated in the UK because the overseas investment, although promising, has yet to produce substantial earnings.

In the UK the group is divided into three divisions - south, midlands and east:

South: GWR FM licences in Bristol and Swindon, the AM licences for those two areas which operate as Brunel Classic Gold, 2-Ten FM and Classic Gold 1431 in Reading, 2CR FM and Classic Gold 828 in Bournemouth and Isle of Wight Radio.

Midlands: Trent FM in Nottingham, RAM FM in Derby and Leicester Sound FM. The AM licences for these cities combine to operate the regional oldies service GEM AM. Mercia FM and Classic Gold 1359 serve Coventry and Beacon and Radio WABC the Black Country.

East :   Hereward FM in Peterborough, Q103 in Cambridge and KL-FM in King's Lynn. The Hereward AM frequency carries The World's Greatest Music Station.

Strategy and management

GWR's strategic approach to its market can be summarised as follows:
. growth by acquisition, building audiences on existing franchises, and applying for new licences. The company believes in taking underperforming businesses and using its management-expertise and economies of scale to bring them into profitability
. continuous audience research for audience development on existing licences and for identifying future business opportunities
. benefiting from the economies provided by new technologies and economies of scale, providing advertisers with a wide geographical target audience
. strong generic marketing for commercial radio

The immediate game plan at GWR is to buy the Chiltern Radio Network which is based in Dunstable and operates nine licences. GWR CEO Ralph Bernard told Broadcast 'Chiltern has consistently underperformed the sector. We believe that we could substantially improve on its potential.'

The headroom of a further seven licences GWR could operate explains why the industry press is forecasting that after a successful completion of its hostile bid for CRN, GWR is considering a move on East Anglian Radio. This includes Radio Broadland based in Norwich and SGR located in Ipswich with licences in Bury St Edmunds and Colchester. There is a compelling geographical logic about the GWR strategy. It would command virtually every licence from Bristol to London, up to Wolverhampton and across to East Anglia. There are certain notable exceptions in this scheme - Capital's stations in Birmingham, Fox in Oxford - but effectively GWR's dominance in the west, middle and east of England would be complete.

Today the Radio Authority has some appreciation of the commercial realities of running such companies. Mr Bernard says that the extent of change which the industry has experienced since 1980 will be replicated in the coming decade. In 1983 when Wiltshire Radio wanted to change any aspect of its programme format, however minute, it needed to ask the permission of the regulator. Mergers between licence holders were looked on with deep mistrust and WR's takeover of the ailing Bristol contractor Radio West was the first which was allowed. The provision of separate services on AM and FM was pioneered by GWR but it is only since the late 1980s that the regulator has been enthusiastic about this development.

GWR has a distinctive approach to commercial radio which provides some insight to how this business may develop. The company is not unlike Stagecoach in that it seeks acquisitions which are underperforming and it injects its unique brand of management expertise. 'GWR places greater emphasis on research than almost any other group,' says one senior industry practitioner. 'Typically it uses listener panels to comment on records used on the playlists of individual stations. For example, GWR-FM in Bristol will operate a panel of 500 listeners who will be asked to say which records they like and those they do not. The results of the panel will directly influence the number of plays which a song will get. '

Mr Bernard says that the use of research has helped to boost listening hours of his stations. 'Our research results showed that only ten per cent of our audience liked rap and that they thought that the presenters talked too much. So we revised the format along the principle of No Rap - Less Chat and that continues to win us audience.' His great research success story is Classic FM. He says that despite all the detractors, the conviction at GWR that a popular classical music station would work has been vindicated. 'We researched the idea heavily before we won the franchise and we repeated the exercise after the award. The station now has 4.5 million listeners. More importantly, we delivered ABC1 listeners, which the advertising industry did not think possible.'

So research will be a key element in the GWR philosophy in years to come - both for existing licences and new stations. At present it runs no big city stations but is keen to apply for a business-news licence in London. Mr Bernard thinks that this may become possible when digital audio frequencies become available. On the programming front, greater coherence will emerge especially on the AM stations. The Classic Gold format - and also on GEM in the East Midlands and Supergold if the CRN bid works - is enjoying the benefits of economies of scale. More and more programmes will be networked on AM which will give the group the opportunity to access some well known broadcasters. Technology advances will also enable presenters to localise common programming while transmitting live to, say, ten different licence areas.

The future

The radio industry is entering another period of radical change. Technology, programming, number and variety of licences, lighter regulation and extent of commercial opportunity will all play their part in the reconfiguring of the sector. Consolidation of key operators will continue apace as will the industry's emancipation as an advertising medium. The two in fact are interrelated. As the bigger groups offer larger and more reliable audiences, so the share of advertising increases. More income - with little increase in costs - means a more profitable and attractive industry.

GWR is well placed to exploit many of the trends which are gathering pace. The greater freedom of operation extended by the regulator will allow the group to add licences to its tally. Wherever it has accumulated franchises previously it has developed them and brought greater value to operating companies. The company is skilled in applying the lessons learned in the original franchises in Swindon and Bristol to other locations. Good market research is central to its market understanding, as well as its capacity to cut costs and put in resources where necessary.

Hanson

Hanson PLC, London

Hanson PLC is one of the UK's and America's largest businesses. It is a diversified industrial management company concentrating in the main on basic industries such as building materials, chemicals, propane and tobacco

Outlook:
This is a tightly managed enterprise which has grown rapidly since its launch. Hanson's corporate finance and research functions are legendary. The greatest challenge for the company will be its capacity to install equally successful leadership as a new generation of management takes the helm

Scorecard:
Structural flexibility	★★★★
Innovative power	★★★★
International orientation	★★★★★
Human resources	★★★
Growth markets	★★★★
Quality of management	★★★★★

Key figures:
Worldwide turnover	£11 billion
Pre-tax profits	£ 1.3 billion
Global staff	60,000

Hanson PLC
1 Grosvenor Place
London SW1X 7JN
Tel: 0171 245 1245
Fax: 0171 235 3455

Hanson plc

Certain management theories argue that conglomerates of the 1980s model are a phenomenon of the past. One of today's central tenets of management philosophy is a return to core; a concept which is apparently at odds with the fundamental platform of diversified holding companies.

A certain interpretation of core would rule out diversified conglomerates on principle as wasteful of management and resources and ultimately unsuccessful. But this analysis fails to take account of several notable and substantial successes, perhaps based on another interpretation of core theory. These successes are businesses that stick to what they do very well: buying and selling other businesses.

The most famous example of a conglomerate in the UK is Hanson. The extent of this group's capacity to pick winners is demonstrated in the fact that in 1995 its market value was £12 billion. The group is among the top ten companies in the UK, top 20 in Europe and top 60 in the US. It owns major businesses throughout the world, especially in the extractive and primary manufacturing sectors. The group is a dominant force in many industrial markets and operates a host of brand names.

Operations and markets

Hanson is truly a global player. It owns major businesses throughout the world, especially in extractive and primary manufacturing sectors with a focus in chemicals, coal, building materials, cranes, tobacco, forest products and propane.

In the year ending September 1994, Hanson reported pre-tax profits of more than £1.3bn on sales exceeding £11bn. Those are impressive figures and a world away from the company's origins as a small Yorkshire-based company called Wiles Group engaged in the manufacture of agricultural fertiliser and leasing of grain sacks. Wiles floated on the London stock exchange in 1964 and was valued then at slightly over £300,000. In 1995 Hanson is valued at around £12bn and is an international business with US subsidiaries accounting for half of last year's profit.

But such statistics do not indicate how Hanson became such a large company - or how its management philosophy is quite different to that of most large UK businesses.

Hanson grew to its present size by making no less than 210 deals over three decades and principally involving the acquisition of business and part disposals. The most important of the UK takeovers were the purchase of London Brick for £245m in 1984, followed by the hotly contested acquisition of Imperial Tobacco in 1986 for £2.5bn. That latter deal led to a number of disposals including Golden Wonder crisps for £87m later that year followed by Ross Young's frozen and chilled food businesses for £335m in 1988. The following year saw the purchase of Golden Fields and a similar dismemberment of several of its overseas interests.

Strategy and management

Perhaps the best way to define Hanson's takeover strategy is to heed the recent words of the company's chairman, Lord Hanson.

He said: 'We are not predators, we go into the game park and get the wounded animal with the tranquilliser, put it right and then set it free again.' So while increasing earnings per share and dividends through profitable internal growth is mentioned first in its management philosophy statement, the key to growth at Hanson has been selective acquisitions and very close control of cash flow.

To understand how Hanson has grown so fast and why it can adopt an extreme form of decentralised management, it is important to remember also that Hanson only invests in businesses which, vice-chairman Martin Taylor says, have 'forecastable earnings'. In other words returns in terms of profitability should be predictable and actual results measured against expectations. In this way action can be taken quickly if the performance of a particular subsidiary appears to be deteriorating.

So, not suprisingly perhaps, the vast majority of Hanson's businesses are in basic industries and in a position where they often dominate that industry too. These two factors make that essential forecasting much easier.

Hanson is, for example, the second largest manufacturer of cigarettes in the UK through Imperial Tobacco and has slightly more than a third of the market. It also controls around a third of the UK brick market through London Brick and Butterly Brick and is the market leader in providing building aggregates through ARC. Not all subsidiaries are in basic industries but most dominate their markets. So, for example, Hanson's Seven Seas subsidiary is the UK market leader in supplying cod liver oil, vitamins and other dietary supplements.

But while Hanson's growth in the UK has been impressive, it has been extraordinary in the US. Since making its first acquisition there in 1974, Hanson has become one of the largest British companies in the US. According to Fortune Magazine, Hanson Industries is now one of the top 60 companies in North America and, as here, dominates certain sectors.

Through Peabody it is the largest US coal producer with 1994 sales of 92 million tonnes from 24 coal mining complexes in nine states. In 1993 it became the largest US manufacturer of polyethylene and other industrial chemicals when it bought Quantum Chemical for approximately $800m in shares and took on $2.6bn of debt. Following what US chairman the late Lord White called 'a comprehensive restructuring programme' which split the business into two, Quantum has been turning in spectacular results. The split of Quantum has also left Hanson owning a company called Propane - the second largest retailer of propane gas for residential, commercial and industrial users. It serves one million customers in 45 states.

Hanson's other major US businesses include Cavenham Forest Industries which operates over 1.75m acres of forest in the Pacific northwest and the southeast. Not many basic industries produce renewable products but Cavenham does: annual new growth of timber exceeds harvesting by a third. Through Beazer US, Hanson also owns the second largest producer in the US of sand and gravel, crushed stone and hot mix asphalt. It sold off Beazer's US and UK housebuilding businesses in the fortunate year of 1989.

Of course not all businesses perform well or badly at the same time. So investing in a group which has interests in different industries can make the overall profit record less volatile. That in turn is a major attraction to investors of a conglomerate like Hanson. So when, for example, its US-based Grove crane manufacturing business produced poor results in 1994, there were plenty of other businesses elsewhere which did better. At the same time Grove almost certainly did better than its rivals as it is the biggest crane maker in the US.

In February 1995 it was announced that Hanson is demerging its non-core US businesses as a tax-free dividend to shareholders. There are 34 non-core businesses and, rather than sell them off piecemeal as has been the case in the past, Hanson wants to get rid of them all at once. The companies are an odd mixture and include Jaccuzzi Whirlpool Baths, Farberware Cookware and Rexair Vacuum Cleaners.

The benefit to Hanson of disposing of them is that it will focus investor attention on seven major business areas, namely chemicals, coal, building materials, cranes, tobacco, forest products and propane.

As Hanson's chief executive Derek Bonham says, this move is 'a major step forward in our strategy to concentrate on our seven major businesses...In addition the reduction in debt will enable Hanson to position itself for major and bolt-on acquisitions as opportunities arise.'

The future

But Hanson's biggest challenge yet lies ahead of it as Lord Hanson, aged 73, looks for a dramatic finale to his impressive career.

What Hanson wants to do is acquire another large business, possibly bigger than anything acquired before. Its available borrowing facilities suggest that it could acquire a business for up to £3bn. That is, of course, not such a big figure for Hanson when it paid a similar sum for Gold Fields in 1989 and close to that figure for Imperial Tobacco in 1986.

But it will undoubtedly be the company's most important bid because it will be made in much more difficult conditions than the 1980s. Then mega-bids and deals were quite commonplace and accountancy rules made it easier to hide rationalisation costs in the balance sheet and conveniently out of the way of the profit-and-loss account.

Nowadays in contrast, all special items however extraordinary or one-off have to appear as a direct charge against profits which makes acquisitions look a much riskier business.

But that said, there is no doubt that Hanson is on the warpath. All the signs suggest that the next mega-bid will come sooner rather than later and that it will have all the classic hallmarks of a typical Hanson bid: the target will be in a basic industry, have strong cash flow and have a dominant share of the market.

There is no doubt that in the annals of UK corporate history, Hanson's meteoric rise from being a small Yorkshire company making agricultural fertiliser to a £12bn conglomerate deserves special attention. It shows how a lean and keen management team made use of a record number of bids and deals to create a diversified and dynamic business based in two countries. Rarely, if ever, has Hanson made a bad deal either buying or selling. That is perhaps the best preparation for the deals of the future.

Hays plc

Hays plc, Surrey

Outlook:

Hays' impressive profit record, the quality of its existing operational portfolio and the strength of its management all point to continuing growth. The company has a leading position in a number of fast-growing business services markets, and is likely to enhance these with further acquisitions

Scorecard:

Structural flexibility	★★★★
Innovative power	★★★★★
International orientation	★★★
Human resources	★★★★
Growth markets	★★★★★
Quality of management	★★★★

Key figures:

All figures are for the year to 30 June 1995:

Turnover	£808m
Operating profit	£116m
Staff numbers	9,000

Hays plc
Hays House
Millmead
Guildford
Surrey GU2 5HJ
Tel: 01483 302203
Fax: 01483 300388

Hays

Since its flotation in 1989, Hays has become one of the UK's largest and most successful business services groups. It provides business-to-business services to industrial, commercial and professional customers under three core activities - distribution, commercial and personnel - and, with over 50 operating companies, currently employs approximately 8,000 people at over 300 locations worldwide.

Much of the firm's growth over the last decade has been driven by the current industry-wide trend to outsourcing and the company has successfully positioned itself as a leading player in a number of fast-growing markets. It has further enhanced its position with a number of astute, strategic acquisitions and, unlike some of its competitors, has successfully diversified overseas, particularly in Europe. It has established a reputation as a well-managed, high-margin business with a good quality client base.

Operations and Markets

Distribution - this is the largest division, accounting for approximately 60 per cent of turnover and just over half of operating profits. It is an acknowledged market leader in the UK logistics market, providing both dedicated and shared-user facilities. Its principal focus is on large-scale dedicated operations for food retailing giants Waitrose (with which it has a celebrated 25-year contract) and Tesco and brewer Scottish and Newcastle. It also offers specialist storage and distribution facilities at its site in Dagenham and through a chain of bonded warehouses to a variety of customers, and has a home/retail delivery service and a home removals business. Some 30 per cent of the division's profits are accounted for by its chemicals distribution business. Although profits have been hit recently by the decline in caustic soda prices, the packaged and specialist chemicals businesses have continued to deliver steady growth.

Unlike some of its competitors, Hays has been successful in diversifying into Europe. Its French operation, Fril, is expanding rapidly, working for Carrefour through warehouses in Paris and Lyon. In Germany, Mordhurst serves a variety of customers through a nation-wide network of warehouses.

The company continues to report major new contract wins and earlier this year announced the award of a five year distribution contract with animal food manufacturer, J Bibby Agriculture, which was estimated to be worth approximately £40m. This was significant not only for its absolute size but also because it provided further evidence that the company was successfully diversifying away from its traditional reliance on the relatively mature food retailing distribution market. Much of the division's revenue is earned under long-term (three to five years) contracts which are structured so as to reward Hays for above-average operational performance.

Commercial - this division accounts for only 13 per cent of turnover but some 30 per cent of operating profits. Its centrepiece is its fast-growing Britdoc business, a unique document exchange service. Britdoc provides a nation-wide overnight business mail service to professional users in the legal profession, government and financial institutions. It has a network of 2,500 document exchange centres and 28,000 members and handles nearly 200m documents annually. It is now looking to expand into the public sector, in particular the NHS, and provide mailroom management services. The company has operated in Belgium for ten years and is now setting up a similar operation in France.

The division also provides document storage and data services. The Records Management Services business is the UK market leader in document storage and retrieval and 1994's acquisition of Rockall Data Services made the company the largest in the energy records storage market and facilitated entry to Continental Europe and the US.

Personnel - due to its cyclicality, this is probably the weakest of the three divisions, currently accounting for 19 per cent of operating profit. Accountancy Personnel is the UK's largest accountancy recruitment consultancy, offering both permanent and temporary placement facilities. The company operates a similar accountancy-based agency in Australia. Its Montrose business provides technical and professional staff to the construction industry. It also operates specialist information technology and insurance and financial services agencies.

Despite its somewhat less attractive growth prospects, the division has the merits of requiring relatively little capital and having a strong cash flow.

Strategy and management

Under the chairmanship of Ronnie Frost, Hays' development has been based on the principle of the three-legged stool. This has served it remarkably well over the years and the company has indicated that it will not be changing in future. However, it seems clear that much of the future growth will come primarily from the Distribution and Commercial divisions.

Hays' strategy is to concentrate on businesses which demonstrate most of the following characteristics:
  · leading position in growth markets
  · provision of essential and value-added services
  · repeat business
  · long standing customer relationships
  · high quality customers
  · significant barriers to entry
  · advantages of scale
  · strong cash flow
  · high return on capital

The company places great stress on business development and aims to achieve growth both organically and by acquisition. It is also prepared to make substantial capital investment - in the year to June 1994, it invested over £100m in acquisitions and capital expenditure - particularly where this can be used to give the company a competitive edge. This seems likely to continue, especially given the substantial cash flow from the Personnel division.

Much of the investment has been hallmarked for its thriving logistics business. Hays is recognised as earning the highest margins in the industry and much of this is the result of its success in offering more value-added services (e.g. packaging, labelling, recycling) to increasingly sophisticated customers.

This·success is itself the function of the substantial investment the company has made in IT over the years.

Britdoc will be another major recipient of funds. Its existing network already confers a significant competitive advantage and with its most obvious potential rival - the Post Office - considered unlikely to enter the market, it is ideally placed to continue to dominate a fast-growing market.

Hays is widely considered to be one of the best-managed business services companies in the UK. It has a decentralised approach to decision-taking and has recently re-organised its management structure in order to shorten reporting lines.

The future

Hays is strategically very well-positioned in the majority of its markets and can expect to be a major beneficiary from the continued growth of outsourcing. On the distribution side, the expansion of the third-party logistics market - it is currently estimated that 70 per cent of the potential UK market is untapped - suggests considerable growth opportunities. In particular, it is likely that Hays will move into the higher-margin area of industrial logistics. The Commercial division is also likely to experience substantial growth. Britdoc, in particular, will benefit from a growing business market, while its position as industry leader seems unassailable.

HEWLETT®
PACKARD

Hewlett Packard, Berks

Hewlett Packard is a world class high technology company which operates in many markets including printers, computer systems and advanced technology

Outlook:
HP is a true company of the future. It makes world technical standards as a by-product of research into new areas of future customer demand. Its flexible culture created the opportunity to allow printers to emerge as the substantial contributor to profits which has proved invaluable. This business invests heavily in long-term research and its people

Scorecard:

Structural flexibility	★★★★
Innovative power	★★★★
International orientation	★★★★
Human resources	★★★★
Growth markets	★★★★
Quality of management	★★★★

Key figures:

Global turnover	$31.5 billion
Global profits	$2.4 billion
Global staff	102,300
UK turnover	£1,700 million
UK staff	5,000

Hewlett Packard UK
Cain Road, Bracknell
Berks RG12 1HN
Tel: 01344 360000
Fax: 01344 363344

Hewlett Packard

If this book is about any one company that business is Hewlett Packard. It scores full marks on every measure of future success. This is the only world class computer industry manufacturer which has emerged from the sector's trauma years with its head held high. It is a widely respected company which is repeatedly cited by businesses across the UK as a standard setter for the whole of Britain's industrial and commercial environment.

Talk to companies as diverse as Sony, 3M and Granada and they will tell you how much they respect HP. This is a business which changes lives - and creates the future. Business Week in a recent feature commented: 'Hasn't anyone told Hewlett Packard, computer companies aren't meant to make profits like this any more.' Alone among the giants HP has survived the bad times by being exceptionally good at what it does. Management is at the heart of the Hewlett Packard vision.

HP is multinational with global capacity and expertise but it behaves like a small company. Light, nimble, responsive to markets, entrepreneurial, intelligent and forward looking, it sounds too good to be true but this is a business which know its strengths and plays to them. And the company doesn't become complacent about it. CEO Lou Platt told a meeting of international managers in January 1995 to kill complacency. 'What makes us highly successful this year could be our downfall next year.'

Operations and Markets

Bill Hewlett and David Packard created the business in 1938 as a measurement company. It now employs 96,000 people worldwide. The entrepreneurial spirit which characterised the original business remains at the heart of HP in 1995. It also reflects the founders' commitment to technical accuracy and their determination that their products should be absolutely applicable to their markets. Serving customer and market need with excellent standards of service quality were a hallmark of HP before they became fashionable management theory.

Typical of a success story within Hewlett Packard is the printer business. At the end of the 1980s Hewlett Packard made large printers for large computers. The company had three per cent of the global computer market and therefore three per cent of the global printer market. One of their managers in an unfashionable location in the eastern United States asked if he could go after sales of the other 97 per cent of the market. Eventually the manager went to the board of Hewlett Packard with a plan. He wanted to take the printers that were being manufactured by Canon in Japan, add some Hewlett Packard technology and repackage them. He then believed that these printers should be sold at a much cheaper rate than HP were selling their existing printers. So was born the famous Deskjet. Over the next few years the Deskjet became the largest single item in Hewlett Packard's $32 billion income. Today printers account for more than 40 per cent of global revenues but the story is exemplary for many reasons.

It shows how somebody with an idea can go to the top in Hewlett Packard and produce a world-class business.

The commitment to market, the investment in research and the perception of opportunity is something which characterises Hewlett Packard. From the Deskjet came the Inkjet and from the Inkjet came the laser printer. Last year in North America Hewlett Packard launched its Officejet. The Officejet combines a printer, a copier and a fax machine which retails at only $800. Hewlett Packard can now no longer keep pace with demand. Clearly this is the next step in the development of the printer business.

HP in the UK was founded in Bedford in 1961. At present it is based in Bracknell in Berkshire and it employs 5,000 employees throughout the UK in 19 sales and support offices and nine research and development and manufacturing operations. Hewlett Packard has offices in Bristol, in South Queensferry near Edinburgh, in Ipswich and in Pinewood. The company's latest acquisition is the fibre optic components operation which is based in Ipswich. It was formerly known as BT&D Technologies which was set up as a joint venture between British Telecom and Dupont. The aim of the operation is to take advantage of the rapidly-growing fibre-based communications market.

Strategy and management

'There are two overriding principles which govern the selection of business opportunities in Hewlett Packard,' says UK managing director John Golding. 'These are undefended hills and core competency. The idea of undefended hills is that we should seek areas of market and technical strength which have so far been neglected by other companies in the market therefore we are able to build a core strength in that area. Which leads us to the second basic principle - that of core competency. Core competency is our traditional belief in sticking to what we know we can do most cost-effectively and produce most efficiently.'

'Our business divisions operate like start-ups. They are autonomous units where managers have the freedom to take risks. We want them to behave like greenfield businesses where managers believe passionately in their products. Ownership, teamwork, inspiration and energy are key factors in this. After agreeing the strategic direction of their unit they are free to achieve targets in the most effective ways. Genuine freedom of operation is backed by all the resources of a $25 billion corporation.'

The British company is seen by the corporate management in Palo Alto, California, as a model of the HP approach. At least a third of all global research funds ($2 billion a year) goes to the company's laboratories in Bristol and South Queensferry, where it is creating advanced systems in computing, multimedia and telecoms. Investment in the future is paying off. In 1993 the worldwide business increased its profits by 156 per cent and by a further 35 per cent in 1994. Not bad in a flat market, where some rivals produced negative growth. Business Week report: 'HP is expanding at the rate of $4 billion a year. Over the past decade HP has quadrupled in size, creating $10 billion in shareholding value and transforming the business to a strong and profitable number two (among US computer makers).'

In addition to HP Laboratories, the company has invested in the new Basic Research Institute in the Mathematical Sciences. BRIMS is a joint undertaking between Hewlett Packard Laboratories and the Isaac Newton Institute for Mathematical Sciences in Cambridge. The main area of study at BRIMS will be non-linear mathematics. The choice of this subject for investment was made because of major scientific discoveries which have recently been made in this area, the eventual impact of such discoveries as chaos theory, solitons and emergent behaviour on measurement computation and communication and the emergence of new subjects such as quantum chaos with exciting potential. Non-linear mathematics has relevance to many parts of Hewlett Packard's business including optical fibres, cardiac arrhythmia, statistical mechanics in very large networks and the theory of coding schemes.

The benefit for Hewlett Packard - and therefore its customers - is that the new institute can be a testbed for new applications in Hewlett Packard products. And the British HP success story goes on. The UK research laboratories have developed products which will facilitate faster and more efficient telecommunications across the world and recently evolved a standard which will eliminate $15 billion worth of telecomms fraud. This was part of a package which the South Queensferry laboratory created in order to develop new systems for mobile telephone communication.

The rigour and determination to succeed could create an impression of a stiff and relentless management eager to squeeze every last ounce of creative juice out of its employees. Not a bit of it. People queue up to join Hewlett Packard. It has some of the lowest staff attrition rates in industry. Employee attitude surveys consistently reveal a culture which encourages individual and team creativity, locating new solutions to technology problems, visualising - then delivering - the technology of tomorrow.

HP is among the highest payers in industry but remuneration isn't the principal reason why it's such an attractive place to work. Everyone is valued for their contribution. This does not mean that HP does not have human resources issues to work on - the pressure on employees caused by continuous change, handling promotion in a virtually flat structure, and identifying any structural barriers to the advancement of women in HP - are the challenges faced by the current UK national management.

The future

HP is most certainly a force to be reckoned with in the future. It has the resources, the position, the people and the drive to be one of the best in almost any of its markets. Change in these markets will come forth from many sources but HP's laboratories and market approach will be among them. It is truly a company of the future.

HOUSE OF FRASER

House of Fraser, London

House of Fraser is a major department store retailing group

Outlook:
The group has invested heavily based on a clearly defined and well researched strategy plan. It aims to occupy the upper ground in the sector and apply its concept to new retailing opportunities in out-of-town shopping centres. The plan is based on a revival of the customer service concept in a sector which has suffered in recent years from more forward-looking competitors

Scorecard:

Structural flexibility	★★★★
Innovative power	★★★★★
International orientation	★★★
Human resources	★★★★
Growth markets	★★★★★
Quality of mangement	★★★★

Key figures:

UK turnover	£755 million
Pre-tax profits	£35.1 million
Staff	9,587

House of Fraser plc
1 Howick Place
London SW1P 1BH
Tel: 0171 963 2000
Fax: 0171 828 8885

House of Fraser

In the last few years a conspicuous increase in retail competition has called into question the longevity of the department store. If originally the explosion of car ownership gave consumers the freedom to choose where to shop, the last decade has produced more competition than ever. Out-of-town centres and an entity described by Andrew Jennings, House of Fraser's managing director, as the 'category killer specialist' (i.e. offering unbeatable range and prices over a limited area of merchandise) have provided unparalleled challenges.

Yet rumours of the demise of the department store are proving unduly pessimistic. Since the beginning of the 1990s, although the multiple stores have come under pressure, department stores have increased sales. The top five department stores have clawed back market share against the 20 leading multiples.

When House of Fraser returned to the stock market in 1994 it had not entirely shaken off an unfortunate reputation for its old-fashioned and poor quality operational practices. However, it was already two years into updating them. Management was able to improve performance by introducing some relatively simple retail techniques. Beginning with a closer examination of its inventory control and relationships with suppliers, it went on to alter the ranges it stocked and the way it used its floorspace. The process extended to the motivation of its employees and to upgrading the shopping environment for customers.

Its strategy is now to build the business on proven strengths. Its stores, their history and their positioning are the foundation and when you add an identified customer base forecast to grow in size and spending power, you have a business with considerable potential.

Operations and markets

House of Fraser is one of the UK's leading department store groups. Originally floated in 1948, it grew via the acquisition of Harrods and a number of regional department store groups. In 1985 control of the group's more than 100 stores passed to the Al Fayed family who rationalised the chain and reduced it to closer to its current 56 stores.

House of Fraser may no longer own Harrods, but it still trades under many highly visible names. These include Army & Navy, DH Evans, Dickins & Jones and House of Fraser. The mainstays of its business are womenswear, home goods and fashion accessories. In-store brand concessions are also a material (c. 30 per cent) portion of turnover and although House of Fraser no longer owns its chargecard operation, it remains very important to group earnings.

Around 29 per cent of all group sales last year were transacted via the FraserCard chargecard. A massive promotional drive in 1994/95 achieved a 36 per cent increase in membership to nearly 686,000 accounts. FraserCard holders spend on average 28 per cent more than those using other forms of payment and the introduction of the FraserCard Club and the GoldCard in 1994 should further encourage customer loyalty.

Strategy and management

House of Fraser's stated objective is to establish itself as a 'focused, up-market department store group'. Mr Jenning's formula is to bring a collection of specialist businesses under one roof, each appealing to a defined segment of the population. He also wants more consistency across each store. 'If part of the business is aimed at the contemporary customer, the fashion, accessories and fashionable housewares must be equivalently contemporary.'

The refurbishment of all of its selling space is well in train. In the past a laissez-faire attitude produced unfocused layouts which lacked consistency and did not establish the brand in the mind of the shopper. Now more thought is put into the utilisation of space and an identifiable 'look', apparent in the refurbished stores, has already contributed to material sales growth.

Some individual stores, depending on their size and location, will be converted from full historic range stores to speciality or limited assortment stores. Dickins & Jones has been relaunched as the flagship store, transformed by a comprehensive refurbishment of the exterior and the addition of an atrium, cosmetic hall, coffee shop and lingerie floor. Other stores across the country are being given a similar treatment with spending focused on capturing the customer's imagination.

The second stage of the equation is to satisfy the needs of differing customer profiles, i.e. to recognise the distinction between a customer in Glasgow and one in Darlington. It has categorised or 'lifestyled' its merchandise into four areas, high fashion, contemporary, classic and essential. It intends to reduce the number of line options and refocus on the preferences of each particular customer base.

Based on a clear vision of its typical client, House of Fraser has refined its merchandise policy to capture, retain and grow that customer base. Mr Jennings intends to progressively rebalance its merchandise toward ladies fashion, fashion accessories and menswear, all areas in which he feels it can make 'a clear authoritative offer'.

Around 30 per cent of turnover is generated by in-store concessions. These represent an important part of the strategy, improving the merchandise mix to offer the desired branded products customers expect. The risk for House of Fraser, which receives a percentage of sales is well contained, as concessionaires accept the stock risks and cover the running and fitting costs of their units.

If store refurbishment is the visible change, establishing the most efficient IT stock control systems and developing a centralised distribution centre are no less crucial. These should benefit margins and efficiently manage stock turnover and deliveries to cut costs.

Only a few years ago House of Fraser preferred a paper-based purchasing and customer accounting system. Now it is committed to a £20m systems development programme which should eventually help it to catch up on its competitors in this area. Mr Jennings believes that by end 1996, House of Fraser will have a full IT driven planning and purchase order management system. Distribution will be concentrated through a single third party centralised centre. It reduced the number of its suppliers by 19 per cent in the last year, obtaining better terms and raising the efficiency of stock turnover.

Its three year plan is to spend £70m on store refurbishment and development, and £20m on systems, yet all this capital expenditure should not put the group's finances under undue strain. Balance sheet gearing at the last year end was a relatively undemanding 31 per cent, and analysts expect positive cashflow and further reduction in group debt this year.

The aim is to transform the business culture from its historic low sales growth and over merchandised options into a profitable, sales-led and high margin business with excellent stock turnover. This has affected its relationships with suppliers, methods of stock control and the store environment.

Management has committed the group to an investment in employee training to help instill the profit-led culture. It has introduced dedicated training courses for all management and staff. Nearly a third of its buying and merchandising team is new and regarded as younger and more progressive in its buying style. Around 40 per cent of store managers have been changed in the past two to three years, both by promotion and external appointments. This has bolstered the sales and profit led culture, with earnings linked to their own store's performance. All staff are incentivised at shop floor level and made aware of the importance of its loyal FraserCard customers.

House of Fraser intends to retain the name and identity of each of its 17 famous brands. Yet the notion of trading under many separate identities appears anomalous in the face of the advantages that amalgamating brands bring in terms of advertising and buying power. However strong stiff local affection for the stores has been demonstrated in the past.

In the 1920s a decision to change the name of Kendals in Manchester to Harrods had to be reversed after the matter was raised in the House of Lords. If that seems too quaint to be relevant today, a similar about-turn took place in the eighties after stores were renamed House of Fraser. However, it operates and markets its individual stores identically except for the merchandise range, and retains the individual brand names to protect each store's high profile in its local community.

Enhancements to customer service are essential if a store such as House of Fraser is to distinguish itself from the competition. Its eleven GoldCard Lounges are unusual and will be extended to all stores by September. Around 60 per cent of all employees are part-time, something which provides House of Fraser with flexibility to adjust staffing levels to meet customer demand.

The future

The role of department stores in UK retailing is unlikely to decline. They remain very important to out-of-town shopping centres. In the US it is estimated that more than 70 per cent of all mall traffic comes through department store doors, making them coveted as anchors. House of Fraser is represented in many of the UK's major centres such as Meadowhall, Lakeside and the Metrocentre and the challenge is how to make those customers stop and buy.

In Mr Jennings' opinion demographic changes are moving in House of Fraser's favour. Its core customer is the 35-54 year old, categorised as ABC1, a sector forecast to grow by more than around two million people over the next decade. 'The growth of the UK's economic middle class is to our advantage. The rich may not be getting richer, but they are certainly becoming more numerous .'

IBM, London

IBM is a worldwide business solutions provider with extensive
technology expertise, acting as consultant and manufacturer

Outlook:
Despite the problems which IBM encountered in the late 1980s and 1990s, it
remains a formidable global operator. It has moved from manufacturing to a
range of activities especially consultancy and systems integration. Above all
IBM has the critical mass in terms of clients, financial power, technological
capacity, talented personnel and business reputation to be one of a small
group of players which will command the market

Scorecard:

Structural flexibility	★★★
Innovative power	★★★★
International orientation	★★★★★
Human resources	★★★★
Growth markets	★★★★
Quality of management	★★★★

Key figures:

Global turnover	$72 billion
Global profits	$6.3 billion
Global staff	219,000
UK staff	9,040
UK turnover	£4.6 billion

IBM (UK) Ltd
76-78 Upper Ground
London SE1 9PZ
Tel: 0171 202 3000
Fax: 0171 202 3605

IBM

For many years IBM was a business metaphor - an international standard against which to assess other corporations. Until the late 1980s it was the world's biggest computer company. At one point it was four times greater than its largest rival and its global market domination appeared assured. But what followed was a widespread collapse. The company which was more powerful than many governments hit the rocks. The enterprise which never made redundancies sacked a quarter of a million people around the globe.

In essence IBM's business approach was unsuited to new market conditions. Its philosophy, organisation and structure were more applicable to selling expensive mainframes to undiscriminating customers. IBM could not cope with a business environment where cheap hardware proliferates, software applications command greater significance than hardware and customers rather than manufacturers are top dogs.

The inability of IBM to respond to changing market conditions had multiple implications - for individuals, communities and affiliate companies. The extent of the change in the nature of the company since is key to understanding why IBM has found a place in this report. The new IBM is much slimmer, still global but more responsive in its approach. Senior computer industry practitioners say that despite the battering the corporation has taken it will remain a key player in business.

Operations and markets

'The computer industry was synonymous with IBM. That is no longer the case,' says one senior US computer industry analyst. It is nevertheless substantial. In the UK, IBM employs 9,980 people and has revenues of £4.3 billion. It is operational in every sector of the market with clients in government, international industry, national and small business, and, increasingly domestic users. It manufactures hardware systems from mainframes through to personal computers.

George Cox, CEO of Unisys in the UK, says: 'In any analysis of the future of the sector IBM will be a key player. There are several requirements which determine whether a company will be a major international operator in years to come. One of these is critical mass - in terms of geography, technical expertise, product range and clients. IBM is still a powerful force by all of these measures. It remains one of a handful of senior international companies. '

This is at the heart of why IBM will survive and prosper. Its client connections around the world are formidable. Institutions - both corporate and public sector - rely upon their long term relationships with IBM. In many cases, such customers have been with IBM for decades and relationships are intimate. As businesses revert to core, supplier services which previously were important are now crucial. Customers will depend on smaller numbers of suppliers whose influence on their businesses will be vital.

Therefore they will need to know that suppliers have the longevity to keep them supplied far into the future. Longevity breaks down to financial stability, global coverage, technical capacity and partnership. IBM wins in all of these areas. Despite the severe job cutbacks, IBM is still a powerful operator in all key world markets. Recent product launches have restored its status to world class player. The O/S2 Warp in particular - despite the long years of its development and previous false starts - is regarded as a milestone on the company's road to recovery.

Regardless of cathartic upheavals IBM aims to be a world class operator, and a dominant player in all of its markets - whether industrial, commercial or governmental. The new IBM is a company which accepts that genuine flexibility, innate responsiveness to customers and a future built on partnership of equals whether rivals or clients are an absolute requirement of the future.

Strategy and management

As part of a total revamp of its business approach and procedures, IBM has decided to re-position itself in the market. 'We have moved from being a manufacturer to being a supplier of business solutions with a strong technological base,' says IBM UK chairman Nick Temple. This is a radical shift. Mr Temple is a prominent example of the new breed of IBM managers exuding confidence rather than arrogance, willing to admit that there have been failures in the past but assured that the new direction the business has chosen is the future for the company.

His language is more redolent of Sony and HP than the familiar IBM code. 'We want to enable our people to get on with their jobs with the minimum of corporate interference and the maximum of freedom to achieve their objectives. We are here to provide the support and technical infrastructure but they work with the clients to find the most appropriate solutions to their problems.'

The hardware solution is inevitably IBM but the company has moved a long distance in two or three years. 'We have created a strategy plan for the next two to five years which enables us to capitalise on the restructuring which has taken place to date. ' He mentions three key points in the plan:
   . help to set the future - anticipate rather than respond to developments
   . establish the role of management in setting financial and strategic goals
   . enable IBM people to be creative and innovative in client relationships, build internal teamwork and locate new areas for business development.

Mr Temple says that industry is in a period of perpetual change where major structural development is taking place among clients and IBM people and solutions are fundamental to many of these changes. 'The company is in a process of continuous business review where we reduce the business risk and enhance our flexibility and relevance to the customer.'

He says that the old IBM was risk-averse which limited the capacity to act. The revitalised company with its greater reliance on customer dialogue, internal teamwork, inspiration and personal creativity will be more lively in its activities. The restructuring had two principal strategic phases. The first was in 1992 with its immediate physical and operational form - the structure was reformed and numbers (ie people) were taken out of the company. The second which occurred over the following 18 months was behavioural and, Mr Temple, says harder to achieve.

'There was considerable disbelief at first at the extent of the people empowerment changes which we wanted to make. Employees had been used to a defined IBM line. But we re-examined our values. And employees have repaid our confidence in their capacities. Previously, we had significantly underestimated their abilities and the benefit from freeing them up has been immense.'

After widespread job losses it was imperative to ensure that staff motivation was enhanced. And the strategic plan for the development of the business relied heavily on giving employees greater freedom of operation and fewer administrative barriers to dealing directly with clients.

The strategic review set UK management a series of five targets:

. to move to customer orientation
. to halve its administration
. to remove systems which promoted contention
. to create world class quality service (products)
. to become specialised

These five points had a direct bearing on the company's employment policy and the scope with which staff could operate within the business. Mr Temple says that clearing the administrative processes out of the business was a major step to ensuring that IBM customer-facing staff could finalise agreements without referring everything back to headquarters.

Expenses have come down by around 12 per cent year on year by removing unhelpful processes and outsourcing internal functions which are no longer deemed core. IBM's standing in industry has been boosted. There are no reliable figures for the UK. But in the annual Fortune survey of the most admired corporations in the US IBM is back up among the serious players rather than down in the lower reaches of the top 500 which is where it lay in 1994.

Mr Temple reports that the results for the UK company have been heartening. It has moved back into profit, its customer relationships have improved substantially, it has returned to employing people after firing them, the cashflows in the business are promising, the return on investment is good and business control systems are now more relevant to a business of the 21st century.

This helped to engineer the change to a culture which concentrates on providing business solutions rather than selling IBM boxes. The relationship between IBM UK, the European region and the company worldwide has also been rationalised. It means that manufacturing, research and development and centres of global excellence are located where customer demand dictates.

The future

IBM has encountered radical change. It has completely reconfigured the way in which it does business favouring solutions to selling products. Its structure now reflects its revised orientation towards customers and working in partnerships with clients and suppliers. Much of the administrative red tape in the company has been purged and decision making is considerably quicker and more effective.

Above all IBM is recognised by industry - given the contortions it has encountered - as a major player for the long term. Its spread of customer relationships across every field of public and private sector is a strong anchor and it is making valiant efforts to shake off the more self-centred aspects of its culture. The real determinants of its long term vibrancy will be its real dedication to its customers and the future role of Japanese and other Pacific Rim operators.

Iceland Frozen Foods plc, Clwyd

Iceland is a leading British specialist food retailer with a formidable
reputation for frozen food, operating from 750 stores worldwide

Outlook:
In 25 years Iceland has matured into an exceptionally strong and efficient
company. It has plans to double its stores and, together with the industry,
double the turnover of frozen food in the UK. A competitive, aggressive
stylish retailer - no doubt a major player in the high street of the 21st century

Scorecard:

Structural flexibility	★★★
Innovative power	★★★
International orientation	★★★★
Human resources	★★★★
Growth markets	★★★★
Quality of management	★★★

Key figures:

UK turnover	£1.3 billion
Pre-tax profits	£70.2 million
UK staff	17,000

Iceland Frozen Foods plc
Second Avenue
Deeside Industrial Park
Deeside
Clwyd CN5 2NW
Tel: 01244 830100
Fax: 01244 814531

Iceland

The battle for the high street will become fiercely competitive in the next decade. Retailers anticipate further rationalisation and consolidation into the major groups, as leading contenders squeeze out local and regional operators. Competitive advantage will derive from distinctive levels of operation, quality of service and market offerings.

The pattern of retail - especially food retailing - will be characterised by a reduction in the number of companies but growth in outlets and a return to the high street to achieve a better balance between local shopping and out-of-town centres. The quest to secure the most advantageous locations for stores was a key denominator in the last decade. The next ten years will see further refinement of that process but the real challenge for retail management is to ensure that their businesses are truly distinctive.

Food retailing is, perhaps, the most overt example of pure commerce. Its daily dialogue with customers, heavy emphasis on immediate cashflow, direct and vigorous competitive interplay, and reliance on the skills of the entrepreneur represent the hallmarks of a true market economy. The winners of the retail contests of the future will need to be masters of entrepreneurship. Iceland, the frozen foods retailer, is a young company which nonetheless has a remarkable pedigree. It demonstrates many of the qualities which are prerequisites of future success.

Operations and markets

In 1970 Iceland was a start-up. By 1995 its turnover had reached £1.3 billion and pre-tax profits £70.2 million. In recent years the company has acquired Bejam and the food halls of Littlewoods - among other purchases - and now operates 750 stores across the UK. The company is a niche player in the sector specialising in frozen and chilled foods with some groceries and fresh food. There is some comparison between Iceland and discounters such as Aldi and Kwik Save but Iceland maintains that its business is different from theirs and that it is more directly in competition with multiple chains such as Tesco, J Sainsbury and Safeway.

The Frozen Food Information Service suggests that the entire frozen food market in the UK is currently worth £4.6 billion in 1995 and that in a decade this may have increased to around £9 billion. Iceland is one of the biggest players in the market at between 10 and 15 per cent. Chairman Malcolm Walker says that Iceland's growth in profits has previously matched the expansion in the market. 'We have a solid and secure niche, and we are the most profitable specialist food retailer. Frozen food is a growing market, and it will continue to grow,' he remarks. The low inflation climate however means that retailers are cautious about committing themselves to flamboyant estimates of future returns.

The company is based in unostentatious headquarters in Clwyd. It employs around 17,000 nationally - of which two-thirds are in customer-facing roles and the remainder in management, administration and its regional depots. It retains its entrepreneurial character despite its considerable growth as a business.

In keeping with many other well-run companies, it has an open culture and a strong customer focus. The organisation began with one store in Oswestry and now estimates that over the next ten years it will grow to more than 1,500 locations.

Strategy and management

Strategy for the group is characterised by a combination of acquisition and organic growth. 'We will pursue suitable future acquisition,' says group public relations director Jill McWilliam. 'The problem is that there are not any immediately obvious candidates - as we are the largest niche operator. There are regional possibilities but we are engaged in a constant process of examining and assessing opportunities. If an appropriate acquisition becomes available we will certainly move forward. We are hungry to expand and will always achieve our goal of 50-60 new stores each year.'

As the search for suitable takeovers goes on, the company will continue its process of opening new stores. Iceland's spread is national but it sees opportunities for opening further establishments in city suburbs and high streets. The company is a strong advocate of high street shopping for both commercial and social reasons. It believes that the high street can be revitalised and like Marks & Spencer argues that this will be good for Britain's communities.

Margins in food retailing - although substantial by comparison with the US - are low when measured against other UK industrial and commercial sectors. So another key plank of the company's strategic direction is retaining and improving profitability levels. This is done by strong cost control, high quality buying decisions and the inherent leverage offered by size.

Iceland's directors have focused on the size of the enterprise and the profitability of individual outlets as important targets for the future. With other leading retailers at best holding steady Iceland is continuing to spearhead profitable growth. The doubling of outlets over a 10-year horizon is a challenging task for the company but throughout its 25-year history Iceland has consistently outpaced expectations. Its entrepreneurial and discounting character has encouraged City analysts to take a somewhat aloof view of the business. Nevertheless it can confidently point to its record of outstripping expectations in terms of expansion, modernisation, quality of offering and commitment of employees. The Bejam and Littlewoods acquisitions were milestones in the recent development of the company. They lifted Iceland into greater leagues and showed its ability to absorb new outlets into the family. The speed with which these two groups were absorbed into the Iceland brand was impressive.

Another key factor in the Iceland approach is its identification with environmental issues. This is no pious single sentence in the annual report but a real recognition that the fouling of the planet benefits no-one. Besides various initiatives within the community Iceland recycles gases and packaging material and aims to reduce waste disposal costs by 50 per cent. The company recognised in the early 1980s that CFCs and other ozone depleting gases would become a major commercial as well as environmental issue. It developed the first CFC-free freezer and in 1994 opened a state-of-the-art cold store warehouse and distribution centre using ammonia as the refrigerant.

Iceland is a fun company. There's no airs and graces about working here. People work in teams in an aggressive and fast-moving market-place so there is a strong sense of cameraderie. To be able to react swiftly to changes, open communication-lines upward are a prerequisite at Iceland and that is how most employees describe the culture - strong and open. The majority of the management team have been working together for years and it is their belief in their teams which propels much of the success of the company ethos.

Employees are encouraged to seek vocational qualifications and Iceland helps them through. Absolute honesty is a cornerstone of the enterprise, and active communication - either official, through Iceland's newsletters, or informal on a person to person basis - is the way of life. People work hard and are encouraged to take an active role in their communities but the company wants its employees to enjoy their work. It is one of Britain's few genuine equal-opportunities employers and is an active member of Opportunity 2000.

The future

Iceland faces a series of commercial challenges in the coming decade. It has secured a place as the premier frozen food retailer and has created a logical strategy of acquisition, exploitation of new geographical locations and growth in share and margins. The opportunities to realise its expansion targets will be more demanding than in the last ten years. But Iceland is proficient at identifying potential purchases and its entrepreneurial character means that the directors will not let new business slip away.

Its image is bold, clean and bright and it makes good use of its marketing budget with a good family orientation. The company is one of the most genuinely concerned companies in the UK and it is especially active on behalf of its employees, the communities it serves and the health of the planet.

Imperial Chemical Industries, London

ICI is the UK's flagship chemicals company - manufacturer of paints, polymers, acrylics and dynamite

Outlook:
The recent reorganisations have set ICI on its way to become a flexible market-led organisation with the resources and experience to take on any challenge the future may throw at it. Its international experience and management resources are impressive and should continue its success in other parts of the world as demand from those regions grows

Scorecard:

Structural flexibility	★★★★
Innovative power	★★★★
International orientation	★★★★★
Human resources	★★★★
Growth markets	★★★
Quality of management	★★★★

Key figures:

Turnover	£9.2 billion
Pre-tax profits	£514 million
Staff	66,200

ICI plc
Imperial Chemicals House
Millbank
London SW1P 3JF
Tel: 0171 834 4444

ICI

Imperial Chemical Industries is the UK's flagship chemicals company. It has long been viewed as one of the UK's premier businesses. Traditionally, ICI is regarded by graduates as Britain's most favoured employer. But the 1990s have seen remarkable changes in the business. This was formalised by the demerger of its pharmaceutical and agrochemical businesses, which were spun off and launched on the stockmarket in mid 1994 under the name Zeneca. But the demerger was merely the most obvious example of a fundamental review of how the company needed to be restructured in order to remain at the cutting edge in both product innovation and in its markets worldwide.

Though Hanson's interest in bidding for ICI in 1991 came to nought and only ended in focusing attention on the Hanson empire, it did also focus minds inside ICI on the structure of its own empire. Management, led by chairman Sir Denys Henderson (who has recently been succeeded by his chief executive Sir Ronald Hampel), decided that it had, above all, to counter the tendency to look inwards which bedevils very large organisations; basic decisions about strategy had to be made in greater proximity to individual businesses' marketplaces.

Operations and markets

ICI's range of products has gone on expanding since the 1930s. Its activities were cemented together by vertical integration stretching all the way from the research laboratories to the market place. This worked well when there were many exciting new products to be fed through the system. But as the industry got more mature in the sixties and seventies, attention began to focus on working out in detail what different businesses and products were actually contributing to profits. This led to putting a number of businesses in joint ventures - where a better return needed to be made - and it led to the transference of more executive powers to divisional managers.

A basic problem remained. This was the relation between ICI head office and individual divisional groupings of businesses. Head office was overseeing the development strategies of so many different businesses that it was unable to give them the attention they needed, or to prioritise between them in a sufficiently informed way. Cutting the empire in two - into Zeneca and the chemicals operations which now make up ICI - made sense as very little, technically and managerially, was, or could be, shared between the two halves.

ICI is now divided into five main divisions (see below.). Since the demerger, it has lost 20 per cent of its workforce and has cut £474m out of its cost base (operating costs came to £8.7bn in 1994 on sales of £9.2bn). It has got out of the ultra-cyclical bulk polymers market, through the public sale of EVC, its joint venture in PVC with Enichem; it had identified polymers as non-core because it was not a global leader in them.

ICI has 62,000 employees worldwide, more than 8,000 products and manufacturing sites at over 200 locations in thirty countries. It employs over

4,000 people in research, technology and development.

It has five international groups of businesses:
1. Paints
2. Materials - Acrylics, Films and Polyurethanes.
3. Explosives
4. Industrial Chemicals & Polymers
5. Regional - Argentina, Australia, India, Malaysia, Pakistan

1. ICI Paints concentrates on three markets - decorative (Dulux in the UK), refinish of vehicles and coatings for cans. Paints' growth is being driven by regional expansion. It is upping its presence in the Asia Pacific region, with the commissioning in 1994 of a plant in China, a new plant in Malaysia and an expansion in Thailand.

2. In Materials, the recent acquisition of Dupont's US acrylics business makes ICI Acrylics the world's largest producer of methyl methacrylate (MMA), the key component in the manufacture of resins and surface coatings. Demand for acrylics has been strengthening, though raw material price increases have kept the pressure on margins. The group has seen a marked turnaround since 1994 in its Films business where prices have been rising.

3. ICI Explosives is the world's leading supplier of industrial explosives, for the mining, quarrying and seismic exploration industries. It only broke even in the fourth quarter of 1994 due to a sharp deterioration in the trading environment but the outlook is excellent, such is its market strength and innovative research base.

4. ICI Chemicals & Polymers is one of Europe's largest manufacturers of petrochemicals, plastics and industrial chemicals. ICI has an 80 per cent stake - BP has the other 20 per cent - in a joint venture cracker at Wilton on Teeside with a capacity of 750,000 tonnes per annum; it converts gas and oil-based raw materials into intermediates for the production of plastics, fibres and fertilisers. It is involved in various products down-stream of this, notably in producing fertilisers (for which it also produces ammonia). In polyesters, the principal ICI product is 'Melinar' PET used in bottles and specialist packaging. Among other areas in which ICI Chemicals & Polymers is a major producer are catalysts, chemicals for skin care and titanium dioxide (which gives whiteness and opacity to paint, paper). Total chemical demand in ICI's markets grew by about five per cent in 1994, while ICI's own sales volumes grew by seven per cent with prices increasing by only two per cent.

Strategy and management

The company is an integrated chemicals operation that, in the words of new chairman Sir Ronald Hampel, 'focuses on businesses which can demonstrate market leadership, technological edge and a world competitive cost base'. It ranks among the top three producers in most of its businesses. The direction of its strategy in the last five years has been to enhance its position in markets, improve productivity, reshape its portfolio in response to changing market demand, strengthen the corporate culture, keep tight control on costs and expand the enterprise.

The programme of cost reductions since 1990 and the company's strategy of moving closer to its customers go hand in hand. Both are continuous processes. There is an inevitable tension between a product-led ethic and a market-led one in ICI with its huge production cost base and heavy capital requirements strung around the globe; keeping in tune with market demand and keeping plant and production units tuned often pull in opposite directions. The cost reductions now taking place are the logic of market thinking catching up with the production base.

The appointment of an outsider, Unilever man Charles Miller Smith, as the new chief executive, is symptomatic of ICI's determination to get closer to its customers, i.e. to look outwards. By virtue of its markets, Unilever's production is, clearly, consumer tuned to a degree still quite alien to ICI. The most recent non-executive appointment to the board, Lucas's dynamic new chief executive George Simpson, is a move in the same direction. Simpson, who successfully turned around Rover at BAe prior to its sale, has long experience at fine-tuning production to the very particular requirements of customers, making them work creatively together.

Among the board's other aims are continuous improvement in process efficiency, selective investment in growth opportunities, greater penetration of the fast growing Asia Pacific region and ensuring that adequate funds are generated for R&D.

The future

ICI's capacity to extract more value from it businesses as its brings them closer to its customers - refining its analysis of its own costs in the process - is set to drive the group forward strongly over the next ten years. The shift to a more market-led and a less production-led empire will not happen overnight. But with the expertise, funds and research muscle of ICI, a giant which has woken up in time and can recast the die in its own favour, a leaner and stronger commercial organisation is certainly on its way.

JBA, Warwickshire

JBA is a world leading supplier of enterprise wide software products, development tools and services for integrated manufacturing, distribution and financial applications.

Outlook:
Business advisers say that among the most attractive of companies are the fast growth enterprises. JBA is a classic example. It is the West Midland's fastest growing company, it is UK market leader and number three in the world. The company is a technical adviser to IBM on applications and it has an innovative human resources policy

Scorecard:

Structural flexibility	★★★★
Innovative power	★★★★★
International orientation	★★★★★
Human resources	★★★★
Growth markets	★★★★
Quality of management	★★★★★

Key figures:

Global turnover	£90.7 million
Pre-tax profits	£6.1 million
World staff	1500

JBA
Needles House
Birmingham Road, Studley
Warwickshire B80 7AS
Tel: 01527 496200
Fax: 01527 496245

JBA plc

The future of software engineering lies in applications which can be reconfigured by business analysts rather than programmers. This is the view of one of Britain's most innovative software houses, JBA. The West Midlands' fastest growing business is UK market leader and world number three in applications for mid-range computers, principally IBM's AS/400 series. In the next five years JBA confidently aims to lead the sector across the world through its increasing - and outstanding - experience in object orientated software programming, which is the next phase in corporate software development.

Customer demands are changing - and clients now need software which keeps pace with the alarming rate of change in their own businesses. JBA managers are recognised in the industry to be establishing the standards for object orientated software. Many of JBA's rivals are strong in functional software programmes which deliver an appropriate solution for a particular business function. For example, packages may be suitable for finance, sales or administration but they rarely provide effective links between disciplines.

This is where JBA steps into the picture. It has developed systems - primarily for the mid-range computer user (up to 1,000 terminals, typically) - which integrate all the major functions within the business. Its Business 400 package has achieved remarkable success throughout the world. In its home base (the English West Midlands), according to marketing manager Allan Davies, every company which JBA wants to do business with has been signed up. On a broader canvas, JBA now operates in 39 countries around the world. It is expanding by acquisition collecting at least one new company, currently, every quarter. The company has in excess of 2,500 customers for Business 400 - among them Pepsi Cola, Reebok Nederland, Sega, Allied Domecq, Bass, Hillsdown Holdings, Whirlpool, Hoover, Elizabeth Arden, Gestetner, Wellcome, Sony Australia and Mercury.

Operations and markets

JBA was originally Johnson Brown Associates - the UK operation of an Australian company. The founders invited IBM UK marketing manager Alan Vickery to head up their British business but within a year the energetic Mr Vickery had decided he wanted to run his own enterprise and bought out his Australian bosses. He invited an alert IBM software engineer Kevin Jones to join him in the venture. Later they were joined by IBM's West Midlands marketing manager Colin Wells to run the sales side of JBA's business.

Without the benefit of a bank loan, the trio created a company which has capitalised on its intimate knowledge of the need for applications for mid-range computers. 'IBM's 34, 36 and AS/400 series were poorly served by software applications. Building an extensive dialogue with customers, the company identified their principal needs and developed integrated packages to meet their requirements,' says Mr Davies.

The business was established in Birmingham and now operates in several sites in the region. Marketing is based at Alcester near Stratford upon Avon and design is located in Studley near Redditch. JBA also operates from premises opposite the Ramada Hotel on the periphery of Heathrow Airport.

220

Given their business lineage, the founders worked closely with IBM customers. They decided to write their own software - rather than license that of other companies - which proved to be a decisive, and beneficial step. Their technical expertise and commercial innovation allowed them quickly to outstrip other small competitors. Year on year the business enjoyed rapid growth and expanding profits. Revenues rose from around £1 million in 1982 to £22 million in 1989. From then on the increase in income has been dramatic, with the steepest rise coming between 1991 and 1992. Sales increased from £36 million to £56 million. In 1993 turnover went up by a further 40 per cent to £75 million.

At present the vast bulk of the business - around 97 per cent - is geared towards the IBM mid-range computer sector. But since the end of 1994, JBA has responded to customer demand for open architecture software which is suitable for UNIX client/server applications. The sales of these packages are small at present but eventually the company believes they will be as valuable as IBM-based product.

Strategy and management

In its traditional marketplace, JBA is UK number one by a long way. Around the world it stands behind Software Science Associates (SSA) - another IBM supplier - and JD Edwards. But JBA argues that neither of these companies has the expertise in highly flexible applications which are the hallmark of its approach. In the UNIX arena, SAP, a German producer, and Oracle are the top two. However, the UK business is unfazed by either of these competitors. It suggests that its gathering world strength and technical lead will prove substantial enough to overcome their opposition.

JBA has added to its technical leadership by drawing into the business sector companies around the world to be used as a platform for expansion and also the most brilliant software minds from the universities. Recently, a team working on leading edge software engineering at Oxford was tempted to enlist in the JBA adventure. The culture of the business reflects its desire to race towards the most innovative business software solutions.

The move to object orientated software in many ways mirrors the trend towards cell-based manufacturing. The components of object orientated software come in hundreds of small units which are effectively like tiny libraries which can be shifted around to suit the needs of the user. If one particular format does not suit the demands of the business, an analyst - with a minimum of IT training - can establish a more appropriate structure. For example, if a specific billing system based on addresses outlives its usefulness it could be replaced by one which is, say, defined by date of last bill. This is not an exercise in re-programming so much as reconfiguring an existing, but highly flexible, system. Flexibility and ease of adapatability are its key strengths. The technology is so advanced that JBA engineers are working with IBM in the States to advise the computer giant on how hardware and operating systems might change to capitalise on these applications developments.

'The way in which we write software has not changed since the late 1950s. There are many different languages - C, Cobol, FORTRAN - but they are all written in the same way. What we are doing now is inventing a whole new way of writing software. This is a major revolution in the development and application of software,' says Mr Davies. The implications for the software industry - and its customers - if Mr Vickery and his colleagues are right are staggering.

However, one major obstacle stood in the way of progressing down this road. There are no tools for developing the new order of software languages. So JBA tackled the issue head-on and created the first package of machine tools for the brave new horizon. Guidelines is the first-ever graphical, mixed-platform true client/server package of tools. It has been sold to IBM for developing its new operating system and is available to large clients like banks and insurance companies which need to make their own confidential systems. A big debate ensued after its launch within the company as to whether JBA would license Guidelines to direct rivals. 'We decided that we would not allow competitors access to the product until we had established a substantial competitive lead', comments Mr Davies.

JBA operates a defined strategy for creating new business. 'One of our major competitors will deal only with the largest clients worldwide. Our approach is to take in a much larger slice of the market. When we enter a market we deal only with the cream. But we quickly expand to much smaller businesses. Take the United States. We are only the fourth or fifth largest company in the sector in the US at the moment. So we are tackling the largest companies. In other territories, such as mainland Europe, we have a greater market presence so we deal with smaller businesses. In the UK we are filling in the gaps.'

Product strengths exist in four key business areas: manufacturing, distribution and logistics, finance and service industries. A good example is Europa Sport, a rapidly growing winter sports, mountain clothing and ski equipment distributor. JBA supplied a software solution which enabled the company to hold three-dimensional information on size, colour and range. Other vendors offered single function solutions but none could embrace all three. Europa Sport invested in a fully integrated Business 400 package comprising modules for finance, payroll, purchasing, report writing and distribution systems.

Europa Sport subjected the system to a tough commercial appraisal over a seven month period. It capitalised on the strengths of the Style 400 package and as the UK economic environment shifted from boom to recession, Europa Sport's business priorities changed. The system was initially installed to cope with rapid growth but maximum efficiency and improved customer service became major drivers. The package's greatest strength was its flexibility so it adapted to the business' changing objectives.

JBA employs 1,600 people around the world and anticipates that this figure will double in the next five years. MD Alan Vickery places great emphasis on the strength and performance of his people and so believes in maximum empowerment. Attrition rates in the business are minimal and recruitment is a high priority. While the company invests very heavily in research - £30 million in the last three years - it also spends heavily on training, appraisal and performance recognition.

The future

Clearly, JBA is going to be a business of the future. Its relationship with IBM is especially strong and recently JBA won an award from the computer giant for service excellence. JBA is a technical innovator *par excellence* and its contribution to the future of software is difficult to overstate.

LADBROKE
GROUP
PLC

Ladbroke, London

Ladbroke is a hotels and gaming company operating worldwide

Outlook:
Ladbroke has changed radically in the last few years. It is concentrating its efforts on its interests in hotels - through its ownership of Hilton outside North America - and gaming in the retail outlets and a variety of situations outside the UK. The company also supplies management services in both areas

Scorecard:
Structural flexibility	★★★★
Innovative power	★★★★
International orientation	★★★★★
Human resources	★★★
Growth markets	★★★★★
Quality of management	★★★★

Key figures:
Turnover	£4.4 billion
Pre-tax profits	£128.5 million
Staff	68,000

Ladbroke Group plc
10 Cavendish Place
London W1M 0DQ
Telephone: 0171 323 5000
Fax: 0171 436 1300

Ladbroke

In the UK, Ladbroke is synonymous with its high-street betting establishments. Its 2,000 shops command 25 per cent of the racing-related betting here, making it the market leader. Even now income derived in the UK still accounts for more than 80 per cent of annual turnover. In 1994, Ladbroke reported sales of £4.4 billion, with operating profit up a fifth at £128.5 million. Until recently its activities were divided among hotels, betting and gaming, commercial property and the Texas Homecare DIY chain.

Operations and markets

The combination was the product of the leadership of Cyril Stein, Ladbroke's recently retired chairman. For many years the business was characterised by the personality of its leader but times change and the new consensus-orientated board has restructured. Out has gone Texas to Sainsbury's. The group's £1 billion of commercial property has been reduced to £500 million and this will disappear completely in the next two to three years. This has had two benefits: Ladbroke is getting out of a sector it no longer wanted to operate in and gearing has dropped from 74 per cent to 57.

The reconstituted Ladbroke will concentrate on two core strengths: hospitality, and betting and gaming. In the hotels sector, it is fortunate to be owner of the world's leading brand - Hilton International. Outside the US, Ladbroke operates all Hilton hotels. This is not only the best known group, it is also the most profitable. Hilton brings in a 30 per cent return on sales. In the gaming sector, the biggest growth will come outside the UK. Ladbroke intends to build on its existing international capacities to reverse its 80-20 UK-overseas income split by the beginning of the next century. At present it is number one betting shop operator in Belgium, joint number one in Ireland, has interests in Argentina and is present in four states of the USA - Texas, California, Michigan and Pennsylvania - where it owns and operates four racetracks.

Strategy and management

At the beginning of 1994, new CEO Peter George, who had been with the group for more than 30 years, commissioned an extensive review of Ladbroke's activities. What followed was a complete restructuring. He brought in Italian-American Tommaso Zanzotto from American Express to run hotels. Mr Zanzotto encourages managers to think of Ladbroke as an international rather than a British business and is working to loosen up a formerly rigid and hierarchical structure. Former Bowater director Mike Smith was appointed to revitalise and reorientate the betting and gaming business.

In the hospitality sector, Ladbroke plans to exploit Hilton's formidable brand leadership. At present the company runs 162 hotels around the world. It is one of the most profitable hotel groups worldwide but suffers from insufficient size. Ladbroke's management believes that Hilton could achieve far more by expanding its reach and that means increasing the numbers of Hilton hotels. Over the next decade or more, Hilton could expand its chain to beyond 600 depending on the opportunities which become available.

Ladbroke bought Hilton International in 1987. It was demerged from Hilton Hotel Corporation - the parent of the US hotels - in 1964 after a business analyst recommended this initiative to add value to the company. Its owners before Ladbroke took charge were TWA and United Airlines. 'We believe that there are great synergies to be achieved by finding some way of linking the two parts of the organisation as they were before 1964,' says head of public affairs Stephen Devany. 'This could be done in a number of ways. At present no agreement has been achieved with HHC but putting the Hilton brand back together would create a formidable presence.'

The hotel business is highly demanding but the results of good management are paying off for Ladbroke. The Heathrow Hilton was a case in point. The company took over an existing hotel from BAA. Within 24 hours, the branding had been changed. Ladbroke adopted its normal approach of installing its own general manager who first arranged the name change then set about implementing Hilton systems. Occupancy rates - one of the two key measures of hotel success - were substantially up within a few weeks. The hotel immediately benefited from inclusion in the international Hilton booking network. As soon as people were aware that there was a Hilton at Heathrow they shifted into this hotel out of rivals at the airport.

Ladbroke's hotel division is divided into two parts: own and lease, and managed. The first group consists of those hotels where the group runs its own establishments; the second, of those where it is paid a fee for running other people's assets. The group works actively with hotel developers to influence the form which new hotel buildings will take. A five-star hotel costs between £50 and £150 million to build. Ladbroke does not want to invest in all the buildings it needs to expand the chain, so it encourages external investors to commit to such developments.

Peter George and Tommaso Zanzotto developed a series of strategic targets for the hospitality business which were announced at the beginning of 1995:

. Hilton International will continue its expansion in prime city centre locations. It will also develop clusters of properties serving individual countries or regions of the world, where such developments are justified. This would be achieved primarily through management contracts but also through acquisition or joint ventures with local hotel companies.
. The company will aim to segment its brand in the middle market sector, either on its own or as a joint venture partner or master franchisor.
. Ladbroke - through Hilton - will target resort properties, serving the tourist industry and establishing synergies with the betting and gaming division on the development of casinos or related activities.
. Hilton will separate property management from the operational management of hotels.
. The company will aim to extend its leadership in hotel information technology, loyalty programmes and direct marketing to remain at the forefront of new global distribution systems. IT will also be used to improve yield management and promote efficiency throughout the business.

Viewed from the UK the betting and gaming sector is experiencing worthwhile but unremarkable growth. Taken from a global perspective the industry is enjoying a period of great potential. In the US, in particular, deregulation is creating a wealth of opportunity. One of the biggest spurs to the process is the creation of casinos on Native-American reservations which do not have to comply with state regulations. As long as a state allows gaming in some form - lotteries, racetrack betting - operators on the reservations can set up any form of gaming.

Ladbroke says it is investigating the casino business in the four states where it already operates. Casinos in the US bear little resemblence to the internationally familiar model with roulette tables and black jack. Although there may be some of this sort of gaming, most American casinos are huge halls packed with rows of slot machines. They are hugely popular - and profitable. Casino riverboats have become particularly active. For a large scale investor, they are relatively cheap to set up. A landing stage with a vast car park in a development area costs around $15 million, while the boat itself, including fitting out fees, comes in at around $25 million. In the early days of deregulation, operators often went into profit after four months.

Ladbroke is looking at the possibility of seeking licences for riverboats. The company is concerned about over-licensing which could make achieving a return difficult, but if it is able to secure an exclusive warrant then it will want to go ahead in Pittsburg as soon as the necessary law changes come into effect, possibly by the end of 1995. It would also like to build a casino on a racetrack it owns in Michigan. The company has not forgotten its home base though. Ladbroke has bought three casinos in London: Maxim's, the Golden Horseshoe and Chester's.

Mike Smith has developed a strategy for the betting and gaming division which emphasises the increasingly international dimension. 'The opportunities for generating additional revenue, increasing employment, broadening the tourism industry and improving economic conditions generally stem from the demand for properly regulated gaming activities,' he says.

'Our objective is to become one of the world's leading operators of gaming facilities. Our expansion plan will be based on the following:
. The group will create a portfolio of gaming businesses on a market by market basis with particular emphasis on those areas with broad popular appeal. It is likely that these will take many different forms reflecting the vast diversity of demand for gaming and regulation by country and state.
. It will maintain its market leadership in racing and sports betting especially in the UK where the unique betting system and anticipated legislative changes make it a very attractive business.
. The acquisition of three London casinos mark the group's return to casino management in the UK.
. The primary geographic markets for expansion will be those where the division currently operates. In particular, it proposes building on its experience and sound reputation in certain US states.'

The future

When Cyril Stein launched Ladbroke it had a market capitalisation of £1 million. He grew the company to a value of £2.5 billion. Now the group is poised for another dynamic phase of expansion. In the next five years Ladbroke will emerge as a world- leading and highly profitable hotel, betting and gaming business.

LAND SECURITIES

Land Securities, London

Land Securities is one of the UK's largest property companies

Outlook:
The nature of the property markets has changed radically since the early years of the 1990s. Operators can no longer rely on passive management to generate income. There is increased emphasis on high-level customer service. Land Securities is in the excellent position of commanding a large and valuable portfolio but has also recognised key movements in market trends

<u>Scorecard:</u>

Structural flexibility	★★★★
Innovative power	★★★★
International orientation	★★★★
Human resources	★★★
Growth markets	★★★★
Quality of management	★★★★

<u>Key figures:</u>

Value of investments	£5 billion
Rental income	£417 million

Land Securities PLC
5 Strand
London WC2N 5AF
Tel: 0171 413 9000
Fax: 0171 925 0202

Land Securities

Land Securities is one of a small number of UK property companies that have survived the crash with their reputation intact, perhaps even enhanced. As others struggled, it maintained a record of unbroken growth in profits, earnings and dividends throughout the severest property slump since the second world war. That performance was not matched by any other leading UK property company.

Its management demonstrated a keener understanding of the long-term nature of the property cycle than many of its peers and positioned the group and its portfolio appropriately. It was not immune to the downturn. A nationwide portfolio spread across all commercial sectors performed broadly in line with the market. However the group was better able to adapt to harsher market conditions than its peer group. As a result, it was one of few in good enough shape financially to buy at the bottom of the cycle, without calling on shareholders to inject new equity.

Operations and markets

Britain's largest quoted property company (market value approx. £3bn) has a relatively short history. The founder of the present operation, the late Harold Samuel, paid £20,000 for a stake in the company at the end of the second world war. At that point the portfolio consisted of just three houses. Growth was via takeovers until 1971. Thereafter it made individual additions to the property portfolio and expanded by developing its existing holdings.

The group now owns over 700 properties. These were valued at over £5bn at the last year end, an increase of some 20 per cent over the previous year. The portfolio is around 44 per cent in offices, all located in London and the South East. Retail property makes up another 48 per cent, around 3,500 shops in town centres, shopping centres and out-of-town retail centres, including retail warehouses. These are spread fairly evenly across Great Britain. Of the rest, five per cent is industrial property, with the final three per cent hotel and leisure. Total rent from its portfolio totalled £417m last year.

A favourite industry maxim says that only three things - 'location, location and location' - determine the success of a property investment. Land Securities employs very strict criteria for selecting purchases, in order to maximise the potential to increase rents and capital values. It has occasionally been criticised for adhering to these principles too rigidly in recent years. In particular, some felt it should have capitalised on its strength, and bought more property at the bottom of the market. Management, in response, claims that few of the properties available met its exacting criteria and with its record on acquisitions it deserves the benefit of the doubt. Those critics would also have advised it to buy more at the peak.

Because of its commitment to low risk, Land Securities' operation is entirely UK based. The reasons are largely historic, but a change of policy is very unlikely. Overseas markets were seen as more volatile and the experience of UK companies overseas has been almost uniformly disappointing. The UK operates a unique leasing system, weighted towards landlords rather than tenants, although the last few years have seen the balance shift. Finally there was also a more restrictive planning policy in the UK than elsewhere.

Strategy and management

Simply stated, the strategy is to extract full value and rent from each property, while maintaining a modest level of borrowings, sustainable cashflow and interest cover. During the last decade, management focused on cashflow and resisted the temptation to take big risks on speculative development.

Its accounting policies are also more conservative than most of its competitors'. Low gearing is combined with no off-balance-sheet interests and all interest on developments is taken through the P&L account. This means that stated group profits are meaningful, closely related to rental income. This is enhanced by the fact that it does not recognise or seek to generate property trading profits. All property acquisitions are for investment purposes. It therefore outperformed its peer group while maintaining stricter accounting policies. The security of the group income stream is most important. Over 80 per cent of total rental income is secured on leases expiring after 2000 without break clauses and with upward-only rent reviews.

Land Securities' past success lies in its ability to combine financial conservatism with proactive management of its properties. There have been three major strategic moves during the past decade.

In the early eighties it sharply increased its development programme, developing or refurbishing one million square feet of space in central London alone. This was followed by a second programme which began in the late eighties, producing an annual income of £90m, but which was not completed until 1992.

However, unlike most of its peer group it actively sought tenants for developments prior to development. As others held out for a higher rent in a rising market Land Securities chose to secure the eventual income. This produced an excellent return on cost, against the huge development losses made by most competitors. Ironically Land Securities actually secured higher rents this way, as the market was due to plunge.

Two other strategic moves are still underway. The first was the early move into the out-of-town retail market and then, during the last three years, the concentration of acquisitions in town-centre shopping centres. Land Securities was one of the first large investors to acquire out-of-town retail property, and now has around 5m sq ft in this sector. It has bought a number of prime shopping centres in Aberdeen, York, Cardiff and Sunderland. The timing has been excellent. As the value of City office property has fallen by over 50 per cent these acquisitions, plus some selective disposals, have shifted the balance towards retail and away from the worst-performing areas of the market.

The concentration on retail, particularly out-of-town, has also helped reduce the impact of over-renting in the portfolio. The group's rental income from the City is unlikely to grow for three to five years as many of its offices were let or reviewed before rents fell sharply. However, income growth will come through much earlier in the retail and industrial sectors.

Thus 'active management' can make a difference. During 1993 the company stated that it might lose about £50m of rental income through lease expiries before the year 2000. By mid-1994 this had fallen to £35m through lease expiries and new lettings achieved in the following 12 months. Recent management actions suggest that the final impact could be as low as £10-20m.

Management is regarded as high quality and if it has not gone out of its way to win any plaudits among property analysts, investors should be very satisfied with its record in recent years.

Peter Hunt is chairman and managing director. He was appointed chief surveyor to the group in 1973 and has been a member of the board since 1976, managing director for some 17 years. He has set out three key objectives for the group that underline his intentions for the property holdings.

The first is 'to maintain and wherever possible increase rental income, whilst minimising voids, irrecoverable outgoings, administrative expenses and other costs'. Second, 'to increase the proportion of group income flowing from properties that have early growth potential'. It will achieve this by adjusting the balance and spread of its portfolio. Finally he intends to 'maintain the programme of upgrading group properties wherever appropriate so that they are capable of achieving the greatest possible increase in both rent and capital value'.

To these ends it has managed to let almost all the remaining empty space in its development programme. Last year it addressed the second aim by acquiring further retail, industrial and warehouse properties, while disposing of three in central London. It bought around 430,000 sq ft of shops, 440,000 sq ft of industrial or warehouse space and 68,000 sq ft of provincial offices, together costing around £128m.

Land Securities puts an emphasis on building design. This is intended to maximise the flexibility of each building to adapt to any changes of use and occupational demand. These are intended to take into account the latest technological, environmental and energy conservation requirements. All properties are managed in-house and the group, perhaps unusual for a group with such a large portfolio, has a hands-on management style.

The future

Land Securities enters a challenging decade for property companies with a portfolio of the highest quality and in excellent financial shape. Management has put in place a strategy designed to adapt to likely changes in demand for commercial space. The recession fundamentally changed the outlook and operating environment for UK property. The rate of inflation will almost certainly remain below that of the sixties and seventies. That in turn means less chance of inflation pushing up rents and capital values. Low inflation is also making it more difficult for businesses to pass on cost increases to their customers, encouraging them to look for buildings that are inexpensive to maintain. Management will thus have to work harder to add value.

The impact of political change on the industry is not easy to predict; the Labour Party has not revealed any stated policy toward the property industry. Logically it won't be as positive towards development as the current government, but the relaxation of planning regulations was instrumental in the explosion of development in the City and the eventual crash. The Tories have in any case already reined in development of out-of-town shopping, to prevent further attrition in town centres. That is a positive move for Land Securities, whose substantial holding of out-of-town retail should grow in value as the supply of new schemes is likely to be very limited.

LONDON CLUBS
INTERNATIONAL

London Clubs International, London

London Clubs is an operator and manager of gaming clubs

Outlook:
London Clubs is market leader - by far - in the UK and an outstanding operator around the world. The company is standard bearer for the sector and argues for deregulation for responsible operators. Its management is developing into a formidable unit and as the government in the UK allows greater freedom for operators, London Clubs is set for greater prosperity

Scorecard:

Structural flexibility	★★★★
Innovative power	★★★★
International orientation	★★★★★
Human resources	★★★★
Growth markets	★★★★★
Quality of management	★★★★

Key figures:

Turnover	£155.68 million
Pre-tax profits	£29.4 million
Staff	1,919

London Clubs International plc
30 Old Burlington Street
London W1X 2LN
Tel: 0171 637 5464
Fax: 0171 631 3441

London Clubs International

The UK gaming environment is perhaps the most highly regulated in the western world. In 1968 the government acted to clean up the operators of clubs offering roulette, black jack and other public gaming activities. The legislation worked and now the operators in this sector are businesses of high probity and distinctive commercial management. But in comparison with other major markets, the UK legislation is now viewed as highly restrictive to the advancement of the industry.

Few observers seriously believe that the industry will revert to its earlier incarnation and indeed is trying to grow with one hand tied behind its back. Equally, the potential for the expansion of profits - and therefore revenue for the Exchequer - is considerable and the state as well as operators and customers could benefit from a relaxation of the rules.

London Clubs is the market leader and is therefore the strongest voice in the campaign to reform the regulatory environment. It has begun a long term dialogue with government and agencies to create greater operational freedom while ensuring that licence holders are reputable and well conducted businesses. The sector's public persona as an elite pastime for millionaires is being revised to present a truer impression as one which could be available to a wider constituency of solvent but by no means super-rich players and the hundreds of thousands of tourists which pass through the capital each year.

Operations and markets

London Clubs is the best managed, most international and broadest-based gaming organisation in the UK. It attracts the cream of the industry and is operator of the most elegant clubs. It runs The Ritz Club, Les Ambassadeurs Club, The Rendezvous Club, The Palm Beach Club, The Sportsman and the Golden Nugget in London. Among its overeseas operations are The Carlton Casine, Cannes and the Ramses Hilton in Cairo. Its subsidiary Mayfair Maritime operates casinos on liners such as the QEII and The Royal Viking Sun and it has a dining area at Six Hamilton Place. The group is engaged in an ongoing search for further management opportunities in suitable locations around the world.

This is a highly profitable business, regardless of the licence payments it makes to the Treasury. It achieves a 20 per cent return on sales. The bulk of its income (80 per cent) comes from the UK, 12 per cent from the rest of Europe and eight per cent from the Middle East. However the positive impact of the Middle East on the balance sheet is increasing.

The vast bulk of the company's clientele are wealthy individuals who enjoy either gaming or dining in gaming clubs. It produces a high calibre glossy lifestyle magazine - Cachet - which is concerned with the interests of many of its clients such as top range cars, high fashion and exotic locations.

Strategy and management

Neatly summarised, the strategic objective of London Clubs is to grow by broadening the base of its operations. It aims to expand its membership in the

UK and to extend its reach to other upper echelon nightspots around the world. The first objective will be achieved only when the government relaxes gaming restrictions. Alan Goodenough, chief executive, says that London Clubs has been campaigning to allow the sector and his business in particular the freedom to widen its client base.

There are several changes to the present operational basis which the company would like to see:

1) changes in the requirement for membership

'At present we are obliged to operate a 48 hour cooling off period. This means that members cannot play for 48 hours after signing their application form. Apart from smacking of the nanny state, this means we cannot market to the 11 million tourists who come to London every year. The resultant loss in potential revenue is significant,' says Mr Goodenough.

2) lifting advertising restrictions

'The anti-gambling lobby has always been concerned that if we are allowed to advertise this will encourage people to start gambling whereas without advertising they would not have begun. We are not looking for advertising to persuade people to become gamblers. But we do want to conduct information advertising to tell people who wish to play where our facilities are located. This would include inflight magazines, space in Where to go type publications, and notices in hotels.

3) gaming machines in clubs

London Clubs wants to be able to offer gaming machines as well as its roulette or card-based games and at present it is limited in the numbers it is allowed to run.

4) licensing and dining facilities

Many of its clientele want to dine rather than play the tables and the company wishes to offer full restaurant facilities to customers who merely want to enjoy elegant surroundings and soak up the atmosphere.

Mr Goodenough suggests that the National Lottery has put piad to any suggestion that the British people are not gambling-minded. 'Look at the numbers of people who play the Lottery each week. At present the market penetration of the industry is two per cent of all adults. These simple changes to the gaming laws would allow us to provide a service to a much wider population who perhaps thought that our clubs were only for the super rich. These are people who have disposable income but may wish to limit their involvement to smaller sums and enjoy an evening out in pleasant and attractive surroundings.'

He says that the industry, in addition to the regulation, has not served its own best interests. 'We have not been user-friendly. We have not demonstrated to the public at large that our clubs are just as much for them as very wealthy. And we are pleased to welcome a broad range of customers.'

The international expansion of London Clubs is also highly impressive. In terms of overall profitability ventures on the mainland and in the Middle East have yet to make a powerful contribution to group profitability. But this will grow. The company is looking around the world to other centres where its services will prove attractive. Latin America is one area where London Clubs could make an important contribution in the next decade.

Many of these ventures are joint ventures with local companies. Each arrangement is individual but must fit in with the company's philosophy of dealing with the leading businesses in each market and in the most prestigious locations. Opportunities exist in each quarter of the world because the theme of deregulation is gaining ground. In the US, for example, huge new markets have been opened with remarkable potential for owners and managers.

Mr Goodenough is also keen to enhance the quality of personnel in the industry and decision making within London Clubs. 'Part of the reason for the industry not advancing quicker was the restriction on directors of clubs, which limited to people within the industry. We have drawn in professionals in senior roles from outside who are influencing the shape and development of the business.'

The future

This is a simple and direct business. The potential for expansion is outstanding and London Clubs stands at the head of the queue to benefit from legislative changes. It is the best managed operator of clubs in the UK and it provides a service which should be expanded to a wider circle of members especially the thousands of visitors to London each year. This would not only help the London Clubs to even better returns but it could put some much needed money in the public purse.

M&G, London

M&G is a leading financial services company specialising in long term
investment plans

Outlook:
M&G can boast two qualities which many other financial services companies
lack - integrity and performance. It is a substantial combination which will
become even more powerful as investors become more aware of the true
strengths of businesses in this sector. M&G is also highly innovative in its
product range

Scorecard:
Structural flexibility	★★★★
Innovative power	★★★★★
International orientation	★★★
Human resources	★★★★★
Growth markets	★★★★
Quality of management	★★★★

Key figures:
Pre-tax profits	£61 million
Funds under management	£11.8 billion
Staff	775

M&G Group plc
7th Floor
3 Minster Court
Great Tower Street
London EC 3R 7XH
Tel: 0171 626 4588
Fax: 0171 623 8615

M&G Group plc

A major shake-up in the retail financial services industry is anticipated over the next five to ten years. The principal criterion which will shape the change is an increasing discrimination by customers. Those businesses which are structurally flexible enough to be able to detect and respond to the change - and anticipate future customer demand - will be the ones that survive and prosper. M&G is among those survivors.

The company has a consistent and powerful investment record. And investment is the key to this organisation. The values and the culture of the investment section of the business lie at the heart of M&G. For the last thirty years it has employed the same approach to investment and it is one which has been very successful for its customers. Its reputation - and therefore its brand - is regarded in financial services as one of the very best. A leading investment analyst at one of its rivals commented 'If you're looking at M&G you are talking about integrity.'

Long-term is another criterion which describes the approach of the company. Its approach to investment is the exact opposite of many of its competitors' in the sector whose approach is often to go in, to make a quick hit and come out again. M&G prefers the long term. Throughout its history, it has invested in the UK equity market taking a long-term approach to the value of companies. Peter Jones, research director, says: 'There are three themes to our investment policy:
. the first is income where we seek an above-average dividend yield
. a high proportion of small companies in our UK portfolio
. also we have a tradition of investing in recovery companies.'

M&G owns around one per cent of the UK equity market. Its involvement in companies often stretches from five per cent to 15 per cent, depending on its confidence in the management of a particular company and the capacity of that company to realise long-term growth. 'We are stock pickers par excellence. We are not index matchers. Many of our rivals are either index matchers or quasi index matchers,' Mr Jones comments.

Operations and markets

At present M&G has £11.6 billion under management. This is split:
. retail £8 billion
. institutional £3 billion
. international £0.6 billion

The market capitalisation of the company is currently £720 million. The success of the business is seen in the growth in funds under management by M&G which rose 11.7 per cent in 1994 from £10.5 million in 1993. Profit also grew by 20 per cent from £50.9 million in 1993 to £61 million in 1994. The number of unit trust accounts - one of M&G's strengths - rose by 17.5 per cent from 637,000 in 1993 to 748,000 in 1994. It has also experienced substantial growth in the number of life policies that it handles. This has risen by 11.9 per cent. In 1993 the figure was a little short of 290,000. This rose to 324,000 in 1994.

Investment management underpins the business and it is M&G's core competence. Its investment philosophy is neatly summed up by a recent marketing document: 'We believe that sustainable above-average investment performance is ultimately dependent on a proper understanding of each stock in a portfolio, and that this can only be achieved through sound fundamental analysis of a business and its management. This results in a bottom-up investment approach in which stock selection is pre-eminent.

'The thrust of our analysis is the long-term strategic issues confronting businesses rather than short-term considerations. We attach great importance to the integrity of management and we will not back management which we do not trust or which we feel has let us down in the past.'

Strategy and management

It is this belief in management which guides the principal philosophy of M&G. Before an investment is made in a company a visit to the company and a discussion with management will take place. Mr Jones says that without this no investment decision will be taken. Also the company is opposed to contested takeovers. In any contested takeover it is the company's first policy to support the existing management. The thinking behind this strategy is that no investment will have been made initially without full confidence in the management of the company in whose stock M&G is investing. So therefore it would be wrong to suddenly switch horses in the middle of a long-term strategy. However, if the management of the company in which M&G is investing believes that it is in the best interests of shareholders, employees and customers to have a change of ownership then it will re-assess its involvement in that company and possibly choose to go with the new management.

Its investment team meets on average 1,000 companies a year. This means that each M&G fund manager averages 30-50 meetings in any one year. The small company investment analyst visits many more since there is quite a high small-company quotient to the entire investment portfolio. Another key strategy of the investment approach is to stick with recovery companies. Three prime examples of this strategy having paid off for M&G in the past are British Steel, Standard Chartered and Midland Bank.

There is a cautious approach to investment and, implicitly, a cautious approach to acquisition and disposal which characterises the culture of the business.

But the heavily analytical approach to management is not the complete story. The character of the business is also one of tremendous enthusiasm. 'This is a consistent company but it is also a passionate one,' says communications manager Rachel Medill. 'As part of a major investigation into the ethics and principles of our business I talk to many of our managers and other employees. I discovered a passionate belief in the company and the products which it is selling.'

The business at present employs 800 people in the United Kingdom. Some 150 are engaged at the company's headquarters at Tower Hill in London. Another 550 administrative and customer service staff work at Chelmsford in Essex. The rest are dispersed around the country working at offices up and down the UK. Mr Shearer has been with the company since 1988 when he left accountants Deloitte, Haskins & Sells. His aim is to lose none of the traditional strengths of the business while at the same time creating a favourable environment for staff involvement.

'We have a good brand name and we are rightly regarded as a company which operates with great honesty and integrity. Our customer service provision is good and is getting better all the time. But the pace of change is accelerating. The UK financial services industry has previously been product-driven. It has never been customer segmented. This is one of the profound differences which will emerge in the next few years. Neither ourselves nor any of our competitors have traditionally done a great deal of customer segmentation. I believe that this is one of the ways forward for the business. We aim to capitalise on the differential needs of particular market groups. This will mean that we will develop products and services for our customers which will be geared to particular demands of particular groups.'

At the moment M&G has 1.2 million accounts and somewhere in the region of half a million customers. As a predominantly retail - and UK - business it intends to work much more closely with its customers to discover their needs and to meet them. Group marketing and sales director Peter Emms says that M&G will benefit from its reputation as an honest operator. 'Now that we have full disclosure, customers will be able to judge for themselves which are the ethical operators and which offer best value for money.'

Traditionally M&G's biggest source has been independent financial advisers (IFAs) who account for 60-70 per cent of M&G's inflow. The remainder comes in via direct marketing, an area in which M&G has been particularly active. It has been especially successful for the company compared with the rest of the marketplace and it has made good use of the increasing number of personal finance pages in national newspapers and the growing number of personal finance magazines.

The introduction of enforced price disclosure in 1995 will act as a powerful catalyst in restructuring the industry. Success will depend less on control of distribution and more on cost competitiveness. The fortunes of companies will change dramatically as their cost structures are exposed. As this happens, those companies with financial strength, a strong and positive brand image, warm customer bases and competitive costs will be the winners. Above all, the key will be to focus on core skills and to offer better value and performance year after year.

While the international element of M&G's business is comparatively small at present this is an area in which it intends to grow. Mr Emms says that it has two current international links. One is in the United States, where it works with Dreyfus.

The other is in Hong Kong - where it has recently established a joint venture with Hong Kong bank Dah Sing to develop a presence in both unit trusts and institutional fund management. With Dah Sing's local knowledge and expertise M&G expects that both Hong Kong, and in due course China, will provide fruitful ground for its investment management skills.

The future

The company intends to move from its headquarters at Three Quays next to the Tower of London in October 1995. The new building at Minster Court will reflect the innovative pace of change which is going on within the company. It will provide the company with extra capacity to take full advantage of the changes in the markets and the opportunities and challenges which lie ahead of M&G in the next decade. Observers should expect to see a much more customer segmented approach towards its investment management policy - but the principles of the business as enshrined by its investment department will remain at its heart.

MARKS & SPENCER

Marks & Spencer, London

M&S is perhaps Britain's most famous retailer specialising in an increasing range of distinctive clothing, food and financial services

Outlook:
No one would seriously doubt that Marks & Spencer is going to be a prominent feature of the UK's high street in the next decade. Its reputation for quality and reliability is unmatched. The company's real growth plans lie in the external arena where M&S hopes to replicate its outstanding domestic success

Scorecard:

Structural flexibility	★★★★
Innovative power	★★★★
International orientation	★★★★
Human resources	★★★★★
Growth markets	★★★★
Quality of management	★★★★

Key figures:

Sales	£6.8 billion
Pre-tax profits	£924 million
Staff	53,000

Marks and Spencer
Michael House
47 Baker Street
London W1A 1DN
Tel: 0171 935 4422
Fax: 0171 487 2679

Marks & Spencer plc

Marks & Spencer is one of the most highly esteemed companies in Britain today. In 1994 Price Waterhouse ran a survey with the Financial Times among managing directors, chairmen and chief executive officers of European multinational companies. The purpose of the inquiry was to identify those businesses across the continent which European executives regarded with most admiration. Marks & Spencer came top by a long margin.

In the 1989 book _The 100 Best Companies to Work for in the UK_, Marks & Spencer was regarded as a by-word for excellent employment practice. Researchers looking for nominations for inclusion in that top 100 were often told, 'Well, apart from M&S, there is always...' And during the research for this current project several leading executives of British-owned companes cited Marks & Spencer as one of the most excellent. They have arrived at this perception because M&S is seen as a company which is true to its core values, advocates managerial entrepreneurship while adhering to its strong culture, believes in growing and developing its people, delivers excellent value and customer service, shows innovation, practises able financial control and personifies business integrity. It is a tall order to live up to such a billing.

Yet the pattern of development of the UK's leading retailer suggests that it has exemplified much of what its admirers regard as the unique personality of Marks & Spencer for more than a century. The story of Marks & Spencer is a business legend in the UK. It started in Leeds in 1882 when Michael Marks, a young Russian refugee, sold haberdashery from a tray to people in nearby villages. Two years later he took a stall in the city's market. He couldn't read or write English so he commissioned a sign which read 'Don't ask the price - it is a penny'.

In 1894 he formed a partnership with Tom Spencer to own shops in the north east, and in 1903 the company was registered as a private limited company. Things began to develop rapidly after that. As the first world war broke out, the penny point disappeared and in 1917 Mr Marks' eldest child Simon, by then chairman, introduced Israel Sieff to the board.

Between the wars, M&S introduced many of the principles which have guided the company ever since. In 1924 it developed the policy of buying direct from manufacturers and today is regarded by many suppliers as their most valuable client, formative in setting excellent standards of delivery but also the toughest business with which to negotiate. In 1933, in another defining moment, it created a welfare department which was to be the foundation for a range of employee support, development and recognition initiatives. The decision was motivated by a mixture of genuine concern for staff but also the directors were inspired enough - as far back as the thirties - to realise that positive employment practice leads to consistent staff loyalty.

Operations and markets

At present some 83 per cent of revenue comes from the UK stores and operations. The size of the UK share of total income - although it will grow in absolute terms - will reduce in favour of overseas operations. 'We see France, Spain, and Hong Kong as the next phase of our development. For example, we already operate six stores in the Paris region and this will certainly grow to nine and perhaps more. Our store on the Boulevard Hausmann is 80,000 sq ft but in the Rue de Rivoli we have a 40,000 sq ft store, where 30 per cent of sales are foods', the company reports. M&S has 283 stores in the UK. There are a further three in Ireland, 16 in France, five in Spain, two in the Netherlands, three in Belgium, seven in Hong Kong and 49 in Canada. So there are presently 363 wholly-owned M&S stores plus the group in Spain which is a joint venture with Cortefiel.

In addition, the company has franchised the Marks & Spencer brand, store design, products and management approach to a further 17 countries. These include Cyprus, Hungary, Portugal, Greece, Israel and the Philippines. Needless to say, M&S management in Baker Street, London is cautious about awarding franchises and employs a team to monitor operations of its franchisees.

M&S also owns Brooks Brothers which has 104 stores in the US and 51 in Japan, Kings Super Markets which has 19 outlets in North America and D'Allairds with 95 sites in Canada. International operations have not always been smooth for the company but today it sells approximately £1 billion of goods in its overseas stores and supplies its franchisees with a further $100 million of merchandise at cost value. Mr Oates and his team are convinced that international will be the biggest area of development for the company. As well as the countries where it currently has operations, Germany is actively being studied to see where M&S can make an entry. In March 1995, the company announced that its only constraint to expansion there was finding prime retail locations at the right prices.

Strategy and management

Ask any business analyst worth his or her salt what will be the key strategems for major companies in years to come. One will almost certainly be to stick to core competencies. Throughout this report, the reader will note that companies such as Hewlett Packard, Williams Holdings, WH Smith, Smith and Nephew, BP and Ladbroke are strong advocates of core values. Marks & Spencer has never wavered from its core - it is a retailer with a defined approach. It moves into new markets - financial services, out-of-town centres, new territories - but adheres to those original values which make it M&S.

Another important approach for the corporate future is culture. Companies which survive the coming upheaval will need an identity which is readily identifiable by suppliers, employees, managers and customers. M&S culture is one which has evolved over the years but it remains one with which the founders would be comfortable. One of the factors which has had greatest influence in the maintenance of the cultural integrity of the business is the high retention of staff. This is not a jobs for life company - which are, nowadays? - but many start their careers and prosper with the business. So much so that there are many lifers in the business. One who joined the company straight from school is Sir Richard Greenbury, its current chairman.

His deputy chairman and joint managing director is Keith Oates. He joined the company as finance director in 1984, launching the groundbreaking charge card, after service at the widely-admired Black and Decker and IBM. 'Anyone visiting Marks & Spencer in ten or more years will see changes but it will be instantly recognisable as M&S. The values, traditions and style of the company have been consistent throughout its history and they will continue to guide the enterprise.'

Mr Oates is unusual in industry in not forecasting wholesale change in business. But, he argues, transformative change was forecast for retail for the last ten years but the predicted scale of change did not occur. So he is dubious. He says that technology is useful as a tool but he does not agree that everyone will start shopping from their homes on multimedia terminals. 'Shopping is a social experience. People like going out to shopping centres to see the latest products but also make contact with friends and relatives.'

Marks & Spencer is a strong advocate of shopping as a favourite pastime. Its 1994 annual report contains an article which says that shopping has never been more pleasant. 'Going shopping should be a pleasure, with easy access to shops by car or public transport, and a litter-free, safe environment. But these things don't just happen. Making town and city centres pleasant takes time and effort. Since the 1970s, M&S has been spearheading the concept of town centre management. The management philosophy of shopping malls is applied to high streets and M&S joins with local authorities to ensure that the centres of towns are managed as purposefully as malls.

The commitment to the development of stores, of the technology to support M&S business divisions and to innovative products and services requires a high level of capital investment. Mr Oates says that the company will allocate more than £1 billion over three years for investment purposes. In 1993 Marks & Spencer spent £300 million and in 1994 £350 million. 'We stated at the beginning of the financial year that the spend over three years would exceed the billion. It may even reach £1.2 billion but we are being very flexible and reviewing requirements as we go along.'

At present the company is growing at around six per cent a year which is high for retail and analysts constantly question whether M&S can sustain this level of expansion. 'We are adding a business the size of Next to our company every year,' he remarks. Pre-tax return on sales is currently at 13 per cent. Sales grew 10 per cent in 1994 over the previous year. Currently turnover stands £6.5 billion with gross operational profit at £874 million. Profits have risen by around 40 per cent over five years, while turnover has gone up around 16 per cent over the same period.

The UK draws in more than two-thirds of the capital spend in the business. There is greater market segmentation than at any other time in the past. The company plans 50 department store size outlets of greater than 100,000 square feet. It is building regional centres of around 60,000 sq ft and high street branches of 40,000 sq ft.

The future

The idea of the British high street without Marks & Spencer is unthinkable. There is absolutely no doubt that the company - barring acts of God - will be here and making a substantial contribution to the UK economy in years to come. It fulfils all the criteria in our report: it is innovative, it has strong but flexible strategy, M&S is a cultural metaphor, retail sector staffing policy uses M&S as the standard-setter, it sees new opportunities in fresh markets - here and abroad, the company has sufficient financial strength to launch any new product or customer-led initiative which it chooses. The format of retailing may change a little more quickly than the company suggests, but then M&S is sufficiently experienced and flexible to take most things in its stride.

THE MAYFLOWER CORPORATION plc

Mayflower Automotive, High Wycombe, Bucks

Mayflower Automotive is the largest component of the Mayflower Group. It combines two businesses - Motor Panels and International Automotive Design - which provide body panels and interior design for the motor trade

Outlook:
Mayflower is an extremely skilfully managed business. It was established to build an engineering-led conglomerate and has acquired Motor Panels and IAD. Both companies are complementary and are respected within the motor trade for the high quality of their products and contribution to the process of building world class cars and trucks

Scorecard:
Structural flexibility	★★★★
Innovative power	★★★★★
International orientation	★★★★★
Human resources	★★★★
Growth markets	★★★★★
Quality of management	★★★★★

Key figures:
Turnover	£134.75 million
Operating profit	£9.1 million
Staff	1,139

The Mayflower Corporation plc
Mayflower House
Loudwater
High Wycombe Bucks HP10 9RF
Tel: 01494 450145
Fax: 01494 450607

Mayflower Automotive

The future may belong to service companies and suppliers: businesses which are expert in their niche but also sufficiently attuned to markets that they advise and influence customers on the development of core specialities. Throughout industry small networks of approved suppliers provide expert level products and services to precise deadlines. They create such positive rapport with their clients that they become influential in the development of their customers' new ranges.

Business advisers have been forecasting for five years or more that the numbers of mainstream manufacturers will become smaller, that these organisations will become bigger and that tight groups of high quality suppliers will fulfil many of the traditional functions of the customer businesses. As these enterprises strip away their non-core activities, suppliers will move in to fill the gap.

The relationships between mainstream business and preferred suppliers are key to understanding the pattern of economic trends in the next decade. Though supplier and client are distinct entities the integration and intimacy between them will emerge as prevailing factors. Nowhere is this more apparent than in the motor industry. Car companies often lack agility and responsiveness to market conditions. Their design teams are removed from the practicality of buying their products. This is where supplier companies play a vital role. As they integrate more closely with the major players they can bring useful input on technical issues but as smaller businesses, lighter on their feet, and with daily dialogue with customers, they offer insight on practical marketing issues.

Operations and markets

Mayflower Automotive is chief among the new breed in the motor industry. Its managers are highly skilled technicians but also alert to the realities of running a business in good times and bad. Automotive is the larger of two divisions of Mayflower Corporation, which is a diversified holding company. The two principal parts of Automotive are Motor Panels, which is based in Coventry, and International Automotive Design, located in Worthing. Operating profits of the group rose 89 per cent to £9.1 million in 1994 from £5.2 million the previous year. This itself was a 54 per cent increase in 1992.

Motor Panels - always a profitable business - was bought in 1991 from CH Holdings which had gone into receivership during the recession. Panels is one of the truly legendary names in the motor business. It is the world technical leader in developing and forming aluminium body panels for the low to medium volume market. Applications vary from family saloon cars through to truck cabs.

Its customer portfolio reads like a Who's Who of the motor industry - Rover, BMW, General Motors, Volvo, Land Rover, Jaguar, Rolls Royce, Ford, Chrysler and Nissan among others. It has four factories - in Coventry, Wigan and the United States. IAD was bought in April 1993 to complement Motor Panels and the two companies are engaged in a programme of integration. IAD is a full service design company which has offices in Coventry, Billericay, France and the US. Mayflower is keen to extend its relationship with leading German manufacturers and has recently opened an IAD facility in the heart of the country.

Strategy and management

'The motor industry worldwide is moving into an era of fundamental change so radical that the shape of both original equipment manufacturers [OEM] and suppliers alike will be totally reformed by the end of the century,' says deputy chairman and CEO John Simpson. 'One aspect of this change will be globalisation, where one source is demanded for a particular commodity or service while the supply is local to the plant or operation.

'The extremely high fixed cost of new product development and the scarcity of specialist resources is inducing yet more mergers, takeovers and collaborations between OEMs. Globalisation requires the supplier to operate on a worldwide basis and be prepared to enter long term partnerships involving product development. The supplier must also be capable of world class standards of performance in terms of cost, quality, leanness and improvement. To remain a first tier supplier into the future, a company must be more than competent at what it does.'

To state that Mayflower is enthusiastic about excellent standards is to do the group a disservice. It is a way of life. In the best traditions of US and Japanese world class businesses, Mayflower companies travel a path of constant renewal. Managers and employees seek ever higher standards of production quality and delivery achievement. Terry Whitmore, group operations director, says 'Strategically, Mayflower faces a series of challenges. To keep step with the pattern of change in the industry, we need to maintain our performance levels and find new ways for delivering beyond customer expectation. We have strengthened and will continue to improve the quality of our management. The biggest challenge presented to a growth company is the management of that growth.'

The group believes in strong financial controls, eliminating waste, and low cost but high quality production. The industry has a reputation for wholesale waste of resources and Mayflower works closely with some of the bigger sector names to demonstrate how costs can be saved. Inventory is high in the motor business but the group is a casebook example of how quickly turnover of finished parts can be realised. Although the British motor industry likes to think that it is progressive few manufacturers practise anything like just-in-time principles. So warehousing provides security. Other industries have abandoned warehouses and depots altogether and Mayflower, as much by example as anything else, is slowly persuading the OEMs to cut the time that parts lie in warehouses.

The business philosophy of Mayflower is embodied in three phrases:
. openness and trust - which pervade the entire group
. teamwork - Mayflower's management argues that public companies should be run by strong teams, and leadership should not be dominated by any one individual
. quality leadership - the company regards this concept as essential in its field of operations

These fundamental principles provide the basis of its culture which seeks to create an environment where organic growth can thrive. In addition Mayflower plans a cautious and well evaluated programme of acquisitions to build a portfolio of world class specialist engineering and manufacturing companies. Its relationship with leading OEMs has provided the platform for participation in joint ventures to develop the vehicles of the future. For example, Mayflower has been an enthusiastic partner in the Rover consortium to produce the new MGF sports car. Other manufacturers have contacted the company to discuss similar arrangements. Its financial commitment to the MGF has been made, the car has been produced and the orders are outstripping expectations. It is an indicator of the manner in which the division will grow - accelerating its world class performance standards and building closer contacts with senior OEMs leading to lucrative joint ventures.

Mayflower's contribution to the motor industry is based on the quality of its management and employees. Motor Panels enjoyed an enviable reputation as one of the country's best employers when it was independent. Mayflower's approach to personnel management has a different character - being somewhat more rigorous in its application - but it shares a deep belief in people at the centre of the business. This is a straightforward business where expertise is valued and input from all levels in the structure is respected as a key part in the advancement of the business. Training and development programmes are among the finest in the industry. There is a great pride in the enterprise among the staff, partly because management genuinely listens to employee views and also because the company invests heavily in new technology. Staff are acutely aware of the company's traditions and outstanding reputation in the sector.

The future

Mayflower's commitment to excellent standards, its strong financial management, teamwork culture and relationships with the world's premier OEMs integrate to make it one of Britain's most exciting businesses. As a unified force Mayflower is young, but by acquiring and then improving businesses of high performance, it is set to be a world beater. Add to this its potential for valuable joint ventures on leading edge vehicles and the potential for profits growth is enormous. In the relatively near future Mayflower will be a full-service preferred supplier to all of the world's leading motor businesses. Its time of profound influence will have come.

McDonald's Restaurants, London

McDonald's is a world famous restaurant company which has an enviable
reputation for quality and management dexterity in the competitive
burgerhouse market

Outlook:
McDonald's commands the high ground in burgers. It is UK market leader
with 72 per cent of the entire sector and a remarkable capacity to find new
ways of retailing its products. Its professionalism, capacity to plan for market
need and the quality of its establishments all contribute to its continuing
dominance of the sector

Scorecard:
Structural flexibility	★★★★
Innovative power	★★★★
International orientation	★★★★★
Human resources	★★★★
Growth markets	★★★★★
Quality of management	★★★★

Key figures 1995:
Turnover	£822 million
Pre-tax profits	£90 million
Staff	38,000

McDonald's Restaurants Ltd
11-59 High Street
East Finchley
London N2 8AW
Tel: 0181 700 7000
Fax: 0181 700 7050

McDonald's Restaurants

Few commercial emblems have created such a lasting impression as McDonald's golden arches or the ubiquitous Ronald McDonald. Many generations ago, the restaurant company learned one secret worth its weight in hamburgers - long-term business can be created by total application to quality, consistency and value. It isn't physical hunger which drives kids through the doors. Sure they like the shakes, fries and burgers. But the magnet of McDonald's is fun. The place is awash with bright colours, packed with people - especially little ones - and the staff are entertainers as much as caterers.

Even for young teens, McDonald's is still cool. For today's generation, it is the contemporary equivalent of coffee bars for teenagers of the late 1950s and early 1960s. But McDonald's isn't only a fashionable, clean and safe place to hang out. It is one of the great retailing success stories of the postwar period. First at home in the US and then throughout the rest of the world, McDonald's has placed its imprint on the business landscape. The opening of McDonald's in Moscow and other eastern capitals was for many almost as potent a symbol of the collapse of communism as the crumbling of the Berlin Wall.

Operations and markets

The McDonald Corporation which is the Chicago parent of the UK company has a formidable reputation for many of the best aspects of customer service. It embodies quality, service, cleanliness, friendliness, and efficiency which could best be characterised as down home USA. But its British business managers have been shrewd enough to realise that undiluted Americana would be nothing other than a flash in the pan. They were aware that America's strongest successes here are those which have taken the essence of the business back home and translated it for the local audience.

There is a certain operational similarity between McDonald's and Disney - in the sense that both are projecting a powerful brand which has an important bond with theatricality. Getting the delivery right is at least as important as ensuring that the product is wholesome. The financial success of the British McDonald's company is due in significant measure to a definitive adaptation of cultural and commercial exchange. The pedigree of the US enterprise is matched by British management expertise with an astute analysis of factors for success in the UK.

The UK operation is one of McDonald Corporation's most profitable subsidiaries. In 1993 the company reported 13 per cent growth in revenues to £651 million. Pre-tax profits came in at £75.4 million, which was 15 per cent up on 1992. Capital employed in the UK is £910 million, which is largely tied up in property. Andy Taylor, chief operating officer of McDonald's UK, says: 'Shareholders look for a significant return on investment. We aim to deliver in the mid-teens.' He adds that the management prefers to look at return on operational activity which gives them a good idea as to the efficiency of the business.

McDonald's assesses the profitability of each restaurant. Each is set challenging targets and is expected to meet them. Among the most profitable sites for the company are: West Thurrock, Gateshead's Metro centre, Meadowhall in Sheffield, the Merryhill centre in Dudley, Liverpool Street in London, Fosse Park (Leicester), the Strand (London), Stockport and Glasgow, reflecting a nationwide success story.

Most of the UK management team are domestic recruits. East Finchley, the UK headquarters, operates its 579 restaurants on rigorous business lines. Behind the imagery is a well-oiled machine which presides over a tightly controlled business financially and one which generates original commercial development ideas and new flavours for the public to sample. Hard core business logic propels the enterprise. High quality customer service means long term business success.

McDonald's commands an astonishing 72 per cent of the sharply competitive ' burger house' market. This is the commercial restaurant sector which embraces burger, pizza and fried chicken takeaway establishments. It is an arena where the fiercest market share battles are fought. 'We would be pleased with an increase of about two per cent per annum over the next five years,' says Andy Taylor. He is a seasoned veteran of current and formative campaigns. He joined McDonald's from university in 1979, progressed through the company and now heads up the operating side of the business.

Strategy and management

Balance is a key factor at McDonald's - matching short term profit demands with a deep commitment to the long term. 'We are a long-term player in the UK economy,' adds Mr Taylor. He is a personal evocation of this core McDonald's value. He has scaled the heights of the organisation and now takes his place at the UK management team top table. He explains that, for example, some businesses take a premises lease for perhaps five years or ten, with a five year break clause. McDonald's takes long leases or preferably buys freehold. This commitment is demonstrated by its plans for diversification in types of outlets and market segmentation. It intends to construct an even greater presence than it has now.

In 1995 it will open 59 new restaurants, in 1996 a further 69 and in 1997 another 79. But do not expect to see them all in the high street. The composite view of a McDonald's outlet is a distinctively bright and colourful place, packed to the gills with young families but a broad mix of old and young. This vision will change as the variety of outlets will continue to grow. 'Market segmentation will become an important issue for us. For example, we may have two restaurants in each high street - one which caters for young adults and the other for families. The latter will be more overtly child orientated and feature play facilities.'

Roadside restaurants on major trunk and arterial roads is another projected development area for the company, as well as an expansion of drive-thru establishments at out-of-town shopping centres. Among McDonald's most innovative ideas are placements in railway termini, hospital restaurants and even on ferry boats.

'We have set three corporate objectives for the company. All of our initiatives fit into these three. We recognise that our markets are becoming more fragmented and that we need to build on our strengths. We intend to stick to our core business which we know well and have no aspirations to use the McDonald's name to go into other business areas,' says Andy Taylor.

The UK company's corporate objectives are:
. 100 per cent customer satisfaction
. increasing market share

. increasing profitability

Great attention has been given in the press and on television to a perceived shift away from retailing activity in traditional high streets. New out-of-town shopping centres have - apparently - taken an upper hand in the battle with town centres. Merryhill, two miles outside Dudley, is often used as an example of this trend. Mr Taylor explains: 'the Dudley high street restaurant opened in 1981 in the thick of the recession and struggled for two to three years before significant growth and subsequent profitability occurred. When the Merryhill centre opened in 1986 we opened our first drive-thru which performed so well that in 1990 we opened another drive-thru facility 800 metres away on the other side of the newly enlarged shopping centre. In addition to these we trade in nearby Stourbridge and in 1994 opened our third restaurant at Merryhill - this time inside the shopping mall. So, within a three mile radius of the Merryhill shopping centre we have five restaurants. Each is successful and each is profitable. In Dudley town centre, we franchised the restaurant to a former employee who has achieved a 150 per cent rise in total site profit by increasing sales in an area considered by many to be dying.'

Franchising represents an aspect of the UK business which is distinctly different from the US. Only 21 per cent of the British restaurants are franchised, as opposed to 84 per cent in America. The superb 1994 McDonald's fact book reveals that by the millennium the company anticipates that at least 40 per cent of UK restaurants will be franchised. Andy Taylor is more cautious. 'We offer franchises only when we have a good business reason to do so. That does not mean that we will not grant more franchises but we must see realisable gains from this policy. In some cases, local operators with significant experience can find ways to secure increases in sales and profitability even though we have been working hard to maximise returns ourselves.' Franchises are granted to individuals rather than absentee investors so the company is looking for candidates who are going to contribute personal effort to the search for greater value.

The 1990s have also been characterised by extensive innovation. In 1990, the first airport location opened at Gatwick. One year later, restaurant number 400 - the company's first in Northern Ireland - began operations in Belfast. 1992 saw the first railway McDonald's at Liverpool Street, London and the first hospital McDonald's restaurant at Guy's in London. Twelve months later, the 500th outlet was sited at Notting Hill Gate, London, and McDonald's went to sea on the Stena-Sealink line on the Dover to Calais ferry route. By the end of 1995 McDonald's will operate six restaurants situated in UK airports.

The future

McDonald's has been a mouldbreaker in its sector since it opened in Woolwich in 1973. It has set the pace for fast food outlets throughout the UK. It is the brand leader with carefully targeted products. The Company's success is based on its core principles of Quality, Service, Cleanliness and Value. It believes in balance in business activities - achieving good profit margins while reinforcing its commitment to staff and community. The vision and innovation which characterise its business approach support the magic which it delivers to its regular customers.

MEDEVA PLC

Medeva, London

Medeva is a small but highly innovative pharmaceutical company

Outlook:
A proposed merger with Fisons failed to get off the ground in the summer of 1995 but according to most observers Medeva emerged from the encounter with its reputation intact. Medeva has won the esteem of the City by its growth in earnings, the quality of its product base and the scope of its management

<u>Scorecard:</u>
Structural flexibilty	★★★★
Innovative power	★★★★★
International orientation	★★★★
Human resources	★★★★★
Growth markets	★★★★★
Quality of management	★★★★★

<u>**Key figures:**</u>
Turnover	£256 million
Pre-tax profits	£79 million
Staff	2200

Medeva PLC
10 St James's Street
London SW1A 1EF
Tel: 0171 839 3888
Fax: 0171 930 1514

Medeva

Founded only eight years ago Medeva is already capitalised at £616m and is Britain's fifth-largest pharmaceuticals company. The company first reported an annual profit of £4m in 1990 but by 1995 that figure had soared to £79m. By 1996 analysts expect pre-tax profits to have reached £89m and earnings per share to be 19.3p - an increase of 484 per cent on 1990.

Though Medeva's expansion has historically been through astute deal-making, it now has a broad range of products on the market, an exciting pipeline of new drugs and a well regarded management team capable of delivering impressive organic growth. This is the rising star of Britain's pharmaceuticals industry.

Medeva was founded in 1987 as Medirace by two young Australian entrepreneurs, Ian Gowrie-Smith and David Lees. It claimed to be working on a drug called Contracan which it was hoped could cure some cancers and Aids, and raised £1.2m on the Stock Exchange Third Market.

Hopes of a wonder cure evaporated by late 1990 but by then had served to push Medeva's share price to startling levels, which allowed the company to start a series of paper-funded acquisitions. The first significant move came in 1990 shortly after Glaxo's former managing director Bernard Taylor joined Medeva as chairman.

Mr Taylor believed that the emergence of giant players in the drugs industry meant there were many medicines and therapeutic areas too small to interest the big players but which could be pieced together to form a significant business. Over the next three years, 13 acquisitions and four rights issues ensued.

In July 1993 Medeva seemed to slip up. Overstocking at a Californian subsidiary IMS caused earnings to fall. Amidst fears that the paper chase was unravelling Medeva's shares halved and Gowrie-Smith and Lees were forced aside.

The new chief executive, Dr Bill Bogie, is less flamboyant than his predecessor and the City now believes that the Bogie-Taylor team is a safe pair. In 1995 Medeva showed organic sales growth of 7 per cent and managed to increase its operating margins by three percentage points, to 30 per cent. Cash generative, the company is now making some small but potentially very rewarding acquisitions. It's back on track.

Operations and markets

Medeva serves niche markets where a small dedicated salesforce can make a significant impact. In the US it has five operations which together generated sales of £158m in 1995 from a group total of £256m:

1. Methylphenidate. A drug for treating attention deficit disorder children which is Medeva's best selling product. Manufactured by MD Pharmaceuticals in the US it achieved sales of £86m in 1994. This market is growing rapidly - total prescriptions jumped 27 per cent last year - and MD is gaining market share from its branded rival Ritalin. The drug is increasingly being prescribed to adults and Medeva has added extra manufacturing capacity.

2. Respiratory Products. These are manufactured and distributed by Adams Laboratories which was acquired in October 1991 and Armstrong which was bought a year later.

Adams' three major products are: the Humbid range which is designed to treat dry coughs, Deconsal which is also a cough treatment and Atrohist which treats sinusitis and the common cold. In May 1994 Adams added to this portfolio Semprex D which it will market through its specialist 250-strong salesforce. At the same time it also bought the US rights to Dexacort, a rhinitis cure, from Merck.

These two deals are typical of Medeva's cautious, but potentially highly rewarding, expansion strategy. Neither require the hiring of additional salesmen and in the case of the Semprex D deal no capital outlay was needed. But both can generate significant revenues.

Armstrong produces metered dose inhalers on a contract basis for third parties. Again, Medeva has been expanding this operation with clever low risk acquisitions. In November 1994 it bought exclusive US/Canadian rights to market Chiesi's inhaler for the Glaxo drugs Salbutamol and Becotide.

3. Hospital Products. The IMS subsidiary produces and markets pre-filled syringes and devices for anaesthesia and pain management. In its biggest acquisition since 1993 Medeva paid £34m to buy Inhalon which owns a state of the art manufacturing facility and two anaesthetics - Isoflurane and Enflurane.

In the UK Medeva operates through Evans Medical, which achieved sales of £59m in 1995. The company has recently upgraded its manufacturing complex at Speke near Liverpool and produces a number of leading products:

1. Branded goods. Medeva produces a range of branded products many of which were acquired from SmithKline Beecham in 1990. Among its leaders are Coracten, an anti-hypertension drug, and Normax, a laxative.

2. Fluvirin. An influenza vaccine which is gaining market share in the UK and is now being sold in fifteen other countries including the USA.

3. Paediatric vaccines. Evans is an established leader in this market producing vaccines for TB, polio, diphtheria and tetanus. Last year it entered a broad vaccine alliance with SB incorporating the grant to them of exclusive world-wide rights to Medeva's patented protein 69kDa - this should safeguard Evans' pole position in UK paediatric vaccines as new products become available.

In Europe sales grew by 15 % to £32m in 1995. Medeva operates in three markets:

1. France. In February 1993 Medeva paid £11.4m for the Institute de Recherche Corbiere which produced and marketed a range of oral medicines through a 75 strong salesforce. Medeva has used this as a platform to push many of Evan's products, notably Fluvirin, into the French market.

2. Switzerland. The acquisition of Tillotts in December 1995 introduced a new core therapeutic category to the Group. Tillotts has two well-established products, Asacol and Colpermin, but, more significantly, the acquisition also brings a portfolio of new products under development which are focused on Tillotts' proprietary delayed-release technology. This therapeutic area is considered to be largely underserved and presents Medeva with important new product opportunities.

3. Spain. Medeva also sells its vaccines in Spain through Evans Espana. In

1995 the company acquired a number of products together with a salesforce from Glaxo Wellcome.

Strategy and management

Medeva does not engage in primary research. Instead it has bought-in drugs which are already well developed but which industry majors believe won't fit in well with their existing portfolios or which offer too small a return for the big boys. Currently it has a number of major projects in the laboratory:

1. Hepagene. Medeva bought this Hepatitis B vaccine knowing its patent was under attack from the US firm Biogen in all markets except Asia. However, it has recently won a major court case in the UK and, clinical trials are underway.

2. Albuterol Metered dose inhaler. Medeva hopes to launch this in the US this year. In late 1995 it filed a submission in the UK for registration of a novel MDI device, Spacchaler. The dry powder inhalers (DPI) development programme continued in the USA. It added to this programme an exclusive UK and European distribution agreement with ML Laboratories for their new multi-dose DPI for use with salbutamol and beclomethasone. A Product Licence Application has already been submitted in the UK for salbutamol DPI.

3. Attention Deficit Disorder. Two projects to protect the Group's methylphenidate franchise further were initiated during the year. One project is evaluating the chiral form. The second is examining an improved sustained release formulation.

4. Gastro-intestinal Disease. Tillotts has developed proprietary delayed release technology which delivers drugs directly to the lower gastro-intestinal tract. Tillotts has several projects, some using its delayed release and, in certain cases, its controlled, two phase release technology. Other projects utilise Tillott's mucosal adhesive technology in foams and liquid enemas.

Medeva has a three-pronged plan for expansion through acquisition. Firstly it will buy new products at a late stage of development. Secondly it expects to acquire existing products and to push them through its existing sales infrastructure. Thirdly it acquires infrastructure to provide access to major pharmaceuticals markets.

The future

Medeva's existing products are capable of sustaining the current rate of sales growth. The launch of new products, notably Hepagene, and clever purchases such as Inhalon can add to that. Further infill acquisitions, probably in Europe, are inevitable. But by controlling its overheads particularly in sales, and maintaining its policy of minimal research spending Medeva can increase its margins still further.

The general weakness of the global drugs industry means that leading players will be increasingly likely to divest themselves of projects or products which are too small for them. A company of Medeva's size with its low cost-base is ideally positioned to take advantage of that. Bill Bogie says his company is well equipped to take advantage of a rapidly changing pharmaceutical environment. Few would disagree.

MERCURY
COMMUNICATIONS

Mercury, London

Mercury is a division of Cable & Wireless and is a major player in the UK telecommunications market

Outlook:
Mercury had been through a troubled 12 to 18 months in the period immediately prior to this report going to press. However the new CEO appears to have done enough to ensure that the company will be one of the serious operators in the future. Mercury's management has shaken out its unprofitable activities and it is now playing to its strengths as a long distance provider

Scorecard:
Structural flexibility	★★★★
Innovative power	★★★★
International orientation	★★★★
Human resources	★★★
Growth markets	★★★★★
Quality of management	★★★★

Key figures (31/3/95):
Turnover	£1645 million
Pre-tax profit	£203 million
Staff	9,500

Mercury Communications
New Mercury House
26 Red Lion Square
London WC1R 4HQ
Tel: 0171 528 2000
Fax: 0171 528 2181

Mercury Communications

The consolidation in the telecomms market which has been so evident in the United States is likely to occur here, argue many of the leading commentators on the industry. They say that the globalisation of the sector and the need for critical mass has favoured three US players - AT&T, MCI and Sprint. The others in the American business environment tend to be niche players. A similar configuration is likely to occur in the UK. Robert Millington, telecomms analyst at BZW, says: 'The dynamics of the US market - globalisation and a price war - have led to a trio of dominant players. The same could happen here in the next five to ten years. It is hard to tell at this distance whether there will be three or whether this market is too small to support so many but certainly BT will be there. I think that Duncan Lewis has done enough to ensure that Mercury will be the second. After that it is hard to tell.'

Mercury - the first beneficiary of telecomms deregulation - has emerged from a trying period. Now it is has a clearer vision of its market opportunities and performance capacities as a business. This is a leaner and healthier enterprise than it was two years ago. Under CEO Duncan Lewis' direction the company has achieved a revised strategic vision which emphasises its relationships with core groups of customers, flexibility in anticipating and responding to market demand, exploiting developments in technology, enhancing the skills of its people, utilising its links with Cable & Wireless to the full, and forging key joint ventures.

Mr Lewis believes that the company can become the UK's leading telecomms company in the next decade. Even though BT is many times larger than Mercury he argues that his business is more financially efficient than that of its biggest rival. 'BT employs 140,000 staff where we have 8,000, but our revenues are only one sixth of those of BT,' he says. Being much smaller, but with the benefit of a large revenue base and cashflows, Mercury can be more flexible and meet customer need in the most direct and effective ways possible.

Operations and markets

The revitalised Mercury remains part of Cable & Wireless and is largely a UK-driven operation. It provides telecommunications services to business and residential customers, which are tailor-made to specific need. In 1994, the company reported sales of £1.6 billion and profits of £203 million. During the last 18 months, Mercury has been refocused - getting out of those businesses which were not profitable, investing in its key markets and cutting costs. Analysts - and indeed Mercury's management - expect to see the beneficial effects of its restructuring in the 1996 figures. Profitability should be up substantially, to provide a platform for further growth.

Mercury now concentrates on six main business areas which are broken down into subsets for individual markets. These are: corporate business, general business, small to medium sized enterprises, home business services, partner services and international business services, for relationships with multinational companies. For example, corporate includes government, where Mercury is active in defence, health and education, but has stayed out of other public sector divisions. 'We concentrate on those areas where we can deliver greatest strength and give greatest value,' says Mr Lewis. Among its other main business areas are small to medium enterprises (SMEs) and middle market companies.

Its international operations are focused on six market sectors: international finance, pharmaceuticals, oil and energy, travel and transport, manufacturing and logistics, and information technology.

Strategy and management

Mercury's strategy is straightforward. The company aims to be the leading telecomms provider in the UK in the next decade. It recognises that BT provides formidable competition but that Mercury's size gives it the opportunity to be infinitely more flexible in meeting customer demand.

Mr Lewis explains that the approach which Mercury has adopted is based on its belief that flexibility in dealing with customer demand and tailor-making services for specific clients are the key elements of success. These two priorities mean that Mercury must be selective about its markets and about the range of services that it offers. 'Our businesses must be based on an appreciation of which markets are best suited to our range of capabilities. We need to meet corporate need, individual need within corporations and residential need. So Mercury at the centre provides the systems, structure and people to ensure that customers receive a high quality service.

'We see ourselves as a service provider. We work with our customers to identify their needs and locate the best solution. This may involve joint ventures with other companies. For example, upstream oil companies need on-line seismic information on potential oil or gas deposits. Cable & Wireless has a global alliance with Sclumberger, the leading provider of equipment and services to the oil industry. We provide the telecommunications support to the customers which are in a key market for us. Joint ventures and strategic alliances will be important for us in the next few years. As we work with our customers to find innovative solutions to their telecommunications needs we will bring in the most appropriate partners.'

The recent realignment of the business, which the CEO says is putting extra pressure on Mercury's management - from within - to go faster was based on a view that customer needs will change rapidly. 'To keep pace with the growing globalisation of our customers, we need to undergo radical transformation. We have started this process but we have further to go. We are like Microsoft in that we have the scale and the cashflows but we must move faster.' Customer requirements will vary according to specific demand but each customer will require the level of service to meet and exceed expectations. If Mercury can show the quality of business solutions while retaining a flexible approach, then it should show superior financial return.

The latest industry information shows that in the US network voice communication accounts for 60 per cent of all business and data transmission some 40 per cent. Mr Lewis says that by the year 2000 these positions will have changed. So the relationship between computing and telecomms will be vitally important in years to come. 'I see us as the bridge between the data supplier and the end-user,' says Mr Lewis. For telecomms companies generally the PC to PC market is growing rapidly. In the further future there is connection with the entertainment industry - films on demand, virtual reality games on-line and so on - but bandwidth is currently a limitation on growth.

Mercury is in the fortunate position that as part of the Cable & Wireless federation it can access knowledge, ideas and systems in place around the world. Additionally, Bell Canada - a 20 per cent shareholder - has some of the most advanced laboratories in the world for telecomms products research. 'This means we can draw on our parent and Bell Canada for the latest developments and invest in customer service. We can demonstrate innovation in our customer relationships by finding the right technical, pricing and quality solutions for our customers. This is how we will differentiate ourselves.'

Key to the future of the business is the quality of its management. Part of the reorganisation has been finding the right people to carry the company forward. Also Mr Lewis and his colleagues have invested a good deal of time in succession planning to ensure that high quality management will be around in the next generation. The shake-up within Mercury meant that some people were dissatisfied and they left to join smaller, perhaps quieter companies. But the Mercury management was delighted by the numbers of reapplications from those people who had left six weeks earlier, discovering that the revitalised Mercury was an exciting place to be.

Mr Lewis says that strong leadership is crucial within any business, he stresses that teamwork - the creation of problem solving teams - is essential to success in the new business environment. Mutual trust and respect must be the foundation of such working relationships, he suggests.

The future

The Mercury which exists five years from now will have transformed itself radically from the company as it is today. Mr Lewis predicts product features will soon enjoy a life of 60-90 days, its catalogue - if such a thing still exists - will have changed beyond comprehension. Its markets will move forward and its quality of solutions will advance to meet increasing customer expectation. Mercury is fortunate to draw on the resources of C&W and Bell Canada so that it can concentrate resources on improving service quality and on forging new relationships. If the market goes as the analysts predict then Mercury will be one of two top dogs in the UK. If Mr Lewis is right then through cost efficiency, targeted service delivery and flexibility, Mercury may be number one. It should be an interesting match.

Microsoft®

Microsoft Ltd

Microsoft is the world market leader in computer software systems

Outlook:
Microsoft has already reshaped the way in which we all work and to a great
extent how we conduct our lives. Its reach and influence are going to grow
incrementally

Scorecard:
Structural flexibility	★★★★★
Innovative power	★★★★
International orientation	★★★★★
Human resources	★★★★
Growth markets	★★★★★
Quality of management	★★★★

Key figures:
Global sales	$5.937 billion
Global profits	$1.453 billion
Global staff	19,000

Microsoft Limited
Microsoft Place
Winnersh Triangle
Wokingham
Berkshire RG41 5TP
Tel: 01734 270001
Fax: 01734 270002

Microsoft

'The most powerful man in the world,' shouted the headline in a recent European magazine article describing Microsoft supremo Bill Gates. While that may be an exaggeration, there is no getting away from the colossal influence of the Seattle-based entrepreneur.

The information technology age has arrived with a whirr, rather than a bang, but Bill Gates' company Microsoft is at the forefront of far-reaching changes which will shape our lives for the next 100 years. Chris Smith MP, the shadow Heritage secretary with special responsibility for the information superhighway, believes the group's influence will grow: 'Microsoft is certainly going to change the way a lot of people live and work'.

How can a company which was formed only two decades ago as a tiny start-up, have become so pre-eminent? The answer lies in sound business practices, which have set the benchmark, not just for software companies, but for companies in all areas of commerce. Wherever you go in the world, Microsoft is recognised as a centre of excellence.

Successful business is all about ideas, and Microsoft has been led by a man widely recognised as a genius, in his own right who has had the foresight to recognise the genius in others. Perhaps that is why Bill Gates' baby has not gone the way of many other promising software shooting stars of the seventies and eighties, and either faded into obscurity or been swallowed up by more commercially-oriented predators.

Operations and markets

Incredible as it may seem, Microsoft is twenty years old in 1995. Yet in those few years, sales have risen to $4.6bn (£3bn) in the year to June 1994. But Microsoft differs from many other technology driven companies, by never losing sight of the ultimate aim - that is increasing the bottom line. In its short history the group has racked up tremendous earnings growth. Wall Street analysts estimate that by mid-1995 profits will have snowballed to almost $1.5bn.

Microsoft's humble beginnings have become part of computer lore: in 1975 a 19 year-old Harvard undergraduate named William H. Gates III dropped out of university to link up with a schoolfriend and sell a condensed version of BASIC, a computer programming language.

Further success came when the pair realised the potential in helping others to write programmes. Gates and partner Paul Allen (who left the company through illness in 1983, but remains on the board, and controls over 10 per cent of the stock) developed programs to make software writing easier.

The seminal year for Microsoft was 1980, when IBM commissioned the tiny group to design the operating system for Big Blue's new personal computer. The decision was to have a profound effect on the world computer industry, and was evetually responsible for bringing IBM - at the time perhaps the most powerful company in the world - to its knees. The operating system is a set of programs for organising the resources and activities of a computer. Applications software for items such as word processing are run from the operating system.

Instead of going through the costly and time-consuming process of designing its own system Microsoft bought one, originally named QDOS, for around $50,000. The system was renamed Microsoft Disk Operating system (MS-DOS). IBM PCs containing MS-DOS became a roaring success, of course. At the time IBM could seemingly do no wrong, and appeared set to continue as the dominant company of the computer age.

But what the Armonk, New York company hadn't reckoned on was Microsoft keeping the rights to the operating system. The phenomenal success of the IBM PC attracted plenty of imitators, who were able to produce cheaper machines but nevertheless wanted their machines to be compatible with IBM models. What these companies needed was the operating system, and this they got when Microsoft, in an inspired move which went against standard industry thinking, licensed MS-DOS to other PC manufacturers. Over 100 PC makers bought licences to MS-DOS.

In what was to become a typical Microsoft trait, it delivered a product and marketed it so successfully that it became the industry standard.

Strategy and management

Well aware that the computer industry is the fastest moving business in the world, Microsoft didn't stand still to admire its fantastic success. Another operating system was developed as a refined form of MS-DOS, and this one turned out to be even more successful. The program was Windows, introduced in 1986. It's estimated that Microsoft supplies operating systems to almost 90 per cent of the world's PCs. That's a market with some 150m machines, of which an estimated 46.5m were sold in 1994 alone. The personal computer, driven by Microsoft software, has become the tool of the decade, an essential item in every workplace, and, increasingly, in every home.

But the success of Windows and MS-DOS cannot be explained merely by the growth of the PC. There are other operating systems, and similar machines. Bill Gates' masterstroke was to convince hardware suppliers of the quality of his product, and get them to ship their machines with Microsoft software already fitted. Although other programs could be added on later, consumers rarely found this necessary.

Another Microsoft tactic was revealed when it used its dominance in one area, in this case operating systems, to gain a major presence in a different but related field. Microsoft software such as Excel, Powerpoint and Word sold by the truckload on the back of the operating system excellence.

Although Bill Gates is the company's leading light and driving force, a company of such size cannot rely on one person alone. Commenting on the group's success, Bernard Vergnes, president of Microsoft Europe, notes simply that 'somehow we've been able to foresee the evolution of the technologies and most of the time make the right bets, and work very hard to have the right software at the right time.' Behind this, however, lies the simple fact that Microsoft has attracted, and retained, some of the most gifted people. A Microsoft culture has been carefully cultivated, characterised by a fierce loyalty to the group. The common sense of purpose, even partnership, has been cemented by the atmosphere at the Seattle headquarters. The spirit of academic and commercial excellence is reinforced by the complex being referred to as the campus. Such is the staff dedication and commitment that an all-night restaurant and laundry has been installed, allowing the jeans- and sneakers-clad employees to work through the night if they wish, fuelled by endless soft drinks and pizza slices.

The enlightened approach to employees extends to supporting their charity work. As well as donating huge sums to charity ($22.6m in 1994) Microsoft has also initiated a programme of matching employees' individual charity donations dollar for dollar, up to a limit of $12,000 per employee. 'Microsoft's generosity in matching employee gifts is one of the best benefits the company offers,' said Dennis Abbe, a software developer. 'I am grateful that Microsoft has been a partner with my wife and me in our efforts to address a variety of community concerns.' The company has realised that its people are its greatest asset, and, unlike many others who then make hollow promises, it has backed up this feeling with hard cash and good ideas.

The future

Microsoft has indeed had an exciting past, but all the signs point to an even more dynamic future. The launch of Windows 95 in August will be a great leap forward into the world of multimedia. Windows 95 is going to be the operating system for the rest of the decade. 'It will be an overnight success among consumers,' according to Ben Tisdall, editor of *Personal Computer Weekly* magazine. The introduction of Windows 95 has been far from trouble-free - it was originally scheduled to be released two years ago - but the whole process is typical of the Microsoft approach. Sensing the changing wishes of the marketplace, new functions were continually added to the system, culminating in the facility to access on-line services provided on Microsoft Network, and the global chain of computers known as the Internet. Demand for Windows 95 is sure to be high: in two years Windows 95 is expected to generate sales of £1bn in the UK alone. Backing up this phenomenal expansion is the growth in PCs themselves. One third of US households now have a PC, and in homes with a teenager, over half have a PC. This figure is set to be repeated around the world, especially as the services provided on-line are expanded. In the Microsoft tradition of going right to the top, talks are already under way with the leading media suppliers for programmes on-line, and a deal appears imminent with Viacom, producer of MTV and Star Trek.

In a recent research circular, analysts from Goldman Sachs, the Wall Street investment bank, said: 'The conventional view of Microsoft as the leading software vendor is much too narrow a perspective when looking at the company's future business.' If Bill Gates' multimedia vision is correct, Microsoft will become the biggest company in the world. Now that's a big risk, but given that even rivals admit he's never made a serious business mistake, who would bet against Bill Gates?

Motorola, Slough

Motorola is a world class manufacturer of semi-conductors, cellular telephones, telecommunications systems, satellite systems, pagers and wireless data systems

Outlook:
Motorola is one of the handful of businesses which is regularly cited as an excellent company. Its all round commitment to its customers, its employees and its suppliers, its ingenuity in developing new products and its entirely ethical business approach distinguish Motorola from many other players. The lead which Motorola has established in its markets gives every confidence that its performance will be sustained long term

Scorecard:
Structural flexibility	★★★★★
Innovative power	★★★★★
International orientation	★★★★★
Human resources	★★★★★
Growth markets	★★★★★
Quality of management	★★★★★

Key figures:
Global sales	$22,245 million
Global pre-tax earnings	$2,437 million
Global staff	132,000

Motorola UK
110 Bath Road
Slough SL1 3SZ
Tel: 01753 575555
Fax: 01753 553225

Motorola

Very few companies - in our assessment - score top marks in each of our criteria. It really is a tall order to be excellent in each category. But rather like Hewlett Packard and 3M, Motorola is the model of a modern company. It operates in every major market across the world in industries which many commentators agree are the high-growth sectors of the next decade. In many of these fields, Motorola is the operator which enjoys greatest market share. It is a great innovator generating appropriate and ground-breaking new products ahead of its rivals. As its history shows, it has made and remade itself over the decades since it produced battery eliminators in the 1920s and introduced car radios in the 1930s.

The quality of management required to identify and meet market trends before they emerge has been a consistent factor of the company since it was launched. Motorola management has always believed in close contact with its customer base, exemplary levels of customer service and fast response times to perceptions of changing demand and technological transformation.

In industries which experience rapid and wholesale growth, Motorola stands among the senior players determined to achieve new levels of product and service performance. This sounds like management hype but with Motorola the commitment is genuine. It runs like a thread throughout this business and this core philosophy is summed up by its 'global leadership through total customer satisfaction' creed.

Operations and markets

A glance at the Motorola history gives a snapshot of how this company has reinvented itself and expanded to a world class enterprise. Started in Chicago in 1928, it manufactured devices to link battery-run domestic radios to the electricity main. In the 1930s it created and successfully marketed the car radio and in the following decade produced the two-way radio while beginning contract work for the US government.

In the 1950s Motorola became a leader in military, space and communications technology, established its first semi-conductor factory and became a growing force in consumer electronics. During the next ten years, it moved from domestic to international markets, and from consumer to industry and public sector customers. In the 1970s it invented new products for globally positioned communications satellites. In the 1980s it produced the MC68000 family of microprocessors, handheld two-way radios, smaller pagers, cellular phones and advanced radio equipment.

From its humble beginnings, Motorola is now the 23rd largest corporation in Fortune magazine's top 500 and generates $22 billion in sales. The company is growing on the back of the extensive inflation in the telecommunications market worldwide. To quote the corporation: 'The potential market for Motorola's products and services has increased fivefold in the last five years. We envision the worldwide wireless communications equipment industry growing from estimates of $40 billion in 1994 to $280 billion in 2010.'

The company's largest chunk of business comes from the US (44 per cent), Europe comes next with 21 per cent and Asia/Pacific third at 11 per cent. Motorola then separates out China/Hong Kong at eight per cent and Japan at seven per cent. Its general systems division - cellular radio phones and systems, personal communications systems, computers and computer boards - brings in 35 per cent of sales, Motorola's semiconductor interests account for 28 per cent, communications - digital radio and messaging systems - 24 per cent, government and space technology three per cent and other products, ten per cent.

The European, Middle East and Africa region, which is based in Slough, accounted for $4.9 billion in revenues in 1994. The UK operation opened more than 25 years ago and runs six facilities here at Basingstoke, Easter Inch, East Kilbride, South Queensferry, Swindon and Stotfold. These plants are net exporters to China, Japan and the US, among others.

Strategy and management

Motorola is a great company for summarising its objectives in short, easily appreciated statements. Clarity and precision are key goals, and this determination to speak in plain English comes naturally to the company's people.

'We believe that the major challenge for companies in the 1990s and beyond is the combination of product innovation with total customer satisfaction. To reach this fundamental objective the company acts within a framework of key beliefs, goals and initiatives:
- key beliefs include conducting business with uncompromising integrity and constant respect for people.
- to develop Best-in-Class people, marketing, technology, manufacturing, service and products; increase global market share and provide superior financial results.
- to produce products and services to a Six Sigma standard (99.9997 per cent defect-free), reduce total time cycle in all activities, lead in the areas of product, manufacturing and the environment, improve profitability, and provide a creative and co-operative workplace.'

The organisation has created a culture of continuous improvement to adhere to quality standards in all its markets. Motorola imposes its own quality review which ensures that products and services meet customer specifications.

Motorola has outlined its strategic vision for the next few years as its platform for the Information Age:
- design and manufacture of radio products and systems for voice and data, including two-way private mobile radio, pagers and public mobile telephone services. It is already the world leader of mobile and portable cellular phones.
- a portfolio of 50,000 component products including thousands of discrete semiconductors, microprocessors and memory chips, as well as application-specific integrated circuits. These are the enabling technologies for other Motorola businesses.
- advanced electronic modules and equipment for aerospace, defence, motor vehicle, industrial and other markets. High-tech automotive applications including powertrain and sensor products.

. open hardware and software solutions, including board and system level products for the data information processing and distributed computing markets. Motorola's worldwide business strategy targets technical and commercial markets as well as the telecommunications industry.

Motorola's management realises that without serious long term investment in research no global operator can hope to survive. Each year it has stepped up its commitment and in 1994 it spent $1.9 billion in a variety of locations including its Scottish centres. The company is also aware of its responsibilities in terms of the environment; it has sponsored an eight-hour course for every Motorola employee in environmental awareness. Motorola intends to achieve the total elimination of CFCs from its processes worldwide and demonstrate to other electronics companies how to do this.

The future

Given Motorola's complete approach to its customers, staff and product development, its role as an industry leader and its focus on the issues of the future, this is a business which will stay the course.

Novell

Novell, Berks

Novell is a major manufacturer of network applications and systems

Outlook:
Novell's conviction that the demand for computer networks and applications software is certainly vindicated by its financial growth. Analysts anticipate that one billion people will use computer databases and that Novell is well positioned to benefit from this potential explosion in demand

Scorecard:

Structural flexibility	★★★★
Innovative power	★★★★★
International orientation	★★★★★
Human resources	★★★★
Growth markets	★★★★★
Quality of management	★★★★★

Key figures:

Global sales	$2 billion
Pre-tax profits	$350 million
Europe staff	1,000

Novell UK Limited
London Road
Bracknell
Berks RG12 2UY
Tel: 01344 724000
Fax: 01344 724001

Novell

Each new generation of computers brings a logarithmic increase in power and the possibility of a range of new applications. However that potential can be multiplied many times via a network of individual users, companies and communities across the world. Novell Inc was one of the first to recognise the enormous potential rewards for whoever brought this about and its efforts continue to be directed towards making the ultimate global network a reality.

In the 1980s Novell foresaw the way that the corporate computing world would be turned inside out by personal computers. That revolution fuelled its early success, based on the office networking solutions it provided. Now it is seeking to provide the next quantum leap in the application of computing power to networking. It is looking beyond the concepts that tie hardware and peripherals together to allow people to work where it is most convenient. It now wants businesses to become closer to their customers, suppliers and partners.

'Pervasive Computing' is the future in Novell's mind. It intends that via its products powerful network applications and services will eliminate barriers connecting individuals, companies and communities throughout the world. Pervasive Computing will connect people to other people and to the information they need, and allow them to act on it at anytime. Novell believes its future growth is assured, based on humanity's basic need to communicate and its hunger for information and entertainment.

In the future, says Novell, the boundaries between computers, telecommunications and consumer electronics will become increasingly blurred. By the year 2000 as many as one billion people will be able to connect to computer networks at work, at home or wherever they happen to be, a tenfold increase on five years earlier. Information networks have then to encompass telephone services, multimedia and new types of 'nomadic' pen-based and voice recognition systems.

However it is not enough to simply convey information, as the amount of data already available as computers, databases and TV channels proliferate is itself creating a problem. Novell's contribution is to help users to access only the information they need from these huge data resources. Retrieval is part of the equation, and hence Novell's applications add value by enhancing the way businesses communicate with their customers. From its users' perspective, ease of access and use, and availability of powerful applications to facilitate their use of those data are the key ingredients.

Operations and markets

Novell is a leading provider of computer networking and application software. Its products provide the infrastructure, services, network access and applications required to make networked information and computing an integral part of everyone's daily life.

Approximately 60 per cent of the world's network computing users rely on Novell; 40 million use NetWare, 30 million UNIX system solutions. A series of acquisitions in recent years have also built it into the world's third largest independent software company.

The group's growth has been relatively recent, in line with the penetration of PC-based systems. Novell shipped its first software in 1983 and went public in 1985. By year end 1994 the group had net sales of close to $2bn with pre-tax profit approaching $300m.

Novell's NetWare software is the world's most popular network operating system. It is used by more workers than all other network systems combined, adding a new user every five seconds. In simple terms it connects people with other people and the information they need.

Strategy and management

Perhaps more than any other company, Novell is associated with the process of linking different computers into networks and enabling access to information and applications. It is the only major company entirely focused that way, by building software that spans from network infrastructure and services to network applications, Novell systems recognise and support the momentum behind the trend to shift computing resources from desktop computers and other systems to networks.

Novell helps people communicate, currently mainly through networks of computers, but already increasingly via telephones, televisions, pagers and other intelligent devices. Novell's product suite is the system with the widest industry and public support. It intends that to extend to newly emerging network services.

Networking is more than the general perception of enabling office workers to share devices such as printers, disks, fax machines and scanners. The launch of its NetWare 4 product is intended to take it a huge step further, to encompass shared resources, giving people access to information resources on Novell networks anywhere in the world, whatever the platform.

The company's aim is to dissolve the boundaries between computers, telecommunications and consumer electronics. In this way, it will drive that expansion of the number of computer users from the estimated 100 million worldwide today to as many as a billion by the end of the decade.

Novell has in recent years actively expanded its product portfolio, most notably via the acquisition of UNIX Systems Laboratories in 1993 and WordPerfect Corporation in 1994. It has acquired, invested cash and formed strategic alliances with other technology companies.

These have added extremely well known additions to its stable such as WordPerfect and Borland's Quattro Pro software, both in June 1994. Prior to this, in June 1993, it acquired UNIX System Laboratories Inc. These moves redefined Novell into four product groups, all within the software industry. They are the NetWare Systems Group, the Novell Applications Group, the UNIX Systems Group and the Information Access and Management Group.

Today Novell can deliver products that span the range of customers and their requirements, from the multinational corporation looking for an enterprise wide network solution to the home user wanting easy to use productive software for their newly purchased PC. It has a network of cross-industry alliances covering product development, testing and certification, and post-sales support. These are critical to the acceptance of multivendor networking and Novell has accordingly formed strategic partnerships with companies such as AT&T, Compaq, Dell, Digital Equipment, Ericsson, GEC, Hewlett-Packard, IBM, ICL,

Intel, Olivetti, Oracle, Sybase and Unisys.

From a company's point of view these are delivering tangible benefits. It is estimated that 75 per cent of the cost of owning a network lies in its administration and Novell has put emphasis on the ability of its new products to cut this expense. Very efficient use of hard disk space and memory minimises the need for additional hardware investment, while the improved graphical interface makes operating and administering the system easier.

Novell's latest products are designed to make it easy for manufacturers of office equipment, industrial controls and consumer devices to create NetWare-ready products. Its Embedded Systems Technology will facilitate the extension of NetWare into faxes, copiers, telephones, pagers, set-top cable TV boxes, utility meters and even vending machines, beccoming new resources on NetWare networks.

In Novell's vision the home will be just another node on the global network. As networks spread from the workplace into the home it expects to see electronic commerce with interactive systems in the home. Manufacturers will communicate directly with consumers, fundamentally changing the face of shopping, product distribution and financial services.

What will make this happen is easier and more efficient access and retrieval of corporate data. For example, Novell talks in terms of enabling a person working at home in the Cotswolds to access corporate information stored on a server located in Tokyo, automatically, and without the person needing to know the address of the server.

The future

As personal computing evolves into Pervasive Computing, Novell believes it can meet the challenge of creating useful information from the growing bulk of data available through networks. It simultaneously needs to demonstrate that those networks are easier to access, simpler to use and more effective through Novell access software, operating systems, network services and applications.

The market is enormous and growing fast. Networks are expanding as computing power extends to telephones, TV set-top boxes and the many other devices from copiers to utility metres. A vast range of organisations are recognising the importance of access to and integration with outside information sources.

More than three million employees in the UK alone spend over 50 per cent of their working day away from the office and the trend is increasing. All this is good news for Novell, perhaps the leading experts on the detail and logistics for remote access, Internet working, and host connection for access to corporate data.

It has launched a system of software to transform local area networks (LAN) into a global LAN. In partnership with AT&T and other telecoms providers its objective is to deploy a commercial information highway built around its own NetWare 4 technology.

As networks expand, they become more meaningful to more people. This is what Novell means by Pervasive Computing. Networking has become much more than linking up different pieces of hardware. Now it means connecting people with people, providing a conduit for information and ideas which can be accessed and manipulated at any time or any place.

NYNEX CableComms, Surrey

NYNEX is the second largest cable television operator in the UK

Outlook:
Cable is growing rapidly. Within the next few years the vast majority of UK homes will have access to cable facilities. NYNEX offers both telephony and television services. NYNEX is US owned and the UK company benefits from the resources of the parents. It is licensed in 16 franchise areas in the UK

Scorecard:

Structural flexibility	★★★★
Innovative power	★★★★
International orientation	★★★★
Human resources	★★★★
Growth markets	★★★★★
Quality of management	★★★★

Key figures:

Global turnover	$13.3 billion
Global assets	$30.1 billion
UK investment	£331.6 million
Staff	4,000

NYNEX CableComms
Tolworth Tower
Ewell Road
Surbiton
Surrey KT6 7ED
Tel: 0181 873 2000
Fax: 0181 390 9993

NYNEX

Cable TV in the UK has come a long way in a very short time. At the beginning of the 1980s, it was basically only used to relay existing broadcast TV channels over narrowband cable networks to homes which, due to their location, were unable to receive such services by conventional methods. The scope for extending this was limited, as the system generally lacked the technical sophistication to be extended to telecommunications or a wide range of programming.

The Cable and Broadcasting Act in 1984 established the Cable Authority with responsibility to award broadband cable TV franchises for particular geographic areas. By October 1990, 135 such cable TV franchises had been awarded. Each franchisee was also required to obtain a telecomms licence which authorised it to provide certain telecommunications services which included, inter alia, cable TV and a voice telephone service.

The enormous investment required to set up a network to supply an unproven market explains the slow early progress. But the Duopoly Review of 1991 was the spur to much more rapid growth. This allowed cable operators to provide all forms of wired telecomms services in their own right, rather than under agreements with existing public telephone operators such as BT.

The UK has now become an attractive environment for cable TV operators. It is one of few countries in which private sector companies are allowed to provide both cable TV and telecomms services directly to customers over an integrated network on a commercial basis. In addition, under current UK licences only one cable operator may provide both cable TV and telecomms services in any one franchise area.

Operations and markets

NYNEX is a leading telecommunications company with its headquarters in New York. NYNEX's history dates from 1984, when it was formed from various subsidiaries of the leading US telecommunications group American Telephone & Telegraph Company (AT&T). For the purposes of this article, the company under examination is UK CableComms, 67 per cent owned by NYNEX.

NYNEX's largest two subsidiaries are the New York Telephone Company and the New England Telephone and Telegraph Company, which provide telephone services to business and residential customers in the north-eastern US. It also provides communications services in selected markets overseas extending to programming, directory publishing, video entertainment and information networks. In its last financial year, NYNEX had assets of $30.1bn and sales of $13.3bn.

Due to the front-end costs of installing its UK network (at 31st March 1995, NYNEX had thus far invested £331.6m of capital in its UK operation), results in that market in the last three years have produced a growing operating loss. However, turnover from cable television and both residential and business telephone services has been growing at a much faster rate, and was approximately eleven times higher in 1994 than it was two years previously.

CableComms is now one of the leading providers of both cable television and telecommunications services in the UK. It is licensed to provide these services in 16 franchise areas covering 2.7m homes, equivalent to approximately 17 per cent of the total homes in the UK for which franchises had been awarded at 31st March 1995. It also covers approximately 167,500 businesses. Approximately 1.7m of CableComms' franchise homes are located within the ten North West Franchises in and around Manchester, the UK's second largest business community.

Strategy and management

The key to appreciating the potential for cable operators lies in their ability to provide incremental revenue generating services on their existing networks, for minimal additional investment.

CableComms is one of the largest cable operators in the UK which means it is able to obtain favourable terms on services, equipment and programming. Being able to provide both cable TV and telecomms services over an integrated network gives it a competitive advantage over single services providers such as British Sky Broadcasting and BT. That combined with its advanced network design, means that while it is already able to deliver a wide variety of entertainment, telecommunications and information services, it is also well placed to offer new services in the future without incurring significant additional construction costs to adapt or upgrade its existing underground network.

CableComms therefore regards the UK as an attractive environment for the cable TV and telecomms industry. As private sector companies can provide both cable TV and telecomms services directly to customers, the costs of their networks are spread over two important sources of revenue. And under existing regulations, cable TV and telecomms services provided by cable operators are not subject to direct government price control.

There are other attractions to the UK. Consumer demand for entertainment programming is very high, as revealed by high average TV audiences, the wide access to video cassette recorders and the frequent video cassette rentals and sales. The public has rapidly accepted telecomms services offered by cable operators. There has been an increase in residential and business cable telecomms lines from 21,225 at the end of 1991 to 717,586 three years later.

In the business market, the basic telecomms offered to residential customers are extended to a range of more sophisticated services. For example, its CENTREX central exchange services give the customer the flexibility of their own telecomms system. This means low cost line rentals and free calls between users at one or more locations.

Managed fibre networks can be tailored to a customer's needs to provide dedicated point-to-point fibre links between two or more locations. Powerful private circuits can be provided to allow transmission of data at extremely high speeds to enable computer and data links, or main frame computer lines, video conferences and local area networks between local offices. Other services include closed circuit TV and commercial cable TV for use in hotels, public houses and sports and social clubs.

CableComms also intends to differentiate itself from its competitors by developing a strong local identity. It is committed to providing local programmes to serve the communities in which it operates and it intends to increase this as its franchises become further developed. It is also entering into co-operative agreements with other cable companies to enhance and extend the programme range and generate cost savings. Wire-TV is an example of such a joint venture, leading to exclusive broadcasts such as the 1996 Cricket World Cup, exclusively on cable.

NYNEX also has two strategic links to generate programming opportunities. It has invested in Viacom, one of the leading US entertainment and publishing companies which produces the music video stations MTV and VH-1. Viacom owns Paramount Pictures, Showtime Networks, Spelling Entertainment, Blockbuster and Virgin Interactive Entertainment. This joint venture will explore opportunities for obtaining rights to special events, developing channels and licensing agreements covering impulse pay-per-view and video-on-demand.

Its other link is with Creative Artists Agency. NYNEX announced at the end of October last year that it had formed two joint ventures with Bell Atlantic and Pacific Telesis Group, one media, and one technology and integration. The media partnership is with CAA, which will provide strategic advice and other assistance in the development of programming and interactive services.

NYNEX can only speculate as to what extent potential customers will accept TV or telecomms services from cable operators. Although initial consumer acceptance has been encouraging, it is unable to predict with certainty how consumer demand for its services will develop. Actual results will depend on many factors, including whether it can meet its construction schedule, the number of customers (and the products and services they subscribe to), the rate of churn and the nature and penetration of new services that may be offered by CableComms in the future.

The ongoing development of its network should lead to increased revenues and customers, higher penetration levels and lower churn rates. CableComms believes that these results will be achieved by, among other things, offering combined cable TV and telecom services in innovative, competitively priced packages, developing and offering new products, including interactive services and providing quality customer service.

It also has plans to expand its franchise base as opportunities arise by acquiring other existing franchises and/or by bidding for new licences and then developing and operating these newly acquired franchises to increase revenues and economies of scale.

The future

The future is expected to see a range of new services. These include video games, which might allow customers to play interactively with other customers on the network. CableComms is currently in discussions on carrying the Sega Channel, which would offer that company's games and should be launched this year. Impulse-Pay-Per-View would see customers choose to view feature films or special events such as concerts or sporting events. Video- and Near-Video-on Demand would provide customers with a choice of programming, which they could view when they chose. Interactive home shopping, financial, travel, education and training services are also all possible.

Oxford Molecular
Solutions for Integrated Molecular Design

Oxford Molecular, Oxford

Oxford Molecular is a major biotechnology company

Outlook:
The prospects for biotechnology companies are always hard to determine. But through the quality of its work and the relationships it has established with leading pharmaceutical companies, Oxford Molecular is among those with the best chance to capitalise on the demand for new sources for drugs of the future

Scorecard:

Structural flexibility	★★★★
Innovative power	★★★★★
International orientation	★★★★
Human resources	★★★★
Growth markets	★★★★★
Quality of management	★★★★

Key figures:

Turnover	£6.2 million
Pre-tax (loss)	(£3.7 million)
Staff	104

Oxford Molecular Group plc
The Magdalen Centre
Oxford Science Park
Oxford OX4 4GA
Tel: 01865 784600
Fax: 01865 784661

Oxford Molecular

The scientific advances which generate substantial new business sectors are often immensely complex and difficult to penetrate for the non-technician. Yet these can be precisely the areas which can lead to products to enhance life or make the conduct of business more efficient. None fits this description more appropriately than biotechnology. It is an aspect of research which many would consider pure science and certainly among the most difficult to evaluate in strict business terms.

Oxford Molecular is a biotechnology company with a better than average chance of becoming a major force in the industry. Its business is the provision of computer software programmes to help in the process of drug design and discovery. This market known as computer-aided molecular design (CAMD) is already worth $200 million a year, and grew by 25 per cent in 1994.

There are two types of companies involved in CAMD. One camp involves companies such as Merck, Glaxo and Zeneca which have invested in the area as one of the many ways of discovering drugs. The other group is the specialist producer of drug design software. Most are small US companies which are limited in their capacity to bring new technologies and innovations to the market. They simply do not possess the resources or the contacts to maintain a technological edge. Contract software houses enjoy lower risk by capitalising on new technology rather than the hit or miss business of the actual drug design. Tony Martin, chairman of biotech outfit Tepnel Life Sciences, notes 'in a goldrush the only people guaranteed to make money are those who sell spades'.

Operations and markets

Ex-Zeneca man Dr Tony Marchington, Oxford Molecular CEO, created the company in 1989 after pinpointing a remarkable market opportunity. The development costs of new drugs are frighteningly expensive. On average, £400 million is spent taking a new drug from test tube to market launch. Worse still for every 10,000 compounds investigated, only one will prove commercially viable. Dr Marchington and his colleagues realised that tools to assist in the discovery of new drugs would be especially lucrative.

This company, in 1995, still capitalised at only £24.3 million, could have several key advantages over rivals. Through unique links with the pharmaceutical companies and the academic research community, Oxford Molecular is in the forefront of technology. Its research base has been created by a world-wide network of 30 academic teams. The academics supply raw ideas but are often employed to create individual software packages for specific projects. Oxford Molecular thus acts as a clearing house in a two-way exchange of ideas and products.

In return for their services, cash strapped academic institutions receive royalty payments from the programmes which Oxford Molecular has the contacts to market. Dr Marchington stresses that Oxford Molecular's strong relationships with its academic contacts represent a 'high barrier to entry' to the CAMD market.

However, Oxford's other route to success is via link-ups of various sorts with other companies. In 1993 Oxford Molecular took over BioStructure SA, a small Strasbourg based competitor, which gave it a stronger European presence.

In September 1994 it paid £5.2 million for the US company Intellegenetics which specialised in DNA analysis - an area Oxford Molecular had little expertise in. Crucially Intellegenetics came with net cash and Oxford Molecular funded the deal with paper.

In January 1995 Oxford Molecular bought again. In another paper-funded deal it paid almost £6 million for CAChe Scientific of Oregon USA which brought net cash of £5 million and several more CAMD software products to the party. It also meant that, for the first time, Oxford Molecular's customers were able to access its software through both Macintosh and Windows platforms.

CAChe and Intellegenetics gave Oxford access to, and contacts in, the crucial US market. CAChe also had a presence in Japan and Oxford has bolstered this by signing distribution agreements with the local firms Sony/tek, Teijin and Toray Systems Centre.

Strategy and management

Though distribution, marketing and research infrastructure are already in place, Oxford Molecular is still looking for growth opportunities through corporate agreements. In March 1995 it announced a deal with Immunogen of Massachusetts under which the two companies agreed to cross-license rights to proprietary technology for the design of humanised monoclonal antibodies. Oxford Molecular's expertise in this field of anti-cancer technology derives from the work carried out by Professor Tony Rees of the University of Bath, and Immunogen holds the US patent on the technique he developed - known as resurfacing. Dr Marchington describes the deal as being part of Oxford Molecular's 'strategy of leveraging its software and scientific know-how'.

Further complementary acquisitions and joint ventures are on the cards. But most of Oxford's growth will be organic. The company already owns a stable of 20 products which are generating revenues.

Customers can either purchase particular programmes or through the MERIT scheme can gain access to all of Oxford Molecular's technology. It currently costs around £20,000 a year to join MERIT but that figure is expected to rise steeply as more products are added to the catalogue. By the end of 1994 Oxford Molecular had almost 100 fee-paying customers.

But the company does not only generate revenues from the licensing out of its technology. Many pharmaceutical companies are too small to set up their own in-house dedicated CAMD teams. So companies such as British Biotech plc hire Oxford Molecular to carry out specific molecule evaluation projects on its behalf.

Larger companies, such as Pfizer, Glaxo-Wellcome, Hoescht, Roussel Laboratories and SmithKline Beecham are also on Oxford's client list. Though many of these firms also run internal CAMD teams, Oxford's often holds a technological edge. As importantly, it is often cheaper for the giants to outsource certain specialist tasks such as some CAMD functions.

Typically, Oxford Molecular receives an up-front fee for its evaluation work, but in the future it is possible that it will negotiate a royalty share from specific projects. Richard Lucas of stockbrokers Henry Cooke, Lumsden stresses: 'All such contracts are profitable in themselves (often highly profitable) and Oxford Molecular takes no risk.'

By the end of 1994 Oxford Molecular already had almost 100 fee-paying corporate and institutional customers.

Oxford Molecular now employs 104 people of whom 29 are employed directly in research. Attractive staff share-option schemes both enhance loyalty and incentivise the workforce. Key personnel from the acquired companies have also been 'bound in' via this route. For instance, the management and scientists of Intellegenetics now own 15 per cent of Oxford following the paper-funded take-over by the British company.

Among Oxford's senior board members, chairman Roderick Hall, chief executive Tony Marchington, and finance director Diana Audley have all held senior positions in industry and commerce.

However the key to this company's potential remains its academic ties. And the joint technical directors Professor Anthony Rees and Dr Graham Richards are both drawn from this background. The links with academia are now firm and, in most cases, long established. That guarantees a stream of new product ideas.

The future

Unlike many high-tech companies Oxford Molecular can already boast significant and rapidly rising revenues. By the fourth quarter of 1994 its income was already running at an annualised rate of £4 million. The CAChe deal will enhance sturdy organic growth and could mean that revenues reach £15 million in the calendar year 1995 and analysts look for dramatic growth from 1996 onwards.

Just as importantly, Dr Marchington predicts that from the fourth quarter of 1995 the company will be cash neutral and it will start to generate cash, acquisitions notwithstanding, thereafter.

In the longer term, Oxford Molecular has positioned itself as a world leader in a field which is set for dramatic growth. Unlike many 'blue sky' companies it already has an impressive client list which is helping it to achieve substantial revenues. And its finances are in good shape.

Above all, Oxford Molecular's unique links with the global academic elite mean that it seems set to maintain a distinct technological advantage over its competitors. And it now has the marketing infrastructure to fully exploit this.

Increasing pressures on research costs in the pharmaceutical industry mean that the environment for technologies such as CAMD has never been better. The future belongs to companies such as Oxford Molecular.

 Packard Bell

---

Packard Bell, Berks

Packard Bell is a manufacturer and distributor of PCs

Outlook:

This is a company which surprises people. Set up more than 75 years ago as a maker of radios, the company has passed through several phases. It is now the number one US manufacturer of PCs and the fourth largest in the world. It is also the fastest growing PC - and especially desktop - producer

Scorecard:

Structural flexibility	★★★★
Innovative power	★★★★★
International orientation	★★★★★
Human resources	★★★★★
Growth markets	★★★★★
Quality of management	★★★★★

Key figures:

Global sales	$3 billion (1994)
	$5.5 billion (estimated 1995)
Staff	3,000

Packard Bell UK
Windsor
Berks
Tel: 01753 831914

Packard Bell

If ever there was a symbol of continuous renewal in industry it is Packard Bell. This business which started in the 1920s as a manufacturer of consumer radios reinvents itself every generation. Now it is the fastest growing manufacturer of PCs in the world. It is fourth largest globally and number one in the States. Packard Bell outsells IBM, Apple and Compaq in its domestic market and is far and away the largest desktop producer.

But despite its standing - and its projected $5.5 billion income in 1995 - Packard Bell is hardly a name which trips off the tongue. Even the US computer industry journal Upside commented in May 1995: 'Packard Bell remains an enigma within a high visibility industry. Though Packard Bell was the most advertised computer brand at retail last year, the computer company has yet to spend a dime on national image advertising.' The article goes on to comment that the organisation is rarely the subject of reports in the mainstream business press and that quietly progressing its work is a cultural metaphor for the company.

Selling through superstore chains, mass merchandisers, home appliance shops and consumer electronic outlets rather than computer stores, Packard Bell grew rapidly. It made listening to customers a tenet of faith. But it has also benefited from the standardisation of computer technology which has been a facet of the last decade and which produced remarkable economies of scale. But the lower-end-of-the-market producers often underestimated the retailers' margins and consumers' progressive appetites. Packard Bell did neither. Its unique talent for perfect timing has meant that it introduced machines sufficiently improved to meet market expectation.

Operations and markets

Some 85 per cent of Packard Bell's sales are still in the US, which is one of the reasons why it is not well known in the UK. However, the assault on European and Asian markets has begun in earnest. President and CEO Beny Alagem aims to substantially increase international revenues. 'We need to balance our revenues so 35-40 per cent comes from outside the US. We have been positioning ourselves in the fastest growing markets around the world. In 1995 we are making a major push in these markets,' he says.

The company now has manufacturing plants in the Netherlands and France and sales offices in 16 other countries all over Europe including the UK (at Windsor). Its operation in Britain is comparatively small at present but it is developing links with the main consumer electronics retailers here (Currys, Dixons and so on) as it has in other markets. Sales internationally grew by 173 per cent in 1994, as opposed to 27 per cent for the industry as a whole. The company predicts that they might add another 30 per cent in 1995.

Strategy and management

To say that Packard Bell is the leanest major computer company in the global market understates its position. It employs only 3,000 people. The managment of the company is in the hands of no more than 20 executives, the vast majority of whom lunch every day in the headquarters building in Sacramento, California. This principle of simple organisation extends through to its approach to costs and markets. Although its products are not necessarily the cheapest in the market, its production costs are. Rivals accuse Packard Bell of stinting on quality and offer poor customer services. Certainly, at one time its returns were considerably higher than the industry average. However Mr Alagem says that Packard Bell is simply better at purchasing components than many of its competitors.

The lower profile of the company - relatively speaking - suits the style of the PB management. But they have achieved their remarkable results from an unswerving dedication to Vision, Spirit and Focus. These are immensely powerful concepts within the company and the directors have an astonishing capacity to generate employee commitment without the beer busts and other razzamatazz of the West Coast computer industry.

They work quietly, listening carefully to retailers and building bonds which will bring returns for retailer and manufacturer. The emergence of other leading players - a revitalised Compaq and entrant Hewlett Packard (no relation) - is considered by sector analysts to be a threat but one which PB can bear. 'In the end Packard Bell has done well for the retailer and the loyalty which this has engendered will probably be the decisive factor,' one told Fortune.

In the next few years Packard Bell intends to build on its strengths in US mass markets by going into relatively unfamiliar territory on two fronts: overseas and the corporate environment. BusinessWeek commented on its corporate adventure: 'This summer the company will launch a new line of PCs called Packard Bell Executive which is expected to include laptops and network servers. It has started building a technical support group dedicated to corporate buyers.'

Mr Alagem told BusinessWeek: 'We have always sold PCs to small and medium sized corporations through our retailers. But as we go forward, we will put more emphasis on our relationship with corporate resellers.' This means that the company will start selling through computer stores as well as directly to corporate customers. The publication was sanguine on the short-term benefits of such a move. 'Low prices are less important to corporate customers. Businesses tend to look at other factors such as the cost of training, software, maintenance, support and upgrades where Packard Bell has scant experience.'

However Packard Bell can claim to be the fastest computer company to build advanced technology into its machines. It has a string of firsts to its name: first to pre-install an operating system, application and entertainment software on PCs (1987), first to offer freefone technical support to customers (US, 1988; Europe, 1992), first to bundle CD-ROM drives with PCs (1991), first to offer full multimedia PC systems in the mass retail markets (1992). In addition it was the first company to launch a PC with Intel's Pentium processor. Its ability to recognise the potential of technological advances has now become legendary.

The benefits of this approach are clear: it has emerged as number one PC manufacturer in the US (by units shipped), market leader in US retail with a 53 per cent share, top US multimedia and desktop manufacturer, leader in the home and home office desktop market, premier supplier of PC monitors and fourth largest worldwide PC shipper. With its projected growth in revenues in 1995 it should strengthen its position further.

Currently the company is selling PCs with surround-sound and twin CD-ROM drives. Tandy president Alan Bush remarks: 'Packard Bell is successful because it builds a quality product and brings it to the market fast.' Given the problems experienced by IBM, Apple and Microsoft in bringing new products to market, perhaps this once reviled company has something to teach them.

The future

Ten years ago Mr Alagem concluded that PCs would become just another home appliance. His analysis has been vindicated. His company is criticised for its support quality - and this may impact its rise in the corporate market - but with US domestic sales still soaring and the overseas markets still relatively untouched, this may not matter too much.

PepsiCo Inc., London

Pepsi is a world famous supplier of soft drinks and operator of restaurants

Outlook:
Things have never looked better for this formidable US operation. Its ambitious strategy plans include employing 1,000,000 people worldwide by the end of the century. This is an exceptionally well managed enterprise with a string of market leader and world famous brands

Scorecard:
Structural flexibility	★★★★★
Innovative power	★★★★★
International orientation	★★★★★
Human resources	★★★★
Growth markets	★★★★★
Quality of management	★★★★★

Key figures:
Worldwide sales	$30 billion
Worldwide operating profits	$6 billion
Global staff	470,000

Pepsi Cola UK
63 Kew Road
Richmond
Surrey TW9 2QL
Tel: 0181 332 0332
Fax: 0181 332 4042

PepsiCo

Wherever you look across the group, Pepsi Cola International's (PCI) management is driven by a consistent passion for its products and employees and for change. It encourages its employees to take risks and reinvent even its most cherished lines. Nothing is sacrosanct. Its aim is to remind consumers constantly that its products fit their lifestyle and aspirations.

In part, this is driven by the fact that its flagship product competes head-on with one of world's most valuable brands. But if the group is permanently number two it doesn't act like it. PCI regards its powerful rival as a large and attractive target and 'Competitive Jujitsu' is its approach to dealing with larger competitors. According to Simon Calver, area Vice President for Pepsi Cola International, UK 'we always try to use our opponent's weight to our own advantage'.

Operations and markets

PCI is the beverage branch of PepsiCo Inc. which contains three of the world's largest, most dynamic and fastest growing consumer businesses: beverages, snack foods and restaurants. Pepsi-Cola soft drinks are available in more than 190 countries and territories and the Pepsi brand is the leading cola in nearly 50 of the world's markets. The group has a remarkable record of growth since its formation, doubling sales and profits every five years on average.

PepsiCo was formed in 1965, the amalgamation of two successful companies, Pepsi-Cola of New York and Frito-Lay of Texas. Pizza Hut and Taco Bell were added to the group in 1970, KFC in 1986 and there has been a flow of acquisitions since.

Over the last thirty years it has grown to own many of the world's most valuable brands, including products over 100 years old. Annual worldwide sales are approaching $30 billion and the group is one of the world's leading employers with around 470,000 staff.

Strategy and management

PepsiCo has a clear aim to be number one in consumer convenience snacks, restaurants and beverages across the world. The prognosis is encouraging. In the US it is close to achieving its target, supported by hugely successful brands such as Pepsi-Cola and Frito-Lay. In the UK it is getting there with the leading crisp manufacturer Walkers-Smith, the second largest beverage company PCI and the restaurants of KFC, Pizza Hut and Taco Bell.

Management is determined to fulfil its commitment to its workforce. As it is making products that appeal to all ages, economic classes and nationalities, its people are the key influence on the group's future, not the economy or demographic trends. What it needs is the innovative leadership to produce the ideas.

The business generates enormous amounts of cash which it invests in existing and innovative new brands to maximise organic growth. It also acquires competitors who provide synergies with its leading products. Finally it buys back its shares, an effective use of its resources considering that PepsiCo shareholders include a great many of its own employees, granted stock as part of its SharePower scheme share options scheme.

The group philosophy is to devolve responsibility to its management. As Simon Calver says: 'Our strength comes from building up the individual pieces in order to produce the whole. Local management has complete responsibility and autonomy to deliver the bottom line. Every individual operation functions that way.' In the UK it has become relatively decentralised and now it is looking for ways to drive synergies between the 'little islands', i.e. between Walkers and Pepsi. In the search for cross promotion it is sharing information and research and now approaches customers as a joint proposition, for drinks, snacks and restaurants.

Pepsi is also committed to a strategy of eliminating non-essential work, designated 'Make waste our enemy'. According to Simon Calver, 'anything not driving PepsiCo in the UK, or anywhere else in the world, towards our vision is dispensed with, a particularly big priority at Walkers, and the restaurant division'.

All new initiatives are tested and benchmarked across the world, to focus on minimising costs in every market. 'We aim for a symbiotic relationship with our partners, bottling plants for example, looking for innovations which can be exported around the world. That helps drive continual revenue growth and market share. We are not just cutting costs in a mature market.

'In the UK, PCI has a clear vision. We want to be the finest and fastest growing total beverage company in the UK. There is much stronger potential as we branch out of soft drinks into a total beverage mentality. As people travel they experience new products overseas which they want to buy in their home market and we hope that in time, whether the consumer is buying tea, juices or water it will be a Pepsi product.' A recent example in the UK is the launch of Mountain Dew, a neon coloured, carbonated citrus drink.

'We seek to develop a calculated risk-taking culture, to encourage our people to think bigger and take advantage of bigger opportunities. At the same time we don't innovate for its own sake, it must add value and be clear to our customers in what way it adds value.'

One of PCI's strongest innovations has been 'The Pepsi Challenge', a powerful comparative marketing campaign which has dramatically raised its profile. It says, in blunt terms, 'we are the best tasting cola, and we can prove it'. Pepsi risks going head-to-head with the competition and if there's any doubt that it works, look at Coca-Cola's response. It has challenged the legality of the campaign, rather than simply rely on the taste of its drink.

According to Mr Calver, The Pepsi Challenge allows consumers to clearly rationalise why they buy Pepsi rather than Coke. In markets where Pepsi's market share is behind Coca-Cola, the consumer image is that Coke tastes better. The Pepsi Challenge disputes that.

The results of the challenge consistently show Pepsi beating Coke. It is a massive effort. In the UK in 1995 it plans 800,000 challenges and at the halfway stage 61 per cent of consumers consistently prefer the taste of Pepsi. Pepsi's UK market share at 18.5 per cent is well short of that, but campaigns like the Challenge are moving it in the right direction.

Growth will flow from innovations such as this which stimulate its marketplace. If it can add value to consumers it can ensure that the UK does not became a pure price-fed market. Supermarket own brands have demonstrated that barriers to entry are relatively low.

Pepsi Max is another superb example of product innovation. PCI's research showed that Diet Pepsi is more popular with female than male consumers. Yet it also revealed that these men were very concerned about their sugar intake.

Apparently, men wanted the taste of a regular cola but secondly, they perceived diet drinks as a feminine product. Launched initially in the UK, Pepsi Max was the solution to PCI's dilemma: a masculine, full tasting, but no-sugar product which has carved out a substantial niche in a short time.

'High Performance Leadership' is its plan to develop a culture of accepting change quickly and doing bigger things. This is designed to produce the big opportunities to grow the business ahead of the market. 'This organisation has a real buzz about growth, innovation and the search for big changes and HPL sets out to engender the spirit of "entrepreneurial leadership". In a big relatively mature market like the UK, 4-5 per cent p.a. growth is all you can normally expect. If we are to get to 15 per cent we need to think harder about how to achieve those big changes.'

PCI is also passionate about operating excellence, minimising the time it takes to get its innovations to market, maximising the effectiveness of all its marketing efforts. Such growth is not driven by head office, but by the success of separate operating companies in local markets. The feedback is, however, exported worldwide.

It takes the success of its partners very seriously. The more profitable a bottling partner is, the more it can invest in the development of PCI in each region. That promotes a true partnership culture which in turn allows PCI to share and similarly benchmark its experience in a particular bottling plant across the world with its other partners. It wants to be perceived as the preferred supplier within each category. By adding value to retailers, they will in turn give it the investment and the shelf space it requires. PCI works with them to constantly grow.

'If we are to achieve brand superiority, quality is vital. Hence we have an absolute dedication to driving quality of product, taste, carbonation, packaging. And when we meet our performance targets, we simply raise the bar, that way we continue to drive towards closeness to perfect product quality. We manage complexity to maximise quality, revenue and profits, that way the customer will take for granted that quality wherever they purchase any PepsiCo product, anywhere in the world.'

The future

PepsiCo is driven by the demanding targets it sets itself. For example, 15 per cent growth in soft drink revenues year on year, in addition to the fact that by the year 2000 it intends to be the first corporation on earth with one million employees. Considering the freedom, authority and responsibility it gives its people, the logistics of running a company that size would tax many governments. But PepsiCo is better focused than most governments.

The highly competitive, dynamic environment in which Pepsi operates demands that it constantly remind customers why its products are their preferred choice. A branded manufacturer can never take its eye off that ball. It must continually offer value to the customer because if superior taste and the perception of the product isn't greater than the price difference between it and say, supermarket brands, people won't buy its products. PCI has taken this fact on board more effectively than many others.

Price Waterhouse

Price Waterhouse, London

Price Waterhouse is a major worldwide firm of business advisers which supplies audit, accountancy, management consultancy, tax, corporate finance and insolvency services

Outlook:
The markets for business advisory firms are becoming more competitive. Industry is becoming more global and PW has constructed a strategy which emphasises European and global service provision. It is an audacious plan since many of its rivals continue to stress their national, as well as international, strengths. Like all the big six operations, PW casts itself as a business adviser rather than an accountancy practice

Scorecard:

Structural flexibility	★★★★★
Innovative power	★★★★
International orientation	★★★★★
Human resources	★★★★
Growth markets	★★★★★
Quality of management	★★★★

Key figures:

UK fee income	£400 million
European fee income	£894 million
Global fee income	$3.98 billion

Price Waterhouse
Southwark Towers
32 London Bridge Street
London SE1 9SY
Tel: 0171 939 3000

Price Waterhouse

The face of modern accountancy has changed radically in the past decade. A group of six firms has emerged worldwide to lead the sector. Increasingly their share of multinational business has grown to commanding levels and the scope of their operations has broadened beyond its original audit, accountancy and tax functions into advisory and consultancy roles. The big six, as they are commonly known, have become the trendsetters for the industry, providing world class service for their clients.

The influence of the big six on the companies and institutions which they serve is expanding rapidly. This has shaped the development of the businesses themselves so that they need to anticipate the future pattern of client demand and to prepare services which will exceed client expectations. Forecasting among the specialist press about the likely format of the largest organisations in coming years has been a spectator sport for more than ten years. Many observers believe that as many as six firms will be unable to supply excellent service in all disciplines and in all markets around the globe. The globalisation of industry suggests that clients will make additional demands on their preferred suppliers and that professional services providers will be obliged to enhance the quality of their output even further.

Operations and markets

PW is one of the most respected accountancy firms in the UK today. It is a world class player with British origins and the UK - especially London - operation remains a powerful force within the world firm. Its fee income for the British practice is around £400 million and it employs around 6,000 people in various offices around the country. It is one of the most potent brands in the world and repeatedly market research in the global business community has shown that the organisation enjoys commanding stature.

The organisation's strategy emphasises blue chip clients and those businesses with the potential to be world class enterprises. It is perhaps more selective in its approach than the other big six partnerships. PW also offers substantially greater operational freedom for its partners than many competitors, advancing meritocratic values.

Among its services are audit, management consultancy, tax, corporate finance, insolvency and a wide range of advisory functions. PW is associated heavily with growing businesses - but only those with the capacity to be outstanding contributors to industry. Its expansion has been achieved without significant merger, although it has acquired affiliates for its regional and global networks.

Strategy and management

The strategy which PW is currently following was constructed after detailed appreciation of the trends within industry worldwide and especially among multinationals, which form a key group of clients. Consequently it has conducted a strategic plan which is global in orientation and which identifies the service provision necessary to meet the demands of clients whose operations are worldwide. Ian Brindle, UK senior partner, says that within the global plan there are regional variations, dependent on the different pace of development of the Americas, Europe/Africa/India, and Pacific Rim. 'The longterm aim is to have a single strategy for all regions.'

John Barnsley, PWE's managing partner, argues that industry as a whole has taken on a global dimension. 'Whereas previously we have seen significant players in national markets, the current trends within business suggest that a premier group of players will emerge worldwide. These will be the dominant forces. Companies whose operations are limited to national markets will become less important as the scale of these top class operators will exert greater influence in their markets. Our services will need to be tailored to the requirements of these clients. We have been moving closer to the decision makers in these global businesses during the last decade. This will accelerate as the managers of these companies will look for higher value input from professional services advisers.'

PW perceives a second major macro-economic trend in the next ten years: the increasing importance of three major undeveloped markets. These are Eastern Europe with a population of six million, the Pacific Rim countries with 1.2 billion inhabitants and China embracing a massive six billion people. Each of these markets is growing by quantum leaps - albeit at different speeds. The firm is also focusing attention on India, black Africa and South Africa in particular because the growing demand for products and services in these areas will mean that clients will require services from the firm in these locations.

The practice is being selective about its activities in each of these areas but in certain Eastern European and former Soviet Union countries business is so strong and of sufficient quality that demand is very high for PW to be active throughout the area. 'The sheer magnitude of these markets and the demand for consumer and industrial products and services is such that our personnel are engaged in a wide range of high value assignments.' One of PW's largest ever audits was won in 1995 at GazProm which will generate $12 million in annual fees. At Togliatti in Russia PW has captured the audit of the Lada car company; a business which produces more vehicles a year than General Motors. Two areas where PW excels in industry knowledge - financial services and oil and gas - are especially active and so the firm's recognised expertise is greatly valued by locals and multinationals.

Another crucial strategic issue for Price Waterhouse is providing the correct structural and operational forms to get the best out of its people and to exploit the benefits of technology. 'We recognise that technology enhancements are changing the nature of the work we do. For example, the audit as we know it today may be redundant in ten years' time. We need to be insightful about how technology will alter what we do and to show our people new ways to deliver our services to clients. We have always been a meritocracy and we believe in letting our people have the fullest freedom to provide their services in their own way. One of the hardest tasks is achieving a balance between achieving the effectiveness of scale and granting greatest personal freedom. We know that we must operate as an effective global and regional force but our effectiveness is built on personal qualities. We will never succeed if we attempt to impose from above.'

Culturally there are four principles which drive Price Waterhouse:
. 'we are obsessive about providing superb client service
. 'we are also obsessive about finding the right people
. 'the firm believes in professional leadership wherever it operates
. 'we are highly selective about the assignments we take on'

The future

PW aims to be the best rather than the biggest. If size - or market leadership - comes with high quality then the firm is delighted. It has made a major gamble in investing in growing markets and concentrating on the regional and global rather than the domestic. But in doing this it is reflecting the future pattern of industrial development. Its culture also argues for success, wich a dedication to client service and employing the best people, giving its teams and individuals greatest scope for performance but at the same time exploiting the benefits of scale.

Procter & Gamble, Newcastle

Procter & Gamble is the world's largest manufacturer of detergents, soaps, toiletries and other household items

Outlook:
P&G has long been regarded as one of the most professionally and aggressively managed enterprises in the world. It operates in one of the toughest marketplaces and is head to head with Unilever across the globe. P&G has made significant leaps in logistics and manufacturing economies of scale which will offer longterm benefits. Coupled with its heavy investment in innovation, product quality and advertising, these factors will be key for its future success.

Scorecard:
Structural flexibility	★★★★
Innovative power	★★★★★
International orientation	★★★★★
Human resouces	★★★★
Growth markets	★★★★★
Quality of management	★★★★

Key Figures:
Global turnover	$ 33.43 billion
Pre-tax profits	$ 2.65 billion
Staff	99,200

Procter & Gamble
St. Nicholas Avenue
Gosforth
Newcastle upon Tyne NE99 1EE
Tel: 0191 279 2000
Fax: 0191 279 2282

Procter & Gamble

One might forgive a venerable old company, in sight of its 160th birthday, for taking its market leadership for granted. Very fortunately, considering the challenges of the current decade, that has never been Procter & Gamble's style.

According to the group's Statement of Purpose, the key to P&G's success has been its in-depth understanding of consumers. The development, technological improvement and marketing of its brands has been a constant throughout its history which has been rewarded with considerable consumer loyalty. However the world recession did what was previously unthinkable; it undermined the value of premium brands and that has forced it to rethink.

Nonetheless the principles by which the company was built remain intact. Energetically develop, protect and market your brands, and invest in the most talented employees. However the turmoil of the current operating environment will continue to test management's ability to innovate and adapt its strategy to a rapidly changing market. The early evidence suggests it has the depth and flexibility to rise to the challenge.

Operations and markets

Founded in 1837, P&G is one of the world's leading household goods manufacturers. It markets its range of laundry, cleaning, beauty care, healthcare, food and beverage products around the world. Its leading brands include Tide, Ariel, Fairy Liquid, Pampers, Crest, Vicks and Max Factor.

From its base in Cincinnati, Ohio, USA, P&G has operations in 56 countries with some 99,200 employees. P&G's international division is split into Europe, Middle East and Africa, Asia and Latin America.

Strategy and management

During the last decade P&G prospered as the world's leading economies grew, but worldwide recession hit sales and intensified competition and a rethink of its early 1980s strategy became a priority.

At the turn of the eighties P&G had recognised that the home market for core laundry and household products had matured and it shifted towards global expansion and the addition of product lines perceived as less mature. As a result it enthusiastically added new products to its range, in areas such as over-the-counter medicines and beauty. During the eighties and early nineties it made more than 40 acquisitions, entered 29 new countries and 20 new business categories. However, 1992-3's losses reflect its need to rationalise those manufacturing operations and cut overheads.

The impact of recession on branded goods drove many manufacturers to turn to price as their key marketing weapon which made cost-cutting imperative. In December 1992 P&G began the most comprehensive ever review of its worldwide work processes and organizational structure. Titled 'Strengthening Global Effectiveness' it set out to improve cost effectiveness by closing plants and cutting employee numbers, setting a precedent for a group whose employees enjoyed a tradition of job security. 1993 saw the biggest job cuts in P&G's history, 12 per cent of its 106,000 workforce, as it restructured its businesses worldwide and closed 30 out of 147 plants. This cost around $2 billion, to save an annual $500m by 1995-6.

These cuts protected its margins when, in the following year, P&G initiated aggressive price cuts to counter competition from generic, own-label products. A more price-conscious consumer has helped sales of own-label products and reduced the premium that can be charged for branded goods. Although some believe that brand erosion is an inevitable result of recession and that consumers will return to recognised brands in due course, P&G chose not to rely on that happening. It has vigorously defended its market shares in nappies, washing up liquid and washing powder, toilet paper and toothpaste.

The market has polarised into the most resilient brands, those with either very strong market shares or clear product differentiation. Since the pressure has stepped up, products which are third or fourth in their sector, or have no clear differentiation, are simply being squeezed out. Some experts believe this is the long-term trend for brands in the UK, Europe and the US where many are being steadily replaced by generic products.

As the need for particularly strong and distinctive qualities has grown, P&G has stepped up the search for technical innovation and differentiation and investment in advertising to maintain market leadership. This has never been more important. Analysts estimate that the premium on consumer good brands has halved since the start of the recession from around 35/40 per cent, to closer to 20 per cent.

Data for the toiletries business are quite poor, but analysts believe there is little actual product differentiation. In a very fragmented market, an enormous amount has to be spent on advertising. Brand loyalty is vital when most of your products are purchased weekly or monthly as each repurchase is an opportunity to switch to another brand. A further problem is that big retailers have chosen this area to introduce generic alternatives and their copycat products are undermining the power of advertising.

In the UK Tesco introduced 500 own-label toiletries brands last year and Sainsburys launched new 'branded' products with advertising. These include new washing powders and nappies which are making inroads on established brands. P&G's response to such threats was to launch 'Value Pricing', a year-round low price campaign, but in effect a series of pre-emptive strikes which has quite successfully blunted the competitive advantage of cheaper generic alternatives.

It has also responded ruthlessly to technological threats such as Unilever's new washing powder in 1994. In this case it caught its arch-rival flat-footed. P&G, mindful of the threat posed by an apparently technologically advanced product, conducted a high-profile campaign against Persil Power which stated that its active ingredient, a manganese-based catalyst, rotted clothes.

Whether or not its case was proven, the publicity ultimately led Unilever to back down and change its formula. P&G's actions blunted the competitive edge of a product launched as the world's most effective washing powder. A spokesperson claims another less devious motive. 'We had to make sure that any of our consumers who tried Persil Power and switched back to our brands, didn't assume a P&G product had done the damage.'

Recently, worrying cracks have appeared in the grasp of P&G's senior management, the most embarrassing of which was $100m-plus lost on interest rate swaps. This involvement in derivatives, well outside of any pure risk-management practice, shows that internal procedures intended to limit exposure were not followed.

However, P&G's attitude to its employees is legendary and its executives are extremely highly regarded. Yet its culture was once described by the FT as 'insular, clannish and secretive, with a policy of promoting only from within and not rehiring those who leave. Employees are barred from disclosing even the most trivial information to outsiders.' This could conceivably be interpreted as sinister or alternatively an effective way to inspire employees and prevent the release of commercially sensitive information. Either way the approach has served P&G well.

P&G's commitment to technnological innovation, quality and value for money remains undiminished, driven by the need to find new products and constantly improve its proven brands. An innocent perception of toiletries and detergents belies the chemistry and science invoved in their development. Technological innovation maintains each product ahead of the competition.

Getting its message across is also vital. Chairman John Pepper regards advertising as 'the lifeblood of P&G's brands. If technological innovation is where a brand begins, advertising is what "gets consumers" attention and persuades them to use our products again and again. There isn't a leading P&G brand anywhere that doesn't have a strong history of effective advertising.'

P&G recognised the importance of advertising to its future when it was recently reported to have formed a strategic alliance with Paramount Television. The plan is to involve the group in TV programming, a defensive response to suggestions that as a multimedia age will increase the number of pay per view channels it will weaken the influence of advertisers.

The future

P&G's immediate future will be to balance the impact of undeniable increases in competitive pressures this decade with the push to increase its global reach and to find opportunities to cut costs. In his last statement the chairman set out four primary business objectives.

These were: to increase the flow of innovative new products to the marketplace, expand the global presence of group brands, offer better value to consumers and increase the efficiency and productivity of its operations. The business is built on a number of simple principles but understanding the needs of the customer is key. Success combines leading product technologies and innovative advertising and marketing to bring its products to the fore. This strategy has built up one of the most attractive stables of products.

P&G also increases the geographical coverage of these lines to maintain its worldwide leadership. Since 1991 Tide and Ariel have been introduced into a range of new markets including India, China and Russia and other developing markets.

Despite growing competition the main task remains building its brands. 'Consumers have to trust that a brand will meet all their needs, all the time. That requires superior product technology and a sufficient breadth of product choices. We should never give consumers a product reason to switch away from one of our brands.'

Psion, London

Psion is a major manufacturer of compact personal and business organisation machines

Outlook:
Psion has a strong spread of sales throughout the world and a solid portfolio of corporate clients. As a highly innovative manufacturer, skilled in detecting likely future demand, Psion seems to be ready for any changes the future may bring

Scorecard:

Structural flexibility	★★★
Innovative power	★★★★★
International orientation	★★★★
Human resources	★★★★
Growth markets	★★★★
Quality of management	★★★★

Key figures:

Global sales (1994)	£61.3 million
Global pre-tax profits (1994)	£6.54 million
Global staff	800

Psion
Alexander House
85 Frampton Street
London NW8 8NQ
Tel: 0171 262 5580
Fax: 0171 258 7340

Psion

For a small company whose products make a virtue of their compactness, Psion has taken on a mammoth job: out-smarting a gaggle of the electronics industry's biggest and wealthiest contenders, from Casio and Sharp of Japan to Hewlett-Packard and Apple of the US. Within Psion, few have any doubts that their company is up to the challenge. More and more experts from outside the company, too, have been won over by Psion's increasingly impressive progress in technical and financial terms, and are backing the London-based company to emerge as a significant force in the industry in the near future.

Psion is the world's leading specialist designer and maker of hand-held computers. Its first commercially produced machine was the Organiser, a combination of an electronic diary, notebook, calculator and word processor. In the mid-1980s, the Organiser caught on as an essential executive accessory - but rapidly proved itself to have far more applications in the commercial as well as the personal sector.

The potential of hand-held computers to increase the productivity and responsiveness of employees who work away from a desk in an office has been recognised, in the UK, by Psion customers from Marks and Spencer and Prudential Assurance to BT and the Post Office. Overseas, Psion counts Motorola, Martin Marietta, BMW and Lufthansa among its corporate customers. The potential market for Psion's technology is huge: according to an estimate which Psion is delighted to repeat, 40 per cent of the UK workforce now spends a significant proportion of its work time away from an office desk. Psion's response has been to follow-up products to the Organiser, which both expand the computing power and adaptability of the earlier machine, and tailor the capabilities of the product to the needs of specific customers and applications.

Operations and markets

Psion's founder and chairman, David Potter, started the company in 1980 with the proceeds of software programs he had written for other people's computers. Psion, too, was at first exclusively a software company. But the breakthrough that set Psion on the road to being a £60m-a-year-turnover company came with the idea of providing the market with a powerful computer that could fit inside a pocket.

The Organiser was the first product of its kind in the world, and created an entirely new sub-sector of the computer industry - one in which Psion, needless to say, was the leader of the pack. Launched in 1984 to almost instant success in the UK, the Organiser, although no longer a leading-edge product, continues to generate some £7m a year in sales.

More innovative products have followed. Psion's latest success is the Series 3 palmtop computer, and its most up-to-date variant, the Series 3a. With 100 times the memory and 20-30 times the processing power of the original Organiser, the Series 3a represents a major achievement in its marriage of high quality miniature engineering, software and design.

A decade after creating the market for hand-held computers, Psion no longer has the field to itself. But the technical excellence of the Series 3 means it is the largest-selling product of its type in every market where it is available. Considering that the main competition is provided by companies with the resources of Sharp, Hewlett Packard and Apple, that fact stands as an accolade to the quality of Psion's product.

Computer industry watchers acknowledge the Series 3's technical edge. 'Psion's expertise is shown in their linking of hardware and software,' says Luke Collins, deputy editor of _Electronics Times._ 'The software in the Series 3 is very well suited to the physical limitations of the screen and keyboard.'

Strategy and management

One of the keys to the production of a market-leading product, Mr Collins explains, was the fact that when the Series 3 was designed, Psion 'started with a clean slate', rather than trying to miniaturise a desk-top computer and its applications. 'Psion has written its own applications, and they're more appropriate (for a palm-top computer) than using a cut-down version of existing software, such as Lotus 1-2-3.'

As the Series 3 range has caught on, sales of the palm-top have boomed - lifting Psion's reported profits in the process. Sales revenue for the Series 3 and related accessories leapt by 77 per cent from £22.1m to £39.1m in 1994, as Psion more than doubled total pre-tax profits to £6.55m. Sales to the corporate systems market represented by the Psion HC, and Organiser II range rose to £14.2m, and an exciting future is predicted for Psion's new entry to this market, the Workabout. As well as the hand-held computers, Psion has a burgeoning side-line in high-quality, credit-card-sized modems, which added to the expansion in turnover in 1994, with sales rising by 55 per cent to £7.42m.

But Psion still has a long way to go before it is established in the global computer industry's premier league. Before it gets there, the company is likely to face ever stronger opposition. Some of the biggest-selling computer manufacturers, such as IBM, Compaq and Dell are tipped to enter the hand-held market, and could soon be competing head-to-head with Psion. How does David Potter expect his company to prosper?

The strategy is twofold. In the first place, continued technical innovation is essential. There is no substitute for identifying the needs of customers and delivering the best products before the competition.

Psion's record here is good - with one exception. The MC laptop computer was launched in 1989 into a market which was already crowded with products from American and Japanese rivals. Despite being technically as good as anything on the laptop market, the MC wasn't as successful as the Organiser - and Psion learnt a lesson in its first attempt to branch out of the hand-held computer market.

Psion's determination to anticipate customer needs in its products of the future is highlighted by two of the key areas it expects to exploit in the medium term: voice-recognition capability, to allow its machines to accept spoken commands, and wireless technology, permitting users to link their hand-held computer, wherever it may be, to public communications networks, thus putting them on-line even when far from the office or home. The latter development is already a reality: Psion, in collaboration with US telecoms equipment supplier

Motorola, has introduced wireless capability to its HC range of corporate hand-held computers, which are used by service and maintenance engineers and others needing to log information on the move. Psion describes this joint effort as 'probably the first remote on-line hand-held terminal'.

The other leg of Psion's long-term strategy is to establish itself as a global player, by expanding the volume of business it does outside its domestic market, and especially in the US. In 1994, 47 per cent of Psion's sales revenue came from outside the UK, and only £7.6m of the annual group total of £61.3m was generated in the US. David Potter believes Psion can build its presence in the US to such an extent that that country accounts for at least a third of the company's sales. This will, he concedes, take time. But, on the strength of the technical superiority of its products, Psion is making significant progress in terms of access to US customers. Beginning in 1993, Psion had built its network of retail distributors up to over 1,500 stores by mid-1994, and the total is still rising.

So can Psion really expect to hold its own against the computer industry's giants? David Potter has been asked the question many times, and his answer is to point to the company's dedication to its niche in the market. 'We probably have more resources in palm-top computers than Hewlett-Packard,' says Mr Potter. 'The chairman of the main board [at Hewlett-Packard] isn't going to focus all his resources on beating us.'

At Psion on the other hand, resources are indeed tightly focused. And the company recognises that making the right products won't be enough by itself: they have to be marketed at the right price, which means production has to be cost-effective in the extreme. This is one department where Psion has turned the lazy assumption of inefficient and costly British manufacturing processes on its head.

Psion's manufacturing facilities at Greenford have been the subject of substantial investment in the past three years, and now both the production facilities themselves and the team-based organisation of manufacturing staff are recognised as state-of-the-art for the microelectronics industry. As a result, Psion's labour costs account for only five per cent of the company's total costs, compared with an average of 127 per cent for other profitable computer manufacturers, according to McKinseys, the management consultants.

The future

'In sophisticated automated assembly of this type, the United Kingdom is now one of the lowest-cost producers in the developed world, and the group's competitive position is strong,' comments David Potter.

Psion's founder sees his company becoming, over the next ten years 'a major British enterprise'. He sees no contradiction between Psion's current small size and the extent of his ambitions for the company. In an industry which is moving as fast in technological terms as the computing sector is, everything is possible for the companies which make the really significant breakthroughs. 'If you look at the history of the computer industry, new innovations have always come from smaller companies,' Mr Potter points out. 'The good ones - Microsoft, Digital - grow into big companies. There's no reason why we can't be a $1bn-sales company within a few years.'

Ramco, Aberdeen

Ramco is an independent oil company and an oil industry services company

Outlook:
Ramco's services business is destined to grow incrementally. The potentially much bigger oil independent role also faces notable significant political risk. Nevertheless if Ramco succeeds in this venture it will be a turnkey player in the last remaining unexploited oilfields in the former Soviet Union

Scorecard:
Structural flexibility	★★★★★
Innovative power	★★★★
International orientation	★★★★★
Human resources	★★★
Growth markets	★★★★★
Quality of management	★★★★

Key figures:
Turnover	£5 million
Pre-tax profits	£1 million
Staff	106

Ramco Energy plc
4 Rubislaw Place
Aberdeen AB1 1XN
Tel: 01224 626224

Ramco

Every successful business story contains some magic - and the Ramco adventure is magic personified. Here is a company which started in the oil services sector in 1977 and was so proficient that it rapidly became world market leader of its sector. It is so light on its feet that every few years Ramco's management has engineered a quantum leap forward, forestalling any entrance by a potentially significant competitor. It has patented and automated its processes, invented a distinctive portable production system, established increasingly high levels of service quality, created the industry standards for cost- effectiveness, become the most reliable source of industry research and opened one-stop shops for cleaning/coating, threading and ultrasound scanning of pipe with Hunting and Tuboscope - both sector market leaders.

Operations and markets

Most finance directors would give their right arm for Ramco's results. The company has made 20 per cent return on sales and more than 40 per cent return on capital employed. On annual sales of £5 million, it reports pre-tax profits of £1 million. Many of its clients are triple A-rated, they pay on time and the last time it experienced a bad debt was in 1986. Ramco has no gearing of its own. It commands 75 per cent of the North Sea market, and it sees tremendous potential for developing and expanding its reach. Its achievements since its inception in 1977 are legion but among the most impressive are: convincing conservative oil industry bosses that cleaning and coating oil pipes was a distinct need and that Ramco would be the most effective supplier; to be the first services company to win more than 50 per cent of the manufacturers' cleaning/coating business, even that of Nippon Steel; to be preferred supplier to all world class major oil companies; and to establish lucrative joint ventures - rich with market potential.

Ramco's trim office building in central Aberdeen is replete with black and white photographic portraits which graphically depict the nascent US business of the 1920s and 1930s. The energy and determination which are principal drivers of start-ups are present here but this is no greenfield venture. Instead this is a world class company, developing a huge potential opportunity in a new market. Its reputation as an excellent supplier is the foundation from which it starts in this enterprise. Ramco is entering the oil business, as an independent with an initial outing in the Caucasian republic of Azerbaijan.

Strategy and management

Business analysts accept that the petro-chemicals industry is in its endgame. By the year 2050, new sources of energy will need to have been found but at present one last - vast - oil-bearing region is still to be explored. The former Soviet Union countries are now inviting leading western oil companies to join with them to locate and exploit their oil. The first country which is up and running is Azerbaijan. Mr Remp was the first western oil industry boss to be asked to talk to the Azeri government in Baku. 'I was asked to work with SOCAR, the government's oil agency, to create a consortium of international oil companies. It is an exciting opportunity because it is our first venture as an oil independent. We could not have had a better start - Caspian crude is pure and easy to extract.' Mr Remp is clear that this is the springboard to the role of a facilitator - and de facto key player - in other former Soviet Union oil ventures. 'I am a great believer in the calculated risk. Whenever we have analysed our position, accepted a risk and led from the front, Ramco has been successful. It is inherent in our culture. We have failed only when we have followed others.'

Analyst Tim Baldwin in the London office of broker Greig Middleton characterises Ramco's latest calculated risk: 'In September 1994 Ramco announced that as a member of a consortium of ten oil companies and SOCAR, the Azerbaijan state oil company, it had signed a production sharing agreement for the development of major oil fields in the Caspian Sea.

'The contract is of immense significance to Ramco. It transforms Ramco from being a small oil service company into an independent oil company. This will make Ramco one of the largest independent UK oil companies. Since its interest in the giant oil field is being carried until project payout by its partner Pennzoil, the value of the reserves is further enhanced. The carry is particularly important to Ramco - this alone could be worth $100 million to the company.'

Mr Baldwin's comment is particularly appropiate because it goes to the heart of the Ramco achievement. The company comes to the consortium table as a fully-fledged player alongside many of the global oil titans while its investment costs are being carried by another player. This means its two per cent holding - in strict cash terms - is probably worth about ten per cent. At peak - in around ten years - Ramco will be drawing 15,000 barrels a day from the Azeri field which means in sheer profit terms it will add $50 million a year to the balance sheet. Ramco confidently expects that it will be able to add at least another three such projects which, in 12 to 15 years, together with the Caspian initiative, will generate $100 million a year. Assuming the services business triples in size over the next three years, Ramco, as a whole, would turn a profit of perhaps £70 million a year from the oil business and £3 million a year from services.

So, is Ramco only the first of a series of well-managed, lithe independent operators which will take small but central roles in consortia to exploit the last great oil development in fields in the former Soviet Union? No. Ramco is special, even unique, because it is unlike any other small oil sector operator. It is a player precisely because it has an extensive network of contacts based on a formidable reputation for quality and customer service as a provider in the market and an existing dialogue with oil companies. None of the other independents shares Ramco's zeal in prosecuting its cause. It owes much of its success to the personality of its chairman and CEO, and by extension to Ramco's team of fluent and committed managers. This is not a one-man company, but it does owe much of its management style to its chairman.

For the best insight into how Ramco works, the services business is worth close examination. Established in 1977 in Aberdeen, it was created to capitalise on the need for oil and gas pipeline cleaning and coating. At every stage in the life of downhole and linepipes, tiny fragments of metal are eroded from the walls. From shipment through putting in place to active operational service, pipes experience wear and corrosion. The silt that develops inside impedes the flow of oil and gas. This clearly has direct commercial implications for operators.

Stewart Cumming, managing director of the oil services company, is well aware that his team are at the heart of a great Scottish success story. Mr Cumming, from Cape Town, South Africa, was present at the onset of the company. So were many of his colleagues. There is virtually no staff turnover. 'We are immensely proud of this business, we all work together to achieve our common goals. Steve Remp and his team leave us alone to do what we are best at. We establish annual targets which are reviewed every quarter and, unusually, we have comprehensive weekly P&Ls. Everyone talks about every aspect of the business, and, regardless of who they are, if they have a useful contribution to make then that is genuinely welcome.'

The services company now operates from a purpose-built facility at Badentoy on a wind-swept hill overlooking the city. It had been there for about a year when we visited in March 1995. The site is three times too large for Ramco - that's because the company wanted Hunting and Tuboscope there as well. 'Several years ago, Ramco's management team dreamed up the idea of a one-stop shop on this site. We talked to several companies in the pipeline services business but we are delighted that Hunting and Tuboscope should be our partners as they are both market leaders. The idea is simple. That manufacturers or users could ship their pipes to any one of us and the others would benefit from the proximity of a world class neighbour. Typically an oil major will say to us, "we want you to handle the cleaning and coating, and then send the load on to another company for scanning or threading elsewhere". We respond by saying that significant costs can be saved by placing the threading with Hunting or scanning with Tuboscope then all we need to do is load-up on a forklift and carry the load over,' says Mr Cumming. Its two partners joined the complex in mid-year 1994 and he estimates that the initiative has prompted a ten per cent sales growth all round. The next step is to take the concept to overseas locations.

The potential for market growth is exceptional. The price of steel is expected to rise so both manufacturers and operators will want to achieve greater efficiencies from their existing pipes. Equally, Ramco's apparently endless capacity for purposeful innovation ensures that clients will be getting better value for money for their current contracts. Constant dialogue with manufacturers and operators suggests that steel pipe technology will continue for the foreseeable future. Ramco is also moving into pipe and joint tracking and logistics, which it already does for Chevron in the UK. In addition, Ramco wants to do more Badentoy-model one-stop shops, more on-site work for the Japanese and extend its reach with the Latin American steelmakers to do work inside their plants.

The future

The characteristics of flexibility, open and creative management, valued-added customer service and high levels of profitability have carried through to the oil business. Its market dynamics are different from the services company but Mr Remp applies his own distinctive brand of leadership which has energised the core business.

Ramco enjoys a superb 40-50 year horizon. The services company will continue to grow and its influence will expand. If the oil business develops as projected, in a decade, Ramco will be an active partner in four or five large former Soviet Union projects. Mr Remp's sense of business timing, Ramco's capacity for achievement and delivery, and, of course, its excellent financial results will guarantee its position as the UK's largest independent.

Environmental Services

Rentokil, East Sussex

Rentokil is a profitable services company with operations in more than 40 countries around the world. Services are committed to improving the environment and protecting health and property. Main activities are in pest control and hygiene services

Outlook:

If this company remains as committed to growth, financial performance and quality of service as it has been in the last decade, it should be able to penetrate new markets as they emerge and maintain its 20 per cent growth figures

Scorecard:

Structural flexibility	★★★★★
Innovative power	★★★
International orientation	★★★★
Human resources	★★★★
Growth markets	★★★★
Quality of management	★★★★

Key figures:

Global:	
Turnover	£860.1 million
Pre-tax profits	£214.5 million
Staff	43,000
UK:	
Turnover	£358.5 million
Pre-tax profits	£91.3 million
Staff	19,221

Rentokil Group
Felcourt, East Grinstead
W. Sussex RH 19 2JL
Tel: 01342 833022

Rentokil

If cash is king, there is a lot of royalty at Rentokil. This company, which is consistently voted as one of Britain's most admired companies, brings in a lot of the green stuff and more and more of it every year. For the last decade this group has met its objective of 20 per cent growth per annum in profits and earnings per share in each of the ten years.

This target growth figure is seen as 'declared corporate objective' or as the company says, 'it is not a promise with the Rentokil stamp on it, but we believe shareholders have a right to know what the company is trying to do!' This emphasis on profits growth is key to chief executive Clive Thompson's thinking. As he is quoted in an article in Director magazine, 'Many companies say "quality is all", but quality is not necessarily complementary to financial performance - in fact they are often in conflict. We have managed to develop an aggressive profit orientation, together with an overriding desire to deliver quality of service.'

One of the most astonishing things about Rentokil's performance is the small amount of money tied up in the business. Its value lies in its people and the quality of its service which is well demonstrated by the fact that a company valued by the market at around £2.8 billion has net assets of only £200 million (August '95).

Operations and markets

The company's focus is on business to business services in developed economies. This comes from the chief executive's belief that in developed economies where material needs are all but satisfied, services will flourish.

Rentokil is a household name in many markets. Its operations run from hygiene services and pest control through building security and office to maintenance.

Charles Grimaldi of corporate affairs remarks: 'The common thread through this range of services is that they take a load off our customers minds in something they need taken care of to high standards all of the time. It is no use for instance to have good security five days a week or a hygienic hospital on every other day.'

The split of the business can be seen as follows:

Healthcare, hygiene, medical services	30 per cent
Pest control	25 per cent
Security/cleaning	21 per cent
Tropical plants services	12 per cent
Other	12 per cent

From the start the company had a presence in all OECD countries - since they represent 85 per cent of the world's wealth. At present almost half of the business comes from the UK where turnover and profit growth figures are in the 30 per cent range and where just over half of Rentokil's people are based.

Strategy and management

The main constructor of Rentokil's recent striding progress is chief executive Clive Thompson. After careers with Shell and Boots he joined the group in 1982 and took over the top job within a year.

As Mr Thompson told Alan Purkiss for the Director: 'We have taken the best of the old businesses - pest control - and built on to it activities which at first sight might not seem complementary. But what they have in common is the ability to deliver quality of service to industrial and commercial premises, through people who are well recruited, trained and motivated.'

He shifted the emphasis from services for households to business to business activities. The improvements were striking and immediate. The improvement lay in increased productivity and profitabilly.

Most of the broader geographical spread, and change in the composition of the portfolio, has been achieved through acquisitions. Rentokil has acquired between 120 and 130 small businesses over the past ten years.

The company consciously searches for small synergetic acquisitions where the new business isn't large enough to dilute any of Rentokil's culture.

All acquisitions are paid for in cash and despite minimal borrowings and the same set of shares it floated with, the company is very cash-rich. Mr Thompson makes it sound simple. 'If you move into cash generating businesses, you can use the cash they deliver to buy more businesses, which generate more cash and on it goes.'

Rentokil does look vey carefully at each acquisition before it is decided on. An estimated nine or ten possibilities are looked at before a decision is made. The company looks for businesses with low working capital and a reputation for quality.

In a company where so much of the value created depends on the people, you would expect to find either best practice or something rather singular in terms of personnel policy. Rentokil delivers both. The company pays in the upper quartile in every area with strong performance related bonuses. It also has no trade unions and no personnel managers. Mr Thompson says, 'A personnel function removes from the line manager responsibilty for understanding and motivating the individual.'

In recruiting, the company seeks people with a drive for being successful individuals. They are given the best training, best tools, best workwear to do the job. Performance is then no hollow demand. 'Rentokil's a wonderful place to be if you're successful, and a pretty rough place to be if you want an easy life, says Mr Thompson: 'We get rid of quite a lot of people. To have a bad apple in the barrel is going to affect the rest, so we take action swiftly.'

Rentokil's structure is designed to align the interests of management with shareholders and those of the staff with management. Responsibilities are clearly and vertically defined which facilitates locating problem areas or underperforming parts of a business.

In his presentation on 'the new marketer' at the CIM annual conference in May '95, Mr Thompson said: 'The structure we developed in the 1980s intentionally broke the mould of specialist functions and disciplines up the organisation and created a structure with minimum reporting lines and profit responsibility devolved as far as possible down the organisation. This structure includes no marketing departments, no personnel staff anywhere and no sales staff above branch level, and a uniform management structure across all businesses which are then run geographically rather than by business stream.'

The future

Demand for services with an environmental focus is bound to grow both in old markets and new, as legislation and consumer awareness move in on this issue. With its excellent spread of businesses both by service and geographicaly and its astounding financial focus Rentokil will be part of that growth. The question is more if it will be allowed to corner and conquer every market than if it will be able to.

REXAM

REXAM PLC, London

Rexam, which recently changed its name from Bowater, is a worldwide group involving businesses in a range of market sectors especially printing and packaging

Outlook:

The group which became Rexam in 1995 is a far cry from the old Bowater of the mid and product quality, 1980s. It is regarded as a highly efficient group of companies with a distinctive management approach and culture. The steady rise in its profitability and improvements and innovations gained from closer integration between group businesses will all contribute to the Rexam's advance

Scorecard:

Structural flexibility	★★★★
Innovative power	★★★★★
International orientation	★★★★★
Human resources	★★★★
Growth markets	★★★★
Quality of management	★★★★★

Key figures:

Global turnover	£2,100 million
Pre-tax profits	£193.7 million
Staff	67,000

Rexam plc
114 Knightsbridge
London SW1X 7NN
Tel: 0171 584 7070
Fax: 0171 581 1149

Rexam (formerly Bowater)

In 1988, barely a few months after his group was reorganised, Bowater's chief executive discovered a concept which radically reshaped the group's vision for the future. David Lyon received a copy of Michael Porter's book *Competitive Strategies*. Reflecting on Mr Porter's principles, the CEO fashioned a coherent approach for managing Rexam's journey towards the goal of a world class business.

It was Michael Porter's model of the Celestial City - as at the end of John Bunyan's *Pilgrim's Progress* - which really struck a chord. The Celestial City represented the goal of what the business - and its individual components - could become. It became a metaphor for challenging targets and a vision of where its executives could take the enterprise if they applied themselves.

One powerful factor in this approach is the genesis of specific visions for individual businesses in the Rexam constellation. The directors of each company in the group decide - based on intimate knowledge of their markets and their own capacities - what their business can become. Group directors take part in the process but the owners of the idea are the teams in each specific business.

'Ownership is very important in Rexam companies,' says Mr Lyon. 'One of my colleagues who recently joined the group from outside said he was surprised to what extent our directors and managers are committed to the future of the companies within the group.'

Vision is critical to the development of Rexam since - in its present form - it is a relatively young enterprise. 'Bowater, as we know it today, came together in 1987. It was a collection of businesses operating independently of each other in markets all over the world.' In 1995 the group name was changed to Rexam so that all companies in the group could carry the same name. (In the US, the name Bowater is owned by a different company.)

Mr Lyon and his team saw the potential to construct a group which had a compelling business logic and where the individual companies benefited from synergies between them. They developed the concept of the Olympic rings to characterise the pattern of integration within Rexam. Several business clusters would be developed from the individual companies. These clusters would form the core strengths of the group. But rather than create, perhaps, five or six pillars which would be discrete, the overlapping rings were envisioned as a more fitting image because they emphasised the concept of cooperation, knowledge transfer and mutual profit.

Operations and markets

Rexam is first and foremost a packaging, print and coated products group. It is not an end-product company but a supplier of components for finished products. Four main business clusters exist within the group:
  . packaging for medical and pharmaceutical companies
  . packaging for toiletries and cosmetics markets
  . packaging for food and drink businesses
  . coated products for mainly industrial consumers

Many of the products start out as fibre or paper or derived from resins for flexible or rigid plastics. Rexam operates more than 50 film lines, 70 coating machines and over 300 moulding presses. Great emphasis is placed in the business on producing technically demanding solutions for customers with precise end-user demands.

Strategy and management

Quality is a key player in all Rexam companies and processes. Every subsidiary is either registered or applying for registration under ISO 9000 - the international quality standard. The group and key operators within Rexam are working with principal customers and industry bodies to achieve industry standards for processes and promote greater adoption of quality procedures. It is also a strong industry advocate of environmental protection.

'To bridge policy and action we are piloting in Europe the Rexam Environmental Management System. This is a computer-based audit tailored for each site, which is being introduced in 66 installations,' says Mr Lyon. The process involves four major elements:
. waste reduction and control
. lower energy use
. economic use of raw materials
. preference for the renewable, reusable, recyclable

In 1993 Bowater set 318 targets in terms of environmental protection and energy efficiency. The first 44 case studies within the group report widespread implementation and action plans for the future. 'We are aiming first for what we call "low-hanging fruit" or the changes which are easiest to implement. Then we plan longer-term innovations and production replacements,' he says.

Two processes take place each year which contribute to the achievement of the balance of profitability - both short-term and long-term - and vision for the future. From mid-October to mid-November, each of the 100-plus companies in the group submits to the budgetary round. This is a rigorous assessment of profit potential, which is soundly based in pragmatic understanding of the ability of each company to meet realistic targets. Rexam believes in having its feet firmly on the ground. It is a direct corollary to the unshakeable tenet of honesty within the business.

At the end of 1993, the group reported turnover of £2.1 billion, with profits of £193.7 million - a return of 9.1 per cent on sales. At reorganisation in 1987, Bowater was bringing in barely four per cent. Its target is in the middle teens. But its achievement is sustained improvement.

The second part of the review process occurs in spring and early summer. This is the visionary programme, which, in the way it is conducted, makes Rexam unique. Group directors spend a day with each company. Managers are told to take the balance-sheet figures out of the equation. They are asked to define the company which they want to create. This is the Celestial City concept at work. 'We set an objective for what we believe the business is capable of becoming. No decisions are taken in these meetings. They are designed to stimulate a clear understanding of the ultimate target for that enterprise.'

While these are blue sky sessions, they are also grounded in sound appreciation of Rexam's markets, quality of personnel and what customers will want in the future. Three values guide the thinking behind these meetings: openness, tautness and innovation.

These are the core values of Rexam, which exemplify its approach throughout the world. It has also developed a mission statement which puts those values into practice. These are its aspirations:
. worldwide cover with world class businesses
. market leadership in all its markets
. recognition for consistent improvement in market-performance

Underlying these objectives is a commitment to understanding customers so well that the business will achieve extraordinary levels of growth by anticipating and exceeding their expectations. Also Rexam intends to employ only those people who are committed to continuous improvement and boldness in change.

The energy and articulation within Rexam companies are high. Executive teams have well defined objectives and they have gained impressive assignments for world-beating companies. The centre provides intellectual rigour, a sense of wholeness about the group, clear strategic vision and a flavour of the personality of the business.

The centre introduced the Free Thinkers - two full-time and five part-time executives whose job it is to promote synergies across the group. Mr Lyon mentions a recent example of their work: 'We have a company which makes own-label diaper [nappy] bags for large US supermarket chains like Wal-Mart. This - until very recently - was a highly profitable business. We saw that there would be a downturn in this market and so the directors of this company went to identify new products and markets. We have another business which has considerable expertise in bottle tops and fasteners. So we put the two technologies together and now the original company is making disposable bags for markets in the gardening and home cleaning sectors. The difference is that these new products have closures which means that they can be used over an extended period. The potential market opportunities for these new products are vast.'

The future

Rexam demonstrates all the elements for sustained business success in the future. It is a creative group, powered by a central management with vision, leadership, concern for the environment, the drive to consistently improve the quality of its products and a strong sense of profitability. They have set a strategic plan for further integration of business clusters inside the group. Managers of individual businesses reflect this determination to success and enjoy the autonomy to make it happen.

ROVER GROUP

Rover Group Ltd, Birmingham

Rover is Britain's largest motor manufacturer, producing approximately half a million vehicles a year. The group designs, manufactures and markets Rover small, medium and executive cars, MG sports cars and Land Rover specialist four-wheel-drive vehicles

Outlook:
As part of the BMW group, Rover enjoys the financial flexibility to develop new markets. Its parent's experience in continental Europe should provide Rover with the market intelligence to succeed there. The US and Far East markets are high potential areas where, through joint ventures and the new MG sportscar, Rover should be able to establish itself as a global player before the end of this decade

Scorecard:
Structural flexibility	★★★
Innovative power	★★★
International orientation	★★★★
Human resources	★★★★
Growth markets	★★★★
Quality of management	★★★

Key figures:
UK turnover	£2.5 billion
Pre-tax profits	£83 million
UK staff	38,500
Turnover (global)	£4.9 billion
Global staff	40,000

Rover Group Ltd
International House
Bickenhill Lane, Bickenhill
Birmingham B37 7HQ
Tel: 0121 782 8000
Fax: 0121 781 7000

Rover

The rapid transformation of the Rover Group from lame duck to manufacturing paragon is startling. In one expert's opinion, at the beginning of this decade Rover was 'probably in irreversible long term decline' with an 'image too poor to succeed in upper niche markets'.

That report, written by stockbroker Laing & Cruickshank, was not optimistic about the group's chances of future success. 'If Rover were to succeed in establishing its brand name in an upmarket niche within ten years it would provide a case study worthy of inclusion in every marketing textbook published subsequently.' History supported this opinion; yet for a process which took BMW three decades, Rover needed scarcely five years.

Operations and markets

Rover's management transformed a loose amalgamation of parts of the British motor industry, brought together during the sixties and seventies, into a successful modern car manufacturer capable of leading the market. Perhaps best known for Minis and Land Rovers, the group manufactures a range of cars encompassing the full extent of small, medium and executive markets.

The merger of British Leyland, Triumph, MG and parts supplier Unipart assembled a group with no focus, making a range of dated and unimpressive products. Work practices encapsulated the worst examples of UK manufacturing strikes, bad management and government interference. The group had lost its reputation as a maker of quality executive cars as the fine 3-Litre model of the sixties had become the disappointing SD1. Generally, Austin Rover did not keep pace with the quality improvements of Japanese and German manufacturers.

Losses peaked at over £350m in 1986. It made a £66m pre-tax profit in 1988, its first for ten years, but only because the government had recently forgiven all debts in an effort to smooth the sale to British Aerospace, saving it an average annual interest charge of around £70m. The quality decline continued and its UK market share fell from over 24 per cent in 1977 to below 14 per cent in 1989. By the early 1990s the group was again losing around £50m a year.

Yet by 1994 pre-tax profit was £83m, more than twice 1993. Car sales rose 11 per cent, exports 22 per cent. With output of around 475,000 vehicles, Rover became for the first time in a decade the largest car maker in the UK with output forecast by some to grow to 750,000 by the year 2000. Yet Rover now has 36,000 employees, compared with 77,000 ten years ago.

Annual group sales are approximately £4.9bn, with more than 50 per cent exported to about 100 countries across Western Europe, Japan, North America and Australia. It is also increasing its presence in Asia and the Pacific Rim with a growing range of international joint ventures and technology transfer initiatives.

BMW valued all this at £1.7 billion when it acquired the Rover Group in 1994.

Strategy and management

According to chief executive John Towers, from the late 1980s Rover focused on a series of simple strategies. To begin with, it identified its core business and disposed of peripheral assets. It then established a new strategy and adopted a total quality programme to inspire the workforce to follow common goals and utilise suppliers' particular expertise. However, the primary purpose for all this was to ensure that the customer perceived the group as a source of exceptional quality, style, design, service and value for money.

Firstly the old BL group was refocused. Since the end of the last decade the product range has been rationalised, non-core activities disposed of and £1 billion invested in the group. According to Towers, between 1989 and 1993 Rover undertook the most intensive new model introduction programme in its history. Old models were replaced. New models were moved into new areas in each respective sector, or into niche sectors to create new business opportunities. For example the Land Rover Discovery, which became the market leader in the emerging 4x4 leisure sector.

Rover set out to learn from anyone it identified as world class. It has a thirst for knowledge - BMW's managers have commented that Rover people seem to suck information out of them. A management constantly looking for ways to improve. Rover looked to Japan for ideas, and initiated its 14 year association with Honda. Its Japanese partner taught about best practice within the automotive industry. Towers defines this as the obsessive attention to process detail, empowering all your employees and the focus on elimination of waste.

Visitors to Japan might have concluded that success was due to unique cultural factors. However, when Rover saw Honda's US plant in Ohio it appreciated that there are no cultural barriers to installing any philosophy for success if the ingredients are straightforward. John Towers sums it up: 'Get the design of your products and processes right to the smallest detail, empower your employees to run and continually improve those processes and profits will naturally flow.'

Japanese style management techniques revolutionised not just methods of design and production, but attitudes towards the involvement of employees in every stage of production. In 1987, Rover introduced its total quality improvement (TQI) programme to encourage employees to get involved in the process of improvement. The second initiative, named 'Working with Pride', linked a customer-led approach to TQI.

Generating regular improvement is achieved via benchmarking. This process begins by identifying key processes in a business and establishes who is the best in the world at doing it. Then it finds out how that best performance is achieved and develops programmes which mirror that performance. Ultimately you set out to improve on that performance and become the world benchmark yourself.

At Rover employees know that continuous improvement is an integral part of their job. Rover wants highly motivated people interested not just in doing their job, but in finding ways to do it better and to do this it must create common goals for all its staff. Each employee knows he has a part to play and each 'strategic vision' is communicated so that they understand the need for change and are prepared for the demands that will put on them. In return Rover introduces a 'New Deal' on employee terms and conditions which recognises the needs of individuals and gives them the authority and responsibility for decision making. Rover has introduced flat management structures and makes no distinction between 'blue-' and 'white-collar' workers.

Rover has tried to capture a slot at the top end of each market sector. Each new model range has to provide distinctive, desirable and highly specified prestigious products. All new designs are subject to rigorous research to test customer reaction several years before manufacturing begins. Local research is undertaken in international markets to make certain the design is suited to local conditions.

The future

In order to reduce the group's dependence on a single market, Rover intends to increase the proportion of its output which is exported. The US is a priority, as an area of enormous potential. The new MGF sports car, a great success at the Geneva motor show, could be the product chosen to spearhead Rover's drive into the US. The MGF sports car sees the return of the MG. This marque has been out of production for 15 years (assume you ignore the misconceived rebadging of Metros, Maestros and Montegos). In the past, the MG, the affordable sports car, was a great hit with American car buyers.

Certain far-eastern markets are being targeted through joint ventures. For example Rover is working jointly with the Republic of Indonesia on the development of the local motor industry. Rover will provide the technical assistance to develop a new small car in Indonesia, designed to meet local demand in a region of rapid economic growth. The group is also working with Proton on technology transfer in Malaysia.

BMW should prove a more creative and supportive owner than British Aerospace. Any fears that it bought Rover to neutralise a competitor have been quickly put to rest. BMW is to invest £400m during the current year, twice the sum Rover received from British Aerospace. It has also pledged to invest over £2 billion over the next five years. Rover is now free of unhelpful short-term decisions driven by BAe's desire to generate cash for dividends or to invest elsewhere in that group. BMW has a better appreciation of what it will require for Rover to achieve an ambition to establish a world presence for its niche products, and a commitment to seeing it happen.

Ryder, Slough

Ryder is the largest road transportation company in the world

Outlook:
Despite its significant market share in the UK, Ryder's income here is a small proportion of global sales. Therefore there is everything to play for. The UK operation was established in advance of the opening of the European single market and Ryder is investing heavily to build business

Scorecard:

Structural flexibility	★★★★
Innovative power	★★★★★
International orientation	★★★★★
Human resources	★★★★
Growth markets	★★★★★
Quality of management	★★★★

Key figures:

UK turnover	£120 million
US turnover	$4.7 billion
UK operating profits	£10.5 million
US operating profits	$520 million
UK staff	11,565

Ryder plc
Ryder House
16 Bath Road
Slough SL1 3SA
Tel: 01753 735000

Ryder plc

Across the US Ryder's yellow trucks are commonplace, part of the largest road transportation company in the country. In the UK Ryder is still comparatively underdeveloped. It is number two in contract hire but in logistics - the area of greatest potential for growth - it still has a march to steal on the leaders. However, three acquisitions in the last year show a determination to do precisely that.

Ryder remains predominantly a US operation; UK turnover is about three per cent of the $4.7bn turnover in the US. Based in Miami, Florida, previous attempts to diversify its core US contract hire business have been unsuccessful. During the 1970s it bought aircraft leasing and maintenance, and insurance businesses. However, since 1990 it has disposed of all but its highway transport business. Now its strategy is to focus on proven strengths and expand those outside the US, particularly into Europe where it already operates in the UK, Germany and Poland.

John Hodges joined as finance director in 1989 and became managing director last year. He finalised a strategic plan to expand the business; conveniently timed as the US board was thinking along similar lines. Mr Hodges wants to build Ryder's UK operations in anticipation of the opening up and deregulation of the European transport market. As the UK logistics companies and market are considered the most sophisticated in Europe, Ryder has chosen a challenging environment in which to hone its skills.

Logistics provides a way to free its clients to concentrate on what they know best, leaving their distribution problems to an expert in that field. Discussions with Mr Hodges suggest that he is re-engineering Ryder's UK operations using a similar philosophy: 'What we are doing is not brain surgery. We seek to recognise where our strengths lie'. Recent changes have involved quite simple, even, with hindsight, obvious solutions. He is also proud of Ryder's ethical approach to its employees, which encourages some creative thinking about staff development. He believes this is why Ryder has avoided the layoffs seen elsewhere in the industry. The group invests heavily in training, doubling its budget in 1994.

Operations and markets

Ryder's business is transport, and in the UK (turnover £120m in the last financial year) it provides a comprehensive road transportation service for businesses. Its operations encompass rental, contract hire and logistics; but all three have effectively been integrated into a one-stop shop for customers, saving Ryder costs of duplication in sales and administration. The former could be anything from a van to a heavyweight tractor unit, refrigerated lorry, tipper or a truck with hydraulic cranes. Ryder's fleet even includes tank transporters used in Bosnia.

The contract hire division supplies and operates vehicles on behalf of clients, in their own livery and image if required, including maintenance. Clients save capital tied up in vehicles, and administration costs, and gain the financial benefits of Ryder's purchasing power. Total Logistics takes this service a step further taking over the practicalities of running vehicles and warehouses, and the routing, scheduling and timing of deliveries.

The group is number two in contract hire in the UK, behind BRS. Economies of scale include the buying power to undercut smaller competitors, access to cheaper borrowings and in Ryder's case a nationwide network and a better breakdown service for customers. For these reasons Mr Hodges believes the contract hire business will continue to consolidate and mid-sized companies will be forced out. With a £60-70m logistics turnover Ryder is a medium-sized player but size is not key to successs in a fragmented industry.

Strategy and management

Although Ryder plc has set out to grow all three established divisions in the UK, the main focus is on how they contribute to logistics. This business should benefit from the growing importance of the European market to the UK economy.

John Hodges believes Europe is ready for intermodal transport, i.e. combining train and road transport into and from Europe. Uneconomic for distances below 500 miles, it has worked well in the US but not in the UK. 'With the Channel Tunnel on steam it will make sense for UK freight', says Mr Hodges, but 'someone needs to be fully integrated. This area will be a big future development for Ryder.' Aware that he lacked the strong UK base from which to access Europe Mr Hodges acquired volume and logistics expertise in 1994.

The first two acquisitions grew its contract hire operations. In July 1994 it bought Unilink, a 900 vehicle contract hire company with an annual turnover of £30m. That added to Ryder's own UK fleet of 8,300 vehicles and £100m annual turnover and brought three new locations to its existing 67 outlets. In November, it bought Hallmark Contract Hire Ltd, adding another 720 mainly contract hire vehicles.

These purchases brought it 135 new clients plus expertise in specialist areas such as tanker operation. As a result it now operates tankers for bulk movement of milk, chemicals and petroleum products and has secured new contracts with Milk Marque Ltd.

The next purchases boosted its logistics side. Ryder bought Federal Express's Systemline and Systemcare businesses. The former is an experienced logistics player with an extensive client base including Sanyo, Filofax, Hewlett Packard and Massey Ferguson. The latter has already won new business for Ryder by helping it establish itself an expert in home delivery. Systemcare provides a service for retail, mail order and catalogue sales operations, guaranteeing service levels at a pre-agreed charge. Ryder's clients include Habitat, Ikea and Littlewoods.

By breaking the logistics business into component parts Ryder can tailor packages to a client's individual needs but considerable emphasis is placed on providing expert advice. As Mr Hodges puts it, 'No one is going to be able to do everything in-house-cover the UK, Europe and the rest of the world via road, rail and air. We therefore want to manage, rather than own all aspects of the transportation process'.

He is 'looking for niches, ways to use our particular expertise'. Growth can't be allowed to jeopardise a reputation for understanding the priorities of a customer in their local market. 'Ryder must never become big and faceless': Mr Hodges has made changes to prevent this happening. Since 1993 the group has steadily decentralised into 25 - from an original eight - regional units, a move designed to empower local management and more recently Mr Hodges has devolved more responsibility to them. 'Each area now has a manager with authority to complete all aspects of a deal without referring to head office.'

The figures for the first four months of this scheme revealed that 97 per cent of new business was signed locally, a pleasant surprise for Mr Hodges, and Ryder's own customer satisfaction survey reinforces his faith in the new strategy. He is not complacent. 'We are always checking for creeping paralysis, any sign that the old system is coming back in.' So far he has seen no sign of this happening.

Ryder has found innovative solutions to clients' transport needs. Nissan Motor Manufacturing (UK) Ltd wanted a just-in-time delivery system for its plant at Sunderland Tyne & Wear. By providing this Ryder cut the cost of the parts inventory Nissan needs to hold. Inventory has been reduced by half and vehicle movements by 80 per cent, four million miles each year, cutting fuel consumption.

On Nissan's behalf Ryder collects components daily or twice daily from 36 UK suppliers, in vehicles carrying the car maker's livery. These products are then trucked to Sunderland, with 18 daily deliveries to the plant matching the requirements of day or night shifts producing the Primera and the Micra. The precise routing and scheduling of deliveries is handled by software jointly developed by Ryder and Nissan, integrated with Nissan's own inventory control system.

Another example of innovation is its 'Fast Truck' operation at Leyland Trucks, which has cut delivery periods for contract hire vehicles. 'The previous system of body building, a cottage industry in the UK, was inefficient. A customer would choose a truck, the chassis would be driven to the body builder who would strip off the lights and electrical system, add the bodywork and replace the lights, all unnecessarily time consuming. Ryder has streamlined the process by negotiating for body builders to assemble the trucks in Leyland's own plants. This simple but elegant solution has sped up the process'.

The advantages of managing rather than owning the means of transport are also recognised by Ryder's US parent. Last year it acquired Logicorp, a 'lead logistics supplier' which it plans to bring to the UK.

'Logicorp sells brainpower and does not own any of the means of transport' Mr Hodges explains. Logicorp offers an independent and ongoing consultancy answering specific transportation problems by co-ordinating operators in each market. Logicorp will examine each case individually and find ways to do the job cost effectively. Hired on a no-savings, no fee-basis, the service has proved popular in the US and Ryder is optimistic about its reception in the UK.

The future

Mr Hodges sees other gaps in the market. 'There is another service we can provide between contract hire and full logistics. Some customers don't want the hassle of running a transport fleet, vehicles, maintenance, drivers, etc. However they do want details of the costs involved and therefore require considerable amounts of management information.'

After 1994's strong growth the future is likely to see further integration of the three businesses, to improve the range of services to its customers. Management has a range of specific programmes which will be introduced in the short term, to include an extension of the Fast Truck system for Leyland DAF trucks via a new partnership with Mercedes-Benz.

SAINSBURY'S

J Sainsbury, London

J Sainsbury is Britain's second largest supermarket chain

Outlook:
Sainsbury and Tesco dominate retail grocery shopping in the UK. Together they have eliminated less robust rivals. This trend is set to continue and these two retail giants will dominate more and more of this sector. Their market profiles are different and Sainsbury is aimed at those customers whose priorities are quality products at fair prices for such quality. In some areas this is an innovative business, in others it lags behind. There is no doubt that these two operators will slug it out for the top spot

Scorecard:

Structural flexibility	★★★★
Innovative power	★★★★
International orientation	★★★
Human resources	★★★
Growth markets	★★★★
Quality of management	★★★★

Key figures:

Sales	£12 billion
Profits	£808 million
Staff	65,000

J Sainsbury plc
Stamford Street
London SE1 9LL
Tel: 0171 921 6000
Fax: 0171 921 7610

J Sainsbury

The last 20 years have seen a radical shift in the grocery retail sector. Giants have risen up to dominate high street and out-of-town shopping. The emphasis has moved away from the corner shop and local chains to massive national operators with extensive buying power, capital muscle and extensive spread. In the last decade this movement has consolidated to ensure that national groups take 80 per cent of the market and within this set Tesco and Sainsbury carve out at least half.

For most of that period Sainsbury was the leader. Its capacity to pick sites, offer the widest competitive range, deliver technical improvements and generally enhance its service to the customer ensured its position as kingpin. It also rode the economic trends sufficiently skilfully to anticipate spending power and prepare for shifts in product taste and rising and falling pockets. The company gained a reputation for value for money, high product value and accessibility. Its image remained strong and throughout the recession it pleased the City by continuing to provide excellent performance.

The UK retail market generally gives a return on sales at around six per cent which is a multiple of at least double on its US counterparts. American rivals suggest that their British cousins are less customer friendly but this does not appear to have injured their returns. Sainsbury was the first significant multiple to combine cost effectiveness with high quality and ease of shopping and it has proved a powerful force. In buying power all three large supermarket chains are able to squeeze higher and higher concessions from suppliers and especially in the provision of cashback financial services the supermarkets have had the banks over a barrel.

Operations and markets

Even though Sainsbury slipped marginally to number two retailer in 1995, it is still probably the best known retailer in Britain. Tesco's rise from pile it high and sell it cheap retailing has been clear and purposeful (see pp. 358-61) but Sainsbury has been top dog for longer and it would be unwise to say that the company has been overtaken by a sleeker and faster rival. Sainsbury fought and won the battle for best sites which dominated the 1980s. It was among the first into out-of-town shopping centres and was at the forefront of service innovations such as cashback, health-promoting foods, in-store magazines, own-label cookbooks and the provision of accessible wines.

In terms of the balance sheet it has majored in own-label brands. As much as 70 per cent of the goods on sale in Sainsbury stores bear the Sainsbury trademark rather than familiar brands. And the company has been ruthless about removing brands from its shelves if manufacturers did not conform to the company's tough stance in terms of price. The size of stores has grown remarkably though perhaps not as much as Tesco, though it has a wider spread of operations since as well as its grocery stores which occupy sites in every major high street, it runs a DIY and gardening chain called Homebase, Savacentre and Slaw's, a grocery retailing business in New England.

Strategy and management

The market strategy of Sainsbury is straightforward: to be the most successful and profitable retailer in Britain. This is achieved in many ways. The dominant features of the 1980s were the battle for supremacy through best location, acquisition of smaller chains, price wars and the wholesale adoption of own label. The location battle is virtually over. A balancing initiative to return to the high street is catching on and if Sainsbury detects a real move back to the hearts of town it will pragmatically back the trend.

The two giants now stand head to head over acqustions and Tesco won the last encounter with the capture of a Scottish supermarket chain. But this is by no means the end of the story. Further regional groups will become available. There is also the possibility that in the longer term one of Sainsbury's immediate competitors will lose sufficient ground to warrant the sale of some of its outlets.

Supermarkets periodically engage in price wars to boost market share and Sainsbury is no stranger to this as a tactical device. In the last serious shoot-out Sainsbury was able to achieve its twin goals of dealing a body blow to rivals and suppliers. Price wars can be very effective for bringing back customers who have strayed to competitors or introduce new buyers from other chains or local retailers.

Sainsbury has cornered the market in own-label. Vastly more of its floor space is devoted to own-label products than any of its rivals. This can mean that shoppers buy as many items in Sainsbury as they would in Tesco or Safeway but they pay less. A recent survey of shopping habits by Taylor Nelson AGB showed that Sainsbury was slightly behind Tesco and Asda in average weekly spend. But loyalty may be stronger because prices are cheaper on average. The store has said that it aims to further increase the range of its own label goods.

The company is a heavy net spender on advertising, a product of the fiercely competitive nature of supermarket retailing and the constant need to remind customers of new offers or facilities. In promotional terms Tesco stole a march on Sainsbury with its Clubcard but Sainsbury quickly responded. Also Safeway and Tesco have been in the vanguard of childcare facilities in stores and Sainsbury has needed to take up the rear. But in areas such as cashback, newspapers and magazines, wines and recipe books the company has been ahead of the pack.

The real challenge for Sainsbury will be its capacity to compete with a cash rich Tesco. Tesco has scaled down its investment in new sites and therefore its cash position will be even healthier. Tesco has notched up some notable gains its bid to be market leader. Sainsbury however is a long-term player which studies its markets with consummate skill and is sufficiently agile to be able to respond with remarkable speed.

This is a national business and incursions into mainland Europe are at present limited but German discounters are already in Britain and discount clubs, such as the ones which are popular in the US, are starting up. So Sainsbury also needs to watch the cheaper end of the market. Sainsbury can continue trade successfully on its value for money, high quality strategy to its markets. But if mainland chains take a real interest in this arena, backed by major capital investment, they could represent a threat in the next ten years.

Leo David Sainsbury comments: 'We have also some of the savings we made last year to improving our performance in customer service. In 1994 we thoroughly researched the views of supermarket shoppers about customer service. This revealed areas where we could improve, and we have introduced changes in all these areas as well as putting in place a major staff training programme. For example, we are now investing an additional £10 million per year to provide additional checkout queues; we open up further checkouts until all checkouts are open. We are dealing with the problem of wonky trolleys and we have introduced a produce bag that everyone can open. We have also launched a major new marketing campaign which will publicise these improvements under the headline of "Sainsbury's, everyone's favourite ingredient". There is no doubt that, increasingly, customer service will be a key to competitive success, and I am confident that with these new initiatives and the enthustiastic response of our staff we will provide our new customers with the best service they can get.

'The final leg of our strategy for the Sainsbury supermarket business is to secure profitable opportunities for growth. As a result of tighter planning restrictions, the number of new Sainsbury's supermarkets will fall from 20 openings last year to 12 in the current year. However, the effect of a lower number of store openings will be almost entirely offset by a large increase in extensions of existing stores and a lower number of store closures. In the current year we plan to remodel 80 stores and extend 20 stores. We are particularly keen to give a new lease of life to stores in town centres. Even with continued planning restrictions we expect to continue growing Sainsbury's sales area by more than five per cent each year. In addition to this we have recently announced our proposed expansion into Northern Ireland with the development of seven stores throughout the province. This will involve the investment of approximately £100 million and the creation of around 2,000 new jobs.'

The future

Sainsbury is not to be underestimated. This is a powerful and alert operator. It has dominated grocery retailing for many years but it needs to watch out for new competitors and it is certain to want to recapture the top slot from Tesco. Sooner rather than later, it is anticipated that it will begin its assault to win back the customers who have deserted the store for Tesco's inducements.

ScottishPower

ScottishPower, Glasgow

ScottishPower is Scotland's largest industrial company and it is engaged in electricity generation and distribution

Outlook:
ScottishPower is a long-term business builder. Year on year, profits and dividends have increased and it has invested significantly both in its energy businesses and in new ventures in retail, gas and telecommunications. The management team has a wide range of business experience which gives the company greater capability to achieve progress in the search for new growth opportunities

Scorecard:

Structural flexibility	★★★★
Innovative power	★★★★★
International orientation	★★★
Human resources	★★★★
Growth markets	★★★★★
Quality of management	★★★★★

Key figures:

Turnover	£1,716 million
Pre-tax profits	£375 million
Staff	8,000

ScottishPower
1 Atlantic Quay
Glasgow G2 8SP
Tel: 0141 2488200
Fax: 0141 2488300

ScottishPower

Amid a UK electricity industry dogged by regulatory uncertainty ScottishPower, Scotland's largest industrial company, offers welcome stability. It has agreed an electricity pricing regime with its regulator which will run for the next five years giving the management plenty of leeway to plan the company's future.

ScottishPower has clear ideas about how it will build its existing businesses of electricity generation and distribution and is not afraid to test itself in potentially more exciting markets such as telecommunications. But the company is not chasing pipe dreams. With its vertically integrated structure which allows it to deliver electricity from power station to power points in its customers' homes, it is sitting on a huge and valuable asset. To make the most of this it is installing fibre optic lines alongside overhead power cables to build a telcomms network. Its well-honed customer service skills are not wasted on just the electricity business either. It has taken advantage of market liberalisation to set up a gas supply company to rival British Gas.

Unlike other electricity companies which poured their excess cash reserves into the pockets of shareholders for want of anything better to do, ScottishPower has a clear investment programme. It has foregone the short-term affection of the stock market and is using its cash to build returns for the future.

With a core business that generates a substantial cash pile capital expenditure is set to continue to grow for the rest of the decade. By then ScottishPower will be seeing the fruits of its endeavours.

Operations and markets

ScottishPower's core business encompasses electricity generation, transmission, distribution and supply. Of these, the distribution and transmission of electricity in its south of Scotland region are monopoly businesses. Its wires network covers an area of 23,000 square miles and serves a population of 3.9 million customers. Profits are determined by a regulated price formula applied to customer tariffs and its own best efforts at cost control. Generation and supply are subject to open market competition and normal market disciplines apply.

Cost cutting will be the key to future profits growth in both regulated and free markets. In order to stretch the business, the company aims to attain best practice standards across all its core activities and is keenly aware of international benchmarks. The intention is to drive ScottishPower to a position among the top ten per cent of the world's best performing companies, including leading US and Japanese utilities.

Strategy and management

ScottishPower has a three-pronged strategy for growth:
. Optimising the profitability of its core electricity business by cutting costs and improving efficiency
. Steppingup electricity exports to England, Wales and Northern Ireland by cementing links with its own electricity grid system

. Using its expertise as a utility supplier to build a presence in other utility markets such as telecomms and gas

The company has already acted on its principal source of cost - labour. Through manpower reductions, which have seen the workforce contract by 3,000 since 1991, and externally purchasing materials and services, the company has already achieved annual savings of £69 million compared with 1991.

The current round of pay negotiations includes further working-practice improvements and should lead to additional headcount reductions of around five per cent a year until 1998. Stockbroker Morgan Stanley expects that these efforts will yield extra cost savings of £20 million a year by 1998.

In the generation business, the main cost is fuel. ScottishPower operates its own generation plant with a capacity of around 4,000 megawatts. On top of this it is contracted to purchase 2,800 MW of power from nuclear and hydroelectric generators.

Purchases of electricity from Scottish Nuclear make up the largest component of fuel costs, accounting for slightly less than 60 per cent of the total. The price it pays to Scottish Nuclear, however, will converge with the cheapest levels prevailing in England and Wales over the next few years.

With its own power stations the generator has great flexibility to switch between coal, oil and gas fuels according to prices. Morgan Stanley expects that a deal with RJB Mining to buy 13 million tonnes of coal up to March 1998 will produce real cost reductions of 17 per cent over the period of £10 million a year.

These cost savings will keep profit growth on track to the end of the century. Potentially more exciting rewards, however, will come from a surge in electricity exports in the late 1990s. Unlike other power generators in the UK, ScottishPower has tremendous growth prospects. Two key factors are working in its favour. It is a very low cost producer of electricity and it has a substantial surplus generating capacity in its power stations. That means that it has huge potential to sell electricity in markets outside its south of Scotland heartland.

When ScottishPower was privatised it was entitled to use 350MW of the 850 MW interconnector which links the Scottish grid with the electricity system in England and Wales. An £85 million upgrade in 1994 increased the interconnector's capacity to 1,600 MW. Now ScottishPower, which is entitled to 75 per cent share of any new capacity, is planning to further upgrade to add 600 MW of power.

Earlier in 1995, ScottishPower recorded a two per cent share of the market in England and Wales. According to finance director Ian Russell, by 1997-8, when the interconnector is in place, ScottishPower will be exporting one third of its electricity outside Scotland. It is targeting a five per cent share of the English market by this stage. Morgan Stanley is more optimistic and estimates that by 1999 it will have tripled its supplies to England.

In concert with Northern Ireland Electricity, ScottishPower is planning to invest £20 million in a 250 MW interconnector between Scotland and Northern Ireland. The Irish market suffers from capacity shortages and this would provide ScottishPower with a lucrative export opportunity.

In addition the company has launched Scottish Telecom with the aim of capturing 20 to 30 per cent of the Scottish telecommunications market. This is presently estimated at £1 billion and is anticipated to grow to £2.3 billion by 2003. So far £30 million has been invested on fibre optic cable installation.

ScottishPower controls one of the country's most extensive private telecommunications networks and the company has received a very good response from existing electricity customers. CEO Rod Matthews says that they see benefits in receiving both electricity and telecomms from one supplier. The company is also active in gas supply with its subsidiary Caledonian Gas.

The future

This company is ambitious and very capably managed. ScottishPower has a wide spread of interests where it is expected to achieve solid and improving profitability. In a sector which is poorly managed, ScottishPower stands out as a business with wisdom and intelligence.

Shell UK Ltd, London

Shell is the largest company in Europe, specialising in petro-chemicals

Outlook:
Petro-chemicals is not a long term business. Shell is astute enough to realise
that the future needs effective planning and has commissioned McKinsey to
deliver an in-depth study of future options. This is one of the most skilfully-
managed businesses in the world and as such will almost certainly locate
substantial new products

<u>Scorecard:</u>
Structural flexibility	★★★
Innovative power	★★★★
International orientation	★★★★★
Human resources	★★★★★
Growth markets	★★★★
Quality of management	★★★★

<u>Key figures world wide:</u>
Net income	£4,375 million
Capital expenditure	£6,951 million
Staff	106,000

Shell UK Ltd
Shell-Mex House
Strand, London WC2R 0DX
Tel: 0171 257 3000
Fax: 0171 257 1084

Shell

In the world of international oil, the Premier League consists of only two teams : Exxon and Shell. For many years the latter seemed content to merely tread water, happy in its reputation as the company that's only ever made one mistake. Since 1990 Shell has lagged behind Exxon badly in terms of return on capital employed. However, earlier in 1995, after suffering the humiliation of being overtaken by BP, its management finally seemed to have grasped the concept of shareholder return.

The company is now set to implement the sort of restructuring programme that BP put in place several years ago. But Shell starts from a much stronger position. It's almost ungeared; is generating vast amounts of cash; and is heavily invested in the growth areas of oil. The possibilities for a company which is already worth £63.1bn are endless.

Operations and markets

In 1907 Britain's Shell Transport & Trading and Holland's Royal Dutch merged to form the Royal Dutch Shell group. The company was quickly integrated but the legacy of the merger can be seen in the share structure. Three fifths of the RDS group are owned by the Royal Dutch Holding Company, shares in which are traded in the Netherlands. The rest of RDS is owned by Shell T&T, shares in which are quoted in London. This part of the business alone is capitalised at £23.3 bn which makes this Britain's fourth largest company.

The net income of the RDS group is distributed proportionally to the two holding companies which then pay dividends to their shareholders. The RDS group has traditionally employed a matrix structure of management. In each country in which it operated, the local management team enjoyed considerable autonomy; there were also operational units based on activity that crossed national borders. But this structure has proved incapable of introducing the cost-conscious atmosphere Shell desperately needs. According to human resources manager Ernst Mourik-Broekman it fostered a committee culture. On March 29 1995 a dramatic overhaul was announced.

From autumn 1995 five business organisations (exploration and production, oil products, chemicals, gas and coal) and Shell Oil in the US will report directly to the board. The eight-person committees which run each division will take charge of strategic issues but day to day control will still be in the hands of national units.

Like all major oil companies during the 1970s and 1980s, Shell feared that oil was a mature sector and diversified into industries such as coal and copper mining. In the 1990s it has largely reversed the process.

1. Exploration and production (E&P). The largest of Shell's divisions, in 1994 it accounted for £1.54bn of the group's total net income of £4.07bn. Though production rose, that was more than offset by the fall in oil and gas prices.

In 1994 Shell produced an average of 2.19m barrels of oil and 7.32bn cubic feet of gas per day. Production of both commodities is expected to increase over the medium term. Shell is an established player in the US, the North Sea, Nigeria, in the big Dutch gas fields such as Groningen and in 25 other countries around the world.

It has continued to discover big fields such as Mars in the US Gulf. It is also expanding its Far East Liquefied Natural Gas operation. Over the past five years its discoveries have exceeded its output by eight per cent. With reserves already in excess of 17.5bn barrels of oil equivalent (boe) Shell is the world's largest non-governmental owner of oil and gas.

At present 35 per cent of production is gas but Shell's reserves are split almost equally between oil and gas. The latter is more environmentally friendly and it continues to steal market share from oil.

2. Oil Products. This division controls Shell's extensive refining and marketing operations. It owns or has interests in more the 50 refineries in 3 countries and has a retail presence in more than 100 countries. Its refineries handled 3.7m barrels a day in 1994 while Shell sold 5.7m barrels of oil products in1994. Products contributed just over half of group net income last year.

More than 40 per cent of Shell's refining capacity is in Western Europe, even though it has shut 7 of the 20 plants in which it had an interest over the past decade. That was in response to industry-wide overcapacity and has left its remaining plants running at high capacity levels.

More exciting are the growing economies of Latin America and more crucially the Far East where oil demand is growing at around 500,000 barrels per day. Shell's biggest single plant, Pulau Bukom, is in Singapore and has a capacity of more than 400,000 barrels per day. Heavy investment is underway in both regions.

In the US Shell Oil lagged behind its competitors for many years but is now showing the rest of the group what can be done. Richard Slape of stockbrokers Charles Stanley notes: 'over the past couple of years its performance in refining and marketing has improved dramatically, moving from last place amongst its peer group to second'. By closing small sites and upgrading plants and cutting costs elsewhere, Shell Oil's utilisation rate has soared to 95 per cent, impressive by any standards.

On the marketing side Shell's power is awesome. In more than 50 countries its market share exceeds 20 per cent and in a further 23 it is between10 and 20 per cent. Such size allows it to achieve significant economies of scale.

3. Chemicals. More than 11 per cent of Shell's assets are tied up in chemicals, which after three years of losses, moved into the black in 1994. An underlying profit of £502m, of which £196m came in the fourth quarter, was partly due to a cyclical recovery in both volumes and margins.

However, Shell has also instituted a major cost-cutting and rationalisation programme. Between 1991 and 1994 it took restructuring charges of £627m. As a result profits should reach £1bn by 1997.

Shell's rationalisation programme is not simply a matter of closing less efficient plants and shedding jobs, though this has happened. For instance, its polypropylene and polyethylene business has been spun off into an 8,000 employee joint venture with Montedison.

As a result of these measures, Nick Antill of stockbrokers BZW expects divisional return on capital to rise from a 1980s average of 10 per cent to around

15 per cent.

4. Coal and other operations. Last year Shell's non-core operations made an underlying profit of just £25m (£10m). Shell is keen to divest itself of these remaining operations and recently announced the sale of its Collahuasi copper interests in Chile.

Strategy and management

In 1994 Shell's return on capital was 10.39 per cent. That put it behind Exxon, as usual, and BP for the first time. The causes are numerous. Its huge cash balances obviously put it at a disadvantage in terms of ROCE, when compared to more highly geared rivals such as BP. But Shell is also inefficient.

Its dual headquarters in London and the Hague employ 5,000 people and cost £600m a year to run. Total staff numbers fell from 117,000 to 106,000 in 1994 but the group still looks overstaffed. More fundamentally an £8bn capital programme in 1995 suggests that Shell doesn't always cost its investments as carefully as its less well resourced competitors. For instance, in E&P the costs per barrel produced are $5, significantly higher than those of its rivals.

To tackle these issues Shell hired the management consultants McKinsey to review all aspects of its organisation. Cor Herkstoter, chairman of RDS, says he wants to see a ROCE of 15 per cent for Shell's existing assets and 12 per cent on all new projects.

As a result further redundancies, starting at both head offices, are inevitable. It also seems likely that capital spending will be slashed, as all new projects are costed more carefully. Shell also seems set to follow BP in outsourcing more functions and further disposals, possibly into joint ventures, are on the cards.

Few analysts doubt that in the biggest corporate restructuring to hit Shell since the 1950s, Mr Herkstoter's targets won't be achieved by the millennium.

Under Dutch law Shell is obliged to consult its workforce about the planned restructuring. Indeed the company is noted for fostering a co-operative atmosphere. This is unlikely to change despite the dramatic overhaul currently underway.

Human resources manager Ernst Broekman says the current changes will only 'alter the feel of the place over time'. And many of Shell's staff welcome the proposed changes since there will be a shift of power and responsibility from old baronial regional fiefdoms to operational managers. Those at the coal face should be empowered.

The future

With net assets of £36bn and minimal gearing Shell has one of the strongest balance sheets in world oil. The ongoing programme of disposals and an operational cashflow of £10.8bn in 1994 means Shell can finance both its expansive capital programme and a progressive dividend policy. By 1996 net income should be approaching £5bn.

Shell is heavily invested in all growth areas of the oil industry: natural gas and refining, and petrochemicals in the Far East. Now that it has also grasped the concept of shareholder value, there seems to be little to challenge its pre-eminence on the world oil and gas stage.

Smith✚Nephew

Smith & Nephew plc, London

Smith & Nephew is one of the world's leading healthcare manufacturers

Outlook:
In the next decade healthcare manufacturing will become a global business. Only three companies - two North American and one from the UK - will command sufficient capacity to be truly global players. As the only UK global player, Smith & Nephew is poised to become one of the top three. Its heavy investment in long term research and development is a key differentiator for the company

Scorecard:
Structural flexibility	★★★
Innovative power	★★★★★
International orientation	★★★★★
Human resources	★★★
Growth markets	★★★★
Quality of management	★★★★

Key figures:
Turnover	£965 million
Pre-tax profits	£172 million
Staff	12,250

Smith & Nephew plc
2 Temple Place
Victoria Embankment
London WC2R 3BP
Tel: 0171 836 7922
Fax: 0171 240 7088

Smith & Nephew plc

Radical forces are reshaping the global healthcare manufacturing sector. Demands from clients for excellent quality products, supplied to hospitals, clinics and doctors around the world, require long term investment and superb marketing structures. Few of the current players are able to meet the challenges which lie ahead in providing full service organisations.

Market analysts argue that the sheer extent of funding needed to support the research functions of truly competitive world class businesses, coupled with the maintenance and enhancement of a supply network are beyond the reach of most companies active in the sector. Three multinational companies will emerge from the processes currently in play to dominate healthcare. Two are American but one is British.

Smith & Nephew is a company with a distinguished pedigree. It depends for its current success on investment decisions made a decade ago or more. In common with the pharmaceutical or computing industry, healthcare manufacturing requires continuous long term funding for research and development to foster its continued viability. Smith & Nephew has always understood this prerequisite and devoted extensive resources to creating new healthcare technologies.

Operations and markets

Customers - hospitals, health authorities and private healthcare groups - demand leading-edge products delivering cost-effective solutions to the increasing healthcare problems of caring for patients as a whole, and elderly patients in particular. Intense competition characterises the relationship between the sector protagonists. As rivals strive to be first with the latest advances in medical technology, the drive for improvement becomes more imperative.

Smith & Nephew has an enviable record as an entrepreneurial innovator. It has invented new mechanisms for advancing the healing process, committed considerable sums to pure medical science research and promoted extensive dialogue with academia to strengthen the range and depth of its research initiatives.

It is also extremely strong commercially. In 1994 global sales rose two per cent to £965 million (underlying sales growth increased by seven per cent), while pre-tax profits grew by nine per cent to £172 million. In the main Smith & Nephew achieves a return on assets of around 38 per cent. The company has six major product divisions, each product area has a global headquarters with its own laboratory. Each is termed a centre of excellence. Every centre of excellence is responsible for its own business plan worldwide. This means that product launches and development can be co-ordinated centrally by people who can see the complete picture for the sector. The main product divisions are:

> wound management (Hull,UK)
> casting and support (Hull)
> trauma (Tennessee)
> endoscopy (Massachussets)
> orthopaedic implants (Tennessee)
> consumer healthcare (Birmingham,UK)

The company is structured globally with the corporate headquarters in London and division headquarters operating with some autonomy, around the world. This is a unitary organisation with clear management lines. The executive team are not remote holding company bosses, invisible when profits meet target but omnipresent when the figures fail to please. Strategic direction, especially research projects, is very much the remit of the centre.

At present the country drawing the biggest slice of income is the United States. The worldwide income split is roughly: North America 40 per cent, Europe (incl. UK) 40 per cent, Africa, Asia, Australasia 20 per cent.

Chief executive John Robinson says that although income will grow rapidly in coming years the biggest growth will come in the Pacific Rim. 'We anticipate that the far east will become much more important to the company.' In perhaps ten years the income split will probably move to: North America 35 per cent, Europe 35 per cent, Africa, Asia, Australasia 30 per cent.

The company's strength in North America and Europe is comprehensive but John Robinson wants to extend its scope in the Pacific Rim. 'We previously operated through distributors in Japan, but now have a wholly owned business employing 150 Japanese nationals. At present, its turnover is only £27 million but we expect that it will grow at 30 per cent a year. In the rest of Asia we have strong positions in a number of countries including Thailand, Taiwan, Korea, Malaysia, Singapore, Hong Kong, Indonesia, Pakistan and India. We are currently setting up an operation in China, where we already have two sales and marketing centres', says John Robinson.

Strategy and management

The key to the company's survival and prosperity was always - and remains - its reliance on the excellence of its research. Research has become a core strength of the business and gives the company its distinctive competitive edge. The combination of its innovative power and the quality and spread of its sales and marketing teams have fashioned an enterprise of unique strength.

John Robinson says that at any one time Smith & Nephew focuses its research on twelve key research projects: 'at least two of these are expected to transfer into manufacturing each year to provide us with radical new products and business areas for the future.' In 1994 the company spent £29 million pounds on R&D.

Smith & Nephew makes a clear distinction between research and development. 'Development is the incremental improvement in existing products and ranges,' says the group director of research and development Dr Alan Suggett. This takes place in laboratories at its centres of excellence.

Research, in contrast, is inquiry into new areas of medical and healthcare technology which the company conducts - in the main - at its research centre in York. It is also engaged in a series of joint ventures with academic departments and participates in an ongoing dialogue with the scientific and medical community.

Mr Robinson mentions three major areas of research which could provide Smith & Nephew with highly remunerative new business areas:

<u>Tissue engineering</u>: The surface of joints are covered in cartilage. Cartilage, when damaged or diseased through arthritis, does not regenerate itself. Normally when joints fail they are ultimately replaced by artificial implants. 'Scientists are very optimistic about our latest technology which - if it is successful - will enable cartilage to regenerate itself. If it does happen it will create a product line which will be as big as the current Smith & Nephew Group. I shall be cautious and say that we have a 50-50 chance of bringing this off.'

<u>Biological orthopaedics</u>: The company has funded a new chair and associated research unit in tissue repair in the Biology Department of the University of York. The main area of interest in the first instance will be bone repair.

<u>Visualisation technology</u>: This is one of the key and most exciting areas of medical technology. Smith & Nephew has sponsored a chair at Imperial College to create advanced visual imagery technology. This group at Imperial College is one of the world's leaders with a close working relationship with MIT and Tokyo University.

Another key element of the company's strategy is the co-ordination between the different businesses around the world. To enable a real, global 'Smith & Nephew culture' to exist, worldwide management information systems and global steering committees facilitate the essential sharing of ideas and information.

Although brand names are important to the company the Smith & Nephew group identity is the most important of all. Consumer brands, such as Elastoplast, Lil-lets and Simple are well known to their public and within the medical professions, Opsite, Richards, Allevyn and Dyonics are equally well known brands.

The company has excellent relationships with the various communities it works in and the Smith & Nephew Foundation funds education and research in the healthcare sector. In addition, its marketing teams regard themselves as educators as much as sales people. They are engaged in promoting new understanding of original processes and technologies.

But to imagine that Smith & Nephew is solely pursuing an altruistic vision is to miss the point. Only by providing leading edge science and pragmatic medical solutions does the company believe it can achieve and sustain profitability. Inquiry, creativity and risk-taking are generic to the long term prognosis of excellent health for the business. Its markets are demanding.

The future

Smith & Nephew is set to be one of three dominant players in an increasingly tough global health sector over the next decade. Its management's commitment to long-term profitability in an industry which is both extremely competitive and sociopolitically sensitive, is manifested both in a strong emphasis on research and in a culture of concern for the interests of patients, their hospitals and their communities, as well as the interests of shareholders. This balanced company will be a guiding light for British industry in the next century.

SB
SmithKline Beecham

SmithKline Beecham, Middlesex

SmithKline Beecham is a major international pharmaceutical company

Outlook:
This company is the product of the merger of two internationally reputed pharmaceutical companies. SB has a highly respected management ethos, and a portfolio of brand names and market-leading products. As such, the company is in a substantial position to be one of the handful of players which dominates the sector

Scorecard:
Structural flexibility	★★★★
Innovative power	★★★★
International orientation	★★★★★
Human resources	★★★★★
Growth markets	★★★★
Quality of management	★★★★★

Key figures:
Sales	£6 billion
Pre-tax profits	£1.3 billion
Staff	52,000

SmithKline Beecham plc
New Horizon Court
Great West Road
Middlesex TW8 9EP
Tel: 0181 975 2000

SmithKline Beecham

The global healthcare market is rapidly turning from one where the physicians call the shots and the cost of medicines is secondary, to a payer-controlled environment. This development is most noticeable in the United States, which has seen the emergence of powerful buying groups like health management organisations (HMOs) and insurance companies, that demand discounts from the big drug companies. In Europe, the governments of Germany, Italy and Britain have started imposing direct price cuts on selected medicines, something Japan has been doing for years. In response, the big healthcare companies have started to consolidate, both horizontally like Glaxo, which has taken over smaller rival Wellcome, and vertically, by buying drug distributors, the so-called pharmacy benefit managers (PBMs), which can often determine whether a certain drug gets on the HMO's formulary list. Both Merck and SmithKline have done that, but the latter is trying to do even more: to evolve a strategy that encompasses healthcare all the way from prevention, through diagnosis and treatment, to cure.

Operations and markets

SmithKline Beecham has been transformed since the merger of America's SmithKline Beckman and Britain's Beecham in 1989. Having grown into one of the world's largest healthcare companies over the past five years, a series of bold corporate deals totalling some $8 billion during 1994 has focused the group entirely on human healthcare and pharmaceuticals. With a value of over £10 billion, SmithKline, which is quoted on stockmarkets in London and New York, is one of Britain's 10 biggest companies.

Despite its size and partly, no doubt, due to its American heritage, the group retains the drive and flexibility of a much smaller company. This is something that chief executive Jan Leschly, a former Davis Cup tennis player for Sweden and largely responsible for last year's whirlwind of acquisitions, has been intent on developing. He talks with almost religious fervour of: 'the new SB, which we are proud to call The 'Simply Better' Healthcare Company. It is built on a foundation of science-based innovation with an absolute commitment to develop and exploit the synergies between our businesses, add value for our shareholders, and fulfil our 'promise'- to make people's lives better.'

This 'promise', according to Mr Leschly, is the reason why SmithKline exists and it is against this that the company's success over time will be measured. To achieve success the company is focusing its resources and energy on three targets: developing a winning strategy; treating its people as its most important asset; and measuring performance and rewarding accordingly.

Strategy and management

The first step, as Mr Leschly says, came in May 1993 with the $125m alliance between SmithKline and Human Genome Sciences, part of the project to map the human genome. That has thoroughly integrated the world's largest database of human gene sequences into the group's discovery programme and today its scientists in eight countries have immediate on-the-desk access to this information.

This has helped SmithKline become the partner of choice in biotechnology and over the last three years it has signed 130 agreements and collaborations on emerging treatments. Coupled with the commitment to maintaining a high level of research & development funding - £638 million in 1994 - is a drive to bring new products to market more quickly and effectively than rivals. Drugs launched in the past few years, including Famvir for shingles, the hepatitis B vaccine Engerix B and Paxil against depression, totalled sales of £810 million last year, helping to offset the decline of ulcer treatment Tagamet, which has lost its patent in America.

A total of seven new chemical entities and four new vaccines were in late stage development at the end of 1994 and this could expand to 20 products by the end of 1995. But the group's boldest move was the acquisition in May 1994 of Diversified Pharmaceutical Services, for $2.3 billion. Diversified is one of the three biggest PBMs in the United States, which contract with employers and insurance companies to manage their healthcare costs by using formularies and buying in bulk and at vast discounts from the pharmaceutical manufacturers.

Mr Leschly argues that the purchase of Diversified gives SmithKline a closer link to the all-important managed care market and that this type of purchasing will spread to Europe and international markets in the next few years. He says: 'With the acquisition of Diversified, we took a giant step towards managing 'total healthcare' which involves the ability to conduct outcome studies and develop disease management protocols.' Profitable in its own right, Diversified has also brought the group over two million members of HMOs it works for.

Another step towards 'total healthcare' was the $2.9 billion purchase of Sterling Winthrop's worldwide consumer business, Sterling. This brought with it a valuable group of over-the-counter (OTC) medicines, which can be bought without prescription; and even after selling the North American division to Germany's Bayer, SmithKline is now the third largest OTC company in the world. Driven by government efforts to control soaring healthcare costs, the OTC market is growing much faster than the prescription market, though margins are also generally lower.

Finally, SmithKline has retained its clinical laboratories business, which provides diagnostic products and services. The rationale here is that with effective healthcare management focusing on prevention and early diagnosis, clinical services and testing will become ever more important. Mr Leschly also points to the collaboration between the clinical laboratories division and the human genome collaboration, since many testing services initially have genetic applications and the fact that lab supplies and services could be marketed through Diversified, alongside conventional drugs.

SmithKline recognises that the ongoing commitment and support of its 52,000 employees worldwide is as crucial as the strategic moves made by the company. As a result, it carried out a major survey among staff during 1994.

This showed, according to SmithKline, that to a large degree it has succeeded in creating a new culture dedicated to continuous improvement through an empowered workforce. The cultural initiative, termed, perhaps inevitably, the

'Simply Better Way', has established hundreds of self-directed teams, working together across functions, businesses and national borders to solve problems and improve the enormous number of processes that go into making a company the size of SmithKline run smoothly and efficiently.

Mr Leschly comments: 'It is no surprise that people perform better when they are empowered and listened to, and when they understand how their individual roles can help SB achieve its strategic goals and fulfil its "promises" to make people's lives better.'

But the survey also showed that much work needs to be done in areas such as rewarding people who take risks, acknowledging failures more openly and dealing with poor performance. Special attention is being paid by the taskforces to how employees should balance work and personal life.

On top of that, SmithKline is asking its managers to develop measurable objectives which can be linked to compensation. Even now, however, the company has one of the highest levels of executive remuneration in Britain, with its 15-man board taking home a total of £9.2 million in 1994. A good part of that went to Mr Leschly himself, who was paid a total of almost £2.5m in salary and bonus, although around £800,000 of that was a one-off relocation expense for moving from Britain back to America, where the bulk of the group's business is now located. Mr Leschly's predecessors, Henry Wendt and Bob Bauman, who oversaw the original 1989 merger, were regularly the highest-paid due in British boardrooms and the latest annual report from the group reveals that they are still being paid, despite retiring in April 1994.

The future

SmithKline's profits have been rising steadily over the past six years and just as surely strong cash flow has reduced the heavy borrowings taken on at the time of the 1989 merger. In 1994 sales from continuing operations rose eight per cent to £6 billion and trading profit grew 15 per cent to £1.2 billion. Pre-tax profits increased 9 per cent to almost £1.3 billion and the dividend was raised 18 per cent.

Two thirds of sales and profits came from the pharmaceuticals division and another quarter from consumer healthcare, which includes brands ranging from Tums anti-acid tablets and Panadol headache pills to Beecham's flu remedies and Aquafresh toothpaste. It is in this division that Sterling's OTC business will be integrated. The remaining profits came from clinical laboratories. The group has set up a £580 million restructuring fund to cover the restructuring and integration of its new businesses, which will be spent over the next three years.

Last year's buying spree has raised gearing through a combination of higher borrowings and goodwill which had to be written off against net assets. But the disposal of the Animal Health businesses for almost £1 billion in early 1995 has already reduced financial gearing to 99 per cent. SmithKline expects gearing to be eliminated within three years barring further acqusitions.

SONY®

Sony, Surrey

Sony is a world class manufacturer of high quality electronic goods for professional and domestic use

Outlook:
Sony is world market leader in the vast majority of its sectors. It is one of the world's true innovators. The company's processes are benchmark standard for many companies around the world and it invests heavily at regional level in co-ordinated research and development programmes. This is not only one of the UK's best companies but one of the world's finest

Scorecard:

Structural flexibility	★★★★★
Innovative power	★★★★★
International orientation	★★★★★
Human resources	★★★★★
Growth markets	★★★★★
Quality of management	★★★★★

Key figures:

Worldwide sales	$36 billion
Global profits	$6 billion
Staff	130,000

Sony UK
Weybridge
Surrey KT13 0XW
Tel: 01932 816000
Fax: 01932 817000

Sony

Few manufacturers hit the quality standards which Sony achieves. In its operations around the world this corporation provides processes and management expertise which are respected throughout world business. Its capacity to innovate, to locate and prosecute new markets are legendary. Above all else this is a business which understands markets and people. But it is not prescriptive. It allows an astonishing amount of freedom for individuals to run their own show and contribute to the greater good of the whole.

In UK industry there is a tendency to view Japanese companies as mechanistic anthills with employees operating within tightly formulated regulations and searching after increasingly high and demanding targets. To extend this analogy to Sony would miss the point completely. This is a business which reflects the true heart of Japanese business culture. That is, it provides a framework where people are genuinely free to create new products and markets, to improve existing products and to contribute to their communities. Sony was the first major Japanese company to come to the UK and in its wake other leaders of Japanese industry have decided to invest here. The impact of Japanese inward investment on the UK's economic recovery is substantial. Major players such as Nissan, Toyota, Hitachi and National Panasonic all have factories in Britain, and Wales and the north east in particular are net beneficiaries.

Japanese business has created direct employment in its offices and factories in the UK but suppliers have also benefited from the arrival of major electronic, engineering and motor companies. Sony's state-of-the-art plant in Bridgend, South Wales uses the services of a range of preferred suppliers - some local and some Japanese which have opened up in Wales to supply Sony. The quality of the development work done in Bridgend is now so impressive that engineers from the plant have been invited to headquarters in Japan to advise systems there.

Operations and markets

Sony Corporation is the world number one in consumer and broadcast electronics. From the Walkman portable cassette player through to its latest complete television stations, Sony is market leader. The organisation is active in domestic and professional television receivers and CD systems; it makes high definition screens for leading computer hardware manufacturers. It is also a key player in multinational joint ventures with the General Magic alliance and also more intimately with Oracle with whom it is generating a new digital electronic news gathering system.

In the UK, its headquarters are in an impressive building on the outskirts of Weybridge. There are further installations in the Thames valley and its massive plant in south Wales. Sony UK is part of the European region and most decision-making for its UK activities tends to take place at European level. The days of reporting directly to Tokyo are almost at an end. The manufacturing business has a direct link to the film and record industry activities but these strictly speaking are not part of Sony UK.

Sony was formed in 1946 as the Tokyo Telecommunications Engineering Corporation. Globally its sales are $36 billion and the company employs 130,000 people worldwide. Research and development projects are decided internationally after intensive market research shows the likely future pattern of market demand.

Strategy and management

Sony aims to achieve four customer benefits in its introduction of new products: greater speed, flexibility, cost effectiveness and creativity. The corporation is committed to pushing back the barriers to technological advancement and to ensure that each new product takes the customer further along the road to service excellence. Kaizen - continuous improvement - operates throughout the business. In Bridgend, for example, Sony has done away with quality circles and made the line responsible for elevation of quality, elimination of waste and refinement to the product. No artificial barriers exist and each member of the team is rewarded for notable achievements.

It is hard to overstate the extent to which this business is committed to serving its customers. It is a driving force within Sony and rather like Hewlett Packard or Microsoft breaking new ground is an inevitable consequence of its business approach. Its catalogue of Walkman products, for example, includes almost 100 variants. The company derives the vast majority of its profits from a handful of lines but it is determined to supply every possible variety of proven demand. Each of these products is profitable - and must be so - but there are certain powerhouse items. The strategy is clearly that Sony will be the first choice when a customer wants to add new electronic devices to his or her collection.

Nowhere is this more evident than in broadcast. As market leader for television and radio stations, Sony has stated that every new product will be fully compatible with all earlier Sony generations. This means that if a television or radio station has bought Sony equipment in the past, it can continue to use its older tape recorders, video machines, cameras or consoles. It also intends to develop new technology in partnership with each of its customers. Its theme for the last National Association of Broadcasters show was Defining the Digital Future. Sony talks to its customers and is satisfied that it knows where the industry is headed. It has therefore been progressively building a platform to take the sector to its technological goal. And Sony has innovated across the board: in acquisition, post-production, transmission, archiving and pro-audio.

Recent product innovations include a new family of broadcast cameras which feature digital signal processing, a growing line of hard-disk-based non-linear hybrid editing workstations, a powerful compact digital broadcast switcher and a new portable Digital Betacam VCR. They use state-of-the-art digital signal processing.

These cameras are extremely flexible, capable of being tailored to any application from studio to outside broadcast and electronic field production. Aimed at high-end production and broadcasting applications, these products were designed for the highest picture quality in the industry at a cost-effective price.

Sony is committed to the fully integrated digital environment for the broadcaster, which means systems, software and infrastructure to support a completely tape-free station. Newsroom reports are no longer recorded but sent in digital form to the control centre. Programmes are mixed electronically and a signal is sent digitally to the transmitter. To achieve this the company is expanding aggressively around the world with manufacturing plants operating worldwide.

There is enormous enthusiasm for this technological initiative especially in the convergence of audio, video, communications and computer technology. Continued growth in the capacities of digital technology means that the distinction between previous industry divisions are becoming blurred. Digital Audio Tape, for example, is aimed at video post-production, radio production and music recording users.

The future

Sony has a strong track record at its European manufacturing operations. At Bridgend it makes colour TVs, displays and cathode ray tubes. Its ambitions are reflected in all its other locations and emphasise Sony's increasing determination to expand manufacturing outside Japan. Bridgend will become the flagship site. There are plans to build Sony Technology Park, with an obsession for excellence carried to the standard of building design which must be of the highest quality in a highly prestigious, well designed well landscaped site.

Other plants in Spain, France, Germany, Austria and Italy make CD players, hi-fi and video equipment, audio and video tapes, laser and compact discs plus other electronics such as robotics, optical pick-ups, printed wiring boards and duplication equipment. Sony is one of an elite group of companies which will not only be making advanced products but determining the shape of technological progress.

It is also an active and positive force in its communities. Sony chairs the Welsh Small Business Council. It also pioneers progress in children's education through the Sony Foundation of Science Education. Elsewhere it supports musicians, museums and projects for the disabled. On the environmental front, the company is acutely aware that some of the residues from its processes are damaging and it is working at a strategic and individual process level to make the company friendlier to the planet. This has become a vital issue and the company's directors established a global environmental policy in March 1993.

All ozone-depleting substances in its worldwide manufacturing plants were eliminated by April 1993, much earlier than the official goal of December 1995 - in fact one month after the policy was launched. A Sony Environmental Fund has been established to back outstanding environmental research programmes.

Sony will be a bellwether company in years to come. It represents the finest in manufacturing, technical innovation, human resources management, understanding of its markets and responsibility to its communities. This is a soundly managed enterprise which sets standards for others to follow.

Stagecoach Holdings plc, Perth

Britain's largest bus service operator with operations in the UK and around the world

Outlook:
Stagecoach's distinctive formula for acquiring and managing bus companies has pushed the business into the UK's top spot. The same formula is being tried out worldwide. This is an entrepreneurial company with tight cost controls and a vigorous approach to marketing

Scorecard:

Structural flexibility	★★★★
Innovative power	★★★★
International orientation	★★★★
Human resources	★★★
Growth markets	★★★★★
Quality of management	★★★★★

Key figures:

Turnover	£770 million
Pre-tax profits	£45 million
Wordwide staff	28,000

Stagecoach Holdings plc
Charlotte House
20 Charlotte Street
Perth PH1 5LL
Tel: 01738 442111
Fax: 01738 643648

Stagecoach plc

Britain's passenger transport industry is in a process of transformation - a pattern which will continue through the next decade. As quality of service and economy of scale issues predominate, many of the hundreds of smaller operators will merge, disappear or be taken over. Analysts anticipate that around 80 per cent of all business will be conducted by 10 to 12 large suppliers.

There may well be further rationalisation among the big players but since the industry is such a recent recruit to the private sector, the future composition of the UK business is hard to forecast with any great clarity. Certainly the inherent inefficiencies among local companies would suggest that much of the sifting out will occur without further delay and the population of operators in the UK private bus sector will be much smaller by the year 2000.

Ultimate supremacy will rely on several key factors which taken collectively will offer operators distinctive advantage. Among them are: critical mass, scale of enterprise, innovative and competitive approach to customer service, capacity to keep operational costs low, strong financial management and concentration on core. Few of the existing larger companies possess these qualities in sufficient measure to fulfil the criteria for sustained success. The size of these players may provide an adequate bulwark against the challenge of more agile rivals. But in the end management resilience, flexibility of action and capacity for original ideas to meet customer demand will differentiate the long term winners from the also-rans.

Operations and markets

Stagecoach Holdings plc is the UK's largest private bus company. It occupies 12-13 per cent of the national market, and runs seven divisions which embrace 38 local bus companies. Its rapid rise to premier bus operator in the UK is a remarkable story. In 1980 it was a family partnership, based in Perth, concentrating on long-haul coach services. Thirteen years later it was floated and in 1995 commands a market capitalisation of £325 million with a turnover of £400 million. By the year 2000, finance director Derek Scott estimates that the annual turnover of the company will have risen to one billion.

The flowering of the business came with the privatisation of local bus services. It has adopted a relentless acquisition strategy which, matched by its undoubted commercial zeal, has allowed it to grow unchecked. Throughout the country - from its home base in Scotland to the English south coast - Stagecoach has acquired local operators. Given the trading indisciplines of many smaller suppliers, Stagecoach has been able to apply its unique management philosophy to bus companies of all shapes and sizes. Since privatisation it has tripled in size reporting 1995 sales of £330 million and a typical 18 per cent return on sales in its better-performing companies. At present 90 per cent of income comes from UK operations - either bus services or providing aluminium transport tokens for local-authority distribution to pensioners.

Overseas activities account for the remaining 10 per cent of income. This area of the business has been as high previously as 20 per cent but recently considerable management effort has been put into building the spine of the UK business and interests abroad have been reduced proportionately. In some senses this is a cautious company. Although profoundly entrepreneurial in nature, it has retained only those external investments which it has deemed helpful in securing the long-term profitability of the group. In the next five years it plans to expand again outside the UK because Stagecoach recognises that limitations exist on the growth potential in regional British markets.

The company's philosophy is redolent of many successful ventures. It sits strategic decision-making at the centre and devolves executive day-to-day authority to the divisions and individual companies. The founders' evangelical Christianity provides a moral dimension to the group's business ethos. This is the backbone of the enterprise - tough commercialism rooted in an indelible belief in fairness and justice.

Operating costs are 20 per cent lower than the market average, allowing the company to offer highly competitive fares on its services. The breadth of its operations also means that the company is able to negotiate beneficial deals on expenditure such as new fleet. It orders almost all of its new vehicles from Volvo or Dennis, the fire engine manufacturer, and Stagecoach is therefore a valued customer for these two businesses. Administration - which was always flabby in public-sector days - has been slimmed. These factors combine to create a low-cost, customer-orientated enterprise.

Strategy and management

Stagecoach has established a vision for its business in the year 2000. It sees income sourced from its three existing main areas but the proportions of total revenue will shift:
- UK bus   70 per cent
- UK rail   10 per cent
- overseas   20 per cent

The company has developed a unique management style which combines entrepreneurship, pragmatism, a degree of caution, and hands-on devolved operational management. Its gift for understanding its markets and taking existing but underperforming transport companies and turning them into winners is its forte. Finance director Derek Scott says that Stagecoach will stick to core and export its talents in these markets to other parts of the UK, to the domestic rail industry and to overseas transport concerns. 'We have avoided the bureaucratisation which hampers many companies when they grow beyond their initial phase. The founders were determined to retain and promote managers who shared their enthusiasm for the Stagecoach approach and to devolve as much authority to them as possible.'

Rail is a logical extension for the business. The UK government has announced the early phases of rail privatisation and Stagecoach has registered its interest. It aims to secure lines close to existing bus services so that it can provide an integrated service. Prices are fixed for the period of each franchise - seven years - so real revenue growth can only be achieved by increasing the volume of passengers using these services. In its previous limited excursions into rail - in Scotland - Stagecoach learned quickly that feeder services to rail heads can be extremely beneficial to both bus and rail.

Another and perhaps more immediately lucrative growth area is overseas bus services. Stagecoach presently runs services in Africa and New Zealand and has made a commitment to Commonwealth countries as its first target. 'These are pre-eminently left-hand-drive countries, using similar vehicles to the UK. English is frequently the principal language, and bus transport is a familiar idea. So we are minimising the barriers to entry and increasing our chances of success. We believe strongly - wherever possible - in taking over existing companies with some kind of infrastructure. Starting from scratch is heavy on management and can mean selling the concept of bus transport rather than adding value to an underperforming business,' says Mr Scott.

In Africa where many traditional services survive on only one vehicle, which can be in a poor state of repair, engineering strength is a key commercial factor. Unlike in the UK where such services can be handled by external contractors, in Africa Stagecoach more often employs its own engineering teams. In Wellington, capital of New Zealand, Stagecoach first refused the opportunity to run its privatised bus company but was then persuaded and it is strategically well placed to bid for Auckland's rather larger service in 1995. An early adventure in Hong Kong also led to bus services in China run by the company which now provides two routes in the colony.

Latin America could provide stimulating opportunities as well. In Colombia and Brazil, Stagecoach is involved in joint ventures which could emerge as the role model for future collaborations. Volvo invited Stagecoach to enter a consortium with the federation of bus operators in Bogota. This is one of the most over-bussed cities in the world but a well managed, high quality service could assist in the process of thinning out some of the more precarious rivals. Funding is provided by US and Colombian institutions, and Volvo which holds a quarter-share - the same as Stagecoach - may ultimately sell its stock to the Scots.

In mainland Europe, Mr Scott says, Stagecoach is taking a more cautious route. A Swedish company Lingebuss AB may be a suitable partner. 'Lingebuss is in some ways a Swedish version of Stagecoach. We think in the same way and our instincts are alike. However in its domestic market Lingebuss has limited room for manoeuvre. There could be opportunities for joint ventures in the Netherlands, northern Germany, and the Baltic states,' he says.

The future

Stagecoach seems leaps and bounds ahead of its competition in commercial terms. It is the only UK bus company with such comprehensive but well costed expansion plans. What favours the company is its coherence as a business, its strong qualities of innovation, ability to rise to a challenge and its capacity to form blue chip joint ventures. It has the opportunity to transform the bus industry throughout the world in the longer term and may be able to do what few consider realistic - make a profit running train services in the reduced-subsidy or subsidy-free UK.

TADPOLE
TECHNOLOGY

Tadpole Technology, Cambridge

Tadpole Technology is an innovative manufacturer of portable workstations and specialist components for world class computer companies

Outlook:
If it can overcome some structural, delivery and organisational problems, Tadpole will experience a promising future. It enjoys some excellent relationships with leading manufacturers and its portable workstations are astoundingly flexible machines. The present raft of difficulties is a major barrier to its advancement but the quality of its personnel suggests that Tadpole will progress to new achievements

Scorecard:

Structural flexibility	★★★★
Innovative power	★★★★★
International orientation	★★★★
Human resources	★★★
Growth markets	★★★★★
Quality of management	★★★★

Key figures:

Turnover	£32.5 million
Pre-tax profits (loss)	(£1.3million)
Staff	200

Tadpole Technology plc
Cambridge Science Park
Milton Road
Cambridge CB4 4WQ
Tel: 01223 428200
Fax: 01223 428201

Tadpole Technology

Business leaders often say that the future of British industry will spring from the entrepreneurial sector - those young and vibrant companies which have the power and capacity to emerge as world beaters. Since hundreds, even thousands, of greenfield ventures open each year the task ahead of any business analyst is to discriminate between the candidates. Those which possess sufficient originality of thought, production capability, understanding of markets and customers, and management expertise will be the standard bearers of tomorrow.

Since forecasting is a tricky business, professionals look for certain telltale signs which will give reasonable indication that a particular business has what it takes to become something special. Possession of any one special strength is not enough. The competitive pressures of modern day business are such that, say, an innovative concept alone would be scant guarantee of commercial viability. A combination of skills and attributes which involves the mechanism to locate, deliver and sustain market demand - and to achieve a worthwhile return - is a prerequisite for a long-term contribution.

Many new businesses open in what is loosely termed high-tech. This is the industrial sector which embraces computers, electronics, telecommunications and a range of other engineering-related disciplines. The spiralling demand for computers and telecomms systems with increasing processing capacity and ever-widening links to other users has created in its wake scores of infant technology ventures. Some are suppliers of the intricate components which larger manufacturers assemble in computers, printers, scanners, and modems. Others fashion products which they release to the markets themselves. Rarely do they do both.

Operations and markets

Tadpole Technology is one that does. This high end portable computer designer and manufacturer, based in Cambridge, could well replicate - in the UK - the formidable success stories of small US leading-edge technology companies. The company is not there yet, but all the signs are in place and the next two years will be a very telling and exciting period for its management, employees and shareholders.

The company is a specialist designer and developer of powerful portable technology. Already, the business is the global leader in workstation-class portable computers, a supplier of circuit-boards and software products to other manufacturers and it recently entered the PC-notebook market at the top-end with an Intel-Pentium based portable, the Tadpole P1000. Expanding into a second facility in Cambridge, Tadpole also operates a US headquarters which is sited in Austin, Texas and subsidiaries and sales offices throughout Europe and the Pacific Rim.

From the onset in 1984, growth has been a major business objective for management . This is why its strategic changes in direction have been the outcome of a conscious planning process. Part of the reason for this lies perhaps in the background of co-founder and current chief executive George Grey. With a first class degree from Cambridge in electrical sciences, he didn't rush into raising Tadpole but took a few years to obtain the insight and business acumen needed to lead a rapidly growing organisation through the ever-changing marketplaces of high technology.

As one of the most useful stepping stones Mr Grey cites his period with one of the leading investment banks where many of the world's high-tech set-up proposals passed his desk for his assessment of their technical and business merit. Thus well-prepared, Tadpole Technology was launched and from the start combined front-edge engineering skills with market-insight and a strategic sense of direction. The first product to flow out of the company's doors in Cambridge was a UNIX-based motherboard that outperformed anything available at the time and quickly established Tadpole as a supplier to the big names in computing. Tadpole's ambitions, however, stretched further and managers felt strategically uncomfortable being dependent on only a few clients, however large. Their next step therefore was to establish an alliance with the leading workstation producer Sun Microsystems in order to develop an end-user product. Capitalising on its ability to create increasingly powerful components in yet smaller boxes Tadpole developed the world's first portable workstation; the SPARCbook.

The SPARCbook now has a third generation successor - the SPARCbook3 - which is used by such clients as Lockheed Sanders for the US Airforce Mission Support System, Reuters for real-time data analysis/risk management and BT for its on-site analysis and support. One of the most striking applications is its use in monitoring one of the America's Cup sailing yachts on board during the race.

Strategy and management

The SPARCbook's success led to further strategic alliances with IBM in 1992 and Digital in 1994 to develop portables using their respective high performance processing systems. Alliances are an important part of Tadpole's strategy, even - suggests Mr Grey - one of its competitive core competencies. Tadpole has been able to share development costs while acquiring experience with other microprocessor architectures and diversifying into the associated markets.

Another alliance which may prove to be of pivotal importance in the future is that with Solectron Inc. In order to grow exponentially and yet retain its lead in development and technology, Tadpole plans to outsource the big production runs of a proven product to Solectron. This enables the company to remain focused on developing and perfecting that proven product's next generation. Tadpole has a leading edge and is not going to lose it because it wants to grow. Solectron's existing production lines in all main market areas add to the structural flexibility in meeting demand.

At present Tadpole's main business is in the portable work-station market (79 per cent of revenue in 1994) and it has shown growth exceeding 70 per cent year-on-year. The original business of supplying custom-made circuit boards to original equipment manufacturers (OEMs) such as Texas Instruments and Rank Xerox continues unabated. As the rate of technology change continues to accelerate, Tadpole's front-edge engineering skills remain strongly in demand to supply the heart and nervous-system of products ranging from flight simulators to multi-media servers.

The largest and most advanced high-tech market is in the United States and almost three quarters of Tadpole's sales at present come from its US head-office in Texas. Although senior management spends most of its time at present in the US, Cambridge remains the company's base and research centre, anticipating the future developments in the global markets. As befits a high-tech company, the latest technologies in video conferencing and communication methods support the internationally dispersed operations.

The workstation market as a whole is predicted to grow from $1billion in 1994 to approximately $2.5billion in 1996. The portable workstation has yet to make any substantial penetration of this market (estimate of two per cent). But, as the present global leader in this niche, Tadpole seems exceptionally well-positioned to capitalise on the potential for growth in these markets. If this were not enough to keep Tadpole on its toes for the next 12 months, the company has created an even more exciting period ahead by launching a new product which promises to be a world beater. In order to tap into new markets, be strategically prepared for future developments and above all continue to be the creators of new high-tech products Tadpole has given the world its first Intel-Pentium 100-MHz laptop, the Tadpole P1000.

The technical configuration of the Tadpole P1000 is as impressive as its external appearance. It was presented at the influential Comdex/Fall exhibition in 1994 where other companies had slipped 75MHz Pentiums into 486-design notebooks to present a Pentium portable. The Tadpole P1000 however has been developed and designed specifically for Intel's first CPU with workstation-class performance, the 100MHz Pentium. Its elegant engineering presents a number of breakthroughs and was awarded the Outlook Engineering Excellence Award for 1994.

The Tadpole P1000 will almost certainly be creating its own market because nothing this powerful has ever been available at the premium end of the notebook market . In areas such as multimedia presentations, data collection and real-time analysis the range of new possibilities will start generating a new demand. Looking even further ahead Mr Grey sees a merging of the portable workstation market and the top-end of the portable PC market as processing power and portability continue to increase.

An atmosphere of concentrated purposefulness in the air pervades Tadpole's design floors at the Cambridge Science Park. This company is a technician's paradise - and many of the employees enjoy their work so much that they rarely want to go home. Being part and parcel of new developments give people both the drive and the resilience to constantly pursue their tasks with intensity and commitment.

One of Tadpole's foreseeable problems as it expands rapidly is being able to equip itself with the right managers, as some of the technicians with good management potential are reluctant to leave the electronic drawing-board for a managing position. However, Tadpole's advancing reputation in the high-tech sector increasingly enables the company to interest knowledgeable management talent from elsewhere.

The future

Analysts appear to be adopting a positively-inclined 'wait-and-see' approach to Tadpole's development. Its year-end figures for 1994 showed a heartening 42 per cent rise in sales to £32.5 million. The development costs for the Tadpole P1000 created a loss for 1994, but 1995 will be the year in which its profitability should be proven. This - and a number of deals which it has recently secured - should allow Tadpole to achieve the critical mass it needs to be a true global player and to carve out its own piece of the future.

Tarmac, Wolverhampton

Tarmac is Britain's largest aggregates company and the country's second biggest contractor.

Outlook:
Following a £600 million asset swap with Wimpey, Tarmac is now focused almost entirely on contracting and quarrying. Although it is expanding its non-UK activities rapidly, the deal with Britain's biggest house builder has left it with sufficient capital to take advantage of any recovery in the domestic construction industry and to capitalise on the Government's Private Finance Initiative.

It is also a significant player in eastern North America, in key European markets and has a growing presence in the Far East.

Scorecard:

Structural Flexibility	★★★★
Innovative Power	★★★
International Orientation	★★★★★
Human Resources	★★★
Growth Markets	★★★★

Key Figures:

Market Capitalisation	£1.1 billion
1994 Turnover	£2.5 billion
1994 Pre-tax profit	£107 million

Tarmac PLC
Hilton Hall
Essington
Wolverhampton
WV11 2BQ
Tel: 01902 307407
Fax: 01902 305537

TARMAC

In November 1995 Tarmac and Wimpey stunned the construction world with details of a £600 million assets swap. Tarmac picked up Wimpey's construction and aggregates businesses. In return it handed over its house building operation.

The deal was borne partly from the unhelpful trading environment in which Britain's contractors operate. Margins and volumes in both house building and construction have fallen sharply every year this decade. Thus both industries have undergone extensive rationalisation during the past fifteen months - only the biggest and the fittest will survive.

But the transaction is not just a defensive move. Both businesses are by their nature highly cash consumptive and with the Private Finance Initiative will be even more so. Neville Simms, Tarmac's group chief executive, said: 'We simply had too many hungry mouths to feed - now we have the cash resources to grow all of our chosen businesses.'

He added : 'This strategic move fundamentally reshapes the group and will maximise shareholder value.'

Operations and markets

The combined quarrying and building materials business would have generated revenues of £1.165 billion in the 1994 calendar year but needed capital of £1.365 billion to achieve that.

British operations dominate the quarrying operations. In its home market it operates from 419 sites out of a group total of 574. Reserves of stone, rock, gravel and sand total 1,300 million tonnes compared to a group total of 2,885 million tonnes. In the various, fragmented, UK markets, Tarmac's share varies from 19% of the ready mixed concrete market to 31% of coated road stone.

Tarmac actually has marginally greater reserves in the United States and Canada but operates from only 104 sites. A presence is maintained throughout the Eastern seaboard but Tarmac has a heavy bias towards the booming economies of the Sun-belt states such as Florida.

A series of small acquisitions has also helped the company establish a significant presence in France and the Czech Republic where it operates 25 and 20 sites respectively.

More important to Tarmac's future growth is its construction activities. In 1994 these generated revenues of £1.708 billion, although in a dreadful environment operating margins were less than 1%.

Again the bulk of turnover came from the domestic market: building contracts bringing in £692 million while civil engineering generated £373 million. There have been some signs of improvement in demand from the private sector for building contracts since early 1995 but it will take many years before volumes return to the levels witnessed a decade ago. A tightening of governmental belts has hit the market for large scale civil engineering, especially for road contracts. Simms says: 'Work is in short supply and competition is intense.'

However it is in this area that Tarmac should make the bulk of the £20 million annual cost savings it hopes to generate from the merger of its activities with those of Wimpey.

More importantly, for the longer term, the group is well placed to benefit from the Private Finance Initiative, a Government scheme where companies, or consortiums, provide the capital to construct facilities from roads through to hospitals and then earn an annual income stream from the project. This saves the State from an up front cash commitment but means that only well funded private concerns can hope to participate in such schemes.

Administrative problems have meant that the Private Finance Initiative has been slow to move into top-gear. Tarmac has shown it is a serious player by picking up a string of small contracts, such as the £4 million deal to build a new hospital unit in Bournemouth. However, much larger packages are currently under review and should provide a useful source of income for the group.

As exciting a prospect for growing the pure contracting side of Tarmac comes from the booming economies of South East Asia and the Pacific Rim. At present the contribution to group profits from the construction of power stations in Brunei and Malaysia and from a £55 million immersible rail tunnel in Hong Kong may not be significant. However, Tarmac is an established player in these markets and Simms says he will be committing capital into these regions, as well as into Eastern Europe because of their enormous growth potential.

In 1994 Tarmac's highly regarded Professional Services division generated revenues of £96 million but it was only established as an independent unit early in that year and is viewed as another exciting source of growth. Its remit is to be a fee-earning business offering consultancy services in engineering design, construction and project management, materials testing and facilities management. Almost 2,000 employees currently work from twenty-five offices, of which nine are outside the UK.

Major contracts won already, including deals with Victoria harbour in Hong Kong, British Gas and Boots, give added weight to the company's claim that: 'Fee income is expected to grow rapidly over the next few years.'

Strategy and management

Chaired by the veteran industrialist and former Director General of the CBI Sir John Banham the bulk of the Tarmac board are long-serving company men. In 1994 the nine executive directors had served the company for an average of 21 years each.

That does not mean that the board is afraid of taking brave steps. The decision to engineer an asset swap with Wimpey received a mixed reaction initially but in the five months after the news broke shares in the company have soared by more than 40% and have outperformed the sector by almost 30%.

A leading City analyst notes: 'In terms of re-orientating the group and in cutting costs, Simms and his team have done a very good job - now they need to show they can integrate businesses as well.'

The company is well placed for further corporate deals, although on a smaller scale, and for organic growth. Debts of £300 million mean that its gearing is under 30%. However, interest is well covered by earnings and there is no financial reason why the group cannot grow itself. Simms has set three core areas for expansion.

In the quarrying and building materials division Tarmac plans to expand its geographic coverage particularly in concrete and especially in the UK and mainland Europe.

Within contracting, it plans to grow its fee generating consultancy services especially in Europe and the Far East and to win increasing business from the Private Finance Initiative and from the Millennium fund in the UK. The idea of using private funding for infrastructure projects is winning growing acceptance world-wide and Tarmac hopes to use its British experiences as a springboard to win business elsewhere.

The Future

After half a dozen terrible years no sensible analysts will predict when the British construction industry will start to see a rapid pick up in both its volume of work and in its operating margins.

Tarmac will obviously benefit when that happens but it is also well placed to grow even in a flat environment.

Cost cutting will help that process but this company also has the resources and the desire to invest for expansion. A strong balance sheet means that it is well placed to take on large scale Private Finance Initiative projects in the United Kingdom and to bid for major construction projects in the world's most vibrant economies.

The company is also committed to expanding its geographic aggregates coverage both in its core UK and North American markets as well as in fresher pastures such as Europe. Expect to see a string of small acquisitions to further that strategy.

Even assuming that there is no immediate pick up in the fortunes of the British construction industry and no major acquisitions, City analysts expect Tarmac to deliver steady profits growth. In the 1996 calendar year the experts expect pre-tax profits to reach £101.5 million and £140.5 million has been pencilled in for the year after. Earnings per share are predicted to grow from 7.3p in 1996 to 10.2p in the following twelve months.

More importantly the business will generate cash allowing both investment in selected growth opportunities and attractive dividend growth.

It does not matter when the good times return, Tarmac is firmly back on the growth track.

TELEWEST

TeleWest Communications, Surrey

TeleWest is a leading provider of cable television and telephony services in the UK

Outlook:

TeleWest is poised to meet the imminent surge in demand for interactive and integrated entertainment, telecommunications and information services - such as interactive video games, video telephony, video conferencing, Internet services, and on-line interactive services like home shopping and banking - as they become available in the future

Scorecard:

Structural Flexibility	★★★★
Innovative Power	★★★★
International Orientation	★★★★
Human Resources	★★★
Growth markets	★★★★★
Quality of Management	★★★★

Key figures:

Turnover	£145 million
Operating profits UK (loss)	(£84 million)
Staff	2,776

TeleWest Communications
Unit 1, Genesis Business Park
Albert Drive, Woking
Surrey GU21 5RW
Tel: 01483 750900
Fax: 01483 750901/2

TeleWest

Government regulation, however much criticised, is essential to create true competition in the future between different broadband networks once the future's expected plethora of electronic services has arrived. The costs of establishing such networks are simply enormous. In the UK, regulatory policies give a number of cable companies up to 1998 to establish themselves as alternatives for existing communications network-providers such as BT and Mercury. One that will be a force after 1998 is TeleWest.

TeleWest was formed in 1994 to acquire the assets of a joint venture (est. 1991) between Tele-Communications Inc and US WEST Inc, which combined their UK businesses and licences. In September 1995 it is to merge with the fifth largest cable company in the UK, SBC CableComms UK.

The establishment of broadband cable networks is an extremely costly activity, but the rewards will certainly have similar dimensions. Once the information highway is built and the traffic intensifies, the returns are projected to be staggering.

Operations and markets

The UK government grants licenses or franchises to build broadband communications networks to deliver video, voice and data services to homes and businesses. Of the more than 130 franchises granted since 1984, TeleWest owns and operates 16 and has a minor interest in seven others.

Over 14.7 million homes (70 per cent of the UK's population) are covered by cable. TeleWest serves of these 2.8 million (19 per cent), spread throughout Britain: in Scotland, the North East, Cotswolds, Avon, Birmingham and around London and the South-East. Its cable network is still in full development and will have reached all homes in its current franchise-areas in 1999.

After the merger in September 1995 with SBCC, TeleWest will have added eight franchise areas covering over 1.3 million homes in the North West of England and the Midlands.

Using its broadband network, TeleWest delivers a wide variety of cable television and telephony services to its customers: 44 television channels, including most channels available on satellite and some channels unique to cable, as well as BBC, ITV and Channel 4. Cable exclusive channels include Wire TV-The Cable Network, Travel, Channel One and the Parliamentary Channel (which offers live coverage of the House of Commons). A number of FM radio stations are also carried. TeleWest also offers telephony services to both residential and business customers.

The income-divide over the main businesses (1994 figures) is:
- cable television   50 per cent
- telephony residential 33 per cent
- telephony business   12 per cent
- other   5 per cent

In this burgeoning business, growth figures from year to year are predictably high. Revenue from cable television rose 73 per cent in 1994 as both the number of subscribers increased (up 50 per cent) and the average monthly revenue per subscriber (up 3.7 per cent). In residential telephony the number of subscribers rose 130 per cent, pushing revenue up 108 per cent and in business telephony revenue was up 80 per cent with both penetration figures and the average number of lines per client improving.

Strategy and management

The companies that will be the big players in this industry will as much as any other company have to get the basics right: to deliver good service, to generate substantial value for the customer, to adapt to and with the customer's needs and continually look for ways to improve things.

On top of that this industry requires the strategic awareness of a chess-player as at present not all players are allowed the same moves and things will change dramatically once the other side is reached.

In the near term the company's primary focus is:
. to improve operations and customer service
. to construct the network in a cost effective manner

TeleWest believes that maintaining and improving the level of customer service is critical to its success. All new employees attend 'Quality Customer First' training to provide them with 'the techniques, along with the authority and sense of responsibility, both to satisfy and exceed customers' needs and expectations'. In 1994 the company installed a new subscriber management system and expanded customer service operations, allowing subscribers to reach a customer service representative 24 hours a day, 7 days a week.

The company is also proving to be innovative in its marketing and sales approach. Besides through the usual direct-sales forces, TeleWest is reaching new customers through telemarketing and sales from retail stores. Forty-four Granada and Dixons retail stores in the London South, Avon and Scotland franchises are already marketing TeleWest services.

The content of the programming offered on its cable television is of obvious importance. The company continuously extends the number and range of channels available to subscribers. In 1994 it added travel, children's, local news and sports channels and in 1995 is expected to open the promising European Business News, a pay-per-view movie service and a video games channel: the Sega Channel.

The aim of controlling the costs of constructing the network is proving successful. Costs are effectively controlled by fixed price contracts with per metre rates for all excavation work. Tight management of these costs has allowed capital expenditure per subscriber and line to drop from 1993 on 1994 by two per cent.

In the longer-term strategy of the company three main points can be discerned:
. obtaining critical mass
. expandable broadband capacity
. cooperate to develop new services/markets

The most critical aspect of the longer-term strategy for TeleWest is size. It is essential to acquire critical mass in this industry to compete effectively. A larger cable company can:

. operate with increased purchasing power
. spread selling and administrative expenses over a larger franchise base
. reduce telephony interconnect costs (more inter-franchise connections)
. strengthen marketing through national strength and local presence
. attempt to develop industry standards

TeleWest aims to be able to upgrade its network with minimal additional capital expenditure. By bringing fibre optical cables into groupings of 500 homes the network's capacity is ready for services that require higher bandwidth such as the interactive and demand services. As the need for broader bandwidths increases in the future, the current investment in state-of-the-art technology will pay off.

In May 1995 TeleWest, together with Bell Cablemedia and NYNEX CableComms, announced a plan for an interactive multimedia services trial, in order to be at the forefront of the development of On-Demand multimedia broadband services and the creation of the industry's standards. Chief executive Alan Michels commented on the agreement:

'This agreement is a major step in the maturing of the UK cable industry. Not only does it signal a new level of co-operation between the cable operators, but it could lead to new developments in the quality and scope of services we will be able to provide to our customers. It will also provide exciting opportunities for UK content providers for creating innovative and popular new products.'

The future

The industry of providing telecommunication and entertainment services through broadband networks is at the start of an exceedingly exciting period. Up to the new millennium a period of trench-digging, strategic position-taking and generic development may be expected. Into the first decade the players will have to prove themselves to be counted among those stayers that will see part of the rest of the century.

TeleWest has a lot to bring to the party, and it isn't waiting for the future to happen, it wants to bring the future to as many British homes as possible.

‖‖‖‖‖
TESCO

Tesco, Herts

Tesco is Britain's biggest supermarket retailer

Outlook:
Tesco's future is golden. It is the largest supermarket operator and the most innovative business in the sector. The store development programme will slow down and so it will need to reinvest to a smaller degree. Therefore the group will be a net generator of cash and is likely to enhance its current high profitability

Scorecard:

Structural flexibility	★★★★★
Innovative power	★★★★★
International orientation	★★★★
Human resources	★★★★★
Growth markets	★★★★★
Quality of management	★★★★

Key figures:

Sales	£10.1 billion
Pre-tax profits	£595 million
Staff	130,000

Tesco Stores Limited
Tesco House
PO Box 18 Delamere Road
Cheshunt
Herts EN8 9FL
Tel: 01992 632222
Fax: 01992 630794

Tesco

The supermarket, the retail powerhouse of the second half of the 20th century, shows few signs of running out of steam. In the hands of Britain's best food retailers, the original concept of a self-service store has continually evolved to meet the changing needs (and increased mobility) of consumers. The large, out-of-town superstores that have sprung up across the country during the last 15 years offer consumers a choice of food and quality standards almost unimaginable a generation ago.

It is commonplace to say that the rise and rise of the supermarket has forced out of business thousands of small independent butchers, bakers and grocers. According to figures from Taylor Nelson AGB, since 1973 the supermarket groups have increased their share of the total grocery trade from 50 per cent to more than 80 per cent.

Nearly half of that 80 per cent lies in the hands of two companies - Tesco and J Sainsbury - the undoubted victors of fierce competition in the food sector. The number of substantial supermarket groups has dwindled as several of the big two's competitors have fallen by the wayside. Even major rivals such as ASDA, now reinvigorated under new management, have run into serious financial troubles.

In the early 1990s, Tesco was criticised for being slow to trim the huge store-building programme which was the main engine for its growth throughout the previous decade. But it is wise to keep these stockmarket-driven worries in perspective. By most measures, Tesco remained a remarkably successful company.

With the help of a series of marketing initiatives, Tesco has recently overhauled Sainsbury to become Britain's largest grocer. According to Taylor Nelson AGB, it has around 20.5 per cent of the combined market for fresh food, packaged goods and toileteries, putting it marginally ahead of Sainsbury.

Operations and markets

In the 1994-95 financial year, Tesco made pretax profits of £595 million on sales of £10.1 billion. To put this in perspective, ten years ago the group was making profits of £81 million on £3 billion of sales. Tesco operates from 519 stores - around 300 less than it ran in the 1970s. The crucial difference, of course, is that the new stores are much bigger, typically 30,000-45,000 square feet - ten times the size of many shops closed in the 1970s.

The huge building programmes undertaken by Tesco and its leading rivals transformed the shape of food retailing. Since 1980, the combined market share of Tesco and Sainsbury has risen from 26 to 40 per cent of the grocery trade. The latest company to fall victim to the fierce competition was William Low, the Scottish supermarket group. Tesco bought Low in 1994 for £257 million, after fighting off a rival offer from Sainsbury.

Besides Sainsbury, Tesco's other major rivals are Argyll, which owns Safeway, ASDA and Somerfield, formerly Gateway. Kwik Save has also made big strides through its policy of discounting on a smaller range of lines. Improved information technology and distribution systems have allowed Tesco and its rivals to release space previously required for warehousing. This has enabled an assault on selected non-food markets - newspapers and magazines, books, videos and music. Further moves into non- food areas are expected.

The group has started to look further afield, with its first overseas acquisitions. Tesco has bought Catteau, which trades as Cedico from 105 stores in northern France, mainly in a belt between Lille and Calais. Catteau contributed profits of £16 million in 1994 on sales of £430 million. Tesco also owns a 57 per cent stake in Global, which operates 44 small supermarkets in north-west Hungary. Global has already opened the first store under the Tesco name.

Strategy and management

Tesco was famously built on the 'pile it high and sell it cheap' philosophy of the company's founder, Sir Jack Cohen. But the birth of the modern Tesco and the origins of its current thinking can be traced back to Operation Check-out in 1977.

Tesco was hampered by a downmarket image, reinforced by its small cluttered stores, their windows festooned by day-glo stickers. Individual store managers were able to buy stock and set prices locally. And too much of the company's marketing had become dependent on the offer of Green Shield stamps, further undermining its price competitiveness.

With Operation Check-out, Tesco jettisoned Green Shield stamps, adopted a new red and white trading style and launched a price war by offering a wide range of price cuts. Check-out produced dramatic increases in sales, but, more importantly still, it reinvigorated management. Buying, pricing and much else were centralised. Clear directions were given on store layout, what goods to sell and how to display them.

The more coherent Tesco that emerged was much better equipped to challenge Sainsbury on quality. It started to exploit its buying power to dictate terms to its suppliers and to insist on its own standards of quality control.

In common with its rivals, Tesco then embarked on the huge store building programme that was the dominant feature of food retailing in the 1980s. The move to large out-of-town and edge-of-town superstores allowed the leading super-market groups to capture a large chunk of market share from (particularly) independent and Co-operative grocers.

Advances in information technology and distribution skills have allowed Tesco to stock an ever-widening range of food.

By the early 1990s, Tesco was opening 800,000 square feet (or about 20 superstores) a year in the face of growing planning objections and fears of market saturation. At the same time, economic recession put supermarkets under increased price pressure, checking the rise in margins. The company was criticised for being slow to adapt to the changing conditions, and for paying too much for land in a depressed property market. The group finally recognised the problem by starting to depreciate its land and property values in 1993-94.

Having secured its place at the top of the food retailing pile, Tesco is expanding into the non-food sector. It has quickly established a significant position in petrol retailing, an area where it is likely to expand further. Electronic point of sale equipment and automatic ordering have reduced the amount of stock stores have to carry, freeing space for the the sale of newspapers, magazines, books and videos.

Tesco's senior management team has shown remarkable stability. Chairman Sir Ian MacLaurin became managing director of the company as far back as 1973, having originally been recruited by Sir Jack Cohen in 1959. David Malpas, Tesco's present managing director, has been with the group since 1966 and a member of the board since 1979.

Sir Ian is expected to retire from executive responsibilities in 1997. The heir apparent is Terry Leahy, the former managing director who has taken credit for the initiatives that have brought about a resurgence in Tesco in the last couple of years. These include the introduction of Tesco Value, a range of cheap goods in no-frills packaging, and the recently launched Clubcard scheme.

Tesco is committed to developing the talents of its staff through sound management and training practices. The company's enlightened approach dates from Operation Check-out, which demonstrated the need to develop a team of professional managers.

Staff are encouraged to use their own ideas and common sense to serve customers better through the First Class Service training initiative. The company continually stresses the need to listen and respond to its customers' needs. Its head office receives 35,000 comments about its business each year. Further soundings are taken via customer panels, where management invites along a group of customers to give their views on their own Tesco store. Customer comments and criticism provide the stimulus for future improvements.

Tesco cites its recent 'One in Front' service as a good example of its ability to respond to customers. Unsurprisingly, they found customers were unhappy about lengthy queues at the checkout. Tesco has consequently reduced checkout queues by 45 per cent.

Faced with continued opposition to new out-of-town superstores and tougher planning restrictions, Tesco has successfully experimented with new trading formats. It has introduced Tesco Metro to trade from prime city centre sites. These stores, of around 12,000 square feet, concentrate on fresh food and other high-margin offerings.

Another innovation which has had an immediate and big impact on Tesco's performance is the introduction of its Clubcard in February 1995. Clubcard encourages customer loyalty by awarding them points that convert into money-off vouchers. Although the potential savings are modest, Tesco quickly signed up five million members. This encouraged a remarkable burst of sales growth, and seems to have been the main force behind Tesco overtaking Sainsbury's market share for the first time in more than ten years. Although the scheme was derided by rivals as 'electronic Green Shield stamps', other groups quickly began testing their own loyalty cards.

The future

Tesco has been nimble on its feet in the changed retail climate of the 1990s. While Tesco's mammoth store opening programme is not coming to an end, it has been cut back. As a consequence, the company is about to become a huge generator of cash. With its UK position so secure, further expansion in mainland Europe will assume a high priority. Tesco recently acquired businesses in northern France and the Hungary area. These are presently trivial in the context of group profits, but will be the springboard for further development outside the UK.

3i Group plc, London

The UK's largest investment/venture capital house, 3i is also the oldest provider of finance outside the banking sector. It is renowned for the thoroughness of its investment approach and its long term commitment to industry

Outlook:

The emphasis in this sector will continue to be on the quality of investment decisions and 3i's commercial understanding and the rigour of its financing decisions will favour the company's development. The quality of its management and the breadth of expertise are key factors in its continued market leadership

<u>Scorecard:</u>

Structural flexibility	★★★
Innovative power	★★★★
International orientation	★★★★
Human resources	★★★
Growth markets	★★★★
Quality of management	★★★★★

<u>Key figures:</u>

Net assets	£2.05 billion
Pre-tax profits	£257.7 million
UK staff	595
Total investment assets	£3.25 billion

3i Group plc
91 Waterloo Road
London SE1 8XP
Tel: 0171 928 3131
Fax: 0171 928 0058

Investors In Industry, 3i

The concept of a large business which operates with the flexibility of a small enterprise seems to be spreading. One of the role models for the idea is Investors In Industry, now known as 3i. It extends considerable operating autonomy to its offices inside a framework which dictates investment policy, business approach and target return or profitability.

3i is one of the oldest venture capital houses in the UK and is British market leader. Depending on measure - number of deals or size of transaction - it commands around 35 per cent of the industry here. Below 3i, the sector is highly fragmented. Its nearest rival is NatWest Ventures which is substantially smaller than 3i. The company operates from 18 locations in the UK including its trim headquarters opposite Waterloo station in London. Some 80 per cent of its business is conducted in Britain - with the vast majority of overseas investments on the European mainland or in the US. Around 40 per cent of investments go to manufacturing industry. Distributors come next in the pecking order followed by other services providers.

This is a company with a formidable reputation for its skills in selecting new businesses for investment. Whatever the fluctuations in the economy 3i's capacity for accurate, early identification of the winners of the future remains undiminished. Its longevity owes much to the clarity of its purpose and the culture's resilience in communicating its core approach to successive generations of corporate talent spotters. 3i has a singular capacity for getting its core business messages across internally. Perhaps this is, in part, because 3i rarely brings in new blood fresh from academia but usually cherry-picks from business and the professions.

Operations and markets

This company is an innovator with clear empathy for the most effective solutions for the development of businesses. It is a leading protagonist for management buy-outs, management buy-ins and start-ups. 3i's investment portfolio includes both equity and non-equity deals. KPMG's equity deal league table published in the Financial Times in October 1994 recorded that in the previous year the company handled 17 deals compared with eight by NatWest Ventures. 3i invested £346 million whereas its nearest rival contributed £223 million.

According to the same sources, 3i commands 35 per cent of the large MBO market in the UK - these are the deals in excess of £10 million per investment. In 1993, 3i also handled 24.5 per cent of all management buy-ins - a third of all large MBIs and a quarter of all those under £10 million each.

The proven success of the 3i formula in the United Kingdom was the springboard for excursions into corporate investment abroad. The 20 per cent of overall investment which is presently invested in international developments is broadly split into:
. mainland Europe - slightly less than two-thirds
. US - slightly less than one-third
. Pacific Rim - the remainder

Neil Cross, executive director for international investment, anticipates that the ratio of overall revenue international/domestic will move in favour of external results, while income from both sources will increase.

The US excursion, while profitable, was not the substantial victory which the company had hoped for and 3i is consequently winding down its participation in the United States. Continental Europe is, in contrast, performing excellently. Finance for mainland markets - which follows and adapts 3i's domestic policy to each market - comes from two sources:

. directly from 3i

. indirectly from a European investment fund set up and managed by 3i but where the company is a part investor (30 per cent)

The international operation currently has offices in Boston, Paris, Lyon, Frankfurt, Milan, Madrid and Barcelona, and affiliates in Australia, Japan, India, and the Netherlands.

Strategy and management

3i exemplifies balance. It matches long term investment strategy with short term profitability. It seeks balance in its portfolio and within each of its investee companies. The executive board of 3i is a jigsaw of qualities and professional disciplines which have shaped an adversarial, demanding, intelligent and experience-dominated approach to management. This clinical - and deeply researched - analysis of business opportunities omits one salient factor. After all their investigation and skilful measurement of candidates, the 3i directors and managers possess one other quality - instinct. With years of extensive experience in a broad catchment of industrial sectors, the company's professional staff can sniff a potential corporate success within minutes of crossing the threshold of an applicant's offices.

And investment is something which 3i is extremely good at. It has consistently achieved sustained and improved profit performance from a portfolio of investments, regardless of the vagaries of economic conditions. A glance through the list of companies which have enjoyed 3i's input over the years shows a creditable assembly. 3i's latest full year figures show £2 billion in shareholder funds and a growth in revenue profit before tax of 42 per cent to £50.5 million.

John Platt, executive director for investment in the UK regions, puts the success of 3i's investment policy down to the rigour of its approach in selecting candidates for inclusion in the portfolio, the depth of commercial experience of its staff, its innovation with new products and the matching of risk-taking and return in its culture. The mechanics of the approach are straightforward:

. local teams identify investment candidates. Business executives interview prospects and assess the quality of management, business plans and soundness of the commercial concept.

. central departments assess the proposition. The 30-strong industry department, which is based in the West Midlands, draws on people of substantial business and sectoral experience. They utilise all their resources to assess whether the proposal stacks up in functional terms. Accounting and legal teams support in evaluation and implementation.

. the executive approves the investment. Local teams prepare each proposition and the larger of these, by value, are then put forward at twice-weekly sessions of the executive team. The majority, however, are approved locally.

Chief executive Ewen Macpherson: 'One of the issues I wanted to deal with when I took over as chief executive three years ago was the market perception of the company. I wanted 3i to be recognised as one of the most respected businesses in Britain.'

The multiple results of this commitment were organised into the two-year MAC enhancement programme, built around the nine areas identified in the Economist 'Most Admired Company' initiative. The aim of this approach was to boost external awareness of 3i among 30,000 key individuals who were identified as outside influences on 3i's future wellbeing. Several factors emerged as important building blocks in this improvement and awareness-enhancement initiative. One was listing the business on the London Stock Exchange.

This exercise was completed in summer 1994 and was useful because as well as raising 3i's positioning it also had tax benefits. 'We are now the second smallest company in the FT-SE 100 in terms of personnel - 500 in 18 UK offices - but one of the most profitable,' he comments. 'We believe that flotation clarified impressions about us. Some people had the idea that we were either a government department or quango. This probably stems from the fact that we were originally created by the clearing banks after a government committee identified a gap in the market for a venture capital provider. This conclusion - referred to as the Macmillan gap, after the committee - was plugged but it left a residual idea that somehow we were a public sector agency.'

Before listing 3i needed to renegotiate its tax status with the Inland Revenue. 'This has always previously been a bar to us going to the market. The relevant element of this was our exposure to capital gains tax after flotation. Here we secured a significant favourable decision - but it involved a considerable amount of time and effort persuading the Inland Revenue to see the issue from our perspective.'

The future

With expansion coming from increasing activities outside of the UK and also in making investment decisions for large pools of institutional investors, 3i will have sufficient organic growth to become a significant influence in the UK economy in the years to come.

3M, Bracknell, Berks

3M the Minnesota Mining and Manufacturing Company produces products in a wide variety of markets including healthcare, office materials, reflective material, tape, abrasives and protectives.

Outlook:
3M has long been a standard bearer for best practice in industry. It seeks to derive 30 per cent of sales from products introduced in the previous four years. The company is respected throughout the global business community for its quality of management, commitment to innovation, strong human resources approach and knowledge of markets

Scorecard:

Structural flexibility	★★★★★
Innovative power	★★★★★
International orientation	★★★★★
Human resources	★★★★★
Growth markets	★★★★★
Quality of management	★★★★★

Key figures:

Global sales (1995)	$15 billion
UK sales (1995)	£667 million
Global staff	85,000
UK staff	4,400

3M UK plc
3M House
Market Place
Bracknell Berks R12 1JU
Tel: 01344 858000
Fax: 01344 858278

3M

Few companies can claim that every year more than 30 per cent of their sales come from products which did not exist four years earlier. 3M can, and it has made this target a tenet of faith of its corporate objectives. The 3M 30 per cent challenge - as it is known - is the way in which the company measures the success of its continuous innovation policy.

But corporate goals are subject to as much change as its products. Until 1993, the goal was set at 25 per cent of sales from products introduced in the last five years. Many organisations would regard this as excessive. However, 3M as the innovator personified regarded this as insufficient and the company increased the target to reflect higher levels of competitiveness in its markets.

3M is often the subject of case studies and is cited in the commercial press as a definitive example of a coherently managed business which aims to exceed expectations. Companies worldwide use 3M as a benchmark standard in every area of its operation. The company sets itself the objective of benchmarking against the world's best, and aims for a cycle of excellent renewal.

Operations and markets

3M was founded in the US in 1902 as the Minnesota Mining and Manufacturing Company. Mining was dropped quickly and the company began the manufacture of the world's first waterproof sandpaper. From there it began to expand into other markets. In 1925 it invented masking tape, which revolutionised the auto-refinishing business and in 1930 the first all-purpose sticky tape such as is now commonly used in schools, homes and offices. In 1953 its Scotch Weld structural adhesives replaced rivets in aircraft manufacture with a lightweight durable glue.

Since then the company has introduced the first commercially acceptable magnetic audio tape in the 1940s, the first video tapes in the 1950s, the first photocopiers in the 1960s and the first computer tapes. The company seeks to harness as many technologies as possible as it develops different products. For example, 3M produces more than 900 different varieties of pressure-sensitive adhesive tape alone. Its adhesives stick side panels to bus chassis, fillings to teeth and Post-It notes to VDU screens.

3M employs 85,000 people worldwide, and manufactures more than 60,000 products covering a wide range from Post-It notes to pharmaceuticals, abrasives, adhesive tapes, respirators, and carpet and fabric protectors. Any short form description of 3M's product classifications fails to do justice to the extent of the portfolio. 3M's first expansion outside the US was into the UK in 1929. Today it employs 4,500 people in 18 locations throughout the UK and Ireland with an annual turnover of more than £600 million.

Strategy and management

Many companies aspire to be known as innovative but 3M has been ahead of the field for the best part of a century. In a sense, it represents a working example of the science, theory and practice of innovation. Its philosophy is that 3M has a single, simple aim and that is a desire to find new ways to make things better. What takes its innovation beyond any gimmickry is that 3M is always seeking a commercial application.

If innovation is a main contributor to its success, another is quality. 3M's commitment to total quality dates from 1979. Its approach is defined by four essentials: 'measuring quality by customer satisfaction, meeting customer expectations all the time, continuous improvement by building in quality at source, and finally driving quality through management commitment'.

Management identifies certain basic disciplines and specifications as key to the production of quality products and services. Each of its manufacturing locations in Europe has achieved ISO 9002 quality standard and it expects all new acquisitions to meet the same target. All suppliers to 3M must conform to effective and audited quality assurance systems. 3M uses more than 110 different technologies to support and make products for industrial, commercial, healthcare and consumer markets worldwide. Management stresses that these belong not to any individual division, but to the company, and hence are available for all teams to use. The success of this approach is undeniable. Some of 3M's most important lines have been generated by the application and combination of technologies across different operations and businesses within the company.

All the ideas are driven by its customers and 3M takes pride in a culture of close co-operation between itself and its customers. Listening to customers' problems - as a standard procedure - helps it to respond quickly to perceived demand in markets, often adapting or bringing together some of its existing technologies. Examples of this are its scent-trapping technology used by magazines to market perfumes - a process called encapsulation. This is an extension of the principles behind carbonless copy paper - also invented by 3M.

During the depth of the recession sales grew only two per cent which encouraged observers to question the quality of its R&D machine. The company's response has been to revolutionise the product development process - in some cases scaling down the time it takes to introduce new products to less than three years. The shift of emphasis from pure research into product development has been reflected in an upswing in financial performance.

In part this has been achieved by inverting the process by which research is translated into new products. In the past 3M's research efforts produced a mass of technology before its teams considered possible commercial applications. By bringing research and marketing teams together, and shifting the emphasis to customers' appetites, it now takes a more pragmatic approach to new product innovation.

There is a genuine joy in innovation and invention in 3M. It has always been willing to invest in research for its own sake - for 'the happy outcomes which emerge from the most unpromising of starts'. This will not change. It encourages individuals to be responsible for their own actions. This is written into the 3M constitution, which was written as long ago as 1941: 'Those men and women to whom we delegate authority and responsibility, if they are good people, are going to want to do things their own way.' That and the ability to think laterally has generated some real surprises, usually through the cross-fertilisation of ideas. For example, the Buf-Puf skin cleansing pad evolved from its Nomad floor coverings which are designed to catch dirt before it spreads through a building.

3M recognises that the creative process is not without mistakes. 'If a person is essentially right, the mistakes he or she makes are not as serious in the long run as the mistakes management makes if it is dictatorial and undertakes to tell those under its authority exactly how they must do the job. Management which is destructively critical when mistakes are made kills initiative. It is essential that we have many people with initiative if we are to grow.'

3M estimates that it spends around twice as much as its rivals, close to $3.5 billion in the last five years, on research and development. Through this commitment, 3M has developed a wide range of new technologies in fields as diverse as membranes, biotechnology, micro-replication, artificial intelligence, systems integration and super-conductors.

This company was among the first to make the environment a policy issue. As well as the beneficial effect of the products it has developed, it has also generated considerable cost savings. Since 1992 3M employees have submitted more than 4,000 ideas on how to cut waste and recycle material, which have created more than $710 million in savings. Its 3M performance fluids were an early response to the threat to the ozone layer. Light Water foam creates a film which smothers fires and can put out an uncapped well fire in minutes. Other products contain chemical spillages, work the respirators used by rescue workers and filter exhaust fumes and air pollution out of cars.

The future

Since 1992 the company has improved customer service and logistics in its European operation. The goal was to quicken its response to customer needs, requirements and service times. Thus far it has promoted efficiency gains via fewer warehouses (cut from 24 to only five by the end of 1995) and rationalisation of its corporate structure. This initiative has improved inventory management, delivery times and product range availability and should save more than $80 million a year in fixed costs.

Another important step forward is the introduction of EUROMS 2, its new Europe-wide, computer-driven order management system. Originally developed to handle orders from one 3M company to another, a new customer-focused system has been assembled from a series of separate building blocks across Europe.

As ever, this approach is customer-driven. Market research showed that change was urgently required if it were to stay ahead. It needed to enhance delivery times, increase the range of stock immediately available and offer a pan-European service to those customers looking to take a regional direction to business.

3M scores very highly in our survey of companies of the future because it is inventive, shrewdly managed and forward looking.

Group

Tibbett & Britten, Enfield, Middlesex

Tibbett & Britten is the UK's largest distribution company

Outlook:
Increasingly, companies are looking to outsource their non-core functions to specialist suppliers. Contract distribution is a prime example and T&B is a market leader in this growth sector. It provides distribution services to many of Britain's largest retailers and is highly innovative in its approach to serving its markets

Scorecard:
Structural flexibility	★★★★
Innovative power	★★★★★
International orientation	★★★
Human resources	★★★★
Growth markets	★★★★★
Quality of management	★★★★

Key figures:
Turnover	£650 million (annualised)
Pre-tax profits	£27 million (1994)
Staff	16,500
Turnover UK	£300 million
UK staff	10,000

Tibbett & Britten Group plc
Ross House
1 Shirley Road
Windmill Hill, Enfield
Middlesex EN2 6SB
Tel: 0181 367 9955
Fax: 0181 366 7042

Tibbett & Britten Ltd

Tibbett & Britten's (T&B) executive chairman John Harvey is on a mission. His aim is to build the UK-based distribution group, currently valued at £220m, into an internationally acknowledged leader in supply chain management. Judging by T&B's rapid growth in recent years, there's every chance he'll succeed. And his cause will be aided by the fact that contract logistics is an undisputed growth business. Estimates suggest the UK market will grow at an overall compound rate of eight per cent in the next three years, while Europe and North America are tipped to expand at an even faster rate.

T&B has demonstrated it has the capacity to exploit these trends. Since its stockmarket launch in 1986, T&B's annual revenues have increased more than tenfold to £464m and pre-tax profits over the same period have risen from £3.38m to £26.9m.

Operations and markets

T&B provides distribution, logistical support, 'added value' services and the management of international supply chains for some of the world's major retailers and blue chip manufacturers. It focuses on; fast-moving consumer-good sectors such as clothing and textiles; cosmetics and personal products; groceries and food; and do-it-yourself and electrical products.

In 1992 it acquired Silcock Express Holdings, adding motors to the range of business sectors it covers. That deal was followed by last year's £16.4m purchase of vehicle distributor Toleman. The two companies have now been merged as Axial Holdings Ltd and T&B is now able to claim over a fifth of the UK car distribution market.

The company's impressive client base reads like a Who's Who in business. It includes such heavyweights as Marks & Spencer, Unilever, J Sainsbury, Ford, SmithKline Beecham, Perrier, IBM, Johnson & Johnson and Wal-Mart.

T&B has a market presence in 15 countries spanning four continents, employs some 16,000 people and has 16m sq. ft. of warehousing and 4,700 vehicles and trailers. Last year it delivered an estimated 459m garments and 340m cases of food and grocery products. Not bad for a company that in 1969 operated just 10 vehicles.

Strategy and management

Attracting customers of a high calibre is central to T&B's strategy which emphasises trust and partnership with clients. In practice, this is how that works: having forged a close relationship with a company in one country, for example Unilever, T&B hopes to build on that by undertaking additional work for the same customer in different geographical markets.

Around 90 per cent of the company's revenue is derived from contractual or dedicated operations and though UK revenues represented some 67 per cent of group turnover in 1994, its overseas activities are growing rapidly. Last year, T&B's international division grew its turnover by £53.6m to £94.2m and operating profits more than quadrupled to £3m. Given that T&B has a number two position in the UK with a seven per cent share - it trails NFC (17 per cent) but leads Christian Salvesen (five per cent) and Hays (five per cent) - its domestic growth prospects are limited.

Overseas markets, however, provide the company with rich expansion opportunities and this is another important element of T&B's strategy.

After a string of deals and strategic joint ventures, T&B has gained a strategic footing in some big overseas markets. The Silcock acquisition considerably strengthened its position in Belgium, France, Portugal and Spain. Through alliances with other international companies T&B has moved into Germany and Austria while it has a more established presence in markets like South Africa and Canada.

In 1994, T&B generated particularly strong growth in Canada. The company won big contracts with Alberta Liquor Control Board, Neilson Dairies, Oshawa Group and Wal-Mart. Expanding into the US was an obvious next step and T&B entered the country in the summer of 1995.

Unveiling its 1994 annual results in March 1995, T&B said that more than 60 per cent of its £464m in turnover was attributable to organic growth. International operations made a substantial progress and contributed half the additional revenue. There was one note of caution in the results statement. T&B's operating margin fell from 6.6 to 5.7 per cent, though this mainly reflected a number of one-off problems. They included a disappointing performance from the fashion logistics' network, exceptional costs associated with resolving an industrial dispute over working practices at a Lancashire depot as well as a late downturn in performance at Axial.

With strong cash flow, T&B's gearing level of 49 per cent (net debt of £37.1m as a percentage of £75.3m in net assets) is no cause for concern. Indeed T&B is set for another year of high capital expenditure in 1995 and the company's finance director Mike Stalbow forecasts that gearing could rise to over 60 per cent. Given T&B's financial might, he's comfortable with that level, as are City analysts who follow the company.

Mr Harvey reckons the contract logistics market is a $185bn global business, with the UK accounting for about $8bn. 'We have a European lead in terms of the expertise, maturity and development of our market, and we are translating rather than transferring our skills overseas. I think it has become fairly clear that growth both in the UK and overseas varies by sector but the total picture is one still of a market that is growing.'

Eleven companies control roughly 50 per cent of the UK logistics market. Mr Harvey believes that situation is putting pressure on market players to perform more efficiently. 'There's a premium on performance in the future, so there is a lot of innovation going on even within the existing contract logistics market.'

'We live in an environment of contractual sophistication. We've learned a lot, our customers have learned a lot, the contracts today are a lot more demanding and sophisticated than they were five, seven years ago.'

He predicts that T&B together with perhaps three other companies will take an increasingly large share of the UK market as the logistics industry continues to concentrate.

T&B's business is managed on an individual unit/site basis within the framework of five operating companies: Tibbett & Britten Clothing, Textile & Soft Goods (UK & Pan-European clothing operation); Tibbett & Britten Consumer Group (UK & Pan-European FMCG operations); Tibbett & Britten International ; Tibbett & Britten North America; and Axial (automotive).

Each unit has its own annual budget, monthly reporting and variance analysis and quarterly updating. The company works within a three year strategic planning horizon against a rolling medium-term plan. 'The management is deemed the company's prime asset', says T&B's corporate profile document. The bulk of the company's managers are either shareholders and/or option holders. Indeed directors and employees hold approximately 25 per cent of the company's shares.

That is a very high percentage for a company of T&B's size and is an obvious performance-incentiviser for both management and staff.

The company's board is a 'cohesive executive unit' with most members having worked together for many years. 'We have been fortunate in holding together a widely experienced and high calibre team whose talent and background have been the foundation of the rapid growth and development of the business,' the company says.

Most board members and senior managers have professional and graduate qualifications and many have joined from directional and senior positions elsewhere in the distribution industry. The company has maintained a graduate recruitment and development programme, taking about fifteen each year, plus a variable number of MBAs.

In more recent years, T&B has targeted people from across the distribution and retail sectors. For nearly ten years it has been the company's policy to build and diversify from the original clothing business across a wider customer base, developing in specific market sectors and from 1989 to translate that experience in overseas markets.

'To achieve these strategic objectives it is our practice to deliberately over-recruit management to provide the resource to support the growth strategy. Furthermore, a central group development and planning unit is maintained to support international tendering and project development and to reinforce the divisional development teams handling organic growth within the operating companies,' T&B says.

The future

John Harvey is unequivocal on his vision for T&B. 'The group has achieved twelve consecutive years of growth. We believe it will continue to develop successfully. Effective supply chain management has become a critical component of both manufacturing and retailing strategies and this has gained emphasis from the advancement of global sourcing and trans-national manufacturing strategies across the new common market and free trade areas. Contract logistics is a growth sector and this, together with the group's recent contract successes, gives me confidence that there is abundant opportunity for future development within the UK, continental Europe and internationally.'

Unilever

Unilever, London

An Anglo-Dutch conglomerate, specialist in brands of packaged foods and goods

Outlook
With strong presences in the mature markets of Europe and North America, Unilever is looking towards the high growth markets in the rest of the world for its growth in the next decades. Its excellent financial position, strong local presence and ability to generate cash in every phase of a developing economy point towards a future in the new worlds that could easily match its track record in the old

Scorecard:

Structural flexibility	★★★★
Innovative power	★★★★
International orientation	★★★★★
Human resources	★★★★
Growth markets	★★★★★
Quality of management	★★★★

Key figures:

Europe turnover	£16,322 million
Global turnover	£31,516 million
UK staff	21,300
Global staff	304,000
European operating profit	£1,262 million
Global operating profit	£2,526 million

Unilever House
PO Box 68
London EC4P PBQ
Tel: 0171 8225252
Fax: 0171 8225754

Unilever

Even people who haven't heard of Unilever the company will still probably have used one or two of its branded products. More than half of the world's population are regular customers of Unilever plc/nv - the Anglo-Dutch giant that invents, makes and markets branded foods and goods for households around the globe.

The company that came forth from yet another marriage between a Dutch and an English company ranks consistently in the Top 20 of the Fortune 500 list of the world's industrial companies both in terms of sales and net profits. During the coming years Unilever's main strategic focus will be on investing in what are now still considered developing markets. But the phrase 'developing markets' may soon lose its validity as chairman Sir Michael Perry suggests in his strategic review: 'The so-called developing countries are expected to overtake us in the "West" well before the turn of the century. Within ten years they will have left us trailing in their wake.' Unilever has been quick to gain footholds in new markets as they opened up such as China and Eastern Europe and although it remains committed to its other markets it is fully focusing on these 'new' regions for the company's future growth.

Operations and markets

The greater part of Unilever's business is in branded and packaged goods, primarily foods, detergents and personal products. Over 1,000 brands - of which many are market-leaders - are marketed by Unilever companies worldwide. The group's other major activity is in speciality chemicals.

Packaged food and drinks account for over half of Unilever's sales and have developed from the original business of edible fats in the Netherlands in the late 19th century to now include leading brands in margarine, ice cream, packaged teas, pasta sauces and frozen foods. The detergents and personal products divisions originated with William Lever's soap factory in the UK and today include such famous names as Jif, Omo and Lux as well as Signal toothpaste and Pond's skin care products.

Although Unilever is seen as typically a consumer products company, it has a segment of its detergent division that supplies to industrial users in over 40 countries and the speciality chemicals division which - initially set up to ensure high quality supplies of chemicals for its own manufacturing processes - provides these chemicals to industrial customers throughout the world. Unilever divides its operations into three main areas: Europe, North America and the rest of the world. In 1994 around 53 per cent of sales were in Europe, 20 per cent in North America and 27 per cent in the rest of the world.

Two recent trends in the UK - often depicted as threats to companies such as Unilever - are the rise of private labels and the increasing levels of ownership concentration in retail. The private labels do form a threat to poorly performing brands, as shown in the UK where in most categories anything but the No. 1 and No. 2 brands have been effectively eliminated by the best private labels. However, retailers will not be able to provide the focus, specialisation and continuous innovation required to produce the No. 1 or 2 brand as Unilever can, particularly not in the wide range of categories that currently fill a super- or hypermarket.

Retail outlets have become more concentrated, and have seen their bargaining power rise subsequently. Although this poses obvious disadvantages for the manufacturers it can bring advantages as well - especially for top companies such as Unilever and P&G. Economies of scale can save costs, they can increase the availability of customer and market information, and make it easier to reach the customer. Strong growth in the European and North American markets will, however, become more and more difficult as these economies remain vulnerable to recessions and have low annual growth rates of GDP.

Strategy and management

Unilever adheres to certain business fundamentals which are 'common to all operating units, in all the regions of the world.' Sir Michael Perry stresses that they require continuous attention since 'none of our brands are market leaders by divine right, they are leaders because we pay constant attention to these basics, and then only if we do so more rigorously than the competitor.'

At the core, even, of these fundamentals lies a specific notion of innovation. 'It is at the heart of the process and it does not simply mean launching new products. We gain competitive advantage by innovating in all areas of our business.'

For Unilever the business fundamentals are:
. R&D - search for products that deliver superior quality and benefits to consumers
. Low-costs - drive down costs continually, and especially faster and earlier than competitors
. Marketing - effective use of advertising and promotional budgets using best creative talent
. Service - the level of service provided to customer (retail trade) is second to none

The key to Unilever's strength in research lies in its understanding of the consumer's present and future needs and the ongoing ability and commitment to meet them. High levels of investment in detailed market research in all of its markets provide a feel for the tastes and preferences of consumers. By ensuring that the functions of market research, marketing, product development and research work closely together, the company can be quite sure that it creates the products people want to buy. Expenditure on R&D has risen over the years to around two per cent of sales and Sir Michael expects this to rise even more 'as the search for competitive advantage intensifies.'

At the strategic review seminar in London in June 1995, chairman Perry presented what he sees as the need for Unilever to reflect the changes in the world ahead if it is to remain a world class business. By 2020 China will possess the largest economy in the world, and Indonesia and India will have moved into the top five: 'the phrases "rest of the world", "developing world" or "emerging markets" are close to being obsolete. Within a very short time, we in Europe and North America will be lagging further and further behind these dynamic and exciting economies. The businesses that will succeed over the coming ten years will be those that learn this lesson early.'

Unilever has already been building a strong position in these 'exciting' new markets. It is now actively expanding through investments in sales and marketing offices, production capacity, and by acquiring stakes in or full command of local companies. Total sales in the rest of the world region excluding Japan and Australasia have grown from £2.7bn in '85, to £3.3bn in '90 and £8.3bn in 1995. Important countries are China, Brazil, South Africa, Indonesia and India, countries with sizeable populations and strong economic prospects. Unilever's broad product range has the advantage of being able to service customer needs from a basic level upwards, thus allowing the company to enter and gain experience early on in a developing economy.

The European and North American businesses function as a solid platform, enabling the substantial investments into the developing world, while at the same time being an important source of technology, new product ideas and management.

Unilever's finances are in good shape, particularly if you take into consideration that unlike other companies Unilever puts no value on its brands in its balance sheet. Financial director Hans Eggerstedt claims quite confidently that: 'Unilever can contemplate any investment opportunity that may come its way.'

The people make the business. True words in a market as competitive as the world of fast moving consumer goods. But Unilever's management is skilled. As James Capel, the analysts, remark: 'we believe brands will remain vitally important, provided they have leading positions in their particular markets and are well managed. Unilever has a massive portfolio of strong market positions and, in our view, a good management team.' Developing future top management has always been Unilever's way of treating graduates. By giving people responsibility early, stimulating strong competition while providing good guidance and by recruiting from all countries, the company will always have the human resources necessary to lead in the battle for the consumer in tomorrow's world.

The future

Unilever is investing for growth and is well placed to benefit from the opportunities available around the world. It has recognised - in timely fashion - the opportunities presented by new markets and by using its strong product portfolio and management skills it has quickly developed operations in all these countries. As the markets develop and consumer demand expands into the higher quality sectors, Unilever with its considerable expertise in advertising, manufacturing and product development will easily be able to contend for the top spots in those markets.

Its strong financial position and commitment to the continuous search for the competitive edge make Unilever ready to take on any challenge. Thus, as one of the few companies that relish change and create the future rather than react to it, Unilever most certainly has a future we are going to hear about.

UNİSYS

Unisys Ltd, London

A major international computer services company, Unisys has managed the transformation from mainframe manufacturer to systems integrator more completely and effectively than many leading rivals

Outlook:
Unisys has decided to concentrate on four key markets where it can demonstrate substantial market leadership - government, financial services, transport and telecommunications - on a worldwide basis. This is a business with a clear strategic direction - as a business adviser and preferred supplier

Scorecard:

Structural flexibility	★★★★★
Innovative power	★★★★★
International orientation	★★★★★
Human resources	★★★★
Growth markets	★★★★
Quality of management	★★★★★

Key figures 1994:

Turnover (global)	$7.4 billion
Pre-tax profits	$153.2 million
Worldwide staff	46,300
UK staff	1,450

Unisys Ltd
Stonebridge Park
31 Brentfields
London NW10 8LS
Tel: 0181 9650511
Fax: 0181 9612252

Unisys

Unisys UK CEO George Cox believes that there are three factors which will determine whether a company will survive the competitive rigours of the next decade. These are: culture; processes and structure; and systems. 'It is not enough, for example, to produce excellent products. What is important is to create and sustain an environment where excellent products can be generated quickly - again and again. This is a key distinguishing factor,' he says.

This philosophy lies at the heart of Unisys. Mr Cox's perception of a market which is constantly renewing itself is particularly apt for Unisys, a business which has experienced utter transformation in a period of only five years. In 1986 the company was formed from the merger of two mainframe giants - Burroughs and Sperry. At the time of integration - it was the world's largest merger - the combine employed 120,000 people and reported global turnover of $9 billion. Today, the worldwide business brings in revenues of $7.4 billion and employs 46,300 people. It is a profoundly different company after restructuring, providing business solutions rather than solely selling hardware boxes. 'We transform businesses and government agencies by creating innovative solutions that change the way they use information,' says Mr Cox. This is now a systems integrator rather than a hardware manufacturer.

Unisys was the first of the big computer companies to hit trouble in the 1990s. For six quarters in 1990 and 1991, it endured substantial losses. At the time of merger 80 per cent of revenues were sourced from hardware sales. By the end of the eighties, customers wanted a different relationship with technology companies, and clearly the Unisys market profile had to change. Europe and Africa division communications director Martin Sexton says: 'We completely re-engineered the business. We decided to move from being a box maker to become a solutions provider. Our four principal mainframe lines were harmonised into two, and we introduced commonality of as many elements in the manufacturing process as possible. We decided that we would not try to be all things to all men. This meant concentration on four industry sectors where we had - or could easily attain - market dominance.'

Operations and markets

The four principal areas which the business concentrated on after restructuring were:
. financial services
. transportation
. telecommunications
. government

Here the company has developed a substantial presence. In financial services, for example, Unisys is supplier to 45 of the 50 largest banks in the world. Among its clients is the Co-operative Bank in the UK. Here Unisys has won a contract to handle all of the bank's cheque processing. Traditionally, banks have been dubious about engaging external suppliers to handle those areas of the business which they regard as core. But Unisys was able to demonstrate that it could offer improved efficiencies, cost savings and application of the latest - and most appropriate - technological solutions.

Iain Davidson, financial systems director for UK and Ireland, points out that the solutions strategy for the company has focused on the business requirements of retail banks, building societies, and life and pensions providers - an emphasis which pre-dated and capitalised on the current bancassurance trend. Unisys has helped NatWest set up its life subsidiary with an innovative laptop-to-open-systems solution managing the distribution and salesforce. National & Provincial Building Society uses the new Navigator solution for all customer engagement of teller and branch sales on industry-standard (UNISYS) personal computers.

Customer-facing business solutions are the heartland of the Unisys approach. 'It is one of our greatest strengths,' says Mr Sexton. A wide range of banks and building societies have brought in Unisys to implement technology solutions for the dialogue with their customers. This is in addition to the mission critical mainframes where banks cannot afford to allow mainframes to go down.

Mr Cox comments: 'banks and airlines say to us that they need technology which does not go down. For these types of organisations, if the system stops for a few minutes then the institution has a major problem, for half an hour it's a crisis, for half a day and they have gone out of business.'

The tally of clients in the transport sector is impressive. Some 140 airlines across the world employ Unisys - and every airline in Europe, apart from British Airways. BA markets its own computer solutions but recently lost a client, Mexicana Airlines, to Unisys. Telecomms is another area where Unisys has much to be proud about. Some 80 per cent of communications companies globally operate Unisys systems. All Bell Telephone companies, PTT Nederland and Hutchison Orange are three examples. In the UK BT is also a client.

Government remains a strong area for global incomes. Most US state and federal institutions operate on Unisys products, and throughout the world many government departments have selected the company as preferred supplier. Quality of service and price - as in the commercial world - are often main determinants in the choice of provider.

The UK company has always been a strong part of the group; indeed, even in the most difficult trading period it made a profit. It is the largest business in Unisys Europe and has always had a reputation for being well managed. There are 1,450 people in the British business which has its headquarters in Stonebridge Park, next to the North Circular Road in London. The European headquarters are located in Uxbridge and there is a strong contingent of teams at its Milton Keynes logistics centre. Teams handling state-of-the-art site installations for Bass Taverns - 3,500 LANs - and TSB branches - 2,500 LANs - work out of here on extremely tight deadlines.

Strategy and management

The decision to stick to four principal market sectors caused a lot of heartache because Unisys had strong client bases in other market areas. But the company did not - and does not intend to - dump clients, it preferred to concentrate on, and expand, those areas where it was strongest. In the UK, Unisys enjoys a healthy relationship with Bass which is not in a core Unisys industry but applications - in which the company is well versed - are used to solve Bass' LAN problems. In addition, as the transportation sector expands to include leisure, with clients like Bass Taverns, McDonald's and Beefeater, Unisys is well placed to serve this sector.

Unisys confidently asserts that its source of revenues will move from more than 80 per cent hardware in 1986 to 70 per cent services in the next few years. This does not mean that it will stop manufacturing - far from it. Technology is a core competence for Unisys. But the manner in which it does business and the nature of relationships with clients has shifted. Unisys has also differentiated itself from other computer manufacturers which now say that they supply business solutions. 'When we are asked by clients to solve a specific problem as an integrator, we pick the most appropriate technology regardless of who makes it. This could be Unisys but then equally it might not,' says Mr Cox.

The board of the US company had no doubts about the extent of the change it was introducing - and the implications for the business and its personnel. Many of the managers who had come to expect a job for life in the cosy world of selling mainframes received a rude awakening. Global chairman and CEO James Unruh brought in consultants and integrators. Malcolm Coster, president of Europe and Africa, used to run the Coopers and Lybrand management consultancy, which had strong IT credentials. Mr Cox was chairman of consulting and services group PE International (having previously been managing director of Butler Cox, a highly regarded IT consultancy). Stephen Carns, president of information services and systems, was the president and COO of the widely esteemed Cap Gemini America and had also served as the head of the professional services group at IBM. Alan Lutz, president of computer systems, came in from Northern Telecom.

This is one of the criteria which Mr Cox believes will differentiate successful suppliers in the years to come. The capacity to offer flexible but integrated solutions will come from businesses with sufficient experience, resources and critical mass. 'Customers need to know if a supplier has the necessary financial strength to be able to deliver on-going service in a variety of areas on a long-term basis,' he comments. These are the companies which create an environment where excellence can thrive. This is not simply the production of superb products and services but an environment where innovative solutions can be inspired and develop. Capacity also means market strength. 'Take the construction industry. We have as customers three of the top five UK construction companies - Tarmac, AMEC and Trafalgar House,' he remarks.

The future

It is easy to see the shape of the corporation which will be fit to compete successfully in the information systems integration field in the next decade, according to Mr Cox. It will be strong in the following areas: profitability, flexibility, global spread, technological knowledge and experience with the industries, and the cost-effectiness of its solutions.

Few businesses enjoy Unisys' strength in these disciplines. Its impact on the UK economy and its contribution to the development of business here is substantial. It is helping clients, in key sectors such as financial services and telecomms, to exploit the opportunities which lie ahead. This is a positive, innovative and far-seeing enterprise which stands on the threshold of an exciting future.

Vanco Euronet, Middx

Vanco Euronet manages wide area networks for companies all over Europe

Outlook:

Vanco Euronet has perceived a gap - a discontinuity in the words of its MD - for the management of WANs (wide-area networks). Vanco adds value by locating faults in networks and rectifying potential expensive faults. Vanco is the leader in this field and its technology is vastly superior to its clients' and any rivals'. Its future is promising as WANs are growing rapidly, companies derive immediate and extensive benefit from their management being outsourced, and Vanco is the standard-setter for its sector

Scorecard:

Structural flexibility	★★★★
Innovative power	★★★★★
International orientation	★★★★
Human resources	★★★
Growth markets	★★★★★
Quality of management	★★★

Key figures:

Turnover	£4 million
Pre-tax profits	£400,000
Staff	100

Vanco Euronet
John Busch House
277 London Road
Isleworth
Middlesex. TW7 5AX
Tel: 0181 - 380 1000
Fax: 0181 - 380 1001

Vanco Euronet

Every few years a seismic shift occurs in the corporate environment. The force of such changes creates numerous opportunities for new businesses to spring up and capture areas of the market which were previously unexplored. Such a movement is currently underway in telecommunications. The old state-owned national monopolies have been privatised and subjected to the stimulation of commercial competition.

The creation of a 'discontinuity' in the markets provides one of the pre-requisites for business success in the mind of Allen Timpany, chairman and managing director of Vanco Euronet. His company has been formed to manage the wide-area networks (WANs) of companies all over Europe. From a control point in Isleworth, west London, his teams monitor and manage the computer networks of companies such as Otis Elevator, Albany Life, Secure Trust Bank and North British Housing Association.

Operations and markets

Many of Vanco Euronet's clients are middle-market businesses with sales in the region of £10 million to £500 million annually. They value the company's strength as an independent adviser and manager of their networks because Vanco offers them cost-effective quality with a high degree of reliability and innovation. 'We regularly ask our clients which aspects of our service are most important to them and they say the quality of service - which they are unable to match either internally or with any other supplier. By quality, they mean the high level of reliability and the availability of provision,' says Mr Timpany.

Recently, when a British Telecom main cable was severed by workmen in the Midlands digging a trench, many BT subscribers in the north lost their lines for 48 hours. 'We located another route within ten minutes for some customers and a maximum of 35 minutes for the remainder. This meant their computer downtime was limited to minutes rather than days. When computer transactions are a vital part of business activity for our clients, downtime can cost thousands of pounds,' says one of Mr Timpany's senior control room engineers.

In 70 per cent of cases, Vanco's staff spot faults before the customer is even aware of a problem. 'Our procedure is straightforward. As soon as we notice a problem we isolate it here on screen and in most cases we can resolve the issue from here. If it is a problem at an exchange we contact the provider and ask them to check the fault. If one of our engineers needs to deal with the problem we despatch the relevant person. Then we inform the client,' comments one of Vanco's network engineers.

Typically, from identification through resolution to informing the customer can take ten minutes. Some 75 per cent of all faults in the system are dealt with in five minutes. Many of the issues are very simple. ' A cleaner may have knocked a cable from the back of a terminal but this will show up as a fault on our system. This may appear trivial but if our client has one terminal in an office in Vienna and it is not available on his network, this could be a major concern. The fault may be more serious. But the advantage of our system is that we can identify where the fault lies - whether it is a loose cable at the back of a PC or a disruption in the main connection with London.'

Strategy and management

Wide-area networks will grow rapidly in coming years as computer and telecommunication technology advance. Companies will demand high degrees of reliability and flexibility in their WANs. This is where Allen Timpany perceived an opportunity. He knew that existing WANs were supplied by the state monopoly telecommunications utilities (circuit providers) or the main computer companies (box makers). 'I realised that both the circuit providers and the box makers were wedded to their own specific solution. We could create a substantial business by implementing and managing WANs independently. Independence was a key factor in the business strategy. As the monopolies dissolved, telecomms companies such as BT, Deutsche Telekom, AT&T and US Sprint would be competing in the same territories with different services. We are able to distinguish between them on behalf of the customer.'

From the outset, Vanco's directors were determined to recruit only the best personnel who would be able to advise customers on the most appropriate solutions. Each is conversant with the raft of potential solutions for WAN implementation. 'We know within minutes of arriving at a client which is the most appropriate configuration for their needs. This means hardware, software and circuits.' The value of the experience which Vanco can offer clients in the first few minutes of the proposal meeting can be staggering.

But this isn't enough for Allen Timpany. 'Our customers want reliability so we offer financial guarantees which take effect if our service level falls below 98.5 per cent. At present we are achieving in excess of 99 per cent and our aim is 99.99 per cent in three to four years.' The level and extent of these guarantees provides - and was intended to provide - a standard for the industry.

Mr Timpany is profoundly aware of the benefits of exceeding the quality expectations of his customers. He has a history of running successful enterprises. In 1980 he established Guestel, which became the second largest Apple dealership in the country. Three years later he created Tycom, a computer manufacturer, and the following year opened Wakebourne, a computer services company which achieves an annual turnover of around £40 million. He is still a non-executive director of Wakebourne but in 1989 he bought Vanco.

He set clear parameters for its commercial objectives. At present, the market is estimated to be £1.25 billion, at least doubling by the year 2000. CIT Research's report *Value Added Services in Europe* argues that 'the UK will be leading Europe in managed network services in 2004 with a market worth £553 million. The German market will be the second largest at £414 million with the French market in third place at £307 million. The UK also dominates the facilities management sector accounting for £164 million in 2004, Germany will occupy second place with £143.4 million of revenue compared with the French market in third place at £123 million.'

Vanco has a distinctive position in the market. The company is aware that its status as the only independent manager and implementer of WANs cannot be maintained for very long. Mr Timpany says that his business arrived at its perception of the commercial opportunity from an unusual combination of historical, technological and current company perspectives. Its unique view on the market gave rise to its analysis of the possibilities in independent management and implementation. Having demonstrated that there is a market, others will enter.

But Vanco has a head start. From the beginning it chose to elevate standards to demanding levels, to offer customers guarantees previously unknown, and to develop a business strategy based on continual renewal. It also believes in providing added value services such as an annual technology overview with each client and detailed reports on all faults including action taken.

Mr Timpany and his managers are advocates of the 'small is best' philosophy. Work groups within the company grow to no more than 30 individuals. Each group contains account managers, salespeople, finance, technical and administrative staff. Each is effectively a company in its own right.

Unusually, once a manager has grown a group up to an optimum size he or she will be asked to come out of that unit and start afresh. In that way Vanco will keep renewing itself and its managers can concentrate on what they are best at - building business. Tony Nester, business manager, is an example. 'I started the domestic team and have grown it to where I now have a team of 15 people. So, I have now come out of that business and I have recently set up the UK international unit. I am now working to achieve the same with this unit as I did with the first.' In this model, the centre lays down quality guidelines, harmonises the business approach of the operating units and establishes the financial targets. It also has a control function.

Outside the UK, Vanco currently has offices in Amsterdam and Madrid. Francisco Lopez, Spanish business manager, says that he secured contracts from IBM, ICL, Digital, Cray Communications, El Corte Ingles and the Bank of Spain. 'We have a lot of work to do here in Spain. There are numerous problems with the telecommunications infrastructure and we can be of positive benefit to our customers. I term what we do as apostolic work because we are spreading the word about the management of networks as much as winning new business. I believe we can make a great contribution to the efficiency of companies in Spain - and also in Portugal where we will be opening next year.'

Mr Timpany says that southern Europe - Iberia, Italy and Greece - and the former eastern bloc countries provide a great challenge for Vanco. 'The telecomms systems have many problems in these areas and our service can help companies to overcome many difficulties inherent in operating in these territories.'

Vanco plans further expansion in Frankfurt - probably later in 1995 - and perhaps Milan. 'Each country will have its own network control centre which can manage all of the networks in its domain. And there will be a pan-European control centre, based in London, for international management. This means that from a desk in London we can solve the remote problems of a single terminal perhaps in Budapest or Bratislava.'

The future

Vanco Euronet sees itself as a pan-European company not a British one. 'Our markets are European and our networks are transnational so we could not really be anything else.' It is a privately-owned business which currently brings in £4 million with profits of £400,000. Every year since its foundation the company has doubled its profitability. Gross margins are good, so the business can be expected to improve its performance even further.

Virgin Group of Companies, London

Virgin is Britain's best-known private company, comprising 8 separate holding companies, largely due to the remarkable personal skills of its chairman Richard Branson. It has made its name in music and airline operations but the brand can be found in many markets

Outlook:
Virgin is the apotheosis of an entrepreneurially managed business. Richard Branson, its founder and chairman, despite his justified claims to empowerment within the business, remains its heart and soul. It was his inspiration which sustained it, and his family and friends run its various divisions. It is a thriving and intelligently managed operation, unafraid to take risks, but when its leader finally retires its longevity must be in doubt

Scorecard:

Structural flexibility	★★★★
Innovative power	★★★★★
International orientation	★★★★
Human resources	★★★★
Growth markets	★★★★★
Quality of management	★★★★

Key figures:
Turnover	£2 billion
Pre-tax profits	£250 million
Staff	12,000

Virgin Group of Companies
120 Campden Hill Road
London W8 7AR
Tel: 0171 229 1282

Virgin

Amstrad's Alan Sugar was once asked at a shareholders ' meeting if he had any plans to emulate Richard Branson by taking his company private. 'I'm not going up in a bloody balloon if that's what you mean,' quipped the founding chairman of consumer electronics group. In the event Mr Sugar dabbled with the idea, but was unable to persuade other investors. Mr Branson's brief flirtation with the City in the late eighties was an altogether different affair.

He riled against the short-termism of financial institutions and the restraints that placed on him from diversifying the core airline and entertainment activities. They in turn increasingly viewed the fortunes of the publicly-quoted Virgin Group as tied to the daredevil publicity stunts of its unconventional founder. In particular, what would happen to Virgin if Mr Branson was run over by a number eight bus?

Operations and markets

When he finally turned his back on the stock market in 1989 he vowed that one day he would return. In all probability, Virgin would be afforded FT-SE 100 status tomorrow if Mr Branson were to deliver on his comeback promise. As a private company, Virgin's value is almost impossible to ascertain. Virgin has no holding company, accounts are not consolidated, and there is a tax incentive to depress profits. The company is also something of a moveable feast and recent expansion into apparently unrelated areas such as financial products, personal computers and the drinks industry makes an orthodox valuation even more difficult for leisure analysts in the City.

The state of the balance sheet is another grey area. Mr Branson incurred sizeable debts buying Virgin back from the stock market, while Virgin Atlantic's bold attempt to break the stranglehold British Airways held on transatlantic routes put a great strain on the airline's finances.

But the surprise £560m sale of Virgin Music - the business that made Branson his first millions - to Thorn-EMI in 1992 helped clear the decks of debt and eased the pressure on Virgin Atlantic. Further disposals followed, notably the $125m sale two years later of a majority stake in Virgin's video games group, VIE, to American video rental group Blockbuster. Branson rejected the other possible exit route for VIE - a $200m flotation on America's junior NASDAQ stock market.

Virgin Group sales this year are set to rise by 40 per cent to an estimated £2bn, consolidating Virgin's position as one of Britain's top five private companies. And according to the Sunday Times, Mr Branson himself is worth a net £895m, making him the 11th richest person in the UK.

The true measure of Virgin, though, is not so much its actual size as its unique management style, capacity for constant innovation and ability to exploit a well-known brand name. Its chairman hates bureaucracy. 'I do not want to run a conglomerate,' he once said, 'People get lost and don't give their best.' Instead, he advocates empowerment. He prevents the need for bureaucratic control by splitting off business areas larger than about 200 people into separate companies. Note the personal touch here - people rather than revenue determine the cut-off point.

The informal, non-hierarchical structure is deliberately designed to attract people who want to run their own business without the top-heavy, time-consuming and expensive involvement of central management. Mr Branson himself leads by example, eschewing a business suit and tie for an open-neck shirt and woolly jumper.

Strategy and management

To ensure common values pervade the organisation, Mr Branson also surrounds himself with a trusted group of managers, many of whom are family or friends. For example, his most trusted lieutenant is Robert Devereaux, who heads up the communications division and is also Branson's brother-in-law, while the Storm model agency that launched the career of Kate Moss is run by a friend of Mr Branson's sister.

Virgin is fond of making the analogy with the *keiretsu*, or corporate family formation, of Japanese companies. Unlike western organisations, which tend to be hierarchical in structure and dominated by a holding company at the top, the *keiretsu* structure is flat with some communality of ownership, often underpinned by a bank providing financial assistance or loan guarantees. But each of the loosely-related units is free to make its own joint venture deals and aggressive expansion policies.

Equally significant is the importance of the Virgin brand name.

'Virgin's strength is its brand name,' said Mr Branson, launching the Virgin retail brand name last year. 'Apart from the Body Shop, Virgin is the only international brand to come out of Britain in the last couple of decades that has recognition in three continents. But we don't use it in any form of hard products that people can pick up.' All that has changed utterly in recent months with the drive into markets for fast-moving consumer goods bearing the Virgin name.

Virgin says because it is associated with fun, price competitiveness and doing things differently, the brand name can be applied to a wide range of products. A recent NOP poll for the trade journal PR Week provided some independent support for these claims. In two separate surveys, it found that about 80 per cent of respondents associated the Virgin name with friendliness, a slightly lower proportion with high quality and 60-70 per cent with innovation, fun and low prices.

Mr Branson himself is seen as role model, especially among the young, and opinion polls regularly conclude that he is the person most Britons would most like to be. His underdog image stems from British Airway's infamous 'dirty tricks' campaign against Branson and his flagship Virgin airline in the early nineties.

Virgin had carved itself a lucrative niche on some routes of BA's key North Atlantic market. In response, BA spread rumours of financial problems within the Virgin empire, tried to poach individual passengers, and planted negative stories in the press.

Mr Branson complained publicly, but when BA denied everything and accused him of trying to drum up publicity, he sued for libel. In January 1993,

Mr Branson won the case in the High Court after British Airways admitted a series of 'regrettable incidents', apologised to Virgin and paid nearly £4m in damages and costs. He has also taken his case to the US courts, claiming a minimum of $325m in lost revenue over four years, and is still pursuing BA in the UK for breach of copyright, breach of confidence and misuse of confidential information.

It is not only in the courts that Virgin is pursuing its David-and-Goliath challenge to the established might of British Airways. In February 1995, the US Department of Transport agreed a transatlantic code-sharing deal between Virgin and Delta which gives the US airline access to Heathrow, while Virgin will be able to sell tickets to American destinations served by Delta. Virgin describes the Delta deal, worth an estimated $150m a year in extra revenue, as the most significant yet. 'It will seal the future of the airline,' says Mr Branson. A similar code-sharing arrangement was also recently agreed with Malaysia Airlines on the Kuala Lumpur route following the launch of cut-price flights to San Francisco and Hong Kong last year.

A similar, low-risk approach is being adopted in the company's latest scheme - diversification into branded products to exploit the Virgin name. The strategy is simple enough. Using the Virgin name and the operational skills of its chosen partners, markets are targeted where the brand leader enjoys margins wide enough to allow new entrants. This usually involves joint venture partners without the need for a substantial commitment of human or financial resources.

Deals with Norwich Union on personal equity plans over the telephone, William Grant on vodka and Canada's Cott on cola mean Virgin can attack established competitors head-on. It conforms with the Virgin image of taking on allcomers, the bigger the better. And Virgin is setting itself ambitious goals. In global terms, Mr Branson hopes to be breathing down Pepsi's neck within five years, and be on Coca-Cola's coat tails within ten years.

The risks for Virgin are that its well-known brand name becomes diluted and management gets found out in areas it knows little about. But Virgin's chairman is sanguine. 'There's always a risk of failure. But you only live once. If you are afraid of failure, you don't do anything in life.'

Of course, not everything he touches has turned to gold. He was visibly upset at not winning the right to organise the National Lottery. He failed in his bid to win a Channel 3 television franchise in 1992. He may not win the franchise to operate the Channel Tunnel rail link or one of eight British Rail franchises.

The future

But Mr Branson is a master at minimising risks. He leases rather than owns aircraft, he has resisted the temptation to make big acquisitions, he lets others take the strain. Perhaps most of all he realises Virgin operates in service businesses that are being changed radically by technology. Innovation, therefore, will remain a key driver in seizing future business opportunities.

WalkerGreenbank

Walker Greenbank, Hertfordshire

Walker Greenbank is Britain's leading integrated designer, manufacturer and producer of top-of-the range wall coverings, furnishing fabrics, display materials and luxury carpets for both the commercial and consumer markets.

Outlook:
Walker Greenbank is emerging from a six year transformation programme and is widely regarded as one of Britain's most innovative and commercially astute producers of upmarket interior furnishings. It has weathered the slowdown in both corporate and consumer spending on refurbishment well thanks to its flair for design, a keen marketing programme and its well established brand names. The company has expanded consistently within its niche markets both organically and via acquisition. An increasing sales campaign abroad, the benefits of integrating recent acquisitions and an already evident upturn in domestic demand provide a solid platform for further growth.

Scorecard:

Structural flexibility	★★★★
Innovative power	★★★★★
International orientation	★★★
Human resources	★★★★
Growth market	★★★★

Key Figures:

Market capitalisation	£100 million
Turnover in the year to 31/1/1995	£75 million
Pre-tax profits in the year to 31/1/1995	£9 million

Walker Greenbank
4 Brunel Court
Hemel Hempstead
Hertfordshire
HP3 9XX
Tel: 01442 234666
Fax : 01442 213541

Walker Greenbank

Founded in 1899 and floated in 1985 Walker Greenbank was a diversified and heavily indebted animal in 1990 when its current chief executive Charles Wightman joined as managing director. Operating in activities as diverse as engineering and retail products Wightman embarked on a sometimes painful four year long disposal programme. That left the group as a tightly focused producer of wall coverings and fabrics.

In December 1994 Walker Greenbank raised £16.9 million in a rights issue that enabled it to accelerate an expansion programme that even group chairman David Richards described as "ambitious."

In the last six months of 1995 Walker Greenbank paid a total of £8.5 million to acquire five other companies including Topwand from the Netherlands, which significantly expanded its European activities.

Operations and markets

Walker Greenbank is organised into two divisions, commercial and consumer, although within each arm there are a number of distinct operating companies.

Around two thirds of last year's group sales of £75 million were in the commercial division. It is dominated by Muraspec, the UK's leading commercial contract wall coverings distributor with around 65% of a £50 million market. This market has a narrow customer base in that it is the designers, architects and office refurbishers who specify the wallpaper used rather than end-customers. This allows relatively cheap, targeted marketing campaigns.

Brymor, the main supplier of wall coverings to Muraspec was acquired in 1991 for £8.4 million. Around 70% of its £15 million annual sales are to Muraspec. Completing the division is Hartley which designs and manufactures upholstery fabrics for office seating and screening and in the 1995 financial year achieved sales of £3 million.

The consumer division operates through many more units. Zoffany achieved sales of £6m in 1994/5 distributing wallpaper to the hotel and domestic markets. Harlequin generated three times as much revenues designing and marketing quality wallpaper for the top end of the domestic market. Much of the wallpaper production for the arm is done by Anstey, which also sells externally, and is Europe's leading top of the range manufacturer.

Smaller, more recent acquisitions compete in niche markets. Among the minnows scooped up in the past eighteen months are the fabrics designer Warner and Cole & Sons and John Perry which make and distribute superior quality wallpapers. These were long established designers that had suffered from many years of under investment prior to joining the Walker Greenbank stable . Indeed Warner is one of the oldest fabric design companies in the world dating back to 1870.

Charles Wightman believes that in both cases his company can restore these niche businesses to their former glories: "Under our highly focused management both Warners and Coles are capable of generating considerable organic growth and improved profitability."

Both companies bring renowned brand names and assets with hitherto unrealised potential. Coles owned over 3,000 wood blocks for wallpaper production many of which were designed by the famous Victorians Pugin and Cowtan.

In the 1995 financial year 29% of Walker's turnover came from overseas and the company's stated aim is to drive that figure up to 50%. Although a wallpaper showroom was recently opened in New York and the company set up a new US division in 1995 the main export market is in Europe where Walker Greenbank has operated through wholly owned distributors in France and Germany for some time.

The Topwand acquisition will, it is hoped, open up the Dutch market and last year Walker Greenbank added a leading Norwegian distributor with sales of £6 million to its stable.

Strategy and management

Although Walker Greenbank's recent history might give the impression that it is pinning its expansion drive on an acquisition programme that would be misleading.

In the 1995 financial year it ploughed an unusually high percentage of its revenues into an extensive capital investment programme. Funds invested in new state of the art plant machinery and production facilities rose by 35% to £7.5 million in 1994/5 and Walker Greenbank promises that the programme will enjoy "further substantial increases" in the 1996 and 1997 financial years. One direct result will be a significant increase in the number of new product launches.

The company also invests heavily in creating new design patterns in all its operating units. The stated philosophy is that: "Creating the right designs and colorations is essential to the success of each of our niche marketing businesses." Each of the separate companies within the Walker Greenbank group employs its own in-house and consultant teams of designers and colourists. The teams are provided with a wide range of facilities including the latest computer aided design software.

However acquisitions are an integral part of the Walker Greenbank growth strategy. The company's inorganic expansion is being conducted on two fronts.

The primary drive is to grow and to consolidate its international coverage especially in Europe. Hence the purchase of further small distributors with localised expertise can be expected. Similar deals in the United States and the Far East would surprise few commentators.

A secondary drive is to continue acquiring small designers and manufacturers with particular expertise of niche, but related, markets within the United Kingdom. Typically such firms will, like Warners and Coles, be well regarded experts in their field usually sitting on valuable brand names and other intellectual or intangible assets but suffering from several years of under-investment or poor management.

Walker Greenbank has been careful to create a powerful and broad enough management team to pursue its growth strategy.

Wightman and finance director Martin Hynes are the central figures behind Walker Greenbank's revival. Both left exhibitions organiser Blenheim Group in 1990 when it was something of a stock market darling. More recently it has had rather serious problems.

Both men are young and, according to a close adviser "still keenly ambitious."

Beneath them in the organisational hierarchy, since March 1996, are Peter Mostyn and Roger Smurthwaite who are managing directors of the consumer and commercial divisions respectively. However many responsibilities are devolved to individual operating companies and Walker Greenbank has not been afraid to sacrifice short-term profits by recruiting heavyweight managers to run those operations and to be in situ to oversee future acquisitions.

One truly innovative touch was the introduction of a no-cost Personal Equity Plan, one of the first in the country. This has helped to widen the company's shareholder base considerably during the past two years.

The Future

Walker Greenbank's short term prospects are dominated by a rather sluggish domestic marketplace. Though the consumer division is already benefiting from a marked upturn in the upper reaches of the British housing market the commercial operation still faces a corporate clientele reluctant to part with its cash. Sales growth in this market is unlikely to be exciting at least until 1997.

However, helped by its acquisitions and a growing international focus, the company should increase its underlying pre-tax profits in the 1995/6 financial year from £8.8 million to £9.7 million and analysts expect £11 million the following year.

Longer term, the company's underlying growth rates should increase as corporate customers revert to something more like historic spending patterns and as Walker Greenbank seeks to match its penetration in the UK in its targeted overseas markets.

The company is soundly financed. The £16.9 million rights issue of 1994 left the balance sheet in good shape, although the City has taken some time to appreciate the benefits of the investment strategy Walker Greenbank has been able to implement with the proceeds of the fund raising.

Despite its recent acquisitions it has net cash and is predicted to generate £8.5 million from operations in the 1995/6 financial year and £11 million in the following twelve months. That leaves the company easily able to fund its ambitious programme of capital investment for the future without having to ask its shareholders for further support.

Walker Greenbank has shown itself to be innovative and long-termist in its approach. Even in a tough market its well regarded management is laying the foundations for real returns for its shareholders.

W H Smith Group, London

W H Smith is the largest music, book and newspaper and magazine retailer in the UK. It is also the only British retailer to be a market leader in the United States

Outlook:
The group has recently come under criticism for its caution in adapting to market trends in its flagship W H Smith Retail business, but this is largely unjustified. The group has achieved market leadership positions in all of its activities - with the notable exception of DIY. The incorporation of Waterstones, Our Price and Virgin into the group has had enormous benefits and the challenge remains in transforming the W H Smith shops for the 21st Century. Its shrewd handling of its US adventures is a casebook example for all British retailers seeking success in North America

Scorecard:

Structural flexibility	★★★★
Innovative power	★★★★★
International orientation	★★★★★
Human resources	★★★★
Growth markets	★★★★
Quality of management	★★★★

Key figures: (1995)

Turnover	£2.69 billion
Pre-tax profits	£115 million
Staff:	23,143

W H Smith Group plc
Strand House
7 Holbein Place
London SW1W 8NR
Tel: 0171 730 1200
Fax: 0171 824 5563

W H Smith

Retailing will be transformed by a range of factors in the next decade, and perhaps the most influential will be the quality of customer service. The clientele of Britain's stores are more discriminating, knowledgeable and aware than previous generations and this development will accelerate, putting increased pressure on retailers to extend the scope of their service provision. It has elevated the sector to new realms where competitive edge is secured by realising across-the-border improvements in key areas such as clear proficiency of sales staff in their understanding of products, positive demeanour in meeting customer queries, logical layout of outlets and value added in the form of additional and relevant services.

Inevitably, progress in a sector which embraces everything from the high street newsagent to Harrods has been piecemeal. Many establishments, despite their intimate contact with the customer, have failed to register the extent of change in buyer awareness. They do so at their peril. Even many leading chains of newsagents appear to regard the customer as a necessary evil. They would do well to learn from the UK's leading newsagent, book and music retailer - W H Smith. The company aims to make shopping - on what it knows definitively is a discretionary spend - a pleasurable and worthwhile experience.

Operations and markets

There is a W H Smith store in almost every high street in Britain - certainly those of any significance. The product mix may vary from location to location but each will contain newspapers and magazines, popular books and stationery. Many devote significant floorspace to recorded music in the form of CDs and tapes, and also to a catalogue of videos. This is the largest newsagent in the UK and is often first choice for many in purchasing newspapers and periodicals.

But the group does not end here. It also owns the genuine booklover's store Waterstone's, the Our Price music chain and the Virgin megastore network. This gives W H Smith a formidable UK market leadership position in the books, music and video markets:

books   23 per cent (W H Smith 14 per cent, Waterstone's 9 per cent)
music   30.8 per cent (Our Price 18.5 per cent, W H Smith 7.3 per cent, Virgin 5 per cent)
video   27.7 per cent (W H Smith 16.2 per cent, Our Price Video 4.1 per cent, Virgin 4 per cent, Our Price 3.4 per cent).

UK retail isn't the complete picture, there is also UK distribution and US retailing. In total in 1994, the group reported sales of £2.44 billion and pre-tax profits of £124.8 million. These figures represented a 0.2 per cent increase in sales margins which is significant for the sector. Return on retail activities is 6.7 per cent and on distribution 3.7 per cent. UK book sales were up 6 per cent, music increased by 7.2 per cent and video grew by 15.1 per cent. The group is increasingly a second half company benefiting from the upsurge in sales prior to Christmas but nevertheless its policies in brand and store renewal are allowing the company to take market share from competitors.

The US business, which comprises Waterstone's, The Wall and W H Smith

Inc, is a case study for students of British retailing experience outside the UK. The company is the only UK retailer to make a sustained success of its American activities. It is number one book retailer in the north east United States, active in lucrative airport and high class resort hotel and achieving above average returns in its music shops.

Distribution comprises the largest newspaper and magazine distribution business in the UK - W H Smith News, W H Smith Business Supplies and Heathcote Books. W H Smith News serves three principal customer groups - newspaper publishers, magazine publishers and newsagents. Newspapers, which are declining slowly, and magazines, which are advancing rapidly - especially in value terms - are treated separately. In business supplies sales grew by 22 per cent in 1994, partly as a result of the launch of its Niceday brand. Heathcote's book distribution division increased sales by 16 per cent in a flat market. Its achievement was realised partly by growing sales at non-traditional multiples like Boots, John Lewis and Virgin Retail.

The sole exception to the unremitting success of the rest of the group is its adventure into DIY retailing. Do It All - jointly owned with Boots - may or may not play an important role in the future of the group but it has cost W H Smith considerable sums in investment. After marked losses, better market focus and improved cost efficiencies have brought Do It All back into profit.

Strategy and management

Brand leadership lies at the heart of the group's strategic direction. All of its individual businesses are market leaders in their own right - with the exception of Do It All. Each of the businesses derives commensurate benefits from its dominant position. W H Smith fulfils all the criteria of a business which will prosper in fiercer market conditions: it has critical mass, strong balance sheet performance, financial stability, excellent reputation for customer service, high investment in core areas of the business and innovative approaches to the development of markets. Many CEOs argue that people management policies will be crucial and W H Smith has long been regarded as an excellent employer. However, the group faces distinctively different challenges in each division of the business.

Sir Malcolm Field, chief executive, says that one of his major concerns is to redesign the W H Smith brand for the new century. The flagship store will be refocused to meet the new demands of the market. Sir Malcolm says that W H Smith retail has strong brand loyalty but customers will make new demands on the business. He says that increasingly the pre-school age group will provide a growing source of income and he is impressed by the diversity of goods available in the US specialist shops. The success of these niche outlets could be replicated in parts of W H Smith stores. Any brand revamp or realignment would require heavy capital investment.

Stores in the Our Price, Virgin and Waterstone chains have all enjoyed modernisation and expansion of floorspace. Given the size of its market share in its core divisions, any further acquisitions would probably be disallowed by the Monopolies and Mergers Commission. Therefore growth will come from developing the business organically - exploiting scale benefits from market leadership, targeting customers more effectively, providing distinctive services and enhancing the quality of staff and management.

Sir Malcolm says: 'Our long term strategic focus in the retail and distribution businesses will be to retain and develop our market shares by organic growth in our core markets and achieving better levels of performance at lower cost.'

Logistics has been a key focus of the business - improving the quality of service while reducing the costs of getting goods from supplier to customers. With its own distribution division, W H Smith is alert to the main issues in logistics management and it has also substantially enhanced the value of its technology. Its IT is among the most advanced in retailing. W H Smith's EPoS system handles more than one million items which is far higher than any of the supermarket operators. The company is achieving scale benefits from merging the Virgin and Our Price managements and systems.

In W H Smith News, Office Supplies and Heathcote are all capitalising on their market strength. News is integrating with publishers on logistics systems such as electronic data interchange and with customers on EPoS which offsets the decline in volumes from newspapers and enhances the increasing profits from magazines. In business systems rapid advance is targeted. 'We have since seen many companies convert to single sources for supplies where are clear market leaders,' says David Roberts, managing director of distribution services.

The strategic plan for the US operation is characterised by cautious expansion.'We have 93 stores in the airport sector with sales approaching $100 million. Research shows that airport customers want ease of shopping, a clear store identity, a broader range of reading materials and fair prices. We are now represented at 15 American airports and there are at least 70 more which meet our criteria for growth,' comments John Hancock, CEO of the US company. It operates stores in 270 locations in business and resort hotels and plans to expand its formats into other parts of the US.

Retail is remarkably polarised in its attitude towards its people. At one end of the spectrum are Marks & Spencer, W H Smith and Safeway with innovative policies for human resources management and at the other end some of the worst excesses of dreadful employment practice in British industry. The company has been one of the longest-standing good employers in UK commercial history and is especially good at training, promotion, pay and benefits scales and communication.

The future

This business has one key priority: to extend its market leadership in its three key areas of business. Unless it loses its formidable grasp of consumer demand, its enlightened staff management policies, its capacity to see the future of its business and its mastery of financial management, W H Smith will continue to be the UK's newsagent, bookseller and music and video retailer. The growth of alternative entertainment and educational media are key areas where the company may exploit new market opportunities. The US will probably achieve greater importance as the management of the American operation apply their skills of cautious expansion and above-average results. Equally there is plenty of room for growth in the distribution businesses.

Williams Holdings, Derby

Williams Holdings is a diversified holding company which has achieved formidable levels of profitability through its astute management of its businesses in the building products, fire protection and security sectors

Outlook:
Williams is a remarkable example of a well managed business. Its high quality research, corporate finance and reconstruction teams underpin the group's substantial success. It is a favourite of the City because Williams delivers no surprises. Its businesses regularly outperform local markets and its managers are given substantial freedom to exceed group expectation

Scorecard:

Structural flexibility	★★★★
Innovative power	★★★★★
International orientation	★★★★
Human resources	★★★★
Growth markets	★★★★★
Quality of management	★★★★★

Key figures:

Turnover	£1.4 billion
Pre-tax profits	£200 million
Staff	15,500

Williams Holdings plc
Sir Frank Whittle Road
Derby DE1 4XA
Tel: 01332 202020

Williams

Clare Sambrook, writing in the Daily Telegraph in February 1995, neatly summarised the Williams achievement. In 1982 'they paid £400,000 for a 51 per cent stake in a little foundry in South Wales. In just over ten years they had built a £2 billion manufacturing company whose brands include such names as Polycell, Cuprinol, Rawlplug and Yale.'

It is a remarkable feat. While many businessmen in the 1980s aspired to create a mini-conglomerate, the executive management at Williams did it and then reshaped their disparate units into a coherent worldwide group with three principal commercial streams. Their achievement owes a great deal to sound financial management, a realistic but challenging vision for all the businesses in the group, a true instinct for corporate finance and company reconstruction, and the capacity to inspire and motivate managers.

And yet outside the City and corporate management circles Williams is virtually unknown. To the initiated, Williams consistently provides improving profits, challenging management and demanding targets. Against the vicissitudes of economic forces the group remains true to its principles - and consistent with its financial projections. The financial community likes the company because it always offers a healthy return and there are no surprises.

Operations and markets

Sales in 1993 reached £1.2 billion with profits of £174.5 million. Its three main business streams are building products, fire protection and security, which draw their principal revenues from North America and Europe. The geographic profit split is currently 48 per cent North America, 38 per cent UK and 14 per cent mainland Europe. Building products account for £700 million, fire protection £250 million and security £190 million.

Williams is the epitome of a well managed business. Chairman Nigel Rudd and chief executive Roger Carr - with perhaps some help from Brian McGowan, a key player until he retired recently - could write the rule book on contemporary successful management. The philosophy is not difficult to understand. In existing businesses, 19 per cent return on sales is the benchmark. Subsidiaries are expected to achieve this level - and the vast majority of them do. Regardless of sectoral tradition or geographic peculiarities, the holding company wants its 19 per cent.

When the group makes an acquisition, the purchase may be a loss-maker but central management will be convinced that the Williams treatment can transform the newcomer into a highly profitable venture. Mr Carr and his teams realise that new management may need a year or two to reach the standard but they believe in setting stretching targets.

This process suggests that Williams is brutal with subsidiaries; only interested in its return. Nothing could be further from the truth. The team in Sir Frank Whittle Road in Derby believes in testing negotiation over budgets and investments but then allowing management to get on with the business of creating world class companies. Beyond all their financial skill the Williams executive team understands what makes businesses tick.

Williams ensures that the individual companies have sufficient resources to capitalise on their strengths and that their managers have ample operating freedom to secure progress in whichever ways are suitable for each market. Messrs Rudd, Carr and Co. exhibit a deep appreciation of the motivation of managers. They pick teams who will galvanise employees and stamp their own imprint on the company through enthusiasm, creativity and zeal.

Strategy and management

There are two key elements to the Williams operational management approach. These comprise its approach to selecting companies for inclusion in the group and the management of those companies after they have been absorbed.

Williams is rightly respected for its approach to acquisition and the procedure adopted by its post-acquisition reconstruction teams. Its research into potential purchase targets enjoys an enviable reputation for its thoroughness and suitability. The knowledge of businesses which could complement its existing strengths in core areas among its corporate finance and divisional teams is among the best in the industry. Mr Carr and his colleagues have established criteria for policy on acquisition.

Underlying this strategy of purchase is a commitment to buying brands. Brands have been out of fashion for a generation but Williams, specialising in products in its key areas of fire protection, building services and security, has made buying brands a core policy of its acquisition strategy. Typical of this strategy is Yale in its securities division. Robert Gasparini, who runs the world security division, says that when Yale was taken over by Williams it was in poor shape. 'Yale had been world brand leader in both industrial and domestic security products. But somewhere towards the end of the 1950s it somehow took its eye off the ball. Throughout the 1960s and 1970s it rapidly lost its market share and all that was left was its reputation. In fact in the late 70s and early 80s all that kept Yale going was the manufacture of Yale clones by Far Eastern manufacturers. The early stages of the Williams plan to rejuvenate Yale involves focusing on the industrial market.'

'A key part of our acquisition strategy is to buy companies with proven or potential market leadership,' says chief executive Roger Carr. The strategy has paid off handsomely because apart from adding key elements to core divisions Williams has captured some of the most respected managers in their field. For example, Michael Harper, managing director of the fire protection sector, which contributes 37 per cent to Williams' profits, is acknowledged to be the senior figure in the fire protection industry.

The active teams involved in the acquisition of new companies are special operations and corporate finance and the group is structured to exploit advantages in each area. Building products and world security are grouped in one part of the business, and fire protection and special operations are grouped in another section. There are two operations directors, Mike Davies and Chris Davies, no relation, who report to Roger Carr. Each works with a finance director, a corporate finance director and the managing director of each relevant division on a particular acquisition. According to its criteria Williams will seek acquisitions which will add to its product and/or global strength. 'We seek businesses which will add greater strength to our operating division, those which can add to the profitability of divisions overall and add to the strength of the group,' says Mr Carr.

After acquisition the special operations groups move into a company and within a comparatively short timespan will reorganise the business along Williams' lines. 'First we do basic housekeeping and then establish Williams principles. We will need to know the financial strength of the business and in order to do that we establish financial procedures which will give us a clear appreciation. We also talk at an early stage to the existing management. We like to take the inherent management with us if possible but they must feel comfortable with Williams' overall objectives and our way of conducting business,' says Mr Carr. 'In many cases the existing management will want to work with us and to achieve targets that they were unable to do under previous management. Typically for a smaller company a team of three or four individuals from our special operations group will take about three months to complete their task. In the case of a larger company it may take six months. But we wish to be able to hand the company over to the operating division as quickly as we are practically able to do.'

Once the special operations team has moved in the new management can then take the reins of the company which has been transformed. Mr Carr says that in terms of management confidence it is very important that after many of the unpleasant activities have taken place at the hands of the special operations group that the team should feel confident that they can work with the division.

The clarity which characterises the group's activity has been an aspect of its approach since the onset. It is a straightforward business. Great emphasis is placed on close operating units where managers demand absolute frankness. Structurally it's a simple organisation. Group objectives are three. It aims to achieve above-average underlying growth in earnings per share, to maintain a progressive dividend policy and to build businesses of lasting quality. The company has fifty operating locations around the world and employs 14,500 people. Its current market capitalisation including convertibles is £2.5 billion.

The future

Williams is one of the most ably managed businesses in the UK. It has a real understanding of what makes businesses tick. It has evolved substantially from its original inspiration in 1982 through a collection of unrelated businesses into three key product divisions. The business concentrates on the brand strategy which it has believed in since the outset. Many of the currently fashionable management theorems have been in place in Williams since the business began. The group is a profit driven business, it achieves remarkably high standards of profitability. It has a highly talented, able, and extremely flexible management team. The managing directors of its various business divisions and of the individual operating companies are industrialists of world standing. There is absolutely no reason why Williams should not grow and even further develop its outstanding reputation within the financial world. In years to come it will also become a byword for management excellence.

WPP Group plc

WPP, London

WPP is the world's leading group of marketing-services companies operating worldwide under their own brand-names in advertising, market research, PR, and specialist communications

Outlook:
With its more coordinated approach this group will be able to follow the trends set by its large multi-national clients and not only retain that business, but grow ahead of other agencies in the faster growing regions of the world and capitalise on opportunities such as market research and specialist communications

Scorecard:

Structural flexibility:	★★★★
Innovative power	★★★★
International orientation	★★★★★
Human resources	★★★★
Growth markets	★★★★
Quality of management	★★★★

Key figures:

Turnover	£1.427 billion
Operating profit	£112.1 million
Pre-tax profits	£85.3 million
Staff	20,000

WPP Group plc
27 Farm street
London W1X 6RD
Tel: 0171 4082204
Fax: 0171 493 6819
e-mail: open@wpp.com

WPP

Very few companies can appear to represent their sector as WPP does. This group combines such a varied selection of advertising, PR, research, and specialist communication companies around the world that it does indeed at times seem to stand for the entire marketing-service sector.

This sector - worth some $815 billion in 1994 - is expanding and changing as agencies are increasingly faced by clients that are reorganising on a global, multinational, regional or brand basis and thus are forced to re-examine their own structures. WPP was originally conceived to be a financial holding company for a group of over 40 companies. It has now, however, reassessed the role the centre can play as different skills in different locations within the group are to be brought together to create extra value for its clients, its people and its companies.

Operations and markets

The group can boast many an impressive name among its clients, as more than 300 of the Fortune 500 companies work with a WPP company. And many of them have contact with WPP in more than one of its four principle areas of operation and in more than one country. The four main areas are:
. media advertising
  (J Walter Thompson Company, Ogilvy & Mather Worldwide, Conquest, Cole & Weber; around 50 per cent of revenues)
. market research
  (Millward Brown International, MRB Group, Research International)
. public relations
  (Hill and Knowlton, Ogilvy Adams & Rinehart, Ogilvy Public Relations and Carl Byoir & Associates)
. specialist communications services
  (over 30 separate companies including The Henley Centre, Metro Video, Ogilvy & Mather Direct, EWA, Sampson Tyrrell, BDG McColl, SBG Partners, Anspach Grossman Portugal; 23 per cent of revenues)

Among the specialist communications services are: corporate identity consultancy and design; strategic marketing services; multimedia communications; financial and corporate advertising; direct marketing; conferences; and Hispanic marketing.

At the end of 1994 the group had 778 offices in 78 countries. In the emerging markets its position is exceptionally strong: WPP is in the top four companies in the ten fastest growing markets, and number one in China and India. In the western markets, the group traditionally has strong positions, amongst which number one in the US and the UK.

The WPP group owns a number of respected brand-names itself in the form of its companies: J Walter Thompson Company and Ogilvy & Mather Worldwide are two of the most powerful names in advertising; Hill and Knowlton is one of the few PR agencies which is well known around the world and Sampson

Tyrrell is regarded as Europe's leading creative design agency.

Strategy and management

The market conditions and global trends that affect WPP's clients are naturally important to the group itself. As shown elsewhere in this book companies are broadening the geographical base of their operations in order to continue to reach growth targets. The intensified competition and stagnating growth in the mature markets, greater free trade possibilities in the world and the enormous improvements in technology and communications both facilitate and necessitate this expansion.

From agencies and consultancies clients are starting to require a much wider and more co-ordinated approach. This development is at the core of WPP's recent reassessment of the role of the centre and of its strategy for the future. The organisational structure of agencies is undergoing what is probably its greatest restructuring ever. For at least the last 80 years agencies have known a vertical structure organised by geography first, function second and client third. These structures, which are neither flat nor process-driven, will no longer be the best way of servicing clients that have re-engineered their own processes horizontally. In order to provide its clients with the best possible value WPP is creating a co-ordination among its agencies organised around the client, so that in the future it will be client first, function second and geography third.

Martin Sorrell, group chief executive, remarks: 'At the start WPP acted as a financial holding company - effectively the owner of the businesses, leaving management of the operating companies to its CEOs but monitoring financial performance. The aim of the increased co-ordinating role of the centre has been to build on the strengths of the individual businesses and create opportunities to add value for its clients and people.'

The strengths of WPP and its businesses lie in a number of factors:
. A remarkable and long-standing client-base including many of the world's best companies ranging from packaged goods to financial services to high-tech businesses.
. The widespread range covered both geographically and in terms of the skill-base. The group derives only around 55 per cent of revenues from conventional advertising, with competitors that figure exceeds 80 per cent.
. The talents and skills of the 20,000 WPP employees and the organisation's ability to continue to attract and develop highly talented people around the world.
. The ability to draw resources from the group as a whole, through the interaction and co-ordination of the parts of the group, through partnerships, the collective database and research function, the Lotus Notes network of all company executives, cross-company training courses, etc.
. The commitment to exceptional client service through ongoing investment in technology, training and incentive mechanisms.

Mr Sorrell is keen to elevate the understanding of the mechanics and operation of business within the companies. (He has a lot of time for the business practices of management consultants such as McKinsey and investment banks such as Goldman Sachs.) The group has recently formed The 100 Club and The 300 Club of top-performing worldwide management to motivate, incentivise and encourage partnership amongst the people who will most influence the future of the business. Younger managerial talent is being sent to business schools and to new training programmes especially developed for the same reason.

The training programmes within the company are one of the key elements in attracting and keeping the best talent. J.Walter Thompson Company and Ogilvy & Mather Worldwide both have long-established and much admired training schemes, ranging from craft skills seminars and masterclasses to interdepartmental weekends, regional seminars and job exchange programmes. Offering superior training and career opportunities enables the group to recruit the best people but it is also part of its commitment to 'provide clients with a comprehensive and, when appropriate, integrated range of marketing services of the highest quality and represent the finest creative and business practice'.

There is an increasing awareness among large companies and management consultants that even strategic planning should start with the consumer and thus have a marketing orientation. This has made management consultants move more and more in the direction of the strategy side of the marketing-services industry. For WPP this is an impetus to strengthen its strategic marketing capabilities. With the enhanced coordination, the expertise already developed in areas such as corporate identity consulting and the depth and range of client relationships at present, this development is likely to present an opportunity to the group while competitors may experience a push down the value chain towards the more executional marketing services.

One of the fastest growing services in the sector - the market research industry - is becoming a global industry. With three of the few players that have true worldwide capability, and which together constitute the largest custom research company in the world, WPP is well positioned for the growth ahead. Existing clients are preparing to outsource more and more of their research functions and new clients are emerging as institutions, services, and government bodies begin to market themselves with concomitant research needs.

The future

The long-term trends for the market-services industry are that the non media advertising will grow faster and that the industry will grow faster outside of the western world. WPP, with its geographical spread and the breadth of services it offers, is well-prepared for what is to come. As the world economy changes and parts of it leave the recession behind, the companies that can continue to improve as they change with the economy, those that have the best people and deal with the best clients will be the ones leading from the front. This group shows the signs of being one of them.

ZENECA

Zeneca Group PLC, London

Zeneca Group plc was formed from the demerged pharmaceutical, agrochemical and specialties businesses of ICI

Outlook:
The company has key strengths in each of its markets. It has improved profits considerably and it is making the necessary investment in all areas of its market activity. The questions which remain concentrate on its capacity to survive in increasingly demanding world markets

Scorecard:

Structural flexibility	★★★★
Innovative power	★★★★
International orientation	★★★★
Human resources	★★★★★
Growth markets	★★★★
Quality of management	★★★★

Key figures:

Turnover	£4.8 billion
Trading profits	£797 million
Staff	30,000

Zeneca Group PLC
15 Stanhope Gate
London W1Y 6LN
Tel: 0171 304 5000
Fax: 0171 304 5151

Zeneca Group

For an entity that was forced into being rather abruptly, Zeneca has built itself a strong position among the top twenty companies in Britain. The group, which comprises the pharmaceutical, agrochemical and specialty interests of Imperial Chemical Industries, was demerged from ICI in the summer of 1993 in response to speculation that Hanson, the aggressive conglomerate, was going to bid for the old industrial powerhouse and effect a break-up to release shareholder value.

The radical defence implemented by chairman Sir Denys Henderson has produced two companies with a combined market value of over £13 billion, of which Zeneca is the larger part, worth more than £10 billion. With management, led by chief executive David Barnes, free to focus on a narrow range of interests, profits have soared from £442 million in 1992 to £797 million last year, achieved on turnover of £4.8 billion. At the same time, borrowings of over £600 million which were taken on at the time of the demerger, have been almost completely paid off, despite continued heavy investment in capital equipment and research & development.

Operations and markets

Compared with most of its competitors in the pharmaceutical industry, Zeneca has a much broader spread of businesses, encompassing both agrochemicals - principally herbicides, insecticides and fungicides - and specialities, which encompass industrial colours and coatings, resins and developing businesses like the new protein food Quorn.

The pharmaceuticals division is the biggest by far and provides around four fifths of the group's profits, but at a time when governments are clamping down on healthcare costs and cutting drug bills, the smaller activities provide a useful hedge. During 1994, pharmaceutical profits grew by 7 per cent at constant exchange rates, while agrochemicals jumped by 55 per cent and specialities increased its contribution by a quarter following heavy restructuring the previous year.

Recent rumours suggesting that Zeneca was interested in selling off its smaller divisions to concentrate exclusively on healthcare are denied by Mr Barnes and his finance director John Mayo, who point to the advantage of a more balanced earnings base and a greater geographical spread. Rough external valuations of around £3 billion for two combined businesses are dismissed as too low by the Zeneca board.

Another useful inheritance from ICI, has been a cost-conscious culture that, until recently, was unknown in the rather sheltered pharmaceutical industry. Mr Barnes argues that Zeneca has been restructuring itself and cutting costs from long before it became a separate company, while rivals like Glaxo are only tackling cost bases that became rather inflated during the easy 1980s.

Strategy and management

Like the other companies in its industry, Zeneca is having to react to the worldwide pressure on healthcare costs. This is exemplified by the growing trend in the United States, where so called (HMOs) organise healthcare for a group of people, such as a firm's employees, in return for a fixed fee per insured person. These groups seek to limit costs in order to contain premiums and they do this by demanding increasingly bigger discounts from drug manufacturers. In other countries, such as Italy and Germany, the same effect is achieved by creating a limited list of medicines which doctors can prescribe and instituting mandatory price cuts.

So far, Zeneca has eschewed both of the industry's most common responses to increasing competition, as exemplified by its two major British rivals. SmithKline Beecham has chosen to integrate vertically by buying one of the American drug distributors which increasingly manage purchasing decisions for HMOs, while Glaxo's £9 billion takeover of Wellcome is perhaps the boldest example of horizontal integration to date.

While Zeneca briefly contemplated a counter-bid for Wellcome, before deciding that the company was effectively out of its reach, that would have been a logical extension of its focus on the primacy of continued research & development. Only research, according to Mr Barnes, will produce innovative products for unmet clinical needs and only those will continue to be sold at premium prices. Happily, the group has one of the strongest R&D pipelines in the industry, with seven new products in clinical trials, of which up to five could be filed for registration this year and launched over the next two. Those treatments cover all its major therapeutic categories, including cancer, where Zeneca is building up a strong franchise, central nervous system diseases like schizophrenia , anti-infectives and respiratory ailments.

But Mr Barnes is aware of the need to couple strong development with more effective marketing, saying: 'Our products offer benefits to patients and cost savings to purchasers. The strong R&D pipeline will provide a platform for future sales growth. In the current environment, however, innovative products alone do not guarantee success. It is equally important to establish closer, collaborative relationships with healthcare purchasers in order to have an opportunity to demonstrate the cost-effectiveness of the products being offered to them.'

One initiative arising from this approach is the formation of Stuart Disease Management Services in the United States, which works alongside healthcare providers like HMOs to design tailored approaches to improve the quality of healthcare and reduce the cost. Stuart is focusing on cardiovascular conditions and works with customers to design and implement diagnosis and treatment protocols, which include advice on diet and exercise as well as the appropriate medication.

Complementing that move was the acquisition of a half share in Salick Health Care, which provides comprehensive care for cancer patients. Salick is profitable and growing in its own right, but the key to Zeneca, as the number two worldwide in the anti-cancer market, is the huge amount of patient data that Salick can provide the group.

In keeping with its ICI heritage, Zeneca has been more proactive than most pharmaceutical rivals in its whole approach to managing costs and improving efficiencies. During 1994, for example, the group, which has 88 principal manufacturing locations in 22 countries, made notable efforts to improve its supply chain in all three businesses. The aim was to make the divisions more responsive to customer needs as well as more cost effective.

About 70 per cent of the agrochemicals' costs lie in the supply chain and a key goal on this side has been to reduce the amount of money tied up in the working capital, like stocks and raw material. In the United States, new purchasing systems and manufacturing procedures have standardised operations. In Europe, manufacturing lead times were cut from three weeks to one by streamlining information and material flows and speeding up decision making.

In specialities, the textile dyes business has switched from large volumes to smaller batches, thereby increasing flexibility on behalf of fashion conscious clothing manufacturers. At the same time, the more frequent production stoppages have been controlled by manufacturing closely related colour shades in sequence. This will save an estimated £3 million per annum. Pharmaceuticals has just begun a two- year review of its product formulation for individual drugs, with the aim of reducing average production time to four weeks.

The company states in its 1994 annual report that 'Zeneca's prosperity depends on its people making as full a contribution as possible to the success of the business, both as team players and as individuals.'

The group is committed to informing its 30,000 worldwide staff about changes and progress in their immediate business and in Zeneca and its markets as a whole. Profit-related bonus schemes and performance-linked reward feature increasingly in the pay structure and the remuneration system throughout the company is designed to encourage and recognise individual performance. The group's commitment to training and development was recognised in Britain during 1994 when its manufacturing sites at Macclesfield and Huddersfield received accreditation to the Training and Enterprise Council's Investor in People scheme.

Zeneca has developed a safety, health and environment management system (SHE), which is designed to produce continuous improvement in health and safety standards. This programme is consistent with the world chemical industry's Responsible Care standard and is supported by 19 internal management standards, which must be followed worldwide. These cover, among other things, process and product design, communication, training and auditing. Good-practice guidelines provide managers with more detailed information and every site uses the management standards and guidelines to establish responsible procedures. Each SHE performance of every site is then regularly audited and the information is reported in the form of a letter of assurance to the group's executive council. SHE has produced some notable successes, such as a 26 per cent reduction in hazardous waste output in the four years since 1990 and a 50 per cent decline in accidents over the same period.

Zeneca also recognises the benefits of giving staff the skills to manage busy, demanding jobs and lives. In the pharmaceutical divisions, over 1,000 employees have attended stress management workshops, designed to encourage a balanced approach to life.

The future

Zeneca has made substantial progress in the years since its demerger from ICI. It has a broader spread of interests than many pharmaceutical rivals, which can be both a benefit and a handicap. But it has recognised the importance of the increasingly global marketplace and is in a good position to exploit the key trends for continued prosperity.

TECHNOLOGIES IN TRANSITION: CONVERGENCE AND TURBULENCE

Dr John Taylor, managing director of Hewlett Packard Laboratories Europe, spoke to the Royal Society of Arts about the pattern of change and the implications for industry.

One of the main drivers for the changes in today's world is often described as the convergence of several related technologies - including computing, communications, consumer electronics, entertainment, telecoms and broadcasting - all of which are based on a core technology of microelectronics. However I believe we are not seeing a smooth convergence of these areas, but rather a turbulent mixing resulting in several discontinuous changes, precipitated by the relentlessly continuing improvements in performance and complexity combined with reductions in size and cost, of the underlying electronics technology.

Electronics is forecast to be the largest industry in the world by the end of the century when it is expected to account for about ten per cent of world GDP. The capability of the basic silicon technology to continue the present growth curves of price performance for both microprocessors and memory show no sign of slackening in the forseeable future. The processing power and storage capacities available from arrays of these devices and from mass memeory technologies such as CD-ROM are going up even faster. The first cause of a slowdown is likely to be economic rather than technical, as we move towards silicon fabrication plants costing $1 billion and more.

Thus the pace of change we've experienced for the past 20 years may be confidently expected to continue for the next 20 at least. Most of the science, much of the technology and some of the investment decisions are already done and in the pipeline. Twenty years ago, we had as the standard minicomputer workhorse the DEC PDP-11 series of machines which could have up to 64,000 bytes of directly addressable core memory, could process about 100,000 instructions per second and cost tens of thousands of 1974 pounds. The laptop computer has an Intel 486 processor capable of perhaps 10 million instructions per second, 8 megabytes of main memory, 140 megabytes of hard disk and a full colour display - all for $4,000 at 1994 prices. That is about 100 times the processing power and 100 times the storage for less than 100th of the cost allowing for inflation.

The HP 200LX palmtop computer is a real PC with two megabytes of user memory and word processing, spreadsheets, databases, e-mail and many other applications built in. It has 10 megabytes of plug-in card memory, can do around one million instructions per second and costs less than $500. Similarly a CD-ROM disk can store getting on for 1,000 megabytes of data, equivalent to a complete set of the Encyclopedia Britannica, and you will shortly be able to buy a two-hour full-length movie with high-quality picture and full stereo sound as a set of two CDs. The silicon chip technology already in the pipeline will start delivering early next year single memory chips each capable of storing 64 megabits, which corresponds to about eight main characters or a couple of full-length novels. Single chips with four times this capacity will be in production four years later. We should plan on that basis that the rate of change will continue unabated for the next twenty years.

However the quantitative changes of the past twenty years have affected not only computing and data processing but also radio, TV, telecommunications, networks, and so on. In particular we're going through a time now where the combinations of these quantitative changes happening in parallel in several related areas produce a sort of critical-mass effect leading to many qualitative changes which, moreover, are not happening smoothly but as relatively rapid discontinuities. I will mention three of the most important: media, digital communications networks and portability and mobility.

Media

Digital technology now means that it is cost-effective to transform any kind of information medium into a common digital representation which can then be transmitted over a single common digital communications network and stored in common storage systems like computer memories and CD-ROMs.

Perhaps the most visible immediate effect of this ability to turn any information medium into digital form is the way that it has suddenly transformed the way that people think about computers. Until now everybody knew that computers were for data processing. Suddenly we have entered the age of informal information like images, pictures, diagrams, video, speech, handwriting and scribble. With the right kind of transducers, which are now becoming available, we can turn all of these into digital form. We can then use the computers and digital communications networks to store them, retrieve them, display them, manipulate them, communicate them and view them, all without the computer needing to understand their meaning and very often without using a keyboard at all, thanks to the invention of interaction devices like the mouse. This represents the natural extension of the way we use fax machines today, and in my view a great deal of what computers will be used for in the future will be for handling these kinds of informal information.

Digital communications networks

The world's telecommunication networks have been installing digital transmission and computer-controlled digital switching systems for 10-20 years now. Globally they are spending around $100 million per year on this and they are perhaps half to two-thirds of the way to their goal of achieving a global digital intelligent network. This network is also expanding very rapidly. The number of the subscriber phone lines in the world should pass 700 million this year and is expected to exceed 1 billion by the year 2000. More interestingly though the number of lines installed this decade will exceed the total number installed in the whole of the previous hundred years, that is, since the telephone was invented. Moreover the new digital networks will be increasingly capable of so-called broad band services, able to deliver more bits per second than is needed for a plain old telephone or for users who want to start using new kinds of informal information.

The second example is the worldwide Internet which over the past two to three years has become a fascinating sociotechnological phenomenon. Statistics about the Internet are legion. It's a network of networks (hence the name - an internetwork network) and currently comprises 50,000 networks with more than two million computers and perhaps 10-15 million users in many countries around the world. Nobody really knows what the numbers are because one of the fundamental outrageous and fascinating things about the Internet is that nobody is in charge. It is self-regulating, anarchic, decentralised, federated and it is very resilient and capable of high degrees of rapid evolution and growth. This is partly because it is was designed to be and partly because it has been operated up to now by loose federations of like-minded well-intentioned and very intelligent people. What is really startling is the recent rates of growth of the traffic on the Internet fuelled by the joint drivers of the worldwide web and informal information.

Portability and mobility

The third source of discontinuity is that quite suddenly it has become possible to build a serious PC small enough to carry around in a briefcase and to deploy nationwide cellular telephone networks which use pocket digital radio handsets containing two or three times as much processing power as my laptop computer and costing less than £100. According to the Swedish company Ericsson, which claims to manufacture 40 per cent of all the world's mobile telephone handsets, the mobile phone market is growing even more rapidly than the fixed phone network. There will be more than 41 million cellular phones worldwide by the end of 1994, of which 9 million have been purchased in the previous six months. What was impossible five years ago has suddenly become quite commonplace; we can see:

. The emergence of global digital communication utilities both fixed and mobile able to handle two-way interactive traffic at a higher and higher capacity
. The ability to convert any medium into digital form and process, store and communicate it digitally, again with rapidly-increasing capabilities, which is enabling us to create whole new classes of multimedia information objects
. The sudden feasibility of portable wireless information processing and communications systems which I am certain will form the basis of the next generation of information appliances

It is my belief that within the next five years these new information utilities will begin to be widely available domestically, that quite new forms of information appliances will start to become commonplace and will move beyond today's PCs, printers, faxes and photocopiers. As a result we will be discovering:

. New ways of doing existing activities like catalogue shopping and travelling
. New ways of getting existing information objects like books, films, magazines, photos, images, videos and music by converting them to electronic form and sending them across a network
. New kinds of activity such as living room to living room multimedia conferencing and virtual reality visualisation of places and environments
. New kinds of information stuff that we can create and use that have their primary existence inside electronic systems rather than as discrete physical objects and which indeed cannot be accessed or viewed without an electronic system

Info business will take place in the information marketplace which has much in common with today's physical marketplaces. It offers a wide range of goods and services from a wide variety of electronic shops, offices, institutions and businesses. The key distinguishing features are that the customer travels around the marketplace electronically rather than physically and the goods and services he or she purchases are themselves delivered electronically in some of the ways we have just been illustrating. Here is a list of some of the new kinds of info businesses which I have in mind:

Tele-healthcare
Tele-learning
Tele-education
Entertainment media
Real-time information services
Electronic publishing
Info business infrastructures and services
Data mining, extraction, refining, recycling, disposal
Brokering and trading digital imaging and photography
Environmental monitoring and control
Virtual zoos, wildlife experiences
Virtual reality experiences, car driving, flying
Electronic sports and competitions
Security and surveillance
Tele-channel

The economic implications for the UK

Although the UK is presently the fifth largest IT and electronics producer in the world and the fourth largest consumer, IT and electronics currently account for only about three per cent of UK GDP. According to Stephan Garelli at the University of Lausanne the UK economy ranks only fourteenth in global competitiveness and the western economies of the European Union and the US are currently facing real threats of significant deindustrialisation in the face of low-cost, low-tax manufacturing operations not just in Asia-Pacific but also increasing elsewhere as well.

I believe that IT, electronics and communications are an area where the UK could and must do much better to increase both its absolute and relative contributions to national wealth creation. The emergence of a pervasive global digital communications infrastructure over the next ten years and beyond presents a great opportunity for business activity in the UK to reach and serve new global markets in exciting new ways. It also poses a very serious threat because it will make it much easier for businesses elsewhere in the world to compete in domestic UK markets. We can use the future Internet to export electronic goods and services but unless we stay at the competitive edge in exploiting its potential we run the risk that it will instead facilitate the export of UK jobs and revenues.

THE CITY OF TOMORROW

By Jim Clark, Chairman of English & Overseas Properties plc

- 1 -

Considerable speculation exists about the shape of the working and business environment of the future. Forecasting, away from its science fiction dimension, is crucial for business planning. Commercial targets, operational structures, and market performances must meet increasingly demanding levels of effectiveness. So the urban environment will need to respond to and, certainly, anticipate the needs of business in the future. The nature of the urban environment of tomorrow is critical to commercial prosperity.

English & Overseas Properties commissioned a survey of expert opinion on the dynamics of urban change and renewal. For the government, Sir Paul Beresford, responsible for urban regeneration at the Department of the Environment, was firm in his belief that cities are more likely to succeed if they provide a built environment of high quality because only in this way will they prove attractive to residents and investors.

The survey found that working from home will increase - up to 8.5 million of today's jobs could go to teleworkers using modems and computers - but experts do not agree on what impact this will have. Fewer people will work at the traditional office or factory site. Other people will work in services where the customer is prepared to pay a premium for personal contact. A high proportion of people will always prefer to "go to work" but increasingly this will be to work centres, where they can access high capital cost equipment, rather than to employers' premises.

- 2 -

The first group to be affected by these changes will be long distance commuters who will increasingly find their daily journeys uneconomic and inefficient. One expert sees a return to a pattern similar to medieval craftsmen living over their workshops, except in the future the craftsmen will be teleworkers who will be experts at packaging and disseminating information. Even so, working from home may appear financially attractive until people realise they are actually earning less. Sales, marketing, consultancy and senior management functions, where clients are prepared to pay a premium for personal contact, will retain city centre locations.

Office accommodation will become less expensive and although business centres will not disappear they will shrink, retreating from fringe areas where staff find access a problem. New buildings will concentrate around major rail stations and transport interchanges. They will have to be easily modifiable if they are to retain their value. The criteria for choosing new premises will switch from "location, location, location" to "flexibility, location, flexibility".

One view is that the office development tide that shaped modern cities has passed its high water mark. The giant headquarters of the 1980s, many of which were corporate ego trips, will become economic and social dinosaurs by the next century. Major single purpose developments will increasingly not take place and schemes like Canary Wharf will be highly flexible and contain a mix of uses. Such developments are commonplace in most other countries. In Hong Kong one block may be divided horizontally and contain offices, restaurants, shopping centres, cinemas and residential apartments. As older office blocks become obsolete and unlettable, they will be ideal for conversion to housing for students, young professionals and housing associations. London already has 250 applications to switch from office uses to housing.

- 3 -

As part of the survey, a poll of 80 public companies identified lack of investment as one of the major problems in the city of tomorrow, even though the major pension and insurance funds have confidence in the future of property investment. Only 10 per cent of companies surveyed said that they would not be located in cities in the future. Shopping and entertainment facilities were cited as the major benefits of being in a city with unemployment and transport mentioned as major problems. The survey predicted that business centres and office buildings are long overdue for the sort of revolution already seen in manufacturing. They are grossly inefficient: subtract empty nights, weekends and holidays and the result is an expensive asset utilised for only 21 per cent of the year - equivalent to 76 out of 365 days. This may lead to an increase in "hot desking" - the practice of sharing desks with colleagues who are often out of the office for several days at a time - further reducing the need for large headquarters buildings.

Some cities will remain vibrant high quality places in the next century. Others may see the gradual erosion of the social fabric and the creation of "edge cities", where white middle-class professionals desert central neighbourhoods to cluster around shopping malls on the edge of conurbations. This is already a feature of some American cities. In the UK, increasing traffic congestion and crime pose a greater threat to the urban fabric. Better public transport will be fundamental to the success of tomorrow's cities. With less than 400 cars per thousand head of population, car ownership in the UK still lags behind other countries. Yet the density of vehicles is already twice that of France and the US.

It is inevitable that car use will have to be restricted even more.

- 4 -

Serious concern comes from retailers in the high street, fearful about the advent of television shopping and the dominance of out-of-town superstores. However, there is evidence that the threat of the superstore has been exaggerated. Even so, the high street will still have to invest heavily to attract shoppers. Retailers will have to play on the entertainment factor and promote high streets as thriving leisure and recreational centres.

The majority of UK conservation areas feature parts of towns and cities which were developed at a time when there was no planning legislation. A mixture of different activities created the attractive and distinctive environment we seek to preserve today. There is a need for greater flexibility in planning policy which will promote mixed use in our high streets. The studio, workshop, restaurant, retail unit and solicitor's office will then be able to sit side by side once more. To achieve this planning authorities will have to develop a more flexible and visionary approach to the change of use of buildings from a commercial to a residential function.

One of the most interesting ideas concerning urban renewal in recent years has been the concept of the urban village which incorporates many of the themes outlined above.

In an urban village there is a conscious attempt to create active cohesive communities by promoting a mix of uses at several levels: within neighbourhoods; within street blocks; within streets and within individual buildings. The UK planning system will need to adapt and incorporate principles and practices conducive to the creation of urban villages if the concept is to become a reality. This will involve changes in policy, attitudes, and behaviour in favour of mixed use, mixed tenure, and sustainable development which will bring measurable benefits to society. Alongside conventional financial appraisal, urban village projects will use two new concepts: social financial analysis and community impact appraisal. The aim is for urban villages to receive between 70 and 100 per cent of their funding from the private sector.

The requirements of the companies of the future are already shaping the cities of the future. But it is a two way process. Successful companies will increasingly need to be sensitive to the desires and concerns of the communities in which they operate. Working in partnership is the way to ensure that resurgence rather than decay becomes the dominant characteristic of the urban landscape of tomorrow.